The Journey Never Ends

Technology's Role in Helping Perfect Health Care Outcomes

The Journey Never Ends

Technology's Role in Helping Perfect Health Care Outcomes

Edited by
David Garets and Claire McCarthy Garets

CRC Press is an imprint of the
Taylor & Francis Group, an **informa** business
A PRODUCTIVITY PRESS BOOK

CRC Press
Taylor & Francis Group
6000 Broken Sound Parkway NW, Suite 300
Boca Raton, FL 33487-2742

Printed on acid-free paper
Version Date: 20160623

International Standard Book Number-13: 978-1-4987-6144-4 (Hardback)

Library of Congress Cataloging-in-Publication Data

Names: Garets, David E., editor. | Garets, Claire McCarthy, editor.
Title: The journey never ends : technology's role in helping perfect healthcare outcomes / editors, Dave Garets and Claire McCarthy Garets.
Description: Boca Raton : Taylor & Francis, 2016. | Includes bibliographical references and index.
Identifiers: LCCN 2015039104 | ISBN 9781498761444 (alk. paper)
Subjects: | MESH: Electronic Health Records--organization & administration. | Organizational Innovation.
Classification: LCC R858 | NLM WX 175 | DDC 610.285--dc23
LC record available at http://lccn.loc.gov/2015039104

Visit the Taylor & Francis Web site at
http://www.taylorandfrancis.com

and the CRC Press Web site at
http://www.crcpress.com

Contents

Foreword

I'm confident you and I could spend considerable time discussing and debating the advantages and disadvantages of living in a digital world. And despite our debate, I'm also confident we would be able to agree on this impressive transformation on at least two levels: (1) how quickly the changes occurred and (2) how pervasive the impact has been. Literally, after thousands of years without digital data, it's almost impossible to fathom how any business can survive in today's world without automating and digitizing its business processes. Few would argue the point. In fact, it's become an easy strategic pastime of some to equate poor market segment performance with poor market segment information technology (IT) adoption.

Clearly, healthcare has been one such market segment generally attacked as an industry quite late to the digital party. Like far too many generalizations, the criticism can be both quite fair and quite inaccurate. Given the widespread adoption of IT in the form of shared accounting systems as early as the 1960s, healthcare was pretty mainstream at that time relative to embracing IT.

Okay, so where's support for the criticism? Outside fairly isolated instances, in my personal case, LDS Hospital in Salt Lake City, Utah, the healthcare industry has been slow to apply IT to its core business processes, that is, applying IT to the processes and documentation of patient care. For example, it has only been during the past two decades that hospitals and physician practices have significantly integrated clinical information in comprehensive electronic medical record (EMR) systems.

It's hard to overstate the value to healthcare, both as a hugely important industry and as a hugely critical public service, of the pervasive installation of EMRs. It's also easy to understand why the vendor and provider components of the healthcare industry, for the past two decades, have been almost fully consumed with the implementation of EMR systems. By almost any measures, we've made significant progress in digitizing core healthcare processes via EMRs.

It has, however, come at a price—huge expenses, huge energy levels, and massive operational stress. The result? Much of the industry has little appetite to spend more money, time, and energy on "what's next" relative to healthcare IT. There are even some portions of the provider community that believe we don't need anything beyond EMRs.

I can fully appreciate the post-EMR fatigue factor. It also resonates with me when someone says why we need to continue to invest in IT. When will we harvest?

My response is straightforward. The harvest comes when we do two critical things: (1) improve work processes that are made possible because of digitized systems, especially EMRs, and (2) create learning organizations emanating from analytics insights made available as a result of these massively data-intensive digital systems. The data "exhaust" from these digitized operational systems, properly organized in an enterprise data warehouse and effectively analyzed and displayed with exciting new tools and technologies, is already permitting healthcare organizations to eliminate health care waste (operational mistakes, inaccurate diagnoses, and unnecessary orders) and improve patient outcomes.

Major harvesting is now possible from our significant investments in health IT (HIT) operational systems by those seeking to learn from the data! Furthermore, these performance improvement learnings can be codified into agreed-upon rules to drive the alerting and reminding capabilities of installed EMRs. With this feedback loop, we now have an organizational vehicle (EMRs) to "sustain the gains" from our new clinical insights and to make good on our promises to broadly and uniformly improve patient outcomes. And there's even more good to do, and to get excited about, in our post-EMR implementation phase of HIT. This is the notion of the contributions, and IT needs, of the healthcare world outside the walls of the hospital.

The new world of healthcare financing and delivery is forcing care delivery organizations to move further to the edge to keep people healthy rather than continue to inhabit a physician-centric, hospital-centric model of fee for service. Hence, the billions that were spent on hospital EMRs was necessary to ensure the most efficient, effective, and efficacious care when someone, God forbid, is sick enough to go to a hospital, but the goal now is to keep that from happening.

Therefore, all kinds of new systems are going to be required that go way beyond the EMR, for sure using the data from it, but combining those data with other information from the patient, from other care delivery organizations the patient has visited, from remote monitoring devices, and other sources of wellness data. Plus, you'll need investments in precision medicine technologies, including pharmacogenetics. Thought you'd spent all you needed to spend on IT with your EMR investment—think again!

The authors in this outstanding compilation of post-EMR needs and benefits will further prepare you for what's required and what's possible. I'm grateful to say that I know many of these authors personally. I'm also grateful to say that Dave Garets and Claire McCarthy Garets are among my closest professional and personal friends. I'm pleased to recommend the insights of these respected professionals to you as you further your efforts to create the enviable healthcare systems we can now only dream of.

Good luck and Godspeed!

Larry Grandia
St. George, Utah

Preface

We never had to go to "Plan B."

It is generally acknowledged that getting an EMR in place is a starting point, not the end of the journey to becoming a modern healthcare organization. That's what this book is about—the many other things that need to be addressed after your EMR is in place. As you move forward on the never-ending path to increasing quality, excellence, safety, service, and so on, the human change leadership challenges you faced when implementing your EMR continue to be important every step of the way. Why? Because each change you make requires the participation of your people in order to succeed.

As we now know, installing an EMR does not, in and of itself, deliver the anticipated benefits. It takes behavior, attitude, and process changes to generate value from the potential the EMR presents. The same is true when you tackle opportunities presented by Big Data, mobile devices, population health, interoperability, cybersecurity, and the many other things that are becoming requirements in today's healthcare world.

Though this book is not specifically about the human aspects of change, each topic covered presents yet another change that staff, physicians, executives—and patients and their families—must adjust to in some way. As you navigate the path to the future, keep the following questions in mind to help ensure you make the most of your greatest resource—your human capital.

- Do you have a change methodology, and more importantly, are you using it? If not, you are probably missing many of the following questions.
- Is there a clear picture of the desired future state? Does it describe the employee experience, the patient experience? Do people understand why you are changing and what will happen if the changes aren't successful?
- People want to know what they are expected to do. How are you managing expectations and showing people what a good job looks like?
- What is the role of leaders in effecting the organizational transformation, as opposed to their role in installing new technology or a new program?
- Change happens when people let go—what is it time to let go of now?
- How strong is change leadership in the organization? How committed are the executive leaders to significant change initiatives? How do you know?
- What is the most important job of your leaders today? If it's not guiding their teams through change and building change capacity, what is it?
- When time and resources are tight, what can you stop or postpone until the top priority is successfully implemented? Is there agreement about what the top priority is?
- People do what they are rewarded for. Are you reinforcing change or reinforcing the status quo?

- What is the cumulative impact of all the changes underway in your organization? Which stakeholder groups are hardest hit? How can you sequence change to reduce the impact?
- How are you ensuring that your organization is increasingly change enabled so that change goes faster, is less painful, costs less, and achieves the anticipated outcomes?
- How much alignment is there between what leaders say, what they do, and what they reinforce?
- How effective are the feedback mechanisms in the organization? Do leaders pay attention to staff feedback and respond to it in a timely manner?

We ask these questions because the hardest things are often those considered to be soft—ruptured relationships, broken trust, crises of confidence, emotional outbursts, unclear expectations, poor performance, miscommunication and misunderstandings, and so on. Why are these things so hard? It's difficult to predict the outcome of these situations; there is no prescribed, sure path to resolution, and people are weird, meaning they are unpredictable and have their own reasons for the things they do.

Why should you care? Just read the news about implementation failures, executive firings, lost revenue, lost market share, security breaches, mergers and acquisitions, and bankruptcies.

This book describes some of the major initiatives that most healthcare organizations here, and internationally, are involved in now or will be undertaking in the next decade. Most of them are transformational. None of them are IT initiatives. All of them are business or clinical initiatives with an IT component. If you or your board thought you were done spending large amounts of money on IT after implementing your EMR, you're dead wrong. Welcome to the new reality!

When we were contemplating the structure of this book and figuring out the chapters, we very quickly knew who we wanted to write them. Because both of us have been in the industry for more than 25 years and sat in some interesting domestic and international catbird seats, we have prodigious networks of friends and colleagues who rank among the most knowledgeable experts in their fields.

And every one of the people we asked to write a chapter for us said "yes." We never had to go to "Plan B." These people know their stuff, and you are the beneficiary.

We hope you enjoy the book and that it helps you understand what it's going to take to be successful in the transformed healthcare delivery world of the future, starting now.

Dave Garets and Claire McCarthy Garets
Blaine, Washington
www.changegang.net

Editors

Dave Garets, FHIMSS, is an internationally known industry analyst, author, and speaker on healthcare information strategies, technologies, and change. The cocreator of the HIMSS Analytics EMR Adoption Model, he was elected to the HIMSS 50-in-50, the 50 most memorable contributors to healthcare IT in the last 50 years. He is also coauthor of two newly released books—*Analytics in Healthcare: An Introduction* and *Effective Strategies for Change.*

In his 25-year career in healthcare, Dave's been

- A hospital CIO
- Group vice president and head of the healthcare IT research organization at Gartner, Inc.
- President and CEO of HIMSS Analytics and board chair and EVP of HIMSS
- EVP of Healthlink
- General manager and executive director of The Advisory Board Company

He's now failing in his attempt to semiretire, and is general manager of Change Gang, LLC, a healthcare change management consulting firm, and senior advisor at Next Wave Advisors.

What Dave brings to the industry is 20 years of healthcare IT industry analyst experience, having advised not only many of the largest healthcare delivery organizations but also health IT companies and investors in the United States and around the world. He's spoken at conferences and advised clients in 22 countries, and sits on five governing or advisory boards in the United States and Europe.

Claire McCarthy Garets, MA, FHIMSS, is an organizational sociologist and an internationally recognized change management and technology adoption strategist. She has more than three decades of experience supporting diverse healthcare organizations (HCOs) through transformative technology implementations. In addition to her IT work, Claire's change leadership experience includes mergers, downsizings, and reorganizations.

Claire is the CEO of Change Gang, LLC, a boutique healthcare change management consulting firm. She specializes in transformational leadership development; supports HCOs in electronic medical record planning, implementation, and optimization; and advises IT companies. Recent work includes organizations in the United States, Sweden, Australia, and the Kingdom of Saudi Arabia.

Claire spent her career in healthcare, working with organizations such as Cottage Health; Providence Health & Services; Kaiser Permanente; Premier, Inc.; Premera Blue Cross; Group Health Cooperative of Puget Sound; and a variety of private practices.

Claire is the coauthor of the critically acclaimed book, *Change Management Strategies for an Effective EMR Implementation*, and the second edition, *Effective Strategies for Change*. She is a founding member of the Association of Change Management Professionals, is certified in multiple change methodologies, and has served as an adjunct professor at Kent State University. She is widely recognized for her collaborative systems approach to managing large-scale change and has given presentations at renowned healthcare conferences across the United States, as well as Australia, the Middle East, and Europe.

She earned an MA in sociology from the University of Montana.

Contributors

Michael Blum, MD, is the associate vice chancellor for informatics and a professor of medicine in cardiology at the University of California, San Francisco (UCSF). As an active clinician, Dr. Blum is passionate about wellness and prevention of heart disease through a heart healthy lifestyle.

As UCSF's chief medical information officer (CMIO), Dr. Blum led clinicians in the successful enterprise-wide deployment of Epic's electronic health record as well as enterprise data warehousing. He is now working across the University of California system with the other UC chief information officers and CMIOs to establish a UC-wide data warehouse that captures the experience of the University's 13.5 million patients and drives innovation into clinical care, research, and commercial partnerships.

Before his medical career, Dr. Blum was trained as an engineer, and he applies his expertise in technology to health care as UCSF's CMIO and the director of the UCSF Center for Digital Health Innovation (CDHI). CDHI develops, validates, and commercializes novel, impactful digital health applications, devices, sensors, and platforms in pursuit of precision medicine. Dr. Blum serves as an advisor to numerous start-up, early-stage, and established healthcare technology companies and serves as the founding director of the UCSF-Samsung Digital Health Innovation Lab.

Ronnie D. Bower, Jr., MA, director, adoption and sustainment, Applied Clinical Informatics, Tenet Healthcare, has more than 20 years of progressive leadership, training, and support experience assisting healthcare entities through organizational change endeavors. Tenet Healthcare has long been committed to the field of informatics, and Ronnie's current role affords him the opportunity to engage in cultural change activities with more than 80 hospitals spanning approximately 16 states. He is engaged in all informatics communications, cultural/change readiness assessments, change leadership training, informatics orientation, and sustainment efforts and supports additional physician adoption activities.

Ronnie helped develop and cochair the HIMSS Change Management Taskforce, pulling multiple healthcare change leaders together to share best practices and leverage change management tools. He has presented hundreds of organizational change management sessions at every organizational level, from national conferences to individual department sessions, and takes pride in knowing he helps move organizations one individual at a time. Assisting people through change is his passion and he is committed to helping individuals endure and embrace the complexities that change offers.

Jeff Cobb, principal security consultant, World Wide Technology, joined the World Wide Technology (WWT) team in June of 2015. Before WWT, Jeff served as the VP of IT, CISO for Capella Healthcare where he was responsible for the enterprise information security program, ancillary clinical systems for radiology/imaging, meaningful use interoperability/reporting, and data analytics.

With a 15+-year career in IT and security, Jeff has an extensive background covering healthcare, IT and security leadership, enterprise architecture, strategy and integration, risk management, governance, and regulatory compliance. Jeff has held technology and security leadership positions with Ingenuity Associates, UnitedHealth Group, AIM Healthcare, and National Renal Alliance.

Jeff served 3 years as president of the Middle Tennessee Information Systems Security Association Chapter. He also chairs the Metro Nashville Information Security Advisory Board.

Michael W. Davis, MS, MBA, has more than 30 years of healthcare experience in both provider organizations and healthcare solutions companies. Mike assisted in starting a successful research and advisory service for The Advisory Board Company, serving as a managing director. Mike also helped launch HIMSS Analytics as the executive vice president overseeing products and services. Mike held the position of managing vice president of Gartner's Healthcare Research & Advisory Service when he led that division. He has managed clinical departments in healthcare organizations and has held product management and director positions with Micromedex/Thomson, American Express Health Systems Group, First Data Corporation, and Motorola. Mike is the coauthor of the HIMSS Analytics EMR Adoption Model, which tracks the adoption rate of EMR applications in the United States and Canada. Mike has published 2 books and more than 300 research articles on computerizing healthcare information. Mike has extensive experience with the design, development, implementation, and management of healthcare IT solutions for established and start-up companies.

Mike is known as an experienced, accomplished, and respected healthcare professional. Mike earned a Master of Science degree from the University of Nebraska Medical Center and a Master of Business Administration degree from Pfeiffer University.

Doug Eastman, PhD, executive director, Usability Center of Excellence, Kaiser Permanente Information Technology, is an organizational development executive with extensive experience leading large-scale change, pioneering technology readiness, and optimization strategies/programs and unleashing human potential. Dr. Eastman established and oversees the Usability Center of Excellence (UCOE) within the Kaiser Permanente National IT Care Delivery Business Information Office. The UCOE combines usability and user adoption expertise to create and sustain positive user experiences across the enterprise.

Dr. Eastman coauthored the 2010 HIMSS book of the year, *Change Management Strategies for an Effective EMR Implementation*, recently rewritten as a second edition entitled, *Effective Strategies for Change.*

He earned a PhD in organizational psychology from the California School of Professional Psychology (now Alliant University), a master's degree in psychology from Pepperdine University, and a bachelor's degree in psychology from The Ohio State University. Dr. Eastman served as president of the Psi Chi National Honors Society at Pepperdine University and served as board president for SMG, a national child anxiety nonprofit organization.

David Finn, MA, CISA, CISM, CRISC, is the health information technology officer for Symantec. Before that role, he was the chief information officer and vice president of information services for Texas Children's Hospital. He also served as the security and privacy officer for Texas

Children's. Before that, David spent 7 years as a healthcare consultant with IMG/Healthlink and PwC, serving last as the EVP of Operations for Healthlink.

He is focused on creating and maintaining trust in and value from information and information systems. David has presented nationally and internationally on such topics as project management, professional leadership and staff development, and privacy and security. He has contributed to or written articles on IT management, disaster recovery, and security for journals such as *CIO Digest* and *Baseline*.

Finn earned a BA degree from the University of North Dakota and an MA from Angelo State University. During 2014, he worked closely with College of Healthcare Information Management Executives (CHIME) management to create and initiate the Association for Executives in Healthcare Information Security. He also is a long-time board member of Healthcare for the Homeless—Houston (two FQHCs) and is vice president of the Primary Care Innovation Center in Houston.

Richard F. Gibson, MD, PhD, MBA, healthcare IT industry analyst, Portland, Oregon, is a research director at Gartner, Inc. and an affiliate assistant professor in the Department of Medical Informatics and Clinical Epidemiology at Oregon Health and Science University. Formerly, he was chief of healthcare intelligence at Providence Health & Services, Renton, Washington. Previously, he was senior vice president and chief information officer at Legacy Health in Portland, Oregon. Before that, he served 11 years as CMIO at Providence Health System, Oregon Region.

He earned his BS from Stanford University, MD from Case Western Reserve University, PhD in medical informatics from the University of Utah with a fellowship at Intermountain Health Care in Salt Lake City, and MBA from the Wharton School. He is a founding board member of the Association of Medical Directors of Information Systems. Dr. Gibson is a family physician and emergency physician. His interest is in using claims data and electronic health records and their data to improve the quality and reliability of healthcare and to decrease the cost of care.

James Hereford, MS, is the chief operating officer of Stanford Health Care. In his role at Stanford, he is operationally responsible for all aspects of care delivery throughout a system of inpatient, ambulatory, and ancillary care settings. He is also a recognized leader nationally in the implementation and use of Lean and Lean management in healthcare and has led the implementation of Lean as the chief operating officer of the Palo Alto Medical Foundation and as the executive vice president of Strategic Services and Care Delivery Services at Group Health Cooperative.

During his 25-year career in healthcare, James has been responsible for the design and implementation of one of the first and most expansive care delivery patient web portals while at Group Health and for the selection and implementation of the Epic electronic medical record. At Group Health and at Palo Alto Medical Foundation, James led the redesign of primary care and several other organizational transformations.

At Stanford, he is again leading the implementation of the Lean management system and is focused on helping Stanford create the preeminent academic care delivery system in the world, delivering leading-edge and coordinated care.

He has also served on the faculties of the University of Washington, The Ohio State University, and the Institute of Healthcare Improvement and continues to teach in programs at Stanford University.

John Hoyt, MHA, FACHE, FHIMSS, is executive vice president, HIMSS Analytics, at HIMSS, the largest US not-for-profit healthcare caused–based organization focused on providing global leadership for the optimal use of information technology. John is responsible for providing executive leadership and direction to HIMSS Analytics worldwide where he also provides direction for all Stage 6 and Stage 7 validations and derivative research.

Throughout his healthcare career, John has been instrumental in defining business and IT strategy as well as selecting, implementing, and integrating mission-critical healthcare information systems across the enterprise. Before joining HIMSS, John served as a hospital chief operating officer and twice as a chief information officer with various healthcare organizations accumulating more than 22 years of hospital executive committee leadership experience. John also served in consultancy practices, including with IBM Healthlink Services and First Data Health Systems Group.

John earned a BA in economics from Xavier University in Cincinnati, Ohio, and an MHA from St. Louis University in Missouri. He is a HIMSS fellow and a fellow of the American College of Healthcare Executives.

Jacquelyn Hunt, PharmD, MS, serves as the chief population health officer at Enli Health Intelligence. Acting as a knowledge partner, Dr. Hunt advises organizations on aligning strategy, care team design, technology, and culture to deliver Triple Aim results in the market. She oversees Enli's Knowledge to Action health program design, helping organizations reduce clinical variation and gaps in care by ensuring that the most current evidence informs care delivery across the enterprise.

Before joining Enli, Dr. Hunt served as chief quality officer and chief information officer at Bellin Health System. Dr. Hunt completed a Merck Foundation Fellowship with the Institute of Healthcare Improvement (2008–2009) focused on Triple Aim, large-scale transformation, and patient-centered health technology. Before her Institute for Healthcare Improvement Fellowship, Dr. Hunt served as the executive director of Quality & Care Redesign with Providence Health & Services.

Dr. Hunt earned her BS in pharmacy from Oregon State University with a certificate in gerontology. She completed a doctorate with residencies in pharmacotherapy and ambulatory medicine in pharmacy at the University of Texas Health Science Center. She later earned her Master of Science in clinical research design and biostatistics from the University of Michigan.

James Jerzak, MD, is a board-certified family practice physician at Bellin Health. He has been a family physician for more than 25 years in Green Bay, Wisconsin, providing a full spectrum of care for patients of all ages.

He graduated from medical school at the University of Wisconsin in Madison and did his residency in family medicine at St. Michael Hospital, Milwaukee, Wisconsin.

Dr. Jerzak is on the leadership team for the Patient Care Redesign Pilot Program and is currently the physician leading the prototype for this program at Bellin Health.

He has received a number of awards, most recently the 2014 Wisconsin Family Physician Educator of the Year.

J. Scott Joslyn, PharmD, MBA, is the senior vice president and CIO for MemorialCare, a six-hospital system in Southern California with revenues exceeding $2 billion, 1500 inpatient beds, 2500 affiliated physicians, and approximately 11,000 employees. As CIO, Scott is responsible for IT, networking, and telecommunications. Beyond IT, Scott oversees MemorialCare's research function with some 381 currently active studies representing 39 service lines and 28 specialties. He is the executive sponsor for system-wide pharmacy services, including inpatient, ambulatory, infusion center, and specialty pharmacy practices.

Dr. Joslyn is also a board member of Summation Health Ventures, a venture capital fund and joint venture with Cedars Sinai Medical Center that invests in and oversees promising, start-up, and young companies that develop products and services in various healthcare market segments. In that capacity, Scott's service includes membership on company boards and advisory committees.

Dr. Joslyn earned a Doctor of Pharmacy degree from the University of the Pacific and a Master of Business Administration from UCLA. He has taught health care information technology at California State University, Long Beach, and the University of Southern California. He is an active and long-standing member of CHIME, HIMSS, and other industry groups.

Kathy Kerscher has been with Bellin Health for 15 years. In that time, Kathy has served in several operational leadership roles in ambulatory care. Currently, Kathy is the team leader of operations for primary care for the past 6 years. As the team leader of operations, Kathy oversees the operations of 23 primary care clinics, 4 FastCare clinics, and 120 employer clinics with on-site services. Kathy is also the change and operational leader for achieving population health management through team-based care.

Pete Knox, MS, BS, executive vice president, chief learning and innovation officer, Bellin Health System, has been associated with Bellin Health System in Green Bay, Wisconsin, in a variety of leadership roles for the past 35 years. Bellin has been on the leading edge of quality for many years and is recognized nationally for superior results. Currently, Pete is executive vice president, chief learning and innovation officer. In this role, he is responsible for population health strategies, physician networks, employer strategies, learning and innovation, and execution of strategy.

In addition, he is a consultant for health care and non–health care organizations. He is a senior fellow at the Institute for Healthcare Improvement and serves on faculty for a number of programs. He is also on the board of trustees for the University of Massachusetts Health System in Worcester. His book titled *The Business of Healthcare* is being used by a number of universities and organizations across the country and he is currently working on a second book, *The Strategy Execution Playbook*. Pete is a frequent speaker on strategy, strategy alignment, population health, and accountable care in the United States and Canada. In addition, he serves on the strategic advisory board for HFMA related to the transformation of healthcare from fee-for-service to value-based payment.

Brian T. Malec, PhD, earned his doctorate from the Maxwell School at Syracuse University specializing in healthcare economics. He has an extensive teaching background in health administration graduate programs and for the past 25 years has been at California State University, Northridge. He is the past department chair of health sciences and current graduate program coordinator of the Master of Science in Health Administration program. His main areas of teaching include healthcare economics and national health policy, health information systems, and quantitative decision-making. His areas of research include HIT workforce development, measuring and managing the economic value of HIT, and teaching HIT in graduate programs.

Dr. Malec is a frequent presenter and moderator at national and international conferences including HIMSS, HIMSS Europe, and HIMSS Asia Pacific. He is also the leader of the Association of University Programs in Health Administration (AUPHA) Academic Forum, which presents faculty research each year at HIMSS. He has recently written and edited a book on careers in health information technology.

Jan Oldenburg's (FHIMSS) purpose is to support better healthcare through digital tools and practices that help patients participate more actively in their own care. She is currently a senior manager in Ernst & Young's Advisory Health Care Practice, where she supports healthcare organizations focused on improving capabilities for patients. Jan is the former vice president of physician and patient engagement at Aetna Accountable Care Solutions, working in emerging accountable care organizations to create and implement population health and patient engagement programs. Before Aetna, Jan was a senior leader in Kaiser Permanente's Digital Services Group developing and implementing consumer capabilities for both care delivery and health plan operations.

Jan is a past president of the Northern California HIMSS Board, a HIMSS fellow, and cochair of the National HIMSS Connected Health Committee. She frequently speaks and writes about patient and physician engagement. Jan served as the primary editor of *Engage! Transforming Healthcare through Digital Patient Engagement*, published by HIMSS Press in March 2013. She wrote the Patient Engagement chapter of the third edition of *Medical Informatics*, published in March 2015. She is currently working on another book on health engagement, written from the perspective of consumers, patients, and family members.

H. Lester Reed, MD, FACP, served 25 years in military medicine in both the Navy and the Army retiring as the chief of medicine at Madigan Army Medical Center and came to MultiCare Health System in 2001 as associate medical director of the MultiCare Medical Group, where he eventually became medical director. He left MultiCare in 2004 to become a clinical director at South Auckland Health in Auckland, New Zealand, and returned to MultiCare in 2005. Dr. Reed was promoted to vice president of medical affairs, for Acute Care, in 2007, to senior vice president for quality in 2010 and to senior physician executive—practice improvement in July 2014. He then accepted his current role as president and chief physician executive of the Centra Medical Group, Centra Health System on May 1, 2015.

Dr. Reed earned his medical degree from the University of Kentucky and completed his internal medicine residency and an endocrinology and metabolism fellowship at the National Naval Medical Center in Bethesda, Maryland. He has published more than 35 peer-reviewed manuscripts and continues to have a small clinical endocrine practice. He is a fellow of the American College of Physicians, board certified in endocrinology and internal medicine, and is a clinical associate professor of medicine at the University of Washington, past clinical professor of medicine at the University of Auckland, and past professor of medicine at the Uniformed Services University of the Health Sciences.

In his physician executive role at MultiCare Health System, he helped describe clinical improvements that supported the HIMSS Stage 7 recognition at MultiCare in 2015 as well as the HIMSS Davies award presented to MultiCare. He was an integral part of the physician engagement in 2008 that supported the inpatient installation of an electronic medical record. Then, again, he was instrumental during two other facility installations between 2010 and 2013. Dr. Reed has presented nationally for the American College of Healthcare Executives and The Leadership Institute on physician performance and clinical outcomes and published on these topics.

Wes Rishel has more than 30 years' experience designing and implementing electronic health records (EHRs) and other clinical IT systems based on open architecture and advising commercial, nonprofit, and government clients on the design and governance of such systems. He has provided substantial pro bono service to government and nonprofit organizations that support healthcare IT.

He currently describes himself as a "retired health IT nerd" but occasionally provides advice to not-for-profit and for-profit healthcare organizations.

As vice president and distinguished analyst at Gartner, Inc., he wrote more than 100 research notes on the IT manifestations of reimbursement changes such as accountable care and patient-centered medical homes, provider-led care management, the CMS EHR Incentive Programs for the "meaningful use" of EMRs, technologies of healthcare software, healthcare interoperability, standards, health information exchange (HIE), eHealth Exchange (formerly the Nationwide Health Information Network), service-oriented architecture in healthcare, medical device interconnection to clinical IT systems, Continua, Dossia, the personal health record, and Health Insurance Portability and Accountability Act of 1996 (HIPAA).

Rishel was a charter member of the Health IT Standards Committee from its founding in 2009 through January 2016. This federal advisory committee to the Office of the National Coordinator for Health IT advised on the standards regulations related to the meaningful use of EHRs.

Rishel has also been a member of the boards of directors of HL7, the North Coast Health Information Network, The eHealth Initiative, HIMSS, Workgroup for Electronic Data Interchange (WEDI), and Certification Commission for Health Information Technology (CCHIT) and served 2 years as the chair of HL7. Additionally, he served in an advisory role to The Joint Commission.

Alan Smith, MPH, senior vice president, chief information officer joining Capella in May 2011, leads the company in implementing information systems to achieve the most effective enterprise-wide IT operations. With more than 20 years of experience, Al has worked in hospitals, hospital management companies, health insurance plans, and technology consulting firms. In 2013, Al received Capella's Shining Star Award in recognition of his outstanding work in all five of the company's pillars.

Before joining Capella, Al served as vice president of applications and interim CIO for Vanguard Health System in Nashville where he was responsible for IT applications for the company's hospitals and affiliated physician clinics across all geographic markets. Before that, he was a client results executive for Cerner Corporation in Kansas City, Missouri, as well as VP–clinical applications for Carolinas Healthcare System in Charlotte, North Carolina. He began his career with Andersen Consulting (now Accenture) and First Consulting Group in Detroit, Michigan, providing technology consulting.

Al is currently serving as chairman of the HIT Task Force for the Federation of American Hospitals. He is also serving on the board of the Tennessee Health Information Management Society. He completed his undergraduate degree in financial administration with highest honors at Michigan State University. He also earned a master's of public health from the University of North Carolina at Chapel Hill. He was also named to Becker's Hospital Review's "100 Hospital and Health System CIOs to Know" list.

Douglas Ivan Thompson, MBA, FHIMSS, is a leading national expert in defining and measuring the value of healthcare information technologies and translating these technologies into operations improvements and strategic advantage for their buyers.

In his 25-year career as a consultant, Doug has worked with more than 300 leading hospitals, including several Davies Award winners, and numerous vendors including Microsoft, Cardinal Health, McKesson, and GE Healthcare.

As a senior research director at The Advisory Board Company, he has authored dozens of monographs on healthcare information technology and is a frequent speaker to business and professional audiences.

As an IT vendor executive, he founded several businesses focused on IT benefits realization.

Doug earned a BS from Brigham Young University and an MBA from Columbia University.

Brad Wozney, MD, graduated from the University of Wisconsin Medical School in 1995. He completed a Family Medicine Residency Program at the University of Wisconsin/St. Mary's Hospital in Madison, Wisconsin. He has been a family physician at Bellin Health in Denmark, Wisconsin, since 1998.

Dr. Wozney is the medical director for Ambulatory Quality and Informatics and chair of the Ambulatory Clinical Excellence and Safety Committee for Bellin Health, and the physician champion for Bellin's Managing Populations for Triple Aim Outcomes breakthrough initiative.

LEVERAGING YOUR EMR TO DERIVE VALUE

I

If your healthcare organization is typical, you got your EMR "installed" on-time and within budget, declared victory, and collected some money from Meaningful Use. But very quickly, you realized you weren't getting the return on the investment that management and the board expected; you didn't have the frontline clinicians using the technology to its fullest advantage, at least on the basis of the expectations you'd set from vendor promises, and you probably had more unhappy people in the organization than you thought you'd have. So you started the "optimization" process to make refinements, do some stuff over, and get it right this time.

This first section of the book is dedicated to helping you understand how to get value from your investment in the software and the people in your organization. Doug Eastman, executive director, Usability Center of Excellence at Kaiser Permanente, and Ronnie Bower, director, adoption and sustainment, Applied Clinical Informatics at Tenet Healthcare, explain how to most effectively optimize your EMR and sustain the improvements you make in adoption, process, and workflow.

Doug Thompson, senior research director at The Advisory Board Company, shares a structured methodology for getting measureable return on your EMR investment, and Les Reed, president and chief physician executive, Centra Medical Group at Centra Health System, expertly explains how to use the data from your EMR to improve clinical protocols, outcomes, and patient safety.

James Hereford, chief operating officer at Stanford Health Care, takes you through some case studies in how to apply Lean principles and thinking to the workflows and processes enabled by your EMR. Mike Blum, CMIO and associate vice chancellor at UCSF, shares some of the EMR innovations his organization has implemented, and John Hoyt, executive vice president at HIMSS Analytics, describes what some of the lessons HIMSS Analytics EMR Adoption Model Stage 7 organizations have learned and the advanced capabilities they can now bring to patient care.

Chapter 1

The User Experience: An Underexploited Opportunity

Doug Eastman, PhD

> *"Any darn fool can make something complex; it takes a real genius to make something simple."*
>
> **Albert Einstein**

Implementing an EMR is a major undertaking and involves a significant amount of change for HCOs. The overall effort is monumental. The stakes are high and this kind of investment is not made without the promise of a compelling return or benefit to the patients, caregivers, organization, and industry. HCOs seek increases in clinical quality and safety, revenue capture, and operational efficiencies. And ultimately, the EMR not only has to support the organization's current needs but also should be scalable enough to grow with future transformational plans. This is no small feat.

To add to the complexity, the launch of the EMR is really just the beginning. The new system becomes central to a growing body of optimization efforts, the success of which is largely dependent on users being willing and able to change their behavior. Technology solutions must be both **usable** and **adopted** by users to reach their potential. This gets tricky at times, because what we want users to do with the technology may not seem intuitive, convenient, or efficient to them. If the technology is too clunky, users become frustrated and the solution loses credibility. This is where problems arise, and some of these situations are difficult to reverse.

There are many stories in the healthcare industry that describe costly implementation mistakes. These shortcomings can affect an organization's reputation, compound existing inefficiencies, and increase the price tag associated with launching an EMR. But what is often not recognized is that **user experience during implementation can make or break post–live optimization efforts**, because it's the user experience that ultimately shapes how the technology is perceived and whether it is ever fully utilized.

The following list of issues is a sampling of what happens when technology is introduced without the user in mind:

- Workflow workarounds
- Decreased adoption, low utilization
- High maintenance costs
- User fatigue and frustration
- Missed revenue capture
- Incomplete fields, incomplete reporting
- Inconsistent processes
- Increased training and support costs
- Information errors
- User work/life imbalance
- Extra work, rework
- Too many mouse clicks
- Difficulty finding information

Sound familiar? Some of this may be inevitable, but more often than not, these issues can be avoided entirely if user-centered approaches are designed into implementation planning and delivery. Great care should be taken to ensure any technology solution is designed well and introduced in a way that helps ensure users see the value and readily adopt required changes.

There are two important elements of user-centered design: usability and user-ability (or technology adoption). Understanding the differences between the two and how they fit together to create an enhanced user experience are key to avoiding predictable problems and reaching the full potential of your technology.

User-Centered Approaches

Usability and user-ability (or technology adoption) are intertwined requirements of positive and sustainable user experiences. Both disciplines mitigate risk and can translate into significant quality improvements and cost savings. Unfortunately, they are often discounted or overlooked when implementing EMR systems. But when they are formally baked into the planning and development for a new system or other technology rollout, the long-term benefits are significant. On the other hand, when user-centered approaches are nonexistent or minimalized, a lot can (and usually does) go wrong sooner or later.

Let's review these user-centered approaches and how they work together to position your organization to realize the benefits from technology.

Usability

Usability is an important user-centered approach to ensuring users embrace technology to meet the organization's goals as quickly as possible.

There are a variety of definitions for usability, but generally speaking, usability contributes to the overall user experience by improving ease of use. The Nielson Norman Group (Jakob Nielsen, "Usability 101: Introduction to Usability") defines usability by five quality components:

1. **Learnability**: How easy is it for users to accomplish basic tasks the first time they encounter the design?
2. **Efficiency**: Once users have learned the design, how quickly can they perform tasks?
3. **Memorability**: When users return to the design after a period of not using it, how easily can they reestablish proficiency?
4. **Errors**: How many errors do users make, how severe are these errors, and how easily can they recover from the errors?
5. **Satisfaction**: How pleasant is it to use the design?

Another key quality component in usability is **Utility**, which refers to the design's functionality: Does it do what users need?

Usability plays an important role in ensuring that the user experience is positive and that users perceive technology as a gift, not a punishment. Think about the presents you have received in the past for your birthday or a holiday. It feels really good when someone knows you well and gives you a gift that fits your needs and interests. Can you recall times when you received a gift and it left you thinking, "How on earth did this person think I wanted this?" (Editor's Note: I got a $50,000 life insurance policy from my parents for my high school graduation gift when all the other kids were getting cars.)

With an EMR, it requires great thought to ensure what you are implementing is well received by users. The main requirement is to deliver technology solutions that support their operational requirement, and make their work more effective, convenient, and efficient. When this doesn't happen, users wonder if the development team understands their work. This disconnect creates a divide between operations and IT. Users tend to abandon solutions that don't meet their needs, like that awful gift they received. Birthday gifts can be returned, but bad technology solutions unfortunately don't come with a gift receipt. You are stuck with it until it gets fixed … and sometimes it takes forever to make simple changes.

The list below highlights some common distractions with EMRs that invariably lead to low user adoption and utilization. These distractions disrupt productivity and erode confidence in the technology, which, in turn, further negatively affects user adoption. It's a vicious circle.

Common EMR Distractions

- Too many mouse clicks
- Cumbersome navigation
- Inconsistent, illogical, and clunky process flows
- Noncontextual buttons and links
- Lengthy scrolling
- Overcrowding of screen layout
- Missing fields
- Difficult to find information
- Requires too much muscle memory
- Inconsistent button placement on screens

Usability helps ensure that the technology you are implementing is perceived as a welcome gift to users. Typically, usability professionals serve as liaisons between operations and IT, ensuring what is being built (whether a proof of concept/prototype or final solution) is comprehensive and aligns with what the business needs to perform their work successfully. To be most effective,

usability should be factored into the work plan from the very beginning. However, at this point, it is often brought in later to assess root causes of poor adoption and utilization issues, a contributing factor to increased costs and missed opportunities.

User-Ability

User-ability (or technology adoption) is another important user-centered discipline that yields great return for the HCO, because it, too, focuses on the user experience. Where usability aims to increase user adoption through the design of tools that meet user's needs, **user-ability also increases adoption through the assurance that users are ready, equipped, and on board with the changes ahead**. Technology adoption is about effectively introducing, implementing, and optimizing change driven by new and existing technology within the organization. An EMR drives a significant level of change for users, and this change must be managed effectively in order to reap the expected benefits.

Once an EMR is put in place, the journey continues. Users get more acquainted with the system and find ways to incorporate the technology more effectively into their daily routines. A sound technology adoption strategy ensures that, at go-live, a solid foundation for change has been established for the organization. This foundation sets the course for subsequent optimization efforts and helps reduce instances where change slows down because not everyone is on board. As stated earlier, we don't want users to be unduly distracted by the technology and other changes surrounding the implementation. When users are distracted, optimization and transformation efforts slow down or are not sustainable because the organization is playing catch-up with users instead of moving forward.

Assuming the technology meets user needs (it is functional and usable), users must be proficient with the system. This takes time and must be handled strategically. Proficiency improvement does not mean throwing more training at users. In fact, user dissatisfaction increases when training interventions aren't perceived to be relevant.

A common complaint from clinicians is that training isn't targeted to their needs, and frustration is exacerbated because training takes them away from patient access. Because of large patient loads, clinicians simply don't have time to sit through training that isn't addressing their specific requirements. A successful practice is to assess proficiency levels and segment skill gaps by audience groups. Having this information enables the organization to be strategic about its training strategy and to determine how localized or widespread the identified skills gaps are. This also enables the training team to determine the most appropriate training and support method, format, and timing to follow.

Training is expensive. To ensure sustainability, it is important to know exactly what your audience needs and to provide convenient ways to get it to them, when they need it. To meet these requirements, I recommend learning about which training interventions work best for each audience group.

There will be times when it is necessary to deploy on-the-ground resources to train people in a classroom or side by side in the field, but be careful, as this approach can become very costly and places a drain on resources. If you have a large organization that is geographically dispersed, this may require a small army of trainers. Try to determine who would really benefit from this approach.

For other users, it might make more sense to develop an online learning approach where users can access tailored videos and learning materials on their own time. Of course, there are advantages and disadvantages to electronic training methods. They allow users to learn on their own time, but that only works when users have the desire and time to access online materials. It is best to have a variety of learning solutions, tailored to meet the needs of your various user groups.

As a side comment, users don't always know what they don't know. When collecting data to understand audience skill gaps and needs, be wary of relying solely on self-assessments. Although a self-assessment is probably the most cost-effective way to collect data (especially within a large organization), the data aren't always accurate because data are limited to what a user thinks he or she needs to know or is capable of doing. It is always best to observe users interacting with the technology to fully appreciate their strengths and opportunities for improvement in the way they interact with the technology.

A Shared Perspective

Usability (UX) and user-ability (UA) share a common perspective and complement one another extremely well (see Figure 1.1). Both disciplines focus on what users need to be successful as well as bring visibility to practical ways to meet these requirements. The following describes areas where a similar philosophy is applied to establish a positive user experience.

Informed Decisions

Both user-centered specialties rely heavily on data collected from the field. Usability experts need to observe how users interact with the technology (software, applications, and devices) to make suitable recommendations about the user, functional, and design requirements.

Beware of the Usual Suspects Syndrome. This is when you have the same people at the planning table for every initiative, making decisions on behalf of all users on the basis of their individual experience and assumptions of what is needed. Many times, these subject matter experts are more than informed to make these decisions, but other times, these individuals are too close to the project and make decisions that are not aligned with what mainstream users actually need. The pitfall here is that you risk not operating from a complete set of user requirements from the start.

Both usability and user-ability professionals ensure that users are well represented in the planning phases and are involved early and closely enough to guide decisions that affect them. It is always important to check back with representative samples of target audience segments to ensure that decisions accurately reflect the needs of the individuals that will ultimately be expected to use the solutions. This requires a strong engagement strategy with the business side of the organization.

Having good data means that you can be strategic about next steps and ensure the interventions are sustainable. In the case of usability, offering users a solution that meets their needs and is convenient and easy to use has a much better chance of being embraced and utilized effectively. With regard to user-ability, providing tailored training and support reduces cost and time and

Figure 1.1 Looking at user experience.

wins the gratitude from users because they feel understood and respected. Both user-centered approaches leverage data to drive solutions to support the adoption and effective utilization of the technology.

The Whole Picture

Let's be honest, not every solution is perfect the first go-around. Sometimes, solutions don't hit the mark well at all. You could probably guess that when things don't go well, user-centered approaches were lacking. Regardless of the reason for poor outcomes, often an assessment is needed to uncover the root cause for low utilization or why people aren't using the solution as intended.

Usability and user-ability are great companions in the search for answers and are very effective in collectively surfacing the whole picture. It doesn't work to just assume that a problem is a training, workflow, or technology design issue without truly checking under the hood first. Please continue to gather assumptions from the project team, but vet those hunches through field research. There are a myriad of contributing factors that influence any given issue.

Working together, both user-centered approaches have been wildly effective in assessing current state problems in the field or uncovering a comprehensive set of user requirements. For instance, I recall a situation in the recent past when a project team couldn't understand why a group of users refused to use a brand new system. Some leaders sensed it was due to poor training, others felt the situation was a result of bad design. After observing users in the field and working closely with them to understand the challenges, it was found that the system worked perfectly—no known issues. The training was prepared and delivered well, as it focused less on which buttons to click and placed more emphasis on how to leverage the system to support the user workflows. The training also reviewed how to think critically and troubleshoot under certain typical situations. With the whole picture in mind, it turns out that the problem rested in two main areas. First, the system was actually developed perfectly to specifications but the requirements were incomplete and did not reflect the work of the users. Secondly, leadership did not communicate expectations consistently across the department and so users were not performing their work the same way. This led to different results.

The User Comes First

It goes without saying that the patient is the ultimate focus, but in the case of ensuring the EMR and other optimized technology solutions are well received and utilized to their fullest, it is important to always keep the user front of mind. User-centered approaches, such as usability and user-ability, are advocates for the user and for the development team. We want everyone to be successful, but emphasis must be placed equally on the technology and the people side in order to achieve positive, sustainable results.

Coupling of Specialties

Sometimes we innovate and develop solutions to enhance the user experience and sometimes we do it to change behavior. Technology alone doesn't change behavior, but rather enables it. Solid change management sets the tone to develop buy-in and user engagement. Coupling technology with great design and change management is a recipe for successful adoption.

More and more organizations are instituting user-centered approaches in their work from the onset and are finding great success as a result. The progress is still slower than it should be, and user-centered approaches tend to take a backseat to the seemingly sexier and more tangible things like development. It comes down to how much of an appetite leadership has for investing in people, not just the technology.

Five Signs of Trouble...

Here are some warning signs that a project may go south due to user-centered approaches not being fully embraced.

1. Flip-the-Switch Mentality
   Beware of the traditional IT mindset that defines a successful launch as merely EMR (or other solutions) go-live on time and on budget. The flip-the-switch mentality reflects poor definition of success metrics and frequently comes back to haunt the project team. Implementing on schedule and within budget is absolutely admirable, but it's only part of the battle. Not identifying and attending to user needs actually costs more (sometimes much more!) in the long run. The real goals are to meet timeline and budget, with full user adoption that results in desired outcomes.
2. Just Get It Out the Door
   This is very similar to the flip-the-switch mentality but differs in that it is usually associated with a rush job with project leads in such a hurry that they don't think about whether there is a better way to do things or if the solution is even on track. Typically, this frame of mind results when people are swamped, running from project to project, and feeling the pressure to get things done fast at all costs. What they don't realize is that usability doesn't have to slow things down; it even works quite well with agile development. The problem with rushed implementations is that they leave users with a bad taste that isn't easily forgotten. When users don't embrace the solution, they abandon it, resulting in a lot of time, money, and effort wasted to launch something no one will use.
3. Anyone Can Do It
   Bring the right people to the table to ensure success! Avoid the temptation to repurpose someone on the team who isn't user-experience qualified. Their interest or availability and your desire to not add additional resources to the project are not sufficient reasons. Good usability and user-ability professionals are dedicated to their craft and have a wealth of lessons learned and successful practices to leverage to ensure your products and organization reach potential.

   A challenge in the usability field is that, because of a lack of understanding, people can be asked to do usability work when they aren't qualified. For instance, be careful about leveraging designers to conduct research in the field. Some designers are cross-trained, and are effective at this, but some traditional designers are better suited to just use the resulting data to inform their design. Field research uncovers user requirements and looks into more than just design implications. Researchers are trained specifically to understand the user's role and tasks, and how they interact with a solution to determine gaps and opportunities. It requires asking the right questions and careful observation.

   On the flipside, be careful about asking researchers to design solutions unless they have an appropriate background in design and applying the appropriate design heuristics (best practices). Experience has shown that researchers know the heuristics, but aren't as savvy as a seasoned designer in bringing a solution to life. All in all, both specialties are

important and should work very closely together, but not do each other's work unless clearly qualified. Caution is in order when organizations try to place people in stretch roles.

4. Pay Now or Pay Later

   Sometimes the mindset of project leaders is to keep moving forward despite their better judgment and just accept that if things don't go well, they can always be fixed later. This is similar to some of the previous warning signs mentioned above, but historically, paying for something later usually translates into more complexity, resources, time, and, consequently, money. Making the effort to do things right the first time not only builds user adoption and favorable results from the start but also saves you from having to backtrack to fix problems later. Funny how it often seems there isn't time or money to do things right the first time, but somehow resources can be found to do it over. Save your money, boost morale, and build confidence by doing it right the first time!

5. Sacred Cows

   There is a whole book on this topic, called *Sacred Cows Make the Best Burgers*, by Robert Kriegel and David Brandt. Sometimes project leads don't engage user-centered resources because past efforts have been successful without them. There will certainly be times when projects are effective without certain resources and partnerships, but what worked in the past may not always work now or in the future. When available, take full advantage of user-experience resources. The objective should be to bring the right resources to the table and collectively work toward what is best for the organization, the user, and the patient instead of taking shortcuts and winding up with a less-than-desirable outcome.

One last caution. The five warning signs sometimes appear in the form of questions or pushback when user-centered approaches are mentioned. Be on the lookout. When you hear the following, you are headed for trouble:

- Is this going to slow us down?
- Can't you just make it look nicer, a more modernized look and feel?
- Can't you just throw training at it?
- Can't we connect about this after we go-live?
- How can we backtrack now? We're already behind schedule!

...and What to Do about It

From experience, pushback or limited involvement seems to generally come from a lack of awareness or understanding of the user work the technology is meant to improve. There are several things that can be done to minimize the level of resistance, as noted below.

Sponsorship

It's in everyone's best interest to protect technology investments and mitigate potential and costly risks. Strong executive sponsorship of user-centered services is one of the best ways to be proactive. When executives are on the watch for opportunities to intervene early, user proficiency can be accelerated and costly delays in benefit realization can be avoided.

Formalize the Work

Consistency in approach is helpful when focusing on technology optimization efforts. Formalizing tracks of work sets clear expectations and reinforces collaboration. The following steps are key:

- Establish a collaboration model
- Develop good working relationships across the enterprise
- Get the right people to the table
- Set common goals and reinforce interdependency
- Ensure joint processes are followed
- Communicate leadership expectations regarding budgeting, timeline, and implementation

Increase Awareness

One of the best things to do is increase awareness of user-centered services within the organization, especially in large organizations. People leading innovation projects are often unaware of the resources available to them. Developing materials and executing a communications strategy help people understand the benefits of user-centered services and how to engage them. Sharing best practices and accomplishments goes a long way to building street credibility. And remember that brown bag learning lunches are a good way to socialize and network with other groups.

Solid Intake Process

It is extremely important to set expectations regarding project goals and priorities upfront. Asking the following questions during the intake process helps ensure that everyone involved works toward the same end goals:

- What vision or presenting problem are we trying to address?
- At what point are we in the process of achieving this goal?
- What has been done to date?
- What does success look like?
- If there are complications, do we have hunches about root causes?
- How will success be measured and tracked?
- Will users be accessible during the project?
- What is (are) the timeline(s)?
- Is there a budget for this work?
- Are there other groups involved in this work?
- If a vendor is involved, how willing and able is the company to partner on solutions?

Conclusion

Our experiences shape our thoughts and behaviors. It is human nature to seek times when we don't have to put a lot of thought and energy into certain tasks, and we gravitate to things that help us consistently become effective at work. We are creatures of habit and want to rely on things that work, the way we expect them to, every time. We are sophisticated, because we know what we have seen outside of work and expect it to be just as effective if not more so when at work. We want tools that support us to be effective.

When our experiences let us down, it becomes a distraction and we look for alternate paths the next time around. There is a lot at stake for HCOs when users abandon or ineffectively utilize the technology solutions provided to them. It is costly on so many levels. To mitigate risk, think of the user experience whenever possible and ensure you have the right team of resources in place to capture that return on your investment.

Moving forward, it is important to ensure your HCO embraces a user-centered mindset and establishes/maintains a foundation for continued success. The checklist below represents several critical opportunities that can propel your quest for benefits realization from your EMR and other transformative efforts. These opportunities are quite effective at ensuring sustainable outcomes but are strongest when embraced collectively. How many of these opportunities is your HCO leveraging on a regular basis?

- Strong sponsorship
- Clear success metrics (defined upfront)
- Formalized usability and technology tracks of work
- Project managers versed in how and when to incorporate user-centered disciplines
- Project approval and funding process with criteria, including plans for managing change and ensuring optimal user experiences
- Project check-ins and audits that also track progress of user-centered work
- Project teams aware of the value and resources available to them
- Shared development and delivery process between developers and usability teams (i.e., agile)
- Best practices and lessons learned at project debriefs and throughout the organization
- The right people in the right roles
- Decisions driven by data … and when data are not readily available—go get it

Chapter 2

Ongoing Change: Developing Sustainment

Ronnie D. Bower, Jr., MA

"Y'all fly in and gobble up all our free time, meeting rooms and space, and then leave us exhausted and alone."

Anonymous

Moving from Implementation to Sustainment

For the past decade, a great deal of energy has been focused on getting healthcare HCOs live on certified digital platforms. Various vendors have worked extremely hard getting health care providers running on viable EMR systems. Sound implementation plans, project timelines, budgetary projections, go-live schedules, and task capturing spreadsheets have brought most HCOs to a point where implementation of their EMRs is completed. HCOs continue to struggle with the transition from implementation to adoption and sustainment. Focus must shift from merely getting the system live to using system functionality, new/modified workflows, and system-generated analytics to better serve patients and their families. The leap into adoption establishes a new set of issues and challenges. Getting the most out of your data, having clinicians and physicians adopt standard workflows to maximize efficiencies, and having leadership, at all levels, maintain a focus on "lifelong" sponsorship often fall short of desired sustainment outcomes. During this transition, HCOs may struggle maintaining metrics, end-user satisfaction, and positive patient care experiences/outcomes.

The "helper bees" leave suddenly after go-live and leadership often isn't prepared to take on the additional duties of sustaining a healthy EMR.

During the implementation life cycle, there are peaks and valleys related to on-site support with lots of opportunities for project teams, vendors, and consultants to engage with frontline leaders, clinicians, and physicians. It was once described as a swarm of locusts descending on the unsuspecting field of organization leaders. "Y'all fly in and gobble up all our free time, meeting rooms and space, and then leave us exhausted and alone" is a favorite quote from a clinical manager describing the activity that happens during the implementation phase of a project. Project teams are there to remove barriers and keep the project moving forward. Armed with very formal plans, delineated tasks, timelines, and due dates, the intensity and focus are usually straightforward. The entire engagement is charged with excitement, emotion, and energy. It is often overlooked that the frontline clinical leader has just been given more tasks to complete but nothing was ever removed from his or her daily to-do lists. The on-site project team helps guide them during the project life cycle and is there to push when the implementation tasks are no longer prioritized and are not getting completed. The "helper bees" leave suddenly after go-live and leadership often isn't prepared to take on the additional duties of sustaining a healthy EMR. These tasks become yet another daily juggle of regulations, guidelines, complaints, budgets, and quality patient care.

It is always concerning when leadership or end users view the project go-live as a complete success and now move on to the next initiative.

The intensity and level of focus required to keep momentum going on the changes implemented are more than most leaders have found themselves ready to take on. The project teams helped them focus and were an extra set of hands to nudge and complete tasks, but when they leave, these duties fall into the mix of daily tasks, and many are forgotten or pushed aside for more pressing matters. Sometimes this happens because the leader doesn't quite understand the importance of the daily tasks through sustainment, but other times, it's just a product of running lean HCOs with leaders focused on multiple departments and multiple organization initiatives.

A nursing clinical director once stated in a leadership session, "You keep adding to my plate but nothing ever comes off, and now the food is falling off and rolling across the floor because I had to focus on another part of my plate and dropped it." Her message was very clear that project teams have been so focused on getting HCOs to the go-live that we often forget that go-live is the beginning, not the end. Once the goal of activation is met, energy levels needed for sustainment drop significantly. There are many reasons why the momentum slows and it's important to recognize that the reduction in focus naturally drops at go-live, and HCOs must decide how to determine why this has happened in their culture and how to reengage energy levels to assure they maintain a healthy EMR.

It is amusing that leaders often cannot turn the skills they have mastered with patient care around to use within their own departments.

Viewing implementations as ending at go-live will definitely set teams up for failure during sustainment efforts. It is always concerning when leadership or end users view the project go-live as a complete success and now move on to the next initiative. It doesn't matter how you label it (go-live, activation, or conversion), your system may now be "live," but the reality of the next phase of development is just beginning and continues long after you retire or leave the organization. When leadership prepares the organization for this difficult transition, they begin to build strong foundations that foster adoption, increase end-user buy-in, and gain the benefits of efficiencies with better patient care outcomes.

So how does an HCO transition from project mode to adoption mode? This question can take an organization down many different paths on the basis of how well they implemented the initial project and how proactive they were in developing a solid sustainment plan. Post-live leadership sessions with clinical leaders and physicians reveal that leaders frequently miss the insight on how to solve the new problems they are faced with daily. It is amusing that leaders often cannot turn the skills they have mastered with patient care around to use within their own departments. Generally, the first step in patient care is assessing the patient's current state, issues, complaints, and history. Just about every clinician will agree that information/history is needed to formulate an action plan for the patient. Leaders often want to jump right in and "fix" the problems within their department without assessing or understanding the problem. They would never administer a random medication to a patient without assessing allergies or having data to establish the medication was needed, yet leaders often randomly fire solutions at their departmental problems without getting a solid foundation on why the problem exists. It is for this reason that one of the key elements to a successful sustainment plan is to understand the culture, current state, and HCO's history.

Laying the Foundation: Post-Live Assessments

Assessing Current Culture

How successful was the implementation phase at your organization? This question should be the first one asked before jumping into planning a sustainment model. Most project plans have "lessons learned" sessions built into their strategies. These can be formal surveys, brainstorming

> Lessons are "acknowledged" but not "learned."

sessions, town hall forums, or informal discussions. HCOs that benefit the most from these sessions have made them formal processes with well-documented actions tied to each lesson. Too often, a new project quickly takes the place of the one that just ended and leaders fail to realize/complete the actions related to the previous lessons learned. Teams don't have time to implement the strategies that had not gone well or needed improvements, so lessons learned are never truly learned and often repeat over and over again during future projects. Lessons are "acknowledged" but not "learned." If key elements were missing from your implementation (e.g., communication or training), and those elements are necessary for successful sustainment, then the organization will never be as successful, if the past issues aren't corrected. This is common sense, but the reality is, the more complex the organization becomes, the more difficult it is for leaders to focus completely on correcting past mistakes to avoid them in the future. So, if you had completed

Department stakeholder matrix (sample)										
Clinical area	Shift change (12 h/8 h)	# team members in department	Readiness resistance			Manager name	Director name	Early adoption-team members	Highly resistant-team members	Additional comments
			Red (very resistant)	Yellow (mildly resistant)	Green (minimal resistance)					
ED	*12 h*	*45*	*15*	*20*	*5*	*L. Pahl*	*C. Constantinou*	*A. Smith, J. Brown*	*A. Broxton, J. Raines*	*3 directors in 4 years*
Surgery	*12 h*	*50*	*10*	*20*	*20*	*C. Ostrom*	*L. Bower*	*M. Green*	*Dr. Jones*	*Physician group negative, resistant*
Case management	*8 h*	*10*	*2*	*6*	*2*	*K. Waldron*	*C. Limerick*	*B. Singer, J. Capana*	*K. Starr*	*Works well with quality and informatics departments*
ICU	*12 h*	*32*	*12*	*12*	*8*	*M. Ray*	*K. Ellis*	*K. Bower, R. Dean*	*S. Miller*	*High turnover in nursing*

Figure 2.1 Sample department stakeholder matrix.

a lessons-learned session and are now starting to move into sustainment, or your sustainment efforts have stalled, dusting that lessons document off and bringing the issues back to leadership focus is a good place to start. At a minimum, HCOs should review the document or set up discussion groups to determine areas that may be continuing to cause difficulties from implementation to the current date.

Obtaining a list of key barriers and strengths is also very beneficial to see what type of historical struggles the organization has gone through. Past behavior often predicts future behavior so understanding how departments dealt with change in the past (including during the implementation) may help in determining strategies for better adoption success in the future. Some HCOs have implemented a Department Key Stakeholder Analysis grid that they found very helpful (see Figure 2.1). It is a fancy name for a simple spreadsheet that each director completes for his or her department. It lists key change questions across the top row and then leaders place the names of their team members and physicians down the left columns, answering each change question for every team member/physician. Once completed, various data can be pulled based on how the spreadsheet was designed to show trends in resistance, level of commitment, level of influence, or focal areas of concern.

For example, some spreadsheets have been geared to ask about resistance and level of influence to determine how resistant an individual might be within the department and how influential they are to their peers. So, if someone was extremely resistant to change and highly influential in the department, then that person could have the potential to derail any change efforts because he or she will always resist and have others that look up to him or her follow his or her actions. Some directors take this type of spreadsheet a step further and put a column on "why" that individual is resistant. This is an exceptional task to complete because the strategy for combatting the resistance varies greatly based on the why. If a person needs more training, leadership might assign a mentor or super user, or require additional training/competency for the individual. If they have negative baggage from past implementation or leadership, a leader might schedule weekly individual sessions to allow the team member to vent and constructively deal with that past emotion to help them engage in the new change without bringing that old baggage into the new initiative.

Finally, the person may just have an extremely negative attitude that doesn't match the new culture and, after repeated counseling and attempts to assist, may just need to leave the department or the organization. Many leaders don't like to hear this because finding staff can be difficult, but sometimes attrition during change is not a bad thing. All efforts should be made to save employees, but understand that some individuals will not see the future state that the organization is striving for and may never match the behaviors necessary for the organization to reach future sustainment goals. When this is the case, the compassionate thing is to help them move on, either into a new role, or to a new organization.

Assessing Team Member/Physician Levels of Resistance

Another simple way to gauge current resistance is to call your leaders together and ask them to go back to their departments and pull out their most current employee list. Every employee that works in the department should be listed on the document. Then ask them to think of a simple traffic light at any intersection in town (see following figure). The light has a red light for stop, a yellow light for yield/slow down/get ready to stop, and a green light for go. Tell them to imagine each of their team members as red, yellow, or green with the criteria.

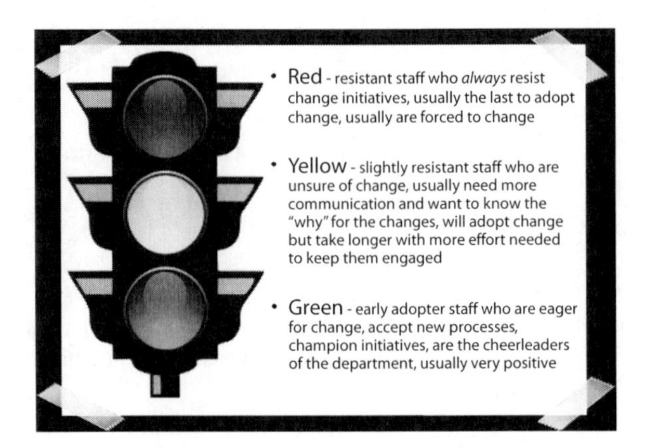

Once they have labeled each team member as red, yellow, or green, ask them to tally to see what percentage of their department is in each category. This helps leaders begin to realize the level of resistance they have within their own departments. Many leaders take the task one step further and put a "why" beside each yellow and red to begin to determine why that particular team member is resistant. These leaders are now prepared to engage their team members in the change process focusing on the best methods to move them forward as the change progresses. Leaders who do nothing to engage and combat resistance can expect no or limited change to take place within their department. A word of caution: Everyone changes when they know they are being watched, so leaders that go headstrong into their departments with an autocratic stance will see change while they are watching their staff closely, but as soon as they relax their grip, staff will regress to what they feel is the norm and changes may not take hold or be hardwired.

Direct supervisors who have good rapport with their team members can work closely to help them gain an understanding of ownership and buy-in at the local level. Helping team members gain an understanding of how their actions (documentation and workflow compliance) are linked to patient outcomes, Meaningful Use compliance, and quality initiatives will help them see the potential dangers of variation.

A real-life example is evident in the following: A nurse was trained to put three assessment levels into a documentation form that then totaled the three elements into a final number. To save time and eliminate a step or two, she quickly realized that she could just do the math in her head and put the total in the final box on the form, finalize, and electronically sign the document. She continued to do the math, left the other sections blank, and felt that she was doing an excellent job in streamlining her work efforts. It wasn't until a near incident that her "workaround" was discovered. The boxes she was leaving blank had rules and alert notifications built in the background of the system that sent messages and alerts to pharmacy and physicians on the basis of certain criteria levels. Even though the alerts and notifications were reviewed during training, she had never gained an understanding of how her removal of steps in the workflow could potentially affect patient care. Once she was brought in to discuss her workflow changes and realized the potential negative impacts of her actions, she became a huge advocate for following appropriate trained workflows and helped others in her department stay true to the standards of training and processes. She also became a strong advocate for helping other team members follow approved enhancement requests for system changes that were escalated appropriately.

Time is often the clinician's enemy and clinicians will try to find solutions that free time for more patient-centric activities. A director once stated: "nobody comes to work to do a bad job," and this statement helps put into perspective that sometimes the system doesn't create the smoothest and most seamless workflow that would be ideal, and end users will always try to tweak and shift workflows to save time. When clinicians understand the downstream effects of their actions, they are more likely to follow approved standards and buy-in to ownership at the department level.

Assessing Leadership Engagement and Resistance Levels

HCOs may wish to also review the level of engagement within their leadership related to EMR adoption. If the organization is live, what percentage of the leadership is actively engaged in the daily operations of sustainment? When there is a new workflow or system change meeting, what percentage of leaders attend? Is it always the same leaders coming and providing input with entire departments not participating? Perhaps there are leaders who are a little resistant to the change and don't wish to participate in further discussions. Maybe their department is one of the unique departments that have to work in two or more electronic systems and they are bitter that the new EMR didn't solve their workflow issues and therefore feel excluded. There are many examples of why leaders disengage when the project timeline ends, but for sustainment to work, the organization must know not only how resistant the department team members and physicians are to change but also how resistant the leaders are to change. This review should include all leaders: executives, senior directors, directors, managers, and shift/team leads.

A story from a training helps illustrate the importance of knowing leadership engagement and resistance level. The story begins with an individual who was attending a family reunion during a beautiful summer weekend. The individual, we'll call him Dean, was sitting outside watching the children run and play through the grass and fields. The wind was blowing a soft breeze, the sun was warm, and it was turning out to be an amazing day. Then, out of nowhere, there came a blood-curdling scream from around the side of the house. A group of teenagers had been playing kickball and one strapping husky teen took a run and kicked the ball with a mighty thud. Just as the ball was taking off and soaring through the air, a young toddler appeared from the corner of the gazebo. She was running downhill to join in the fun. The ball went soaring through the air just as the girl ran right into its path. There was loud smack; followed by a hundred gasps as everyone quickly turned to see how horribly disfigured the little girl must be from the impact. The ball hit her face and shoulder, startling her and making her fall to the ground. The teenage boy was horrified and came running and screaming down the hill to rescue the child.

Dean jumped from his seat and ran to the child, making sure he got to her before the hysterical teen. Dean picked up the child, who was so stunned she didn't know what had happened or what to think. Remember, all she knew was that she was running down the hill and then, bam, she was hit from out of the blue and on the ground. Dean quickly remembered his parent training class and knew the girl would react based on his reaction, so he smiled and rubbed her head and said: "It's all right … you are fine … it just scared you … you can go on and play." He assessed her to make sure she was really fine and she jumped up, rubbed her face a minute, smiled, and ran off playing.

The point of this story is what a difference the outcome was because Dean reached the child before the upset teen who thought he had just murdered his cousin. Had the teen reached the toddler first, the toddler would have looked up to see his hysteria and shock and would have instantly panicked herself. She would have started crying and screaming and then all the activities would have ceased as everyone would have run out to see the drama.

Remember that the size of your footprint increases as you progress through leadership, and more and more team members look for your reactions to help them gauge theirs.

This story always shows that although our team members are not babies (during training sessions, some leaders laugh and challenge that their staff are), they often react just as the toddler did. They are working steadily when, all of a sudden, a change comes that they knew nothing about but now affects them (just like a ball hitting their face) and they don't know what to do or how to react. So, they look to their direct supervisor and they often base their reaction on the reaction of that supervisor. HCOs must take a hard look at their leadership to see what type of resistance exists at those levels, because as long as leaders are resistant to change, the team members that look to them will have similar reactions, and change will not have a chance to flourish within that culture.

When leadership within the organization has great longevity, most leaders wind up supervising team members that were once their peers. Relationships were formed as peers, and now that the individual is a leader, they often forget that the type of interaction they have with their staff professionally must change. Leaders will always have more advance information about what is coming and will always be included in more communication and meetings surrounding initiatives and activities.

When leaders don't like a new initiative or an action needed for sustainment, they must remember to monitor their level of resistance when around their staff. People should feel free to share the types of things they don't like about initiatives: "I don't like that we have to document in two systems either, but that's the change, so how do we make it work." This statement is a great way to help show empathy that you as the leader do not like the change either, but that you are committed to making it work with their help. Remember that the size of your footprint increases as you progress through leadership, and more and more team members look for your reactions to help them gauge theirs.

Resourcing for Sustainment

Another common area to analyze during sustainment is resource allocation. Most implementations are adequately funded to bring in resources or backfill employees to give time to focus on the project. After the project timeline has been met, however, those resources usually disappear from the books. Project team members and consultants leave the organization and super users often go back into clinical care. So, who is left to maintain the work now? So much time and money was invested in getting the system live, but did the organization plan for sustaining all that work? It is a tricky question because now sustainment must become part of the daily budget, and as everyone knows, if it isn't budgeted, it isn't going to happen.

HCOs pay now, or pay later *with interest,* on the investment side of people and organizational change management.

Even the most conscientious leader, who wants to do the right thing and keep a proficient super user engaged in workflow updates and changes, will keep that super user on the floor working patient care if there is not a budgetary item that allows that super user to attend a meeting or upgrade training. It happens every day all around the world. HCOs have to proactively plan and budget for needed resources. There are enough examples out there to show that HCOs pay now, or pay later with interest, on the investment side of people and organizational change management.However, getting that point across to senior leadership may take time and some HCOs will fail or lose the benefits gained before taking steps to appropriately resource.

Each organization may have an exhaustive list of individuals necessary to sustain adoption efforts within their culture, but a few positions that have proven to help HCOs successfully transition through sustainment are included in Table 2.1.

Develop a Sustainment Plan/Charter

Many HCOs have been successful in adoption efforts by creating documents that clearly outline the necessary steps for sustainment. The documents have been successfully communicated to leaders in a variety of mechanisms (PowerPoint, Leadership Talking Points, Project Plans, or Charters). These documents help set the standard for expectations related to all elements necessary for a healthy adoption. Successful HCOs assure that the review and communication of these documents are embedded in the implementation life cycle, usually presented to leadership shortly after go-live. If an organization did not proactively establish such documents to share across leadership, it is never too late! HCOs can utilize sustainment charters to help set expectations long after the initial go-live and still have an impact on improving adoption and aligning staff within the organization. Establishing a collaborative plan and reviewing with all leadership can begin an all-encompassing adoption journey.

Sometimes the organization's culture isn't ready for change or transition during the go-live process, or there is so much transition and change being implemented that they could not focus on long-term sustainment and adoption. The "chaos" sometimes has to settle and then team members are receptive to change. It is always easier when the stars align and HCOs can transition smoothly from implementation to sustainment, but that is not always the reality in the complex cultures that exist within many hospitals across multiple departments. A good sustainment plan is implemented when the culture is ready to receive the information. If presented too soon, teams will be reviewing the information again at a later date, with a significant loss of momentum and a greater focus needed for reengagement.

A CEO once stated, "Timing is everything in making these changes," and his words are especially true when trying to assure the changes you are implementing get hardwired into the culture because *culture will trump strategy every time.*

Table 2.1 Adoption Sustainment Leaders

Position	*Description*
Sponsor	• Senior management (usually CNO or COO) to be the point person for decisions, barriers, enhancements, issue escalation, and resolution • Usually chairs the clinical committee that reviews workflow, policy and procedures, and protocols
Director of Clinical Informatics (CI)	• Director-level team member to assure equal footing with other directors • Usually a Registered Nurse (RN), but some HCOs have been successful with other key clinicians in this role • The main point of contact and focus for all things informatics • Works to bridge the gap between technology and clinical practice • Assists other directors in assuring compliance with EMR practices and accountability of workflow and clinical documentation • Instrumental in deploying system changes and enhancement requests • Assists other directors in communicating system changes
Medical Director of Informatics (MDI)/ Physician Champion (PC)	• Licensed physician who is credentialed to practice within the organization • Usually has been involved in helping physicians through change within the organization and has rapport with other physician leaders • The main point of contact and focus for all things related to physician informatics • Works in close partnership with CI on sustainment issues • Works to bridge the gap between technology and clinical practice for the physician population • Assists other Physician Directors in assuring compliance with EMR practices and accountability of workflow, standardization, and physician documentation • Instrumental in communicating and deploying system changes and enhancement requests to physicians • Works closely with Medical Staff and Training to assure new physician hires have appropriate training before beginning work at the facility/hospital
Training Specialist	• Individual who works either in the Education Department or under the CI who helps assure a sustainment training plan is established, maintained, and appropriate for all new hires (clinician and physician) • Works with CI on ongoing education needed for system enhancements or upgrades

(*Continued*)

Table 2.1 (Continued) Adoption Sustainment Leaders

Position	*Description*
Pharmacy Specialist	• Pharmacist who usually works within the pharmacy but has additional duties to assist with ongoing system changes • The main point of contact and focus for pharmacy informatics-related issues • Works to bridge the gap between technology and clinical practice within the pharmacy • Assists other directors in assuring compliance with EMR practices and accountability of workflow and clinical documentation of pharmacy practices • Instrumental in deploying system changes and enhancement requests within pharmacy • Assists other directors in communicating system changes that affect pharmacy and other departments
Communication Specialist	• Usually a marketing or communication individual already working within the administration • Key to assisting CI in deploying appropriate communication for system changes, analytics updates, accountability issues, upgrades, and success stories
Lead Super User	• A specific super user (usually the best super user in the department) designated to assist with adoption issues post–go-live • Usually one per major clinical area of the hospital or facility • Assists CI in creating a network of communication links where information can flow from the CI to the departments and back to the CI related to system changes, accountability issues, workarounds, enhancements, and physician-related issues • May attend a specific Super User Meeting that could meet monthly, every other month, or quarterly depending on sustainment needs of the organization • These meetings and the time for this position must be budgeted or leaders will not allow them to leave clinical care, even for short durations • Leaders must have a plan to replace these positions because they are often the same individuals who get promoted to other leadership positions. This role often prepares individuals to take on greater responsibility and therefore their traits and abilities make them prime candidates for promotion • *They are the true heroes of adoption and sustainment because they are involved daily in transitioning clinicians, physicians, and other super users to new standards and processes, assuring sustainment is taking hold and being solidified in their departments and culture*

A resistant culture will tear into the most well-founded sustainment plan and make it pop as easily as a kid's balloon being popped with a pin. Everyone can imagine how sad a kid would be to suddenly have their balloon popped (see Figure 2.2), and that's what change feels like to many when it is suddenly thrown at them. *If we haven't prepared staff for change, then there will be greater emotional reactions to the change.* Your staff may feel upset, sad, frustrated, and let down if they are not ready for change, or if the excitement for the change is suddenly stopped. Develop a plan to help you prepare your team. Provide clear expectations so no one comes to the table deflated. Your team will thank you.

Leaders may desire changes in responsibility or accountability faster than the culture will allow. The most successful HCOs move quickly to establish a solid sustainment plan that launches close to go-live, but HCOs must assess their culture to determine the most appropriate time to begin a sustainment plan.

The most important factor in planning is that everyone clearly understands their role in the post-live environment and that accountability is clearly established and can be reinforced at all levels. A successful transition from implementation to sustainment feels seamless to everyone. Support to end users continues across all levels and in every department. There are key meetings to escalate workflow and training issues and address barriers with transparency and involvement across all departments. Resistance to adoption is focused on by all leaders at the department level, with additional super user/training support augmented to match the needs of each department. Accountability to new workflow and system functionality is maintained and reinforced. Leaders are completing chart checks and audits on their staff and physician documentation, getting ahead of workarounds and unauthorized workflow adaptations. The drama/negativity regarding new

Figure 2.2 Change popping my world.

processes is minimized and dealt with appropriately. Sustainment goals and regulatory standards are reported and openly discussed.

A good example of not establishing a clear expectation, which is common among HCOs, is not setting the expectation that every leader (manager/director) attend EMR training. Some HCOs have never required their directors to get trained on the EMR functionality or new workflows. Typically, these departments struggle to meet target goals, Meaningful Use levels, or quality initiatives outcomes. Senior leadership becomes frustrated that outcomes aren't being met but fails to see the connection between lack of training and accountability. The directors can't hold staff accountable because they don't understand the new workflows because they don't understand the software. If the organization's sustainment plan had documented "all managers/directors will complete a training/competency checklist for system functionality/workflow," accountability would be more consistent across the organization. At a minimum, leadership would have received a basic understanding of what their staff was being instructed to document and the new workflows required to meet quality patient care. Directors would quickly know when clinicians were creating "workarounds" to decrease documentation times or skip workflow steps that they did not think were necessary.

This is one small example, but it shows how easy it would be for a clinical director to say "I'm too busy to go to training, and that's why I have super users," never obtaining the information needed to lead their department through this transition, and missing a key leadership opportunity. This director doesn't clearly understand that he or she can't hold the team accountable if they don't know what the team is being asked to document or change in new workflows. This simple example can be avoided if senior leadership will challenge their leadership to all agree to be trained, place this decision in a formalized plan, socialize the idea, and then hold any leaders who do not follow through with the training accountable.

If HCOs focused time on the following steps related to sustainment, resistance would be reduced, alignment and standardization would improve, and cultural barriers/silos would begin to drop:

1. Agree to expectations and standards required for success.
2. Put them in writing in a plan or document.
3. Socialize/communicate them to all parties involved.
4. Hold people accountable for these common goals (at all levels—executives to staff members).
5. Positively reinforce desired behavior, and deal directly with those who do not perform.

The Sustainment Plan

So now that we see the importance of having everyone on the same page with sustainment expectations, what types of elements should be included in a solid sustainment plan? A list of the types of sections and key elements follow, but remember that each organization has a very specific culture and sustainment plans should document all the items that are necessary for setting expectations to help with accountability. This list is but a base to begin, and HCOs should include all items they feel are necessary to communicate to all levels within the organization to make changes successful:

Nobody in this world changes anything until they *feel* the need to change.

- *General Guiding Principles of Sustainment*—Explaining the "why" the project is moving from implementation to adoption. Explaining how everyone's help is needed to make this successful is needed for buy-in. Include quotes or stories or data that make people feel the need for change. Nobody in this world changes anything until they feel the need to change. We forget this as leaders and often jump into "just get it done." If you help team members *feel* why they are needed in this change process, they are more likely to embark on the journey collaboratively with you. Think about your culture and use examples or stories that fit the culture and hook those team members to listen to your message and then want to follow you through this change.
- *Roles and Responsibilities*—This probably is the largest and most important section of the document. It should clearly outline everyone's duties in a post–go-live state. Some roles change significantly from implementation to sustainment and others just a small amount. Don't be afraid to list everyone that is affected by the EMR and specifically identify what the expectations and accountabilities are for their positions. The more specific you can be with key behavioral (observable) expectations, the better your plan will be and the less variation you will have from department to department, clinician to clinician, and physician to physician.

Now, I don't want readers to think that I am naive because just documenting what is expected doesn't take into consideration the complexity of the individuals working throughout your organization. Accountability will not just magically happen. HCOs are full of individuals who have their own personality, background, history, and experiences that place them on a continuum of resistance (less resistant to more resistant). Add to that a department's culture looming over the individual's experiences. Then, all those individuals begin to make up the hospitals/healthcare facility's culture (open/closed, familial, urban, rural, physician-owned, community focused, educationally focused, etc.) and we must consider how recent events have affected the culture (mergers, layoffs, expansions, new service lines, bad/good audits, etc.). All of these complex levels build on one another to create the culture that is lived and breathed each day within the organization. (If you are unsure what your organization's or department's culture is, think "unwritten rules.")

So, assuring roles are clearly outlined is fundamental to aligning everyone, but there is another level of work needed to break through some of the complexities that culture and background have embedded into the entrails of each department. This takes time to sift through and begin to move culturally, but accountability can begin with alignment of expectations, so this section is central to beginning culture shifts and adoption.

Key roles to make sure you always address the roles/responsibilities section of a sustainment plan might include the following:

1. C-Suite/A-Team (CEO, CFO, CNO, CMO, CMIO, COO, etc.)
2. Clinical Directors/Managers (Nursing Units, Education, Quality, Pharmacy, Lab, Rehab, Radiology, etc.)
3. Nonclinical Directors/Managers (HIM, Registration, Medical Staff, Finance, Information Services, etc.)
4. Clinical Informatics Director/Manager
5. Physician Informatics Director/Physician Champion
6. Physician Groups (MEC, Advisory Groups, Department Meetings, etc.)

7. Super Users
8. Helpdesk/Service Desk/Technicians

Once all the roles have been identified, Table 2.2 can be utilized to show role and responsibility.

Committee, Groups, and Meetings

A table or list of all committees, groups, or meetings necessary to keep everyone informed of system functionality and changes is beneficial to include. Remember to review all your stakeholders to see what types of meetings they attend or already have established. Many times, sustainment needs can be placed on other meeting agendas to avoid creating another meeting that zaps valuable time from leadership focus (leverage what you have). The rule is to make sure your stakeholders have a voice and a feedback mechanism to complete the circle of ongoing communication to increase adoption. The following are three examples that often get missed:

Executive/Sponsorship Meeting—Is there a place where key decisions about EMR adoption are rolled up to executives to be able to remove barriers, provide resources, and understand where the organization stands with adoption?

Workflow/Process Meeting—Is there a place where key workflow decisions are vetted; where all workflow decisions are decided, documented, and socialized to keep standardization of processes and training consistent?

Super User Meeting—Is there a forum for lead super users from each major clinical and business area to meet (monthly, bimonthly, quarterly, etc.) to discuss system changes, workflow issues, enhancement requests, training needs, or opportunities for better collaboration?

Table 2.2 Sustainment Plan Roles/Responsibilities Sample Table

Role	*Responsibility*	*Behavioral Expectation*
CNO	• Hold team members accountable for documentation and workflow standards • Remain engaged in committees and updated on system/workflow changes • Provide appropriate resources to assure adoption • Promote continuous process improvement across all departments • Maintain updated workflows, policies and procedures, and protocols • Promote adherence to Meaningful Use, regulatory, and clinical Best Practice standards	• Round floors to interact with team members on system/workflow concerns • Chair workflow/clinical standards local committee, including documentation of meeting and updating of required forms/policies • Review system issues/problems at daily huddle with leaders • Include system performance indicators in direct reports and goals/objectives and review periodically throughout the year • Attend training on system/workflow and additional supplemental training for updates/upgrades • Assure system analytics are being utilized at the department level to reinforce adoption and standardization across departments

Escalation Processes

A section for your organization's escalation process for system/workflow issues needs to be included. Many times, this is left out as it is assumed that the normal past process will be sufficient. However, it is often quickly identified that the complexities of an EMR require a more detailed escalation process that needs to be discussed, accepted, documented, and socialized.

Enhancement Requests

As soon as your facility starts using an EMR, each department will begin requesting enhancements to the system or changes to the workflow because "we are special and you don't understand our workflow."

A section on how your organization will handle enhancement requests needs to be included. As soon as your facility starts using an EMR, each department will begin requesting enhancements to the system or changes to the workflow because "we are special and you don't understand our workflow." This statement almost always arises because within an organization there are various services lines with different needs. **Too often, enhancement requests that flood in at go-live are not valid or helpful for the entire system, and although they would make a few individuals happier, they would not be beneficial enterprise-wide.** This lesson is a hard one for cultures that have always gotten what they wanted (think mass customization and exception mentality). This can be a delicate navigation for specialty groups or physicians that provide niche services to the organization. Having a clearly defined enhancement process will eliminate some of the cultural shift pains because everyone will know the process and then be able to communicate "why" decisions were made and "why" actions were taken or not taken.

Post-Live Training

A section on how the organization will handle ongoing training is extremely important and often overlooked. Usually, a Clinical Informaticist (CI) has helped lead the organization to go-live and is often thought to be the only person responsible for the EMR success. This type of thinking will set the organization up for failure, and training is an area where this struggle becomes a reality in many HCOs. After go-live, many leaders think that the training of new staff and physicians can fall to the CI. After all, this is usually a new position and "what will they be doing now that we are live." Leaders fail to realize that the level of work necessary to assure adoption to meet regulatory standards often completely consumes the CI's schedule. So, HCOs must plan out a strategy to successfully train new hires (clinician and physician) and document it clearly. Also, when upgrades/system functionality changes (which can be often), how is this training completed? Having all this thought out and documented helps managers/directors know what is expected when they hire a new individual and avoids overwhelming or burning out the CI position.

Downtime Procedure

Assuring you have a solid downtime procedure that is either referenced in this document or embedded in it will keep all teams focused on the correct processes when there is planned or unplanned downtime. This issue is often overlooked and chaos and patient safety issues can arise when team members and physicians do not clearly understand the approved downtime processes. Sometimes this document can be quite large and is often just referenced within the sustainment plan, but please assure you have a downtime process that is approved and very well socialized with super users and end users (clinicians and physicians).

Post-Live Communications

A final section to address in your sustainment plan is communication. How and what is needed for communication now that you are live? What types of communication vehicles exist in your organization? What will be shared about system changes, adoption efforts, Meaningful Use success, or upcoming downtimes? Putting responsibility for communication under each role will help with accountability. Utilizing a list or table to capture types of communication, responsible parties, distribution routes, and delivery dates/times will help coordinate post-live communication efforts. Using lead super users, daily huddles, town hall forums, employee surveys, department communication logs, or informal discussion groups to provide feedback mechanisms is key to assuring communications are reaching all levels within the organization and that the messages are being clearly expressed in the most appropriate manner for the recipients' communication needs.

Once expectations have been clearly outlined and socialized, there are some significant activities that have proven to help align HCOs that are working on solidifying their sustainment efforts. Each activity would generally be customized to the organization's cultural needs and a few are listed below.

Post-Live Leadership Session

Developing a session that engages the leaders and allows time to interactively discuss concerns, align expectations, and pinpoint action plans specific to department leaders helps put leaders on the adoption path.

Providing a post-live leadership session is a great way to "kick-start" sustainment efforts regardless of the implementation success level. A leadership session helps reignite the burning platform for leaders within the organization. Developing a session that engages the leaders and allows time to interactively discuss concerns, align expectations, and pinpoint action plans specific to department leaders helps put leaders on the adoption path. A few key elements that have been proven successful in post-live leadership sessions follow.

Just about every leadership session has some form of introduction section, but introductions can be utilized to gauge level of experience and comfort with change and to get more information on barriers or strengths. A good facilitator can utilize information from introductions to gain rapport with participants and gain a better understanding of where the organization is on their change continuum.

An interactive session with open dialogue to brainstorm is an excellent way to get the conversation of change started (see Figure 2.3). Begin by asking participants to openly express barriers that they have seen that hinder the progression of change in the organization. Even if there are less barriers today, participants are encouraged to disclose and discuss all items they feel have

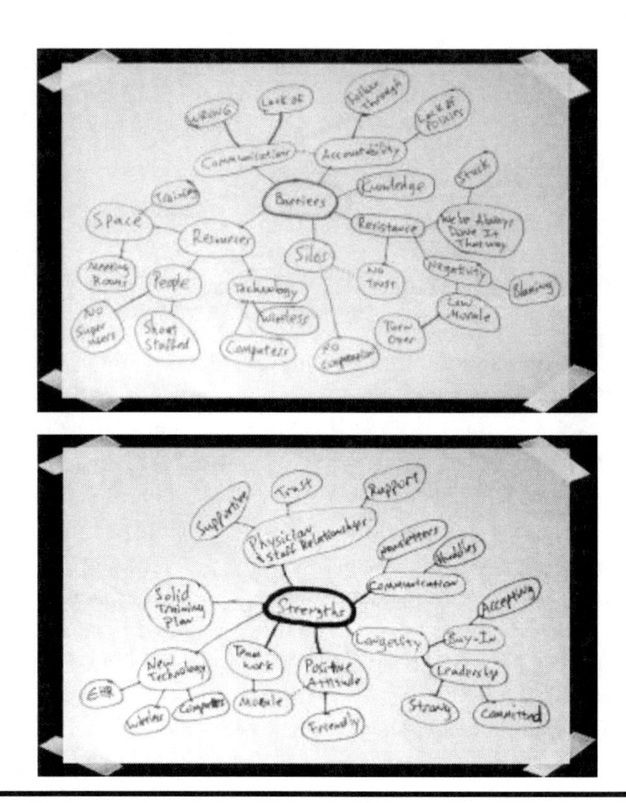

Figure 2.3 Examples of whiteboard barriers and strengths from leadership session.

slowed progress. The facilitator offers assistance and challenges participants to further explain and discuss items as the brainstorming continues and writes them on a whiteboard to show connections and reference them throughout the rest of the session. Next, move to the strengths that have helped the organization through change. This section may start slow and may not come as freely as the barriers. Since we tend to remember the negative emotions more freely, the facilitator must work a little harder during this section to probe and get the strengths from the participants. The wonderful outcome of this section of a leadership session is the audience verbalizing, sometimes for the first time, the true challenges and strengths to change within their organization. One note is to assure the audience that this is a "safe zone" so they feel free to openly discuss any topic expressed. This will help with open dialogue throughout both sections. Another key factor to point out is that what might be a barrier for the entire facility may be a strength for a specific department (e.g., communication may be poor for the whole organization, but the department has worked hard to create clear channels of communication and feedback loops to make it a strength for them).

A review of Dr. Stephen Karpman's 1968 theory known as The Drama Triangle has proven very successful in getting leaders to begin discussing the drama that occurs within their departments during times of conflict and change. This interactive section reviews three specific roles that individuals play during conflict and drama. The drama often centers on the Victim role with someone being perceived as helpless and vulnerable. Then the Persecutor role is reviewed to show how that individual is attacking the Victim and is perceived as evil. To finish the triangle off, the Rescuer role is there to swoop in and save the day.

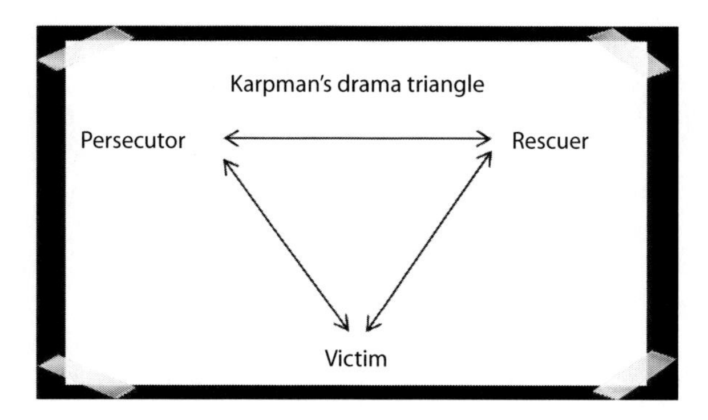

Audience participation regarding times of recent conflict where participants played a role on the triangle has been very beneficial in getting leaders to openly discuss their perceptions about team members, leadership, and physicians within the department or the organization. Once all the roles are discussed and examples explored, the session begins to wrap up by discussing how each role is "not real." The Victim ultimately is not helpless, the Persecutor is not evil, and to be honest the Rescuer does not always need to help or be heroic. Leaders often take on the role of Rescuer and want to "save" their departments but end up creating learned helplessness and codependence within their staff. Team members soon become victims who rely more and more on the leader to fix the problem, thus creating more drama and living more on the triangle.

Sometimes this interactive session is the first time leaders are confronted with the cultural realization that they have been living "on the triangle" for years. The best part of the session is discussing how to help teams live off the triangle, by helping them realize that the roles on the triangle are not real and that "options" are the only way to get off the triangle. After this session, it is not uncommon to hear leaders state "Stop the drama, stop living on the triangle" during key meetings or times of conflict. It is a healthy way to begin to combat cultural factors that have existed through many iterations of leadership. This section does not change culture, but it allows leaders to begin to have a language to talk about changing their culture, which then helps break down old barriers that have fostered resistance and hindered sustainment.

Accountability is another important factor to review at leadership sessions. It is important to help leaders understand that ownership for documentation within the EMR is shared by everyone. Since the CI and Medical Director of Informatics (for physicians) are often viewed as the main points of responsibility for the EMR implementation project, other directors often place more responsibility on those positions for accountability and sustainment. If departments are creating workarounds or not following through with workflow steps, senior leadership often look to the CI to "fix" the problem, when in reality, it is every leader's responsibility to assure that team members and physicians are accurately following standards set forth by the approving committees. If accountability is set early across all directors and leaders, then it will be easy for department leadership to step in and reduce variations in processes while aligning standardization. The CI is usually a single position within an organization and logistically could not possibly hold all departments and team members accountable for all workflow processes. The CI position is to help other leaders, but the entire responsibility cannot fall on this position's shoulders. Executives who recognize the need for shared accountability generally set this expectation early in the project or it is already embedded in the HCOs' culture.

A simple nonthreatening example to use when asking leaders about accountability is to question them about their time clock policies and have them explain their clocking in and clocking out policy. Can team members clock in 3 min early or 3 min late and not break policy? Once this discussion begins, ask them to pay attention to actual time clocks around change of shift as they round the organization. Those departments that have strong accountability surrounding clock in/out will usually have a line around the time clock with staff waiting to follow the appropriate, by policy, time to badge in/out. Those departments that are more relaxed with accountability regarding attendance and overtime won't generally have lines at the time clocks.

This example is an easy one that can get the discussion about accountability started with leadership, but remember that the point is to make sure that, post-live, all leaders understand their role with holding team members and physicians accountable for new workflow processes, documentation, and order entry. Executive buy-in for accountability is essential, as is an appropriate escalation process to address situations when leaders are not pulling their weight.

Leadership (Director/Manager) Toolkit

One of the most successful tools for directors and managers after go-live is a toolkit created specifically to help them lead effectively in an electronic environment. It is important to assure that all leaders have the basic training on system functionality before implementing any additional tools or training. Establishing an online toolkit that can be easily updated and serve as a reference tool for leaders and super users will enhance the organization's sustainment efforts. A toolkit should meet the needs of leadership at the facility level. Some fundamental areas that have proven beneficial include the following:

- A simple **Day in the Life Leadership Checklist** provides leaders with a simple guide to check during the initial transition from implementation to sustainment. Items are listed on a checklist with reference documentation to help the leader understand what to look for and how to get the information. Examples of types of items to initially review are overdue tasks, staff assignments, medication administrations, physician telephone/verbal orders, intake/output reports, and form completion reports. The checklist provides a daily tool that leaders can reference and complete to assure team members and physicians are following approved standards. If your facility is long past go-live, you can still create a reference document for the types of system issues that you may be falling behind on or areas where goals are falling short.
- A **reference to specific job aides** can be quickly reviewed in the toolkit, with links to online videos or cheat sheets. This is extremely beneficial for leadership because it gathers these aides in one place for easy reference.
- Placing a link to the **policy and procedures** that are needed to support new workflows (or placing the actual policy and procedures themselves) is essential for leaders to be able to quickly reference. This assists them when reinforcing the "why" to team members or physicians as they can reference the approved documents as supporting collateral.
- A section that references **regulatory standards** is also helpful. Because leaders can't be experts with all regulations, having a section to reference helps them stay current on regulatory requirements (e.g., Meaningful Use, Core Measures, Magnet Status Requirements, and The Joint Commission). If your organization has experts in these various measures, creating documents that are in user-friendly language further helps leaders. Just referencing regulatory standards or web page references are not as helpful as having local experts create more useful reference documents or tools.
- Since EMR implementations often seem like learning a new language, a **glossary of terms** assists leaders who are not familiar with project management or specific vendor system lingo.

Specific abbreviation lists are also very helpful because sometimes a clinical abbreviation and a vendor abbreviation are completely different in meaning.

- There are usually **complex workflows** that are difficult to master from initial training, so referencing these workflow documents in one location will help leaders navigate their complexity. Many of these workflows cross departments and levels of care, so having one toolkit available online assures that multiple leaders can reference one primary source of truth at any time for clarification. Some common workflows that tend to initially cause confusion include but are not limited to staff assignment, patient handoff and assessments, chart checks (24 h), chart audits, medication administration/reconciliation, and charge-related workflows.
- **System customization and options** on how to quickly change views, settings, and parameters are important elements to be able to quickly reference. Because many people change settings and then forget how they completed the change, a reference section for the most common settings or how to change them based on your vendor selection is helpful.
- **Reports** is the section that many leaders find valuable. Since so much data are available immediately to leaders, utilizing this section to help leaders determine which reports are the most beneficial begins to ingrain accountability at the local level. Armed with data, leaders can make decisions and reinforce appropriate behaviors with their team members and physicians. Parsing this section into daily, monthly, and quarterly reports helps leaders focus their efforts because there is usually an abundance of reporting tools but little reference to how/when to use them. Having a system expert sit individually with leaders to review this section seems to be the most beneficial way to use this portion of a toolkit. Not every leader will be interested in every report, so individualizing this section will improve the likelihood that leaders actually reference and use what they need from the system to increase their effectiveness.
- Getting **new hire** team members and physicians the access to the tools they need their first few days on the job eases the orientation process and lessens the burden on super users and leaders at the department level. Therefore, a section that references new hire requirements, security and credentialing forms, position control, and training requirements helps leaders shorten the time required to gain system access. Having a solid post-live training plan that outlines all training requirements for the various positions within your organization reduces confusion during employee/physician onboarding.
- **Downtime and printing** are always areas of concern after go-live, so having all downtime procedures referenced in one location is extremely helpful for leaders. Also, instructions on what is allowed to print and how to print are good reference tools. Team members and physicians can become very creative in the use of print functionality, which may be outside approved workflows, so providing leaders with easy access to updated printing policies will help with accountability in this area.
- **Devices** are another area that directors sometimes need additional assistance understanding. So many devices are deployed during an implementation that it is sometimes overlooked that many leaders do not understand how to "care for" their devices. A section that references online guides for the various devices you have deployed or a quick care sheet discussing charging, cleaning, location, and dos/don'ts for each device has been found to benefit leaders in maintaining their devices. This also has a secondary gain of reducing unnecessary calls to technicians as many questions are answered in the referenced documents.
- The availability of a **physician-specific** section is beneficial for leaders because physicians often confront leaders with common system questions and complaints. Some focus areas to

include or reference are job aides, pocket guides, patient lists, managing lists, groups and proxy functionality, rounding reports and views, messaging, and order entry tips/tricks.

- Understanding how **charges** work in the new electronic world is an area that confuses many leaders during activation, so referencing key charging decisions or job aides is very helpful. Leaders may forget how items or procedures that are rarely completed or utilized are captured for charging, so having a reference section on how charges are pulled from and input into the system will help reduce missed charges and additional back-end work capturing items later.
- Because leaders are not just leading this change but also directly involved in the details of the change, a section on **Coaching for Organizational Change Management** is helpful. Leaders are change agents during implementation and then throughout the life of the EMR's sustainment. Many leaders have excellent skills in moving their team members along a change curve, but some need additional assistance or tools. Providing tools that help them engage, energize, challenge, and hold their teams accountable is very useful. This section may reference additional training (web based or face to face) that leaders could utilize during staff meetings to help the teams that are struggling with adoption. Many HCOs subscribe to various web-based training modules that leaders could utilize to help individual team members by assigning them specific training sessions to complete (e.g., communication within a team, how to handle negativity, or team conflict management). Working with the education or organizational development (OD) department to find the most appropriate training sessions to reference in this section that would be helpful for leaders is a good plan of action. This section should not be an exhaustive list of all training materials but rather focused on those specific training modules that are the most beneficial. Remember that leaders can reference online catalogs or the education/OD department for exhaustive lists of all training materials, as needed.

Lead Super User Program

Lead super users were referenced earlier. They are so crucial to a successful sustainment program that there needs to be a specific program developed to make sure this role never goes away. Once the project team descends on the organization, leaders quickly get the idea that many of their team members will be pulled from staffing at varying times with varying degrees of involvement. After go-live, leaders often expect that all their team members will return to full clinical care within their departments. This may be true but HCOs must convince leaders that having a key point person from each major clinical area is necessary to remain connected to system changes that may happen daily. Once convinced, leaders may need some guidance on establishing a lifelong super user program. The term *Super User for Life* has been used to describe those individuals that remain as points of communication contact for the CI to and from the departments. Maintaining a strong program after go-live is not easy and there must be consensus across all clinical leaders. Representation must be across the entire organization, so responsibility is not left to a few individuals carrying the burden of the entire sustainment process.

Selection criteria can be reviewed to assure you have the correct person in place as the primary point of contact for each department. Many times leaders choose the same person over and over as the super user, but sometimes that person doesn't have the appropriate skills for the job. There are selection criteria that can be utilized to help leaders choose the most appropriate person for this important ongoing role. The simplest explanations are the best. Figure 2.4 shows how super users are used through the life of a project.

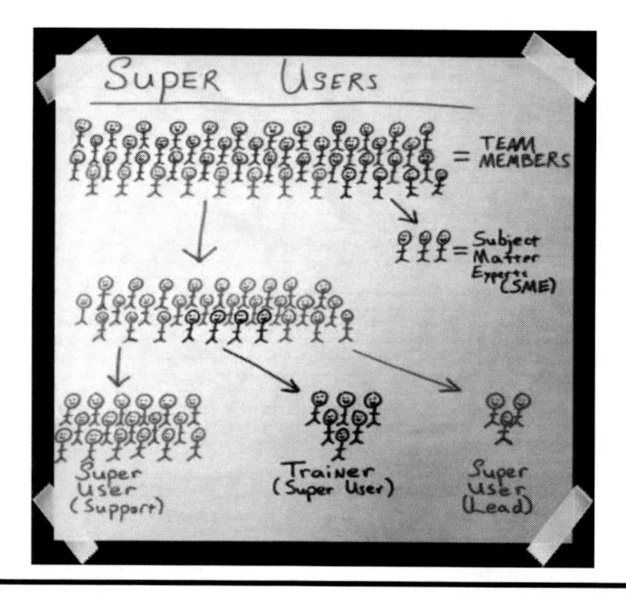

Figure 2.4 Super user model for success.

Thus, looking at the diagram, all the team members are listed first, just like when a project team arrives on-site for the first time. Then, some team members are pulled out of the population to serve as subject matter experts (SMEs) for workflow and design discussions. These are team members that really understand the daily operations of each department within the organization, but they may or may not have the skill set to become a strong super user, so when they are done helping, they go back in the mix of team members. Some of those SMEs may very well have the skill set to be an excellent super user and are chosen by leadership. Out of the super user population, some individuals will rise to the top of the class and may be identified early as those that would help the department after go-live and become lead super users. Other super users are excellent at handling groups and very comfortable in front of a class and may become additional facility trainers during go-live to help get everyone trained. The majority of super users selected during implementation are trained and used as frontline support during all go-live activities. These individuals do return to complete clinical care duties after go-live, but the ones that have excelled in their role are often chosen as super user leads to help the department continue to meet objectives long after go-live.

Figure 2.4 shows how individuals might serve different roles through the life cycle of a project. All the information above had been put into charters and PowerPoint presentations, but until it was drawn quickly on a whiteboard at a leadership session, leaders didn't quite grasp how simple it really was to choose the right person for the right job during different times within the project. An additional lesson here is to avoid making communication too complex, detailed, and overwhelming.

Below are a few of the fundamental criteria used in a selection matrix to help leaders identify super users:

- Consistently displays hospital mission and values
- Ability to motivate and encourage others
- Ability to provide frontline support

- Understands workflow processes
- Ability to handle/reduce resistance
- Familiar with help desk escalation and downtime procedures
- Trains other effectively
- Understands additional duties of super user role
- Successful mentoring/coaching experience
- Demonstrated analytical and problem-solving skills
- Understands project timeline and scope
- Has well-established relationship with local physicians
- EMR or transformation experience
- Strong sense of responsibility and project commitment
- People oriented with sound interpersonal skills
- Displays strong active listening skills
- Experience with computers/technology
- Performs with minimal direction/supervision
- Good oral/written communication skills
- Exhibits a positive attitude

Clinical ladders or incentive programs are great ways to encourage participation as super users. Many super users enjoy assisting during the implementation, but it can be stressful to deal with resistance and extreme emotional reactions from end users and physicians. This experience may make some of them leery to assist in a post-live role. Leaders should have open conversations with potential post-live super users to review negative implementation experiences and discuss interest in continued super user service.

Creating a super user contract or agreement letter is a good way to set expectations regarding the role during sustainment. Leaders can agree on the language of the document as a group and then meet individually with each super user to assure clear expectations are set. Items to include in the letter and discussion are as follows: meetings the super user is required to attend, how communication to the department will happen during times of transition or change, and clinical care duties versus super user duties.

Clinical Informatics and Information Services Partnership

Having an experienced Director of Clinical Informatics and Medical Director of Informatics will guide clinical practices to meet objectives and regulatory requirements, but there must also be an extremely sound partnership with the Director of Information Services to make sustainment successful. Sometimes this partnership comes naturally for the culture, but sometimes the relationship must be cultivated. The two fields must learn to overcommunicate to keep each other in the loop on very complex system issues. Defining scopes of practice early in the relationship helps leaders within the organization appropriately triage issues. CIs often get pulled into issues that are more geared for an information services solution (e.g., troubleshooting desktop issues, printer jams, or network connection issues).

Also, information services technicians often get questions related to workflow decisions or clinical process questions while fixing more technical issues (e.g., why does patient weight have to be put in first, why does this order not include pain medication, or how do I complete this clinical assessment form). Getting clarity over which types of issues are handled by which departments truly helps leaders and super users in navigating and teaching end users and physicians to triage their own problems more appropriately, thus reducing unnecessary help desk calls and end-user frustrations.

Communication Is Forever

The truth is very few clinicians are monitoring their e-mails the way leaders do, so if that is true for that culture, then why would that be the only avenue chosen to send the message?

A leader once described communication as a "contact sport" and that description resonates because communication is action and reaction. Leaders often fail at communication because the message is lost, doesn't make it to the intended audience, is too complex, or is misunderstood. Communication efforts must continue at the same intensity as during implementation to reach sustainment goals. Overcommunication to team members and physicians is often required. Leaders must really look at their culture to see what mechanisms work effectively and then utilize those avenues to communicate. The truth is very few clinicians are monitoring their e-mails the way leaders do, so if that is true for that culture, then why would that be the only avenue chosen to send the message? Leaders need to take a hard look at their role in communication and make sure the message is being sent in a manner that it can be received and understood by all those who need to understand it. But don't stop there—go a step further and ensure a feedback loop is in place to catch instances when communication fails.

Conclusion

Sustainment is a lifelong event that requires planning, resources, and daily focus to stay on track and meet goals. Action is needed at all levels within the organization if sustainment is to become hardwired in the culture. Maintaining focus, alignment, and attention is a constant struggle as

Sustainment topics/focus area	Have we addressed this area?	Action plan needed? (yes/no)	How have we addressed?	Due date for action plan	Responsible party
Resource needs					
Training needs					
Workflow accountability					
Resistance to adoption					
Technical needs					
Physician adoption					

Figure 2.5 Sustainment focus areas table.

new initiatives and priorities draw attention. Everything described in this chapter contributes to building an environment that helps achieve sustainment goals, a better end-user experience, and a safer patient care experience. If HCOs are struggling to engage adoption and sustainment efforts in their facility, a simple review of the table shown in Figure 2.5 might begin to focus efforts in key sustainment areas.

Chapter 3

EMR Benefits Don't Come in a Box: Why Structured Innovation Is Necessary to Realize Strategic EMR Value

Douglas Ivan Thompson, MBA

"Many HCO executives, including IT executives, believe that merely installing the EMR software and using it in a technically competent manner will result in substantial benefits being realized."

Healthcare organizations track and manage many strategic outcomes. These include mortality, complications and other adverse events, lengths of stay (LOS), patient and staff satisfaction, financial results, hospital readmissions, population health status, and many other things. It's rare to see dramatic improvements in these metrics from month to month, or quarter to quarter, because after many years of concerted effort, most of the "low hanging fruit" (easy improvement opportunities) has been picked.

Implementation and use of an advanced EMR system is one of the few remaining opportunities for an HCO to realize breakthrough performance improvement. This is because these systems include new capabilities that most HCOs have not had in the past, which can help drive dramatic improvements in some of these key outcomes (Figure 3.1).

The most commonly reported hospital EMR benefits are listed in Figure 3.2. They include reductions in medication error and adverse drug event (ADE) incidence, shorter hospital LOS, reduction in nursing time devoted to administrative activities, reduced use and cost of lab testing and medications, increased use of preventive care, dramatically faster order communication and execution, reduced paper use, improved charge capture for billing purposes, and reduction in transcription costs. These are just a few of the many reported benefits of the innovative use of EMRs, as illustrated by the case examples below.

	Cumulative Capabilities	Some Potential Incremental Benefits
Stage 7	Complete EMR; CCD transactions to share data; data warehousing; data continuity with ED, ambulatory, OP	Increased data integration and completeness, improved analytics capabilities
Stage 6	Physician documentation (structured templates), full CDSS (variance and compliance), full R-PACS	Improved quality of clinical documentation, reduced clinical practice variation, error prevention, outcome improvements, AE prevention
Stage 5	Closed loop medication administration	Prevention of many drug errors and ADEs, nursing efficiencies (e.g., elimination of MAR reconciliation)
Stage 4	CPOE, Clinical Decision Support (clinical protocols)	Prevention of transcription errors and related ADEs, much faster order processing, improved clinical outcomes, reduced practice variation
Stage 3	Nursing/clinical documentation (flow sheets), CDSS (error checking), PACS available outside radiology	Further improved quality of clinical documentation, prevention of more drug errors and ADEs, radiology efficiencies, easier to access clinical data
Stage 2	CDR, Controlled Medical Vocabulary, CDS, may have Document Imaging; HIE capable	Improved quality of clinical documentation, prevention of some drug errors and ADEs, reduction of duplicate lab testing
Stage 1	Ancillaries—Lab, Rad, Pharmacy—All Installed	Departmental efficiencies and productivity, ease and speed of accessing clinical data, avoid redundant data entry
Stage 0	All three ancillaries not installed	

Figure 3.1 EMR capabilities and associated benefits by HIMSS Analytics EMR Adoption Model level.

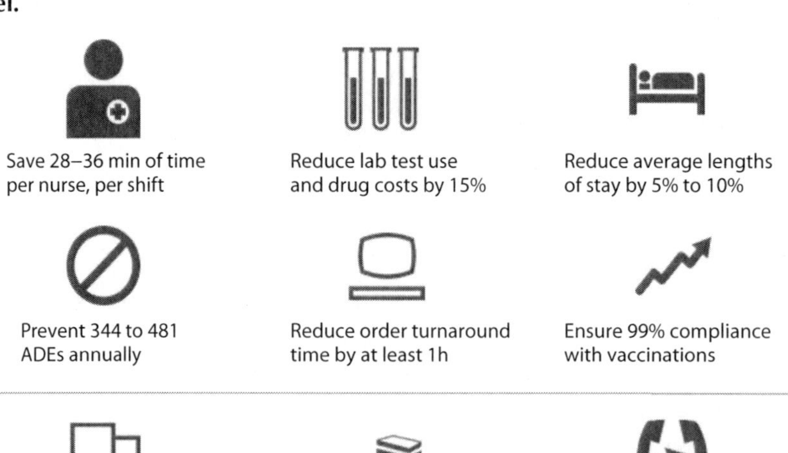

Figure 3.2 Most commonly reported hospital EMR benefits. (From Thompson DI et al., *J Healthc Inf Manag*, 2007, 21:49–60. Also courtesy of HIMSS Analytics and Advisory Board Company survey of EMRAM Stage 6 and 7 hospitals, 2012.)

A Few Success Stories

Sentara Healthcare

Sentara's 2007–2011 EMR implementation at eight hospitals is one of the best-known examples of benefit realization. Sentara achieved a financial return on its EMR investment 2 years earlier than it had budgeted, including 2011 financial benefits of $54 million related to LOS and ADE reduction, increased outpatient volumes, increased nursing unit efficiency and registered nurse retention, reduced transcription expense, reduced medical records staffing and supply expenses, reduced health plan costs, lower IT maintenance expenses, and other cost reductions.

Among many other clinical benefits measured at Sentara were an approximate 50% reduction in mortality ratio across six hospitals, reductions in many patient flow metrics of 25%–40%, a dramatic improvement in its CMS Core Indicators from mostly worse than expected to almost all better than expected, an increase of more than an hour in the time nurses spent on direct patient care, and a 73% reduction in medication administration times.

Texas Health Resources

Texas Health Resources (THR) implemented its EMR in 13 hospitals from 2006 to 2011. Among its documented EMR benefits were ADE reductions of more than 50% 1 year after go-live, a decrease in the time spent by nurses on administrative activities of more than 45 min in three of four nursing units, a $3 million reduction in Unit Clerk staffing, a 50 FTE reduction in medical records staffing after 1 year, dramatic improvements in "perfect care," or the percentage of time its patients received all CMS Core Indicators for their conditions, and a reduction in the time from drug order writing to computer input from 118 min to 0 min.

Allina Health

Allina implemented an integrated EMR at eight hospitals from 2004 to 2007 (other hospitals were implemented later). Allina measured benefits at its first two hospitals in 2005 and 2006. These benefits included a 50% reduction in the time required to move patients from the emergency department (ED) to an inpatient bed and a 91-min reduction in ED wait times. Nursing documentation quality and completeness was dramatically improved. ADEs were reduced. Drug utilization and costs were cut by 29%. Duplicate testing was "virtually eliminated," and "charge on documentation" saved significant nursing time. Transcription volumes were reduced by 25%, scanning workload was cut by 57%, and the number of health unit coordinators was reduced by 20%, resulting in substantial cost savings.

Hospital LOS for pneumonia, circulatory disorders, and other conditions were reduced. Compliance with process quality metrics (e.g., CMS Core Indicators) was dramatically improved, and the use of standardized order sets increased substantially. Allina implemented integrated revenue cycle functionality along with its EMR and saw a 21% reduction in accounts receivable days, a 27% reduction in denied claims, and many other process and outcome improvements.

Vanderbilt University Medical Center

Vanderbilt implemented its self-developed EMR beginning in the 1980s. One of the more dramatic examples of the use of its capabilities is in Vanderbilt's intensive care units (ICUs) and is known as the VAP Dashboard. Taking advantage of the electronic nursing documentation capabilities of the EMR, the VAP Dashboard is a screen saver that appears on every monitor in the ICU. This dashboard shows each patient on the unit and each element of the "ventilator bundle," or best practices for care of mechanically ventilated patients. The elements of the bundle that have been documented as being provided in a timely manner are shown in green, while those elements that have not been provided when needed are shown in red. Nurses see the red and help their colleagues get current on those patients' ventilator care. This relatively simple mechanism was credited by Vanderbilt for preventing 108 VAPs and 16 deaths in Fiscal Year 2009 and saving $2.5 million to $4.3 million that same year.

El Hospital Marina Salud de Denia

Marina Salud is a privately managed provider network in the Marina Alta area of Spain that includes 34 primary care facilities and a 206-bed hospital. Marina Salud implemented hospital and ambulatory EMRs in 2008 and has since seen dramatic improvements in quality and efficiency metrics across their continuum of care, primarily associated with best practice protocols. These include a 33% reduction in congestive heart failure (CHF) hospitalization rates and a 35% reduction in CHF readmissions, a 21 reduction in chronic obstructive pulmonary disease (COPD) hospitalization rates, a 15% reduction in COPD readmissions, and a cost savings of 22 million Euros.

The average hospital does not get measurable value from their EMR.

They have also eliminated many unnecessary chest x-rays, improved early detection of sepsis resulting in a 40% reduction in sepsis mortality (saving an average of five lives a month), and reduced delays in physician consultations by 70%. Medication alerts resulted in order changes 37% of the time, indicating a potential impact on patient safety. Nursing efficiency has been improved, giving nurses additional time to spend with their patients. Unlike many hospitals, Marina Salud has even saved physician time with EMR functionality. And data from the EMR have greatly improved both the efficiency and effectiveness of patient care improvement initiatives such as pressure ulcer and fall prevention.

Why do some hospitals get substantial, game-changing, strategic value from their EMRs, while the majority do not?

Additional examples of EMR benefits achieved by HCOs can be found in the peer-reviewed literature, in other less formal industry publications, on the HIMSS Davies Awards website, as told in conference presentations and on site visits, in the records of EMR vendors, and in the private files of many hospitals. These success stories stand in stark contrast to recent research on the average hospital with an EMR. According to most of these studies, the average hospital does not get measurable value from their EMR [1,2]. Indeed, according to some studies [3], the more sophisticated an EMR is, the higher costs are at the HCO that uses the system.

Why do some hospitals get substantial, game-changing, strategic value from their EMRs, while the majority do not? One possible answer is that most hospitals don't study EMR value—so they may be experiencing value that is not measured. Another possible answer is that most hospitals are not far enough along in their EMR implementation and optimization journey to have achieved substantial value. However, we believe that the most important reason has to do with a difference in their attitudes toward EMR benefits and the approaches or methods used by the successful hospitals—what they did to get value from their EMRs (Figure 3.3).

In the 1990s and early 2000s, most large HCO software implementations were technically driven; their goals were to build and implement defined functionality on time and under budget. Gradually, it became apparent that HCOs needed to pay attention to process changes driven by an EMR in order to have a smooth implementation and satisfied users. The state of the industry today is an EMR implementation that is both technically and process driven; its goals now include the changing of workflows to take advantage of new system capabilities, or in some cases building the system to replicate familiar workflows from prior operations, which could be considered paving cow paths.

However, a technically competent, process-driven design and implementation approach is still not sufficient to ensure measurable strategic value. Process design without an overarching set of outcome goals may emphasize user convenience, conventional wisdom, political considerations, and other factors that do not support improved outcomes.

We studied the methods of more than 200 hospitals that have realized substantial business value from their EMRs and found that they generally adopted a "benefits-driven" implementation and optimization approach. That is, the focus of the implementation was the realization of specific, measurable benefits, aligned with the strategic goals of the HCO, in addition to process changes, technical success, and human change management.

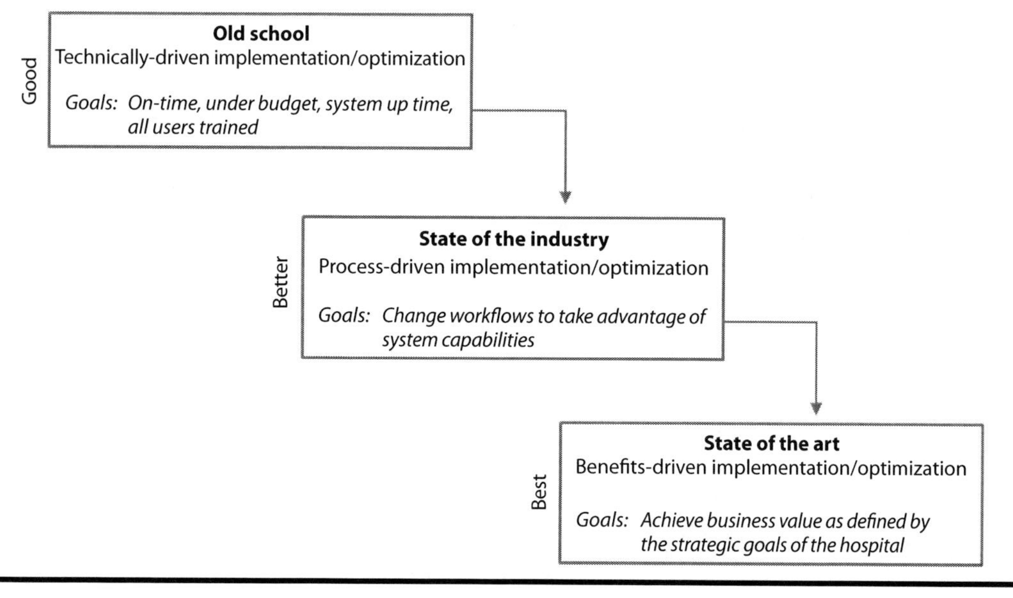

Figure 3.3 Contrasting EMR implementation approaches. (Courtesy of The Advisory Board Company.)

Leadership Beliefs That Promote or Hinder EMR Benefits Realization

Many HCO executives, including IT executives, believe that merely installing the EMR software and using it in a technically competent manner will result in substantial benefits being realized.

Leadership attitudes and beliefs play an important role in whether EMR benefits are actually realized. Below, we describe three "self-defeating" beliefs or attitudes that hinder EMR benefits realization at many HCOs.

- *Self-defeating belief #1: EMR benefits are the result of automation.* Many HCO executives, including IT executives, believe that merely installing the EMR software and using it in a technically competent manner will result in substantial benefits being realized. This leads to a technically focused design, build, and implementation project and to underresourcing the post–go-live optimization of the system. In fact, our experience tells us that the great majority of EMR benefits are the result of innovation—learning to use the EMR's capabilities to support new ways of working.
- *Self-defeating belief #2: EMR benefits realization can be delegated to IT.* Because the most important EMR benefits result from innovation in care processes, the optimization process should be led by operational and clinical executives. IT is responsible for putting in place the technologies that support innovative care processes; however, decisions about how to change those processes must be made by the leaders responsible for those processes, and the overall responsibility for achieving desired outcomes (benefits) is owned by the senior executives of the organization (Figure 3.4).
- *Self-defeating belief #3: Measuring EMR benefits is a waste of time and money.* Many HCOs do not invest in EMR benefits measurement because they feel those benefits will be realized whether they are measured or not, and because benefits measurement can be expensive and time consuming. But what these HCOs do not realize is that most EMR benefits are achieved through an iterative improvement process; the first design and build is almost never sufficient to produce the desired benefits. Therefore, having hard, monthly or quarterly data on the changes in system use, processes, and outcomes resulting from innovative use of the EMR allows the organization to understand where it can improve its approach. Benefits measurement does not just give a reason to celebrate success but is part of the actual mechanism by which success is achieved.

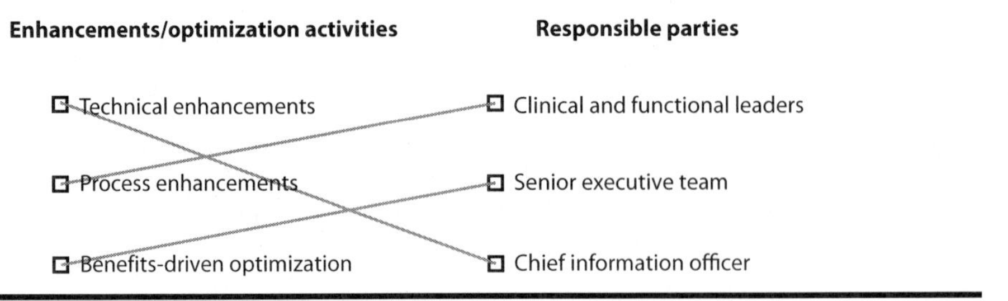

Figure 3.4 Responsibility for optimization activities. (Courtesy of The Advisory Board Company.)

Best Practices for EMR Benefits Realization

HCOs that have achieved substantial strategic business value through use of their EMRs use six best practices, which comprise a "benefits-driven implementation (and/or optimization) method." HCOs can use any one of these best practices, but the most successful organizations use most or all of them together; they are synergistic and sequential. The good news is that these best practices are simple to understand and relatively inexpensive to use; the bad news is that few HCOs use them.

Best Practice #1: Benefits Framework

A benefits framework is a "short list" of key EMR benefits that represents an organizational commitment to achieve those benefits. A benefits framework should be mutually agreed upon by HCO leaders including senior executives, key department leaders, clinicians, and IT representatives. Organizations that did not use a benefits-driven implementation approach should still develop a benefits framework to guide their optimization work after go-live—it's never too late to begin thinking about and pursuing EMR benefits. This is also true for the other five best practices described below.

We recommend using the process illustrated in Figure 3.5 to reach agreement on a benefits framework.

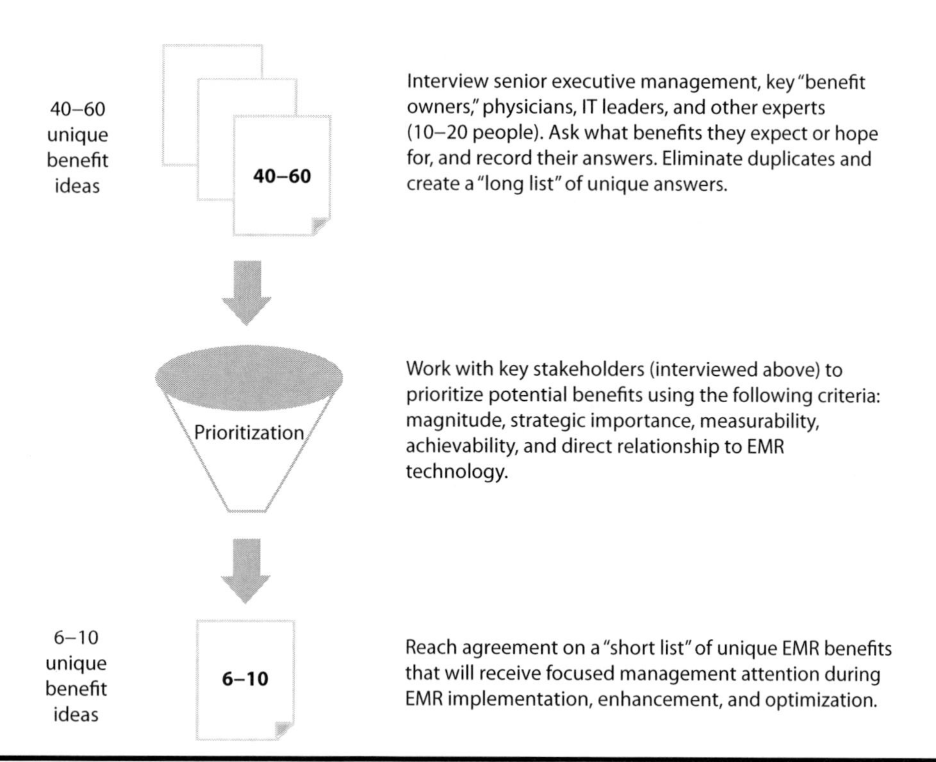

Figure 3.5 Reaching agreement on a benefits framework. (Courtesy of The Advisory Board Company.)

Best Practice #2: Benefits Sentences

Once HCO leaders agree on a list of 6–10 EMR benefits to pursue, these benefits must be defined to ensure that everyone understands them the same way. A useful technique for doing this is the creation of benefits sentences. A benefits sentence has four "parts of speech": the EMR functionality that supports the benefit, the process change that results from using the functionality, the amount of change in outcomes that should result from using the EMR, and the expected amount of time it will take to achieve those outcomes. The development of a benefits sentence is illustrated in Figure 3.6.

Best Practice #3: Benefits Modeling

An EMR benefits model is a spreadsheet that estimates or quantifies the amount of EMR benefit that an HCO can expect in a particular area. The most common reason for creating a benefits model is as part of a business case that justifies the EMR purchase decision. The second most common reason is as part of a benefits study done years after EMR go-live that quantifies the amount of benefit actually achieved. Both of these are good reasons for benefits modeling, but a third reason is much more important. The creation of a credible benefits model requires a deep understanding of performance goals, current performance against those goals, the benefit mechanism by which the EMR affects performance, and the amount of impact that can be expected, given the experience of others.

Having this information makes it much easier to manage the process of benefits realization, and much more likely that desired benefits will actually be achieved. So the most important reason for benefits modeling is as a blueprint for benefits realization—it is the insight gained from creating a credible benefits model that makes it so valuable.

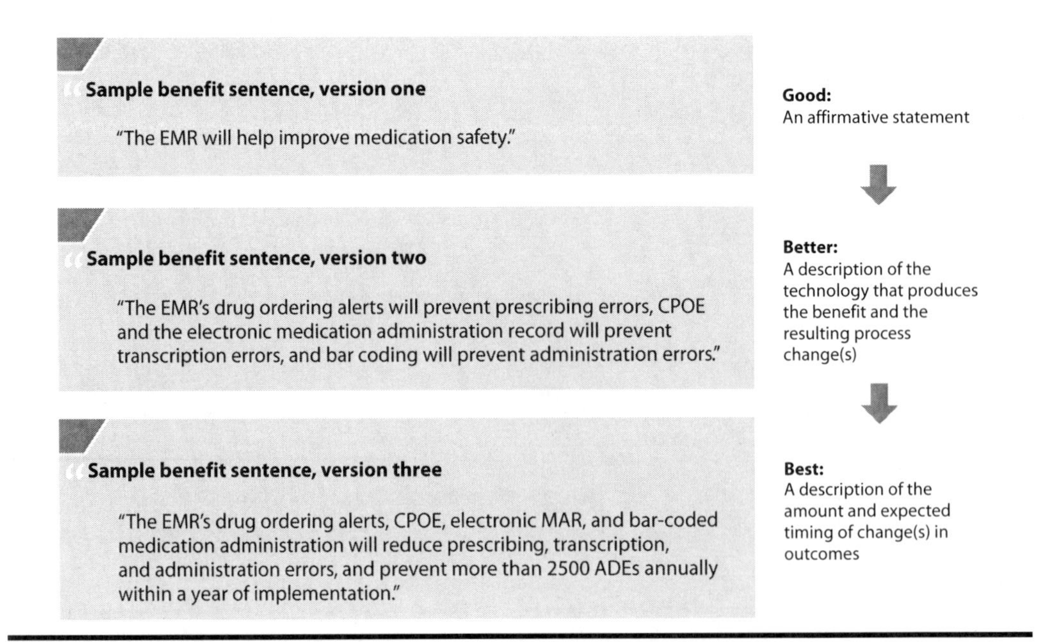

Figure 3.6 Refining a benefits sentence. (Courtesy of The Advisory Board Company.)

Obviously, it is easier to measure EMR benefits if you start with good baseline performance information about the results or outcomes achieved before going live with the new EMR. However, organizations that did not measure performance before EMR implementation can still measure benefits using available retrospective data such as hospital LOS and infection rates (available from historical records), ADE incidence (available through retrospective chart review), direct variable costs (available through cost accounting studies on retrospective financial data), and CMS Core Indicators (available from public reporting).

More importantly, organizations that are live on a new EMR can always measure their current levels of performance on all important outcomes and begin their improvement journey from that point. Most strategic EMR benefits take years to fully achieve, so an organization that has been live on their EMR for a year still has a long journey ahead of them.

Best Practice #4: Benefit Requirements

A typical EMR project plan includes thousands of functional requirements and hundreds of process changes that must be designed and implemented. But each of the 6–10 key benefits listed in the benefits framework (best practice #1) is supported by only a few functional requirements and process changes. Knowing what the "benefit requirements" are for a given benefit allows those functional requirements and process changes to be prioritized to ensure that each of the key strategic benefits are achieved (see Figure 3.7).

Best Practice #5: Benefits Measurement

As noted above, benefits measurement is essential to realizing EMR benefits, because these benefits are achieved over time, in an iterative process that requires regular feedback. A dashboard view, showing monthly progress in achieving each of the 6–10 benefits listed in the benefits framework, is very useful. This report should include not only the outcome metrics that define the desired results but also a few process and system use metrics that help reveal the root causes of success or

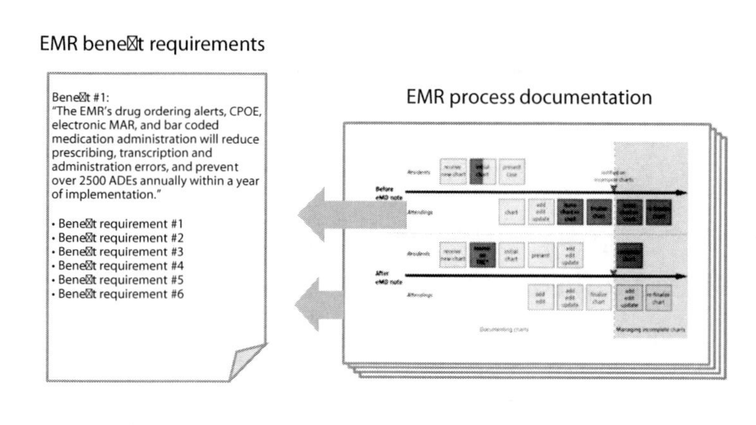

Figure 3.7 Benefit requirements. (Courtesy of The Advisory Board Company.)

Sample "monthly operating report" for benefits tracking

Benefit category	Base	Target	Jan 09	Feb 09	Mar 09	Apr 09	May 09	Jun 09
% fall interventions charted	76.5	95%	79	81	80	84	87	85
Pt falls per 1000 pt days	3.6	2.0	3.5	3.5	3.1	2.9	2.7	2.9
ADE incidence rate (%)	26.5	20.0	27	25	29	23	24	24
# of top 10 OS implemented	5	10	8	10	10	10	10	10
% top 10 order sets used	35.9	75.0	37	43	50	56	60	65
Cost/case, top 10 DRGs	$4500	$3700	$4460	$4250	$4100	$4043	$3987	$3924
Paper forms cost/admit	$9.47	$4.60	10.2	9.50	9.42	8.54	9.28	9.12

Figure 3.8 Monthly operating report: EMR benefits. (Courtesy of The Advisory Board Company.)

failure. Figure 3.8 shows an example of a "monthly operating report" used by one HCO to guide its benefit realization efforts.

This example highlights in red one of the HCO's desired EMR benefits: reduction in practice variation and cost per case for high-volume, high-cost conditions through the use of standardized electronic order sets. The dashboard includes monthly direct variable costs per case for the top 10 conditions selected for order set development and also shows the number of order sets available for use each month and the percentage of time the order set was selected by the ordering physician.

Best Practice #6: Organizing for Benefits

An organization that adopts a benefits-focused approach to EMR implementation and optimization needs organizational structures that reinforce this approach. There are a variety of ways to do this, depending on the HCO's culture, the other structures that are in place, and so on, as shown in the examples that follow. However, there are a number of principles that inform the creation of these structures, including the following:

- A single "benefit owner" is responsible for each "short list" outcome.
- Benefit owners are senior individuals, natural owners of the outcome.
- Cross-functional teams work on improvement initiatives associated with each major benefit.
- Analytical, change management, data, process support is provided to benefit owners.
- Benefit owners meet regularly to review metrics, progress, and tactics.
- Benefit owners are responsible to operational executives for results.

Case Studies: The Link between Best Practices and Best Results

Near the beginning of this chapter, we presented four case studies of organizations that achieved substantial strategic benefits from the use of their EMR systems. Here, we briefly describe how two of these same organizations used one or more of the six best practices to achieve their benefits.

Sentara Healthcare

Before beginning its EMR design, build, and implementation project, Sentara deployed management engineers throughout the organization to identify major opportunities for performance

eCare benefit category	Annual benefit (million dollars)
Improved nursing efficiency	$4.9
Reduced IT maintenance	$3.6
Reduced medical records/transcription	$3.6
Increased outpatient services	$4.8
Reduced length of stay	$3.8
Improved pharmacy process/ADEs	$3.0
Reduced paper/storage	$2.7
Other hospital improvements	$3.6
Home health	$1.8
System health plan	$2.3
Total	$35.5

Figure 3.9 Sentara's projected financial benefits associated with EMR implementation. (Courtesy of The Advisory Board Company.)

improvement and define the role of the EMR in achieving those improvements. Their financial benefit goals are shown in Figure 3.9.

Sentara created an organization structure where corporate executives were the benefit owners, with personal responsibility for achieving major benefits. The performance improvement work at each local hospital was led by individuals reporting to these executives, and support was provided by "optimization teams" at each hospital that included finance, measurement, process analysis, and change management experts (see Figure 3.10).

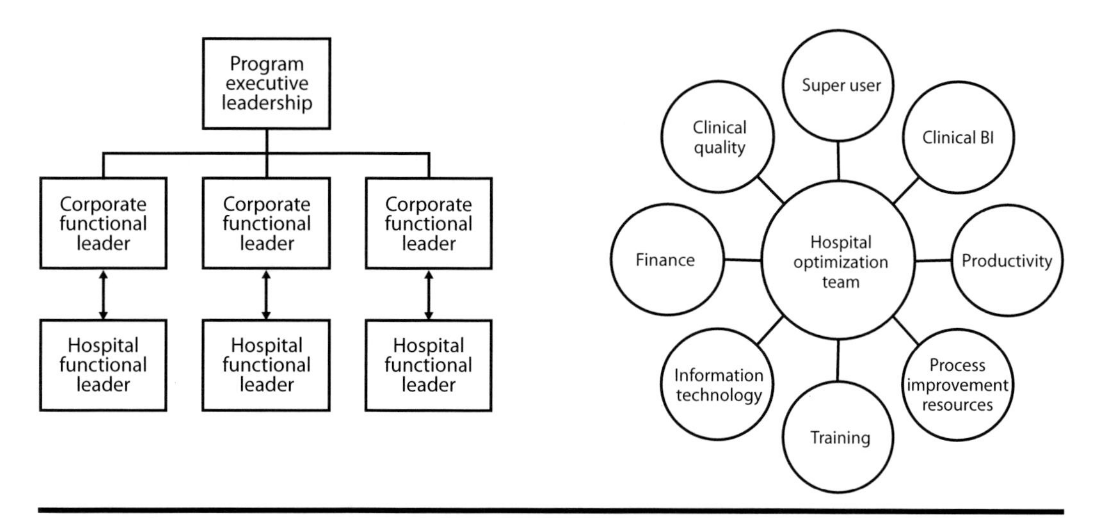

Figure 3.10 Sentara organization structure. (Courtesy of The Advisory Board Company.)

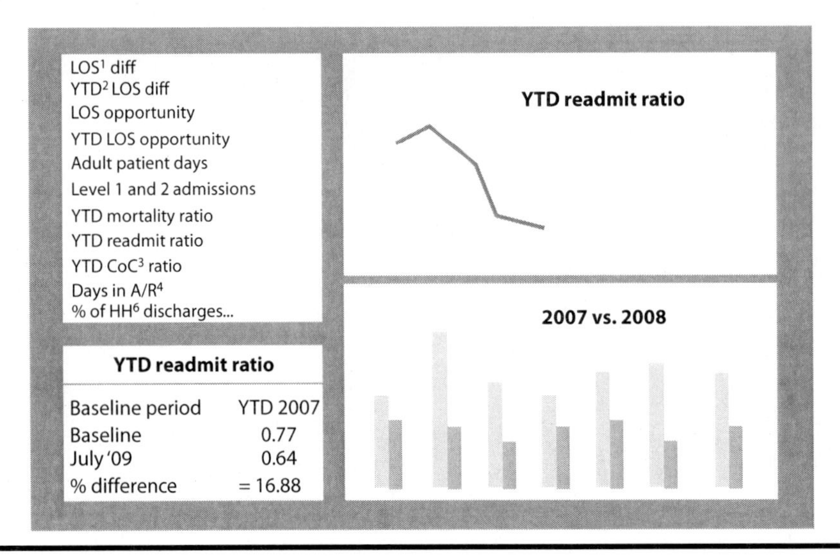

Figure 3.11 Monthly EMR benefits dashboard. (Courtesy of The Advisory Board Company.)

Sentara also created a monthly dashboard report showing each of the major benefit goals and their progress in achieving them (see Figure 3.11).

Texas Health Resources

THR formed a committee made up of senior executives, functional leaders, and clinicians to identify and agree upon a short list of key benefits for its EMR implementation. Their rigorous process of identifying and reaching agreement on these benefits is illustrated in Figure 3.12.

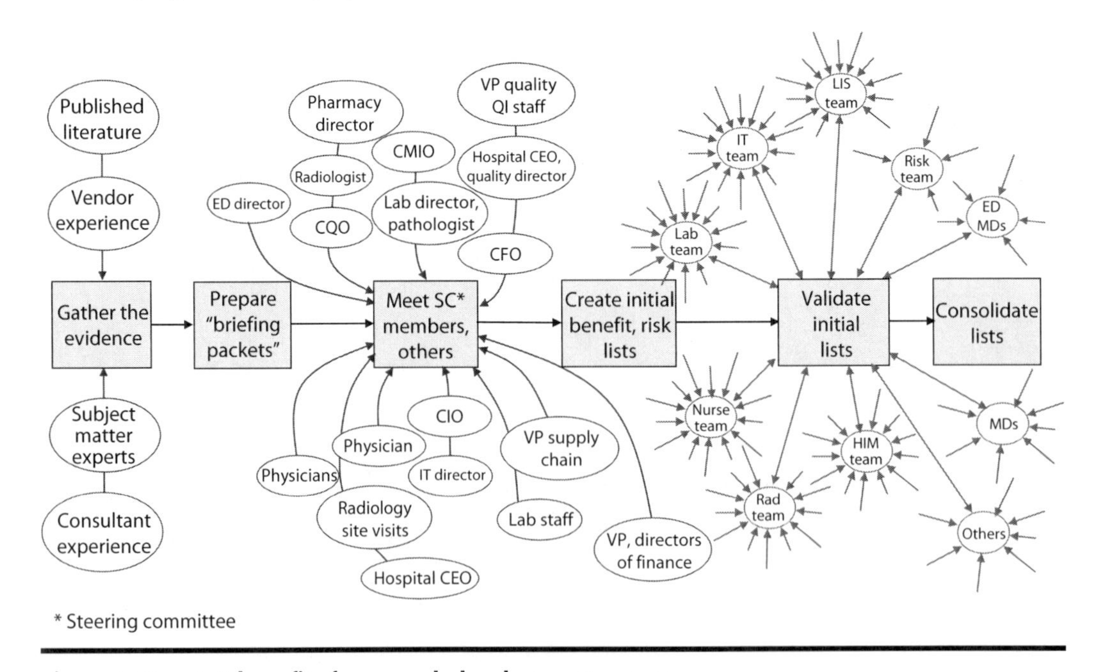

Figure 3.12 THR benefits framework development process.

Benefit Category	Expected Benefits
Promote evidence-based care	High impact on KPIs[a]/P4P, save $50 million annually
Increase medication safety	Prevent 2500–5000 ADEs annually
Reduce complications	Major reductions in patient falls, pressure ulcers
Cut order communication time	Orders received 1–1.5 h faster
Increase staff efficiency	Large impact on nursing, unit clerks, HIM[b]
Increase patient throughput	Significant impact in some EDs on visit, wait times
Reduce use of paper forms	Save $600,000 to $1 million annually
Increase data collection efficiency	Save half of chart abstraction time
Reduce IT support workload	Some impact on lab support staffing
Optimize medication use	Significant impact on spend in some drug categories
Improve charge capture	Significant impact via automating manual processes

[a] Key performance indicators/pay for performance.

[b] Health Information Management department.

Figure 3.13 THR benefits framework. (Courtesy of The Advisory Board Company.)

Through this process, THR created the EMR benefits framework shown in Figure 3.13.

THR also selected a Benefits Director for the project. She was a senior IT manager with a clinical background, who had deep knowledge of the Texas Health organization, process improvement methods, and Epic functionality, and who was also well known and respected by her peers. She was supported by two full-time analysts with nursing degrees as shown in Figure 3.14. THR's Benefits Team engaged clinical and operational stakeholders at the entity and system levels to review the benefits framework, create data collection plans, and establish benefit realization goals

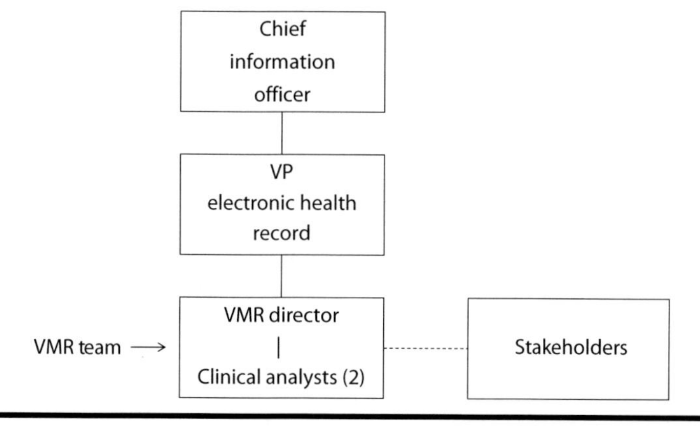

Figure 3.14 Texas Health's EMR benefits realization (VMR) program structure. (Courtesy of The Advisory Board Company.)

and expectations. Benefits analysts worked with stakeholders to outline data collection methodology, measure baseline performance levels, define and model expected benefits, and validate pre- and postimplementation performance data.

EMR Optimization through Structured Innovation

Whether your organization is using a benefits-driven approach to EMR implementation or is working on post–go-live optimization, the principles are generally the same. EMR *optimization* is a term that is used in many different ways by HCOs today (Figure 3.15).

From bottom to top of the pyramid diagram, many HCOs think of EMR optimization generically as "what happens after go-live" (e.g., redeploying EMR project staff). Others have a technical focus on enhancing system design and adding functionality not included in the original build. Still others are focused on workflow or process changes to drive increased use of the system, or to standardize clinical and operational processes. At the top of the pyramid are pioneers in EMR value realization, who are focused on achieving measurable outcome improvements, both in areas where others have shown the way (e.g., medication safety, drug and lab test utilization) and in new applications.

The tactical, technical, and process aspects of EMR optimization are all important and must be efficiently managed and effectively executed. However, many HCOs become stuck in a cycle of technical EMR improvement driven by user demands and never break through to realize more strategic EMR benefits. As we have described above, achieving these strategic objectives requires management focus over an extended period and real changes in the way care is delivered and work is done. In other words, it requires innovation.

Innovation is generally thought of as taking inventions, or new ideas or tools, and applying them to the real world to improve results or outcomes. Innovation is different from improvement—improvement is doing the same things better; innovation is doing something different. While many organizations recognize the importance of innovation, their emphasis is often on the generation of "good ideas" by creating a supportive culture, forming cross-functional teams, brainstorming, and so on.

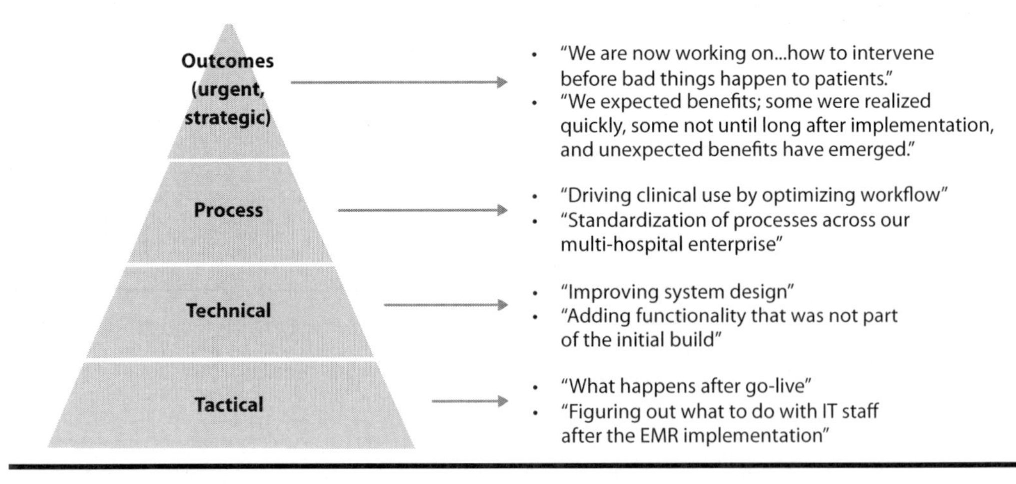

Figure 3.15 How HCOs define EMR optimization. (Courtesy of The Advisory Board Company.)

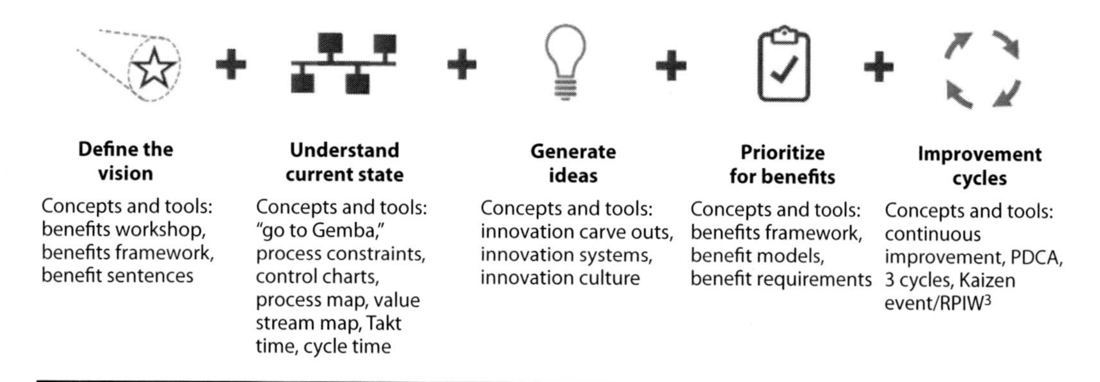

Figure 3.16 A structured approach to innovation for EMR optimization and benefits realization. (Courtesy of The Advisory Board Company.)

In the context of benefits-driven EMR optimization, good ideas alone are not enough, as is illustrated in Figure 3.16.

As illustrated above, we begin by defining the vision of what can be accomplished through EMR optimization using the first two "best practices"—Benefits Framework development and the creation of Benefits Sentences. With that common vision in mind, we then use Benefits Modeling and Benefit Requirements to better understand both our current state and the potential role of the EMR in improving current performance.

With that background, the new ideas that we generate are all relevant to our top organizational priorities and tied to known EMR capabilities. We then prioritize the new ideas on the basis of their expected contribution to the achievement of strategic benefits and implement them in rapid improvement cycles with frequent Benefits Measurement and modification of our approach. This is simply an example of a Lean improvement method with the addition of some specialized information about what EMR benefits have already been achieved by others, the amount of benefit they achieved, and known best practices around benefits measurement and organization of the benefits realization effort.

Moving into the Unknown: Population Health Benefits of EMRs and Other IT

As we have described in this chapter, there is a growing body of evidence about hospital EMR benefits and how they can be achieved. There is also a good amount of evidence about the benefits of ambulatory practice EMRs and practice management systems (see Figure 3.17).

However, very little is known about the benefits of EMRs and other information technologies in population health management and chronic disease management. The increasing focus on noninstitutional patient outcomes and costs, both in the United States and in many other parts of the world, has clearly attracted the attention and investment of EMR and other IT vendors. Many different solutions, including IT elements, are now being developed, tested, and used to help manage population health and patients with chronic diseases.

One implication of this new focus outside the walls of hospitals and doctors' offices is increasing complexity. As illustrated in Figure 3.18, the geographic and organizational scope of population

- Improved patient service levels and satisfaction
- Better communication among the care team
- Better communication with patients
- Improved scheduling
- Improved tracking of preventive care needs
- Reduced chart management effort, staff cuts
- Dictation/transcription use/cost reduction
- Reduced A/R days
- Increased billings and revenues
- Reduced charge entry costs
- Shorter drug recall response times

Figure 3.17 Commonly mentioned benefits of ambulatory EMRs. (Courtesy of The Advisory Board Company.)

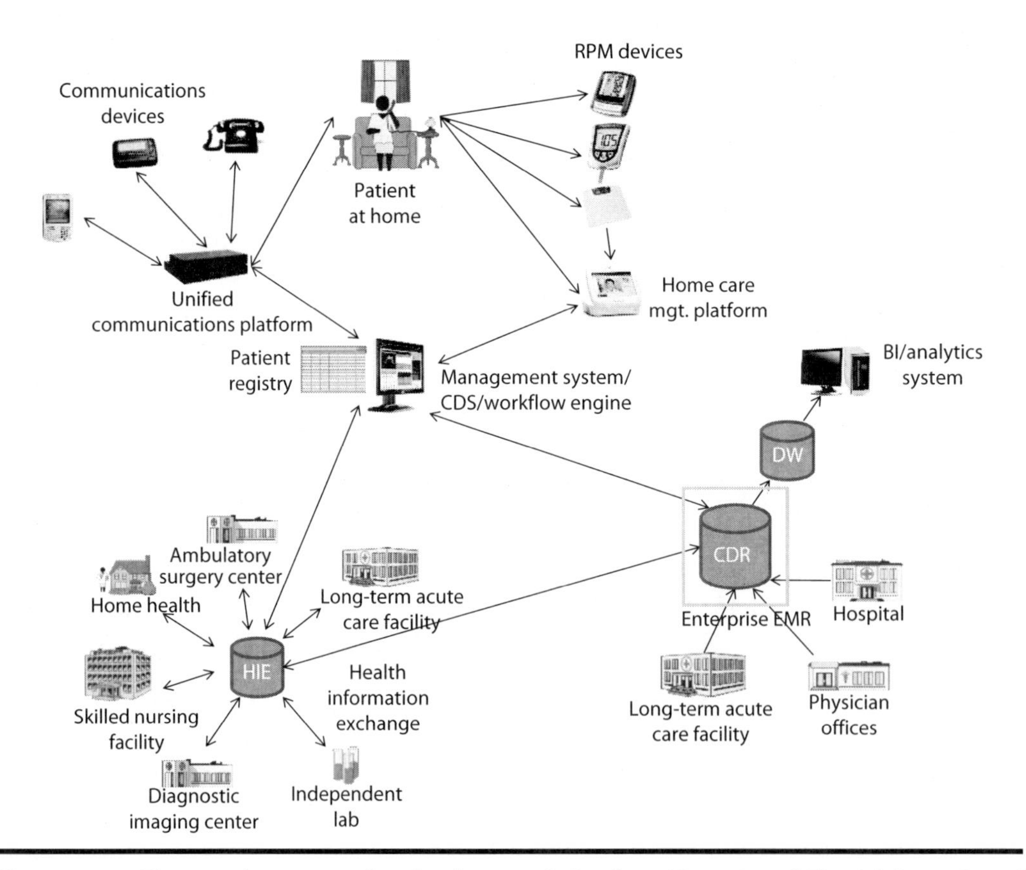

Figure 3.18 The growing scope of technology optimization. (Courtesy of The Advisory Board Company.)

health efforts is much broader than those required for hospital operations, and the potential number of technical and process connections and interactions is much greater.

While in-hospital information technology is increasingly EMR-centric, this is not necessarily true outside the hospital. Optimizing technology to achieve strategic benefits requires managing a large number of possible connections between hospital and physician office EMRs and those same systems at other HCOs, HIEs, public and private registries, remote monitoring and care delivery devices, communications technologies, and more.

It has been suggested that hospital and ambulatory EMRs can help support population health and chronic disease management benefits through functionality such as

- Structured, standardized clinical documentation to improve the consistency, readability, and ease of communication between providers
- Condition/patient-specific care recommendations to improve the clinical condition of patients leaving the hospital or ambulatory care setting, leading to easier patient management after discharge and better patient outcomes
- Integrated patient information for better decision-making across the continuum of care and reduction of duplicative or unnecessary care
- Automated preventive care schedules and reminders to increase the consistency of care delivered in physician offices and other outpatient settings
- Ability to analyze population outcomes leading to recognition of patterns and improvements in the effectiveness and costs of care
- Risk factor tracking for chronic populations leading to better recommendations for ongoing care coming out of hospitalization and physician visits, and more informed and useful care provided in those settings
- Integration of EMR data and decision support capabilities with disease registries and home monitoring leading to a more holistic view of the patient's condition and better care across all settings

Some of the potential population health benefits of EMRs and other IT may include

- Improved reliability of care for populations
- Increased patient engagement and compliance
- Better identification and management of risk factors
- Reduced costs of care
- Improved short- and long-term patient outcomes
- Reduced needs for acute care
- Better identification of fraud and "prescription shopping"

However, unlike many hospital settings, where well-integrated EMRs include most of the IT capabilities required to improve quality, safety, and efficiency, the population health and chronic disease management worlds require many other systems and technologies that are not part of a typical EMR and may not even be owned or controlled by the HCO.

This implies that the principles of benefits realization described in this chapter will need to be applied in collaboration with other organizations (hospitals, physician offices, clinics, IT vendors, public health organizations, and even patients), some of which may be our competitors. Overcoming the technical and logistical complexity that go along with these new partners and care settings, and dealing with potential political and competitive conflicts, will more than ever require a clear, common vision of the potential benefits, a good understanding of the benefit mechanisms, and the ability to recognize and measure benefits as they are realized.

References

1. Congressional Budget Office. Evidence on the costs and benefits of health information technology, May, 2008.
2. DesRoches CM, Campbell EG, Vogeli C, Zheng J, Rao SR, Shields AE, Donelan K, Rosenbaum S, Bristol SJ, and Jha AK. Electronic health records' limited successes suggest more targeted uses, *Health Aff*, 2010, **29**:639–646.
3. Dranove D, Forman C, Goldfarb A, and Greenstein S. The trillion dollar conundrum: Complementarities and health information technology, National Board of Economic Research, August, 2012.

Chapter 4

Using EMR Data to Improve Clinical Protocols, Outcomes, and Patient Safety

H. Lester Reed, MD

"Do not become discouraged: Look again, engage again and try again, fail early and frequently and continue to improve."

Patients receive only approximately 50% of the treatments that evidence suggests they should have been given.[1,2] In the United States, even with this low delivery of systematic care, mortality rates from cardiovascular and cerebral vascular disease fell by more than 40% between 1980 and 2004. This decline can be attributed in part to the increased improvement in blood pressure and serum cholesterol management and early intervention schemes.[1] However, how low could these rates have declined if we as healthcare providers delivered 60%, 70%, or 80% of the recommended interventions to improve clinical outcomes?

There are many limitations to why these recommendations are not delivered. However, some barriers can be overcome, and we have seen this evidence in reduction of patient harm, for example, with near-zero rates of infections from central catheter infections or pneumonias associated with ventilator-assisted breathing (VAP). How can some of these outcomes improve while others flounder in an era where clinical data seem to be available but often not fully utilized?[3] This chapter will outline the steps that are needed to improve clinical outcomes with the use of clinical data and provide four clinical cases that emphasize these points. The 10 key concepts are summarized below:

1. ***Infrastructure:*** Local expertise in the area of database management and analytics is critical for establishing a culture that comfortably uses data to generate information.
2. ***Data governance:*** Exercising a discipline around data governance by emphasizing a central repository for definitions and documentation of methodology is critical for reliable and reproducible data. This is a prerequisite for the use of data to generate information and predict outcomes.
3. ***Explain the Clinical Why:*** Without the focus on the clinical rational for change, clinical caregivers will move slowly with little engagement and the results will be sporadic.

4. ***Process and outcome need to be considered and managed together:*** Engage providers with education and provider- and unit-specific data.
5. ***Use outcomes that are well defined both clinically and objectively and maintain consistent data governance to standardize the definitions:*** Deep venous thrombosis, mortality from sepsis or myocardial infarction, or admission to a hospital for congestive heart failure are examples that meet these criteria.
6. ***Advertise the clinical outcomes:*** These improvements add pride to a group or an institution, and they build teamwork if it was not in place. Case stories with patient details and omitting identifiable information can be a powerful tool for support from all sectors. Both outcomes met and unmet can have powerful clinical stories to motivate clinicians.
7. ***Use teams to change care:*** If in the medical home with patient compliance and satisfaction, or with using a preoperative surgical checklist, the team is exponentially more powerful than any one individual.
8. ***Set goals for the patient's benefit, not clinician comfort:*** Reductions to near zero for VAP and central line infections were thought of as impossible in 2008.
9. ***Keep the clinicians delivering care involved, and locate a clinical leader:*** If we are to change process so the outcome remains improved, it must involve those delivering the care. Physicians must lead these outcome changes.
10. ***Do not become discouraged:*** Look again, engage again, and try again; fail early and frequently and continue to improve.

Introduction

The request for a clinical or nonclinical measurement can come from international, national, local, institutional, or individual sources. With all of these requests, it must be clear to understand the "why." In this regard, "why" would this particular outcome be an important measure to improve clinical outcomes or the potential for improvement? Some are for compliance with national standards, improved patient safety or clinical efficiency, or reductions in observed variation from the standard. However, within all of these there is and must be a clinically important reason for striving for this outcome. Sometimes they are difficult to identify, and sometimes they are not very clear. However, in order to fully engage clinicians in the improvement of care, this clinical "why" needs to be clearly and consistently articulated.

> Changing behavior has well-known steps in the psychological literature, and changing clinician behavior adds additional complexity to these steps.

Start with the clinical question and when possible make this a measurable outcome. What is the hypothesis and what are we attempting to improve should be the direction of the question. In the strictest sense, the application of the scientific methodology helps clinicians support these questions and the process improvements that are needed to bring about the change. **Determine what data** elements are needed and **be precise** in their definitions. Focus also on the governance of data that is needed to support reliable and reproducible information by utilizing data stewards as described by Dr. Gibson in Chapter 9 of this book. **Outline the interactions** and roles of the humans needed to carry out this improvement such as nurses, physicians, patients, receptionists, and analysts. These roles and plans will help provide structure to the improvement plan.

> Unfortunately, too often clinicians argue with the accuracy of the data rather than the implications of what can be dramatic differences between facilities or provider groups.

Engaging Physicians: Physicians and other clinicians can be motivated to improve, but as described by Drs. Don Berwick and Brent James in 2003, the inclusion of these clinicians in the improvement process is a key factor of success.[4] Introducing an educational component carries a much stronger personal commitment in contrast to a more compliance structured system. Some would argue that Dr. Berwick attempted to move in this educational direction during his tenure at the Centers for Medicare and Medicaid Services.

Changing behavior has well-known steps in the psychological literature, and changing clinician behavior adds additional complexity to these steps. However, a common theme that adds leverage in the clinician group is the fact of retaining a continued focus on the clinical care and (1) what improves that clinical care, (2) what is intuitively and spontaneously easy to do, (3) what happens during real-time decision making, and (4) are these reminders pertinent to the case at hand? The challenge is to find topics that excite clinicians about improving care and then to link these to manageable projects that can improve care, as well as compliance measures that may be less engaging but nationally reported. This concept can be seen with reducing sepsis mortality as described later in this chapter.

Infrastructure Needed for Improvement: Comparing results between national targets, between local facilities, between local provider groups, and between individual providers is a critical aspect of reported data to stimulate improvement. Unfortunately, too often clinicians argue with the accuracy of the data rather than the implications of what can be dramatic differences between facilities or provider groups. For example, two institutions have two mortality rates for sepsis defined in the same way with one group reporting 17% and one group reporting 10%. As mentioned by Dr. Gibson in Chapter 9, the accuracy and reproducibility of the data extraction is a key component to the infrastructure. If possible, it is best to report the variance of the measure with a standard error of the mean or standard deviation, which helps clinicians accept true differences when they are present.

This reproducibility requires expertise, attention to detail, and quality assurance testing of data reliability. The standard should include a level of attention one would use if preparing data for a peer-reviewed publication, although fully recognizing some of the trends and subjective data may be a proxy for what is considered the true measure. In other words, a clinical visit for a deep venous thrombosis might be a combination of filtered data elements, such as the encounter diagnosis that did not appear before the visit but after a procedure documented within the previous 60 days and further supported by an order of an ultrasound that showed a discrete data entry reading of venous thrombosis. Establishing a group of these filters to satisfy the definition of a new deep venous thrombosis can increase the reliability, as opposed to depending on a single coded or billed entry.

This type of clinical understanding requires a department that is supported by analysts who have some clinical expertise, data architects who consult with those analysts, database architects who can extract from the enterprise data warehouse (EDW), and finally data stewards, both junior and senior, who continually test the data and outcome reliability against standards for extraction and calculation. A coefficient of variation can be a helpful calculation here to look for variation in the extraction and calculation of a known data element.

Several areas of analytics that can provide improved clinical implications but are advanced and require increasing technical support from the data architects and others on the analytics team are increasingly important now, and this importance will increase in the future. These areas include the following:

1. **Predictive analytics** such as predicting if someone will be admitted to the hospital or readmitted to the hospital or if the patient has a high likelihood of taking their medication
2. **Social determinants** such as knowing if the patients have transportation, if they can afford the care recommended, or if there are other social demands such as a single parent at home or children and parents with special support needs
3. **Combined total cost of care including outcomes** that can be attributed to individual providers and integrating claims data with clinical data from multiple sources

The Concept of Collaboratives

In order to maximize the effectiveness of a clinician's involvement and their time, the concept of a Collaborative has been proposed by several groups, including Intermountain Health Care. These Collaboratives are an organized structure that include support from subject matter experts in clinical, analytic, administrative, and program organization areas. They can improve the efficiency of reaching agreement about protocols and care pathways, key metrics, and analytic extractions. The analysts in this distributed model of organizational knowledge assets will have a deep understanding of the specific question and a more broad understanding of the more general clinical question. Administrative support provides documentation and program management and finally the administrative leadership must defend the use of resources and articulate to senior leadership the benefits of these Collaboratives and the clinical outcomes that are being achieved. A stylistic design for such a Collaborative is provided in Figure 4.1.

These Collaboratives are a combination of a process improvement team, an administrative support team, and a clinical action team with subject matter experts and an analytics group with access to higher analytical capability such as predictive analytics, if that is needed.

The goal of the Collaborative is to improve outcomes and then to articulate these as the authoritative source by emphasizing the combined and respected clinical expertise present in these groups. Work must be done outside of the meetings of the Collaborative and that is the role for the subgroups of working specialty areas who then report back often by e-mail to the group as a whole.

The work on these Collaboratives must be productive and recognized as productive so the time of the clinicians away from delivering care can be justified to the institution and to the clinician. We have chosen to achieve this by direct payment for time or credits toward a total salary based on hours donated to clinical administrative time. The work cannot be done effectively without a recognition for its value and worth. The recognition can take many forms, but a fixed part of an employment agreement or documented benefit toward an administrative academic degree is an example.

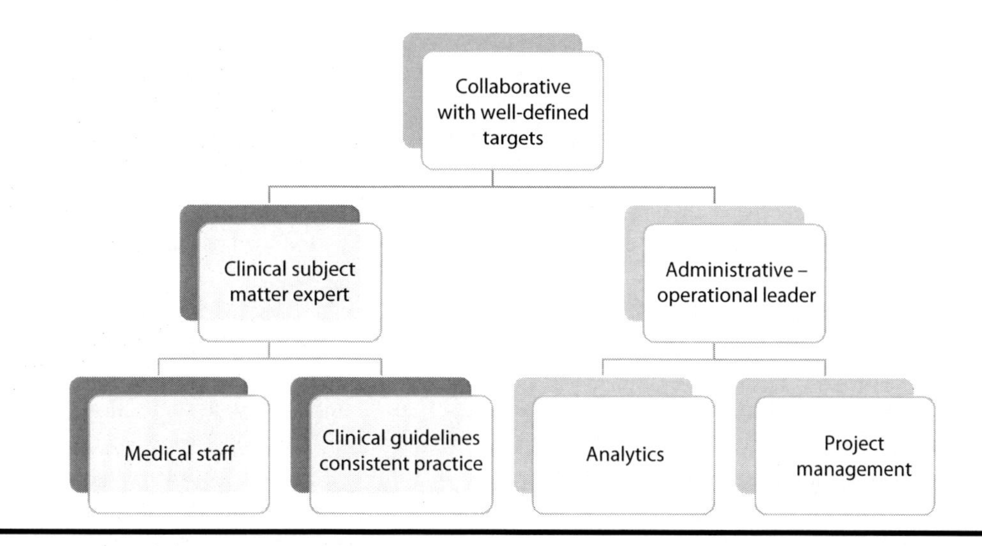

Figure 4.1 ***Collaborative Structure*****—A structure is outlined in this figure with specific supporting elements that are needed to achieve the targets. The line diagram implies leadership responsibilities for management of assets and resources needed to accomplish the tasks assigned to specific areas. (Provided by MultiCare Health System with permission.)**

Clinical Case Reports

#1 Why Are Patients Dying in Our Hospital? Sepsis Mortality

In 2004, the concept presented by the Institute for Healthcare Improvement (IHI) and, specifically, Dr. Don Berwick created a major transformation in clinicians delivering care. Saving 100,000 lives per year and saving them not from poor care but from average care appealed immediately to clinicians. Patients were dying in hospitals from care that was not optimal. The concept has now been expanded to understand that death and injury in ambulatory settings also occur from care that again was not optimal.

> The combination of the emotion of saving lives in a setting of a "preventable" death combined with objective data to help provide feedback has launched clinicians into the area of quality improvement, but often with little training.

These deaths and harm incidents had previously been considered acceptable risks, and they might have included the central line infection that resulted in sepsis; the fall in the hospital or the clinic where a hip was fractured in an 82-year-old man, who now has a 40% mortality rate in the next 12 months; or the lag in timeliness of antibiotics before surgery or a subtle infection that could develop into sepsis. All of these might have received a review by clinical peers in 2005, where the standard of care that was delivered would be considered adequate, but the patient died. That standard has now changed.

All of the examples listed above are now substandard, primarily because the outcome of mortality has been linked to clinical care and clinicians have become motivated, actively involved, and leaders of change. The combination of the emotion of saving lives in a setting of a "preventable" death combined with objective data to help provide feedback has launched clinicians into the area of quality improvement, but often with little training.

In this climate of quality improvement, in 2007, we asked why patients were dying in MultiCare's adult hospitals and attempted to locate a common area of focus. We determined what others had suggested and what is now widely reported. The diagnosis of sepsis is a factor in 44%–55% of the hospital deaths.[5] Additionally, the Centers for Disease Control and Prevention and the National Hospital Discharge Survey reported in 2008 that sepsis was the 11th leading cause of death in the United States and hospitalization for sepsis increased 70% between 2000 and 2008. Even though sepsis only accounts for 2% of hospital discharges, it accounts, as the cause of death, for approximately 17% of the hospital deaths in one report. In our review, we found these same ratios and that sepsis was a leading cause of death in our institution.[6] This was the "Clinical Why?" and this was the engagement feature that stimulated an effort to improving the recognition, multidisciplinary standardized care, and follow-up for sepsis for the next 8 years through to 2015.

A very important concept is the local validation of what the IHI was discussing nationally. We could say "Yes, this is happening here" and there are tools and guidelines for care we need to review and initiate. This was the "learning" portion of what Drs. Berwick and James wrote about in 2003[4] and was the clinician involvement that was critical in the movement and momentum we enjoyed for the next 8 years. It cannot be underestimated that the clinicians need to be involved and the "learning" environment led by physicians with subject matter expertise is key in any change.

We later developed the Collaborative format with help from our consultations with Intermountain Health Care, and it consisted of clinical, administrative, analytic, and program management support (Figure 4.1).

Questions were immediately asked about consistently measuring the coded cases for sepsis (APR DRG 720) and how can "comfort care" and "Do Not Resuscitate" determinations be accounted for. Data governance was being recognized in our institution at this time and the definitions and coding criteria were published. The agreement on IHI recommendations for sepsis care was developed over a several-month working session with subgroups involving all aspects of the care such as emergency room physicians, critical care physicians, inpatient internal medicine specialists, infectious disease physicians, nurses, respiratory care technicians, and administrative hospital and MultiCare system leaders. The target was set at achieving the lowest 10% mortality rate for sepsis in the United States using the Nationwide Inpatient Sample database.

The tracking of the mortality rate data by individual facility using the EDW was a key milestone that allowed comparison between facilities and information that was "real time," updated every 24 h (Figure 4.2). Additionally, our Information Services (IS) Informatics team was able to build an "early warning system" for patients who were decompensating physiologically, initially monitored by a "monitor technician" who was retrained from his original duties of watching for irregularities in cardiac rhythms. This system was eventually automated and placed in the EMR. The system called MEWS was adapted from a paper version and inserted into our Epic EMR. Later, we presented the automated format at the Epic User Group Meeting as an important contribution to our success in this area. The public recognition of this accomplishment helped motivate the team further. Standardization of the coding for sepsis and agreement on the elements needed for definitions of systemic inflammatory response syndrome (SIRS), sepsis, and severe sepsis were agreed upon by coders and clinicians and then published as a "Practice Alert." This step is critical for consistent coding by all clinicians involved in the care of these patients.

Clinical case stories were presented at major employee forums that highlighted real patients who either lived or died based on our care of sepsis as well as other conditions. These cases were

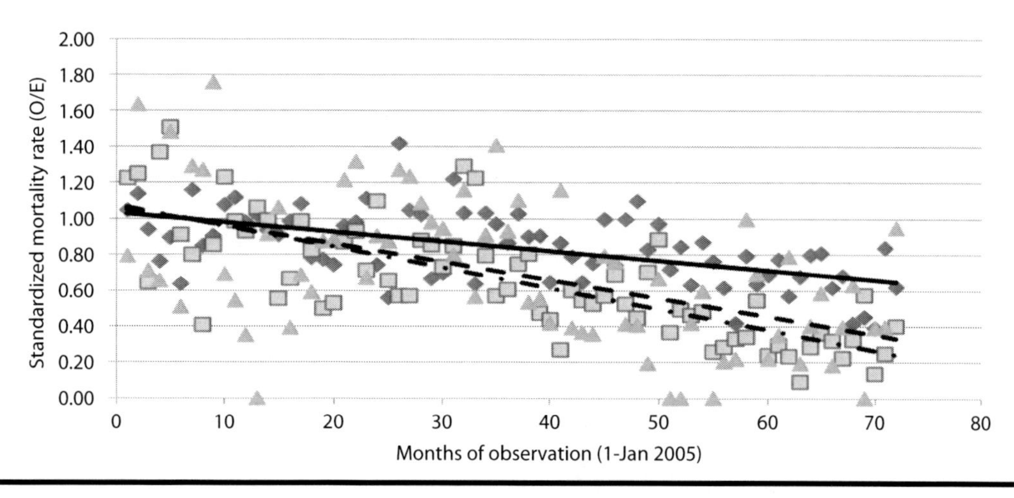

Figure 4.2 Standardized mortality rate (observed/expected) for the highest three levels of risk of patient between January 1, 2005, and December 31, 2010. Risk of mortality (ROM) 4 (diamonds) (highest), ROM 3 (rectangles), and ROM 2 (triangles) (lowest) are shown by month for this 72-month period. Reductions in these three ROMs independently were observed.[4]

told in a way that brought emotion to the factual data and influenced all levels of the organization from the chief executive officer to the coding team in Finance. We opened the Collaborative meetings with a "case story" that continued to bring the reality of what we were doing for those delivering care, as opposed to having it being only a graphic representation.

An important lesson for the team was to retain vigilance on the improvements and continue monitoring these. Improvements in one facility did not always mirror improvements in another. If it was found that a facility was trending over time to drift away from the target, "best practice" techniques were reviewed openly at the Collaborative meeting. Using video conferencing for these meetings, members could attend from four sites and help the facility that was trailing. Unfortunately, sometimes these meetings become quite large, and attendance needs to be managed or action steps assigned to smaller groups.

Actions taken by the trailing facility in our example included developing a very moving video about sepsis and highlighting the key educational functions for clinicians while attaching the emotion. As Drs. James and Berwick would have pointed out in their improvement theory,[4] the clinicians were involved in teaching each other and increasing in a supportive manner the academic importance of early recognition and early intervention of sepsis. The work groups focused on early intervention in the ED and watched the mortality rate for sepsis decline. The use of serum lactate, a measure of worsening cardiovascular oxygen supply, was discussed and education about its importance and the role of an increasing lactate became universal knowledge of a decompensating patient. In a "learning environment," all clinicians from physicians to technicians were learning and practicing what they learned, and the mortality rate was dropping rapidly. Standardized order sets were produced and put into practice, which were especially helpful for those with less experience in managing sepsis and helped as educational aids, as well as what would be discussed classically as "decision support tools."

With this activity, where a consistent team with both an emotional and objective focus on the outcome used reliable data that they trusted, with an EMR as a communication tool and an aid in early detection, coupled with an order set to serve as a checklist, and consistent coding to

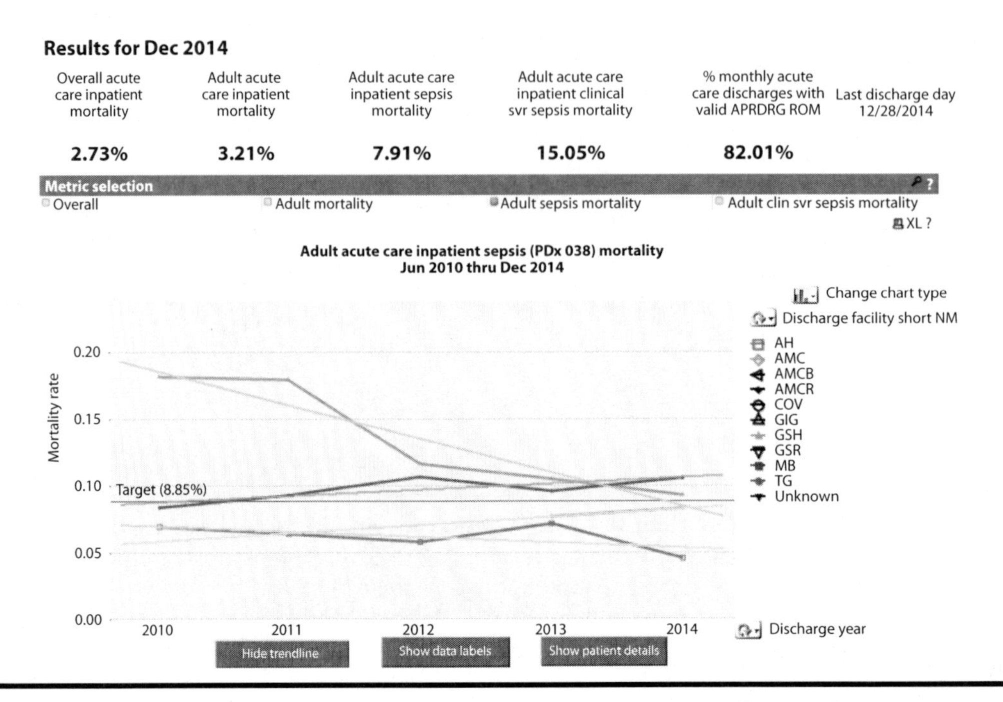

Figure 4.3 Sepsis mortality data by hospital facility between 2010 and December 28, 2014, are shown as they appear on the graphic application available online and updated every 24 h. The overall mortality rate at the time of this isolated summary was 7.9% with the variation in mortality from three major facilities declining from 17%–18% to near 9.0% for GSH and converging near the target of 8.85% for AH and TG. (Reproduced with permission from MultiCare Health System, MultiView Application.)

standardize the data, the variation between facilities began to decline quickly. Figure 4.3 shows the decline in sepsis mortality by each facility and the approach to a similar mortality rate for all facilities of near 8%–9% from rates that were between 17% and 25% initially. This change in mortality translates to real lives saved, and these lives saved were published with the monthly results. Real mothers, fathers, grandmothers, and grandfathers, who would now be able to have another birthday and observe another holiday ceremony, are the patients whose lives were saved and for whom these efforts were the ultimate reward.

In summary, the key points made at the beginning of this chapter were all carried out during this initiative, which started shortly after the final "go-live" implementation of Epic as our EMR in the inpatient setting at one facility. It was continued through implementation at two other facilities with their "go-live" of Epic and demonstrates the power of data for facility comparison coupled with clinician leadership and a structure of the Collaborative.

#2 ED Length of Stay—Does This Affect Clinical Outcome?

In 2013, we became comfortable monitoring overall hospital mortality and its leading contributor, the mortality rate from sepsis. This was an institutional focus, and we identified that sepsis mortality contributes more than 60% of the month-to-month variation in overall hospital mortality and published this finding.[6] Because we had determined this association and validated it with more than 8 years of data, it became a concern when we observed that the relationship began to shift.

We noticed in March of 2013 that the overall total in-hospital mortality rate was increasing beyond seasonal trends and yet the sepsis mortality rate could not explain this difference. The Critical Care Collaborative described above identified a subgroup to investigate the possible causes.

To understand these deaths, more than seven different mortality and morbidity review sheets were collected from areas such as the ED, the trauma service, the pediatric intensive care unit, the critical care unit, and the inpatient adult medicine service. These work sheets were reviewed with clinicians from each of the groups, and then the core variables were extracted to be able to determine several key questions. These questions were straightforward and similar to what the IHI had focused on in the past. There were two key questions: (1) Did the death happen in a monitored bed and (2) Was the death expected? Variables, such as age, "Do Not Resuscitate" or "Comfort Care" status, principal diagnosis on admission, site of admission and site of discharge, risk of mortality, and time in the ED, among several others, were extracted from the electronic record and circulated as a universal summary of the key measures. Clinicians reviewed the records with these variables, and it was difficult for the individual reviews to identify any unifying theme. At that time, an analysis was carried out using the variables sorted by facility and by risk of mortality.

This analysis identified that the majority of deaths were happening in patients designated as high-risk patients (MORT-4); they were admitted through the ED, and it was this group where the mortality rates were increasing. Specifically, there was a strong association with the time spent in the ED and the eventual death in the hospital. After this observation, a review of why it might be happening was launched. Work was begun to identify the particular segments of the ED length of stay and determine which ones had increased. There was intense collaboration between administration and the ED clinicians. The ED time segments associated with the biggest increase were identified; these were tracked by using an application of data extracted from the EDW and published for all to review and understand, if and where improvements were happening. Process improvement techniques were used and a prediction was prepared.

The data were used in a real-time manner to select what part of the ED length of stay was the critical delay and then involve physicians in the emotional trigger and the practical process improvements to bring about change.

It was estimated that if the overall time in the ED for those patients in this category who were being admitted could be reduced to 4 h, from the current target of 6 h, the overall hospital morality for the highest risk of mortality patients could be reduced. More importantly, the overall in-hospital mortality could be reduced from more than 2% to less than 1% by reducing this period in the ED. These predictions were made from multiple linear regression models and were an important stimulus to making changes in the ED that had been very difficult to bring about before now. This reduction in mortality became the "Clinical Why?" and the emotional trigger to help engage the clinicians in care.

The ED length of stay was reduced (14%) and a decline was also noted in the mortality rate (25%) for patients who were admitted through the ED. These patients were in the highest risk of mortality called MORT-4 and a highly suggestive association was found between these two changes compared to a year before. This finding is described in Figure 4.4.

In summary, this case study identified the "Clinical Why?" and asked the question in a way that could be tested, and work was carried out in teams involving clinicians, analysts, and

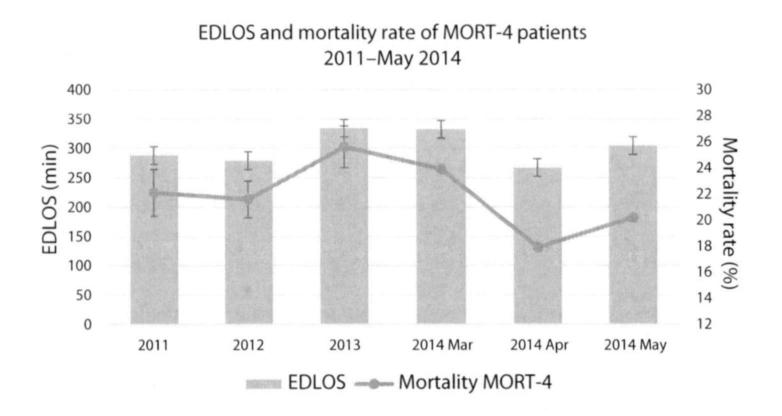

Figure 4.4 The mortality rate for high-risk patients categorized as MORT-4 admitted through the ED is shown (gray line) compared to the ED Length of Stay (EDLOS) for these patients (gray bars). The April 2014 data followed specific process improvements, where there was a decrease in both mortality rate and EDLOS. This value was seasonally lower than the previous 2 years, and as a mean, it was significantly below the 2013 values for both the EDLOS and the mortality rate. There was an individual patient association of this change using the pooled mortality rate.

administrators. The changes were articulated and emphasized with clinical stories describing the particular nature of the patients, who were described to be dying after prolonged stays in the ED. The data were used in a real-time manner to select what part of the ED length of stay was the critical delay and then involve physicians in the emotional trigger and the practical process improvements to bring about change.

#3 Heart Failure Readmission—How Can the Primary Care Physician Help?

Readmission for patients with heart failure has been identified as a key issue for hospitals. Similar to other medical causes for hospital readmission, however, it was not until many attempts had been made to minimize the readmission rate by the hospital that it became very clear that the readmission and, more importantly, the initial admission were influenced critically by the ambulatory physicians and their teams. These teams may have been in a medical home, extended care facility, or single primary care provider office. None of these areas are usually directly under the specific influence of the hospital, even though there may be an employed medical physician and provider group or even extended care facilities within the health care system. Unfortunately, again the educational aspect of understanding the "Clinical Why?" was a concern nationally and with our health system locally.

It took many months to several years to educate ambulatory providers and patients of the clinical benefits of avoiding admission or readmission.

Primary care providers for years had sent patients to the ED for emergent care and urgent care. It took many months to several years to educate ambulatory providers and patients of the clinical benefits of avoiding admission or readmission. The primary financial reward was directed at the hospital for avoiding these readmissions and many hospital systems simply translated this as a message of "help save the hospital the fine associated with the readmission." Even this point was poorly articulated to many providers, who no longer spent time in the hospital.

However, an alternative point of view was to address the complications that can happen when an 82-year-old man is admitted for heart failure to the hospital. Complications such as a fall from a bed with a subsequent broken hip and annual mortality rate of 40% in the year after this fracture is unfortunately not an uncommon scenario. Also, the risk of central catheter infections, decubitus ulcers, and delirium can and do happen, and this patient would be at high risk for these complications. From the cardiology and the internal medicine community about this time, data began to emerge that admission to the hospital for heart failure represented a primary complication of outpatient management and suboptimal care. With these two concepts, the ambulatory provider now becomes a part of the engagement and can help determine answers to the reasons why patients are readmitted.

Educating these points and rebuilding the Collaborative team from an inpatient focus to an outpatient focus was disruptive and took considerable time. Historically, these collaborative teams have been built around cost savings for the diagnostic-related group (DRG)–based hospital system and the ambulatory group is unfamiliar with the structure. Educating well-trained physicians about a stepwise approach to the patient, who was just discharged from the hospital with heart failure in an online available guideline with a simple mnemonic, was invaluable in engaging providers and educating without any demeaning tone. Again, I refer back to Drs. Berwick and James,[4] who emphasize engaging the provider in the care pathways and emphasize the learning environment and education that can accompany these process improvement models.

We began to actively recruit a co-chair of the Cardiovascular Collaborative, which was initially called the Heart Failure Collaborative. We coupled a heart failure cardiologist specialist with a primary care provider to address the concerns of ambulatory providers. The data they needed were different from what the hospital system needed. They needed individual clinic attribution for patients who were readmitted and, if possible, individual provider attribution. The concept of "care as a team" quickly emerged that individual attribution was difficult, but clinic attribution such as Clinic "A" was much easier, and then these could be completed and posted online with the same 24-hour update that the hospital sepsis mortality was published. Comparing all provider clinics with these readmission rates was a start, but there remained discontent over attribution to the correct clinic. Thus, the concept of data governance and reliability of data again became a central theme. The providers in these clinics needed help with a "dashboard" so that they could track and identify who had been discharged and the key clinical features of their care. Multiple values such as their cardiac ejection fraction, their cardiac medications, their body weight, and the date of their last admission were collected together at one site (Figure 4.5).

Finally, it became increasingly clear that social determinants were an important part of readmissions, such as did the patients have a ride, could they afford the medication, did they have dietary complications from a social or cultural aspect? Few of these could be answered by the standard phone call from the hospital. A registry was developed for all patients at high risk for readmission that was linked to providers and a team of trained social workers, clinical nurses, and a process improvement manager. The risk of readmission was calculated both by a simple screen of medication number and age and by an electronic tool developed with predictive modeling

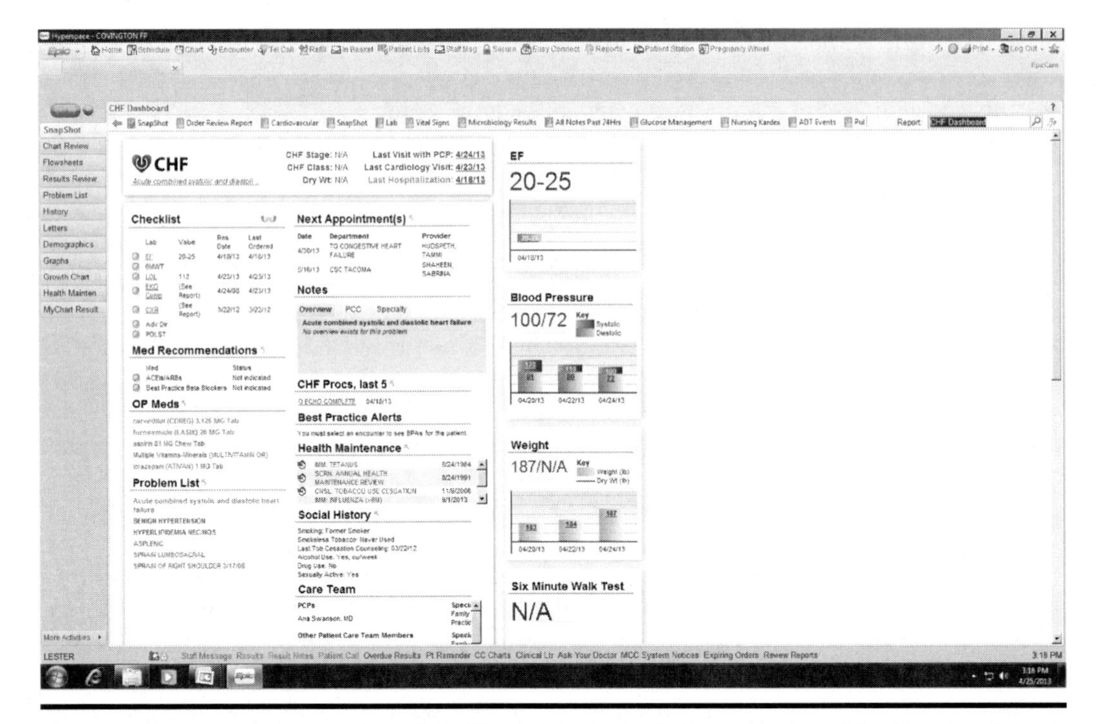

Figure 4.5 The ambulatory clinical dashboard for heart failure was one of the first dashboards developed as tools for the ambulatory group. This dashboard was developed with support by the IS department. Close coordination between the home institutional IS team and any contracted IS services was an important and critical step.

capability. The clinicians were slow to use the predictive model, since it was new and not easily accessible. In addition, having a trained pharmacist work with patients in the ambulatory clinic regarding their medications and when and how to take them helped even well-trained internists reduce their readmission rate below that of the group. In the past, this same internist had been unable reach this target.

In summary, the clinical question of the "Why?" had to be developed, data that were different from those previously used for inpatient groups had to be developed into registries, teams had to be collected to visit the home for social determinate interventions such as rides to the provider office, and, finally, the registries had to be available to all persons.

#4 Ambulatory Clinic Management—How Can We Anticipate What Is Needed in the Clinic?

In this final case story, the data and information were used to improve administrative measures and patient access in the ambulatory clinics. One of the first applications for the EDW was an application to monitor, compare, identify, and predict patient flow and availability for all employed clinical providers. The data extraction and management tool was developed by the data architects and data analysts after the "stakeholders" were gathered and the key objective variables that could be extracted or calculated were identified. The prototype was tested with the "stakeholders," and the "Clinical Question" here was improving access and efficiency for the clinicians.

With the development of the ambulatory application extracted from the EDW, it was able to show within 24-h updates what the clinic availability, productivity, case complexity, and no-show accumulative rates were for any provider, so that proper staffing could be applied on given days or weeks, where they would be predicted to have the need. These reports were generated in the past by a single person and then published to every clinic in a report format and subsequently e-mailed to them. Under the current system, the data are "pulled" by the clinic coordinators, or by the clinicians, and the "no show" rate, vacancy rate, comparison to last year at this time or last week at this time or to others with the same specialty, is available with a 24-hour refresh period.

Variation in production and efficiency can now be better managed. In this particular case study, a 0.5 full-time equivalent (FTE) had been used to generate these reports on a daily basis, and once the application became available, that 0.5 FTE was retrained for other work that can better support the clinical medical group.

Chapter Summary

In this chapter, I have tried to set the stage for what is needed to bring about clinician-driven change with effective engagement of clinical leaders after the initiation of an EMR. The data from the "go-live" in both ambulatory and inpatient areas are critical, but success can occur only with the following supporting elements:

1. The infrastructure
2. Data governance
3. Critical question and the "Clinical Why?"
4. Process and outcome management together
5. Well-defined outcomes measures
6. Advertisement with such mechanisms as clinical stories
7. Use of teams to change care
8. Setting goals for the patients' benefit
9. Having clinicians lead and keeping them involved to find solutions
10. Not becoming discouraged and always looking for improvement because the outcomes of our patients depend upon us

Acknowledgments

I personally acknowledge the following people (both friends and colleagues) for without their help and involvement, none of the outcomes described in this chapter would have been possible. Analysts: Sheila Renton, DVM; Mark Hines, RN; and Albert Marinez, MBA; Clinicians involved with the Collaboratives: Jim Taylor, MD; David Angulo-Zereceda, MD, MBA; and Bruce Gregg, MD; Clinical Administrators involved with the Collaborative and Knowledge Trust and Data Governance: Christi McCarren, RN, MBA; and Christopher Kodama, MD, MBA (Knowledge Trust and Collaborative); the Clinician Administrator involved with Ambulatory Care and Knowledge Trust: Patrick Ward, RN, MPA; and Information Services: Harold Moscho, MBA; Debbie Embree, MBA; and Brenda Bowles, RN, MBA.

References

1. Kover AR, Knickman JR, eds. *Care Delivery in the United States*, 9th ed, Springer Publishing Co, 2008.
2. McGlynn EA, Asch SM, Adams J et al. The quality of health care delivered to adults in the United States. *N Engl J Med*. 2003; 358:2635–2644.
3. Landrigran CP, Parry GJ, Bones CB et al. Temporal trends in rates of patient harm resulting from medical care. *N Engl J Med*. 2010; 363(22):2124–2134.
4. Berwick DM, James BC. The connection between quality measurement and improvement. *Medical Care*. 2003; 41:130–139.
5. Liu V, Escobar GJ, Greene JD et al. Hospital deaths in patients with sepsis from 2 independent cohorts. *JAMA*. 2014; 312(1):90–92.
6. Reed HL, Renton S, Hines M. Dependence of all-cause standardized in-hospital mortality upon sepsis mortality between 2005–2010. *Am J Med Quality*. 2014; 29(4):315–322.

Chapter 5

Using the EMR to Achieve Operational Excellence through "Lean" Thinking

James Hereford, MS

> *"The last thing you want to do is insist that the EMR you've spent thousands or millions of dollars to implement do something it wasn't designed to do just so you can do processes the way you've always done them."*

At the outset, the EMR was held out as a transformational tool for healthcare. A RAND Institute study in 2003 and summarized in *Health Affairs* in 2005 estimated, "Over fifteen years, the cumulative potential net efficiency and safety savings from hospital systems could be nearly $371 billion; potential cumulative savings from physician practice EMR systems could be $142 billion. This potential net financial benefit could double if the health savings produced by chronic disease prevention and management were included" [1].

The difficulty has been that these savings are elusive. Without doubt, the care delivery system has benefited from the adoption of EMR systems. But, documented returns of the transformational effect are difficult to find, with many of the benefits cited being improved coding and quality, and several negative impacts have also been documented [2]. While these are important to a practice or a healthcare delivery system, the results have been far short of the anticipated transformational effect.

The hypothesis that I have formed from these experiences is that health care has not benefited fully from the implementation of EMR technologies because of its lack of knowledge about its own processes.

Why is that? Over the last 20 years, I have been involved in both technology and operational leadership in several large healthcare organizations. At Group Health Cooperative in Seattle,

Washington, long known for both its consumer governance structure and its ability to manage the total cost of care, we were an early adopter of an EMR and of web-based patient portals. I held executive positions responsible for both information technology and operations and was deeply involved in the establishment of the patient portal, in the implementation of the EMR system, and in leading the Lean transformation effort.

As the chief operating officer at the Palo Alto Medical Foundation, in Palo Alto, California, I was very involved in leading the Lean transformation. Now at Stanford Health Care, as the chief operating officer, I'm again in the process of leading a Lean transformation with the goal of achieving substantial operational improvements in quality, safety, patient satisfaction, and efficiency.

It is little wonder that providers largely feel that the EMR has made their practice more difficult and increased the time required to take care of their patients.

These experiences have given me a reasonably informed point of view about the role and relationship of technology and of operations. The hypothesis that I have formed from these experiences is that health care has not benefited fully from the implementation of EMR technologies because of its lack of knowledge about its own processes.

Processes in this case refer to work processes, or the description and shared understanding of how work gets done. One can think of an ambulatory clinic as a series of processes that include the setup and scheduling of a visit, including determining the structure of the visit schedule itself; the registration and welcoming of the patient at the point of visit; the preparation for the visit done by the clinical staff; the visit itself, and the choreography of the events that occur within that visit, including diagnostics such as laboratory or radiology studies; and the after-visit process.

Each of these processes contains the basic elements of content, sequence, and timing. Content comprises the actual steps, including the clinical content and decision making, that occur. Sequence is the order in which they occur, and timing is when they occur. For an ambulatory clinic to run well, each one of the key processes, with their basic elements, must be well understood and executed by all of the people who are engaged in those activities.

Our concern regarding processes is twofold. First, is the process capable, meaning can it meet the requirements specified? These specifications should be deeply connected to the value that is defined by the patient and that is intended to be created, and is typically measured across dimensions of quality and safety, the experience of the patient, and the efficiency or resources consumed per unit of service produced.

Second, is the process reliable? Will it consistently meet the needs with minimum variation, and is it robust to forces that could disrupt it? If it fails at the first hint of higher demand, or the first time one of the individuals working in the process calls in sick, it is not reliable. Deep process knowledge results in processes that are both capable and reliable.

How many of our healthcare delivery services have been studied, documented, and iteratively improved, so that they can run reliably and capably a high percentage of the time? My experience would indicate that, in most healthcare organizations, not many!

To this, we add a sophisticated technology like the EMR on top of what are largely unsophisticated, undocumented, and unimproved clinical processes. It is little wonder that providers largely feel that the EMR has made their practice more difficult and increased the time required to take care of their patients. Now, they must deal with an in-basket of clinical activity including messages from patients and other practitioners, documentation and coding of their charts, responding to diagnostic studies, referring patients to other points of care, and so on.

Representative democracy is not a replacement for deep process knowledge.

In order to fully take advantage of technology, we must truly know our processes so that we can adapt the technology to them or adapt the processes to the technology. The last thing you want to do is insist that the EMR you've spent thousands or millions of dollars to implement do something it wasn't designed to do just so you can do processes the way you've always done them. That has been the downfall of countless healthcare organizations' implementation efforts. So what does it mean to really know our processes?

First, we can describe them, and we can describe the standard work that is required to make them work. And the standard work is agreed to and consistently followed by the individuals who are involved in the process. In addition, we know how our processes can fail. And with that knowledge, we can take steps to prevent failures from occurring, or at the very least, when we can't prevent failures, know how we're going to respond to abnormal conditions when they present themselves.

We should also be able to immediately detect abnormal conditions or unintended deviations in our processes when they occur so that they can be corrected, or we can stop the activity until we can correct the problem in order to avoid passing quality issues downstream or creating unsafe conditions that go unattended.

I would also submit that unless we are doing continuous improvement, through running small, iterative experiments, we aren't continuing to refine the knowledge of our processes. And when we really have command of our processes, we know what to look for that is predictive of future abnormal conditions and can take action to prevent these.

If that is what it means to have deep process knowledge, what is the result of the lack of it when it comes to the implementation and use of EMRs? First, we end up "paving the cow paths" when we implement the EMR, because we use the knowledge we have and build that into the technology, thereby automating our incapable and unreliable processes.

This issue is not one that has been experienced only by healthcare. The so-called information paradox, or the lack of benefits realization to the investment of information technology, was well documented in the late 1990s [3]. This realization gave rise to the concept of business reengineering, whose fundamental view was that processes must be rethought with the introduction of new technology [4]. It is only because health care has been such a late adopter of technology, and specifically adoption of clinical technology in the form of EMRs, that we are facing this dilemma two decades after other industries.

In our approach to the implementation of EMRs, we often rely on the fallacy of representative democracy to determine how things should work when we build our EMRs, meaning that we depend on a small group or even a single physician, or nurse or other clinical professional, to try to represent process knowledge. Because there has been a lack of systematic knowledge development in the organization, and the result is that the misperceptions and biases of that small group of individuals are now perpetuated to the large group of users of the EMR system. Representative democracy is not a replacement for deep process knowledge.

This also results in an asymmetric relationship between technologists and operational representatives, where the technologies are often asked to represent both the technical knowledge of the system and the process knowledge of operations. This is an unfair and an unrealistic expectation. This asymmetry then creates an ineffective dialogue about the nature and direction of adaptation between the technology and its capabilities and the operational processes. We've even invented a class of hybrid professionals, called informaticists, whose role it is to bridge between the technology and the clinical knowledge. However, clinical knowledge alone is not sufficient to represent robust work processes, so it is a bridge that is built on a very shaky foundation.

The result? Our EMRs, and the significant investment that we have made to implement and maintain them, have had only a marginal impact on the capability and the reliability of our healthcare processes. The fault is not of the technology, nor the technologists. It is because we haven't developed the deep process knowledge in order to best know how to use the technology. So how do we best gain fundamental process?

Lean

My belief is that the most effective way to develop this level of process knowledge is through the application of Lean, also commonly referred to as the Toyota Production System.

Lean is best thought of as a systemic approach to operational management. It is built around two fundamental sets of activities: the first is the improvement system and the second is the management system, depicted in the Stanford Operating System "house" in Figure 5.1. It is in this aspect that Lean represents a significant improvement over traditional quality approaches, such as quality improvement or Six Sigma, in that their weakness has been in their lack of attention or specificity to the role and function of management in supporting continuous improvement and

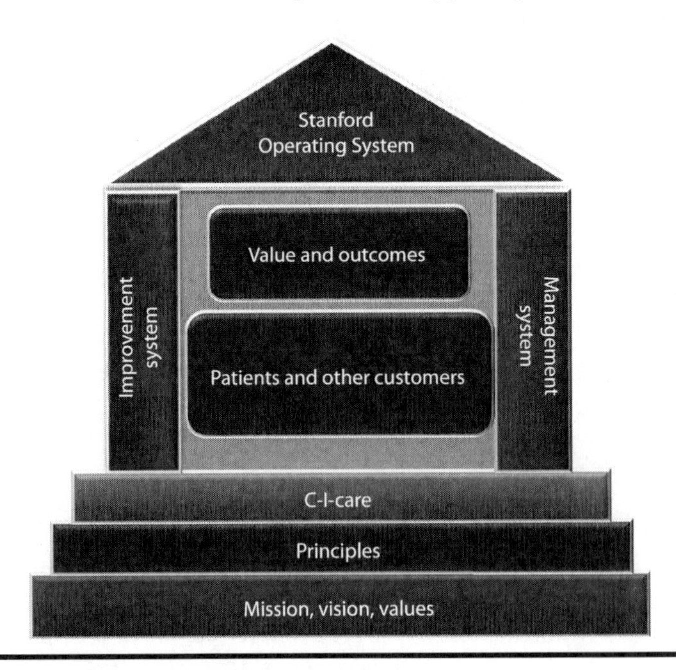

Figure 5.1 Stanford Health Care Operating System.

holding the gains that are achieved through improvement activities. A Lean-based operational system includes all the elements of traditional quality improvement but adds to this an articulation for the management system.

> The goal is that every member of the organization knows exactly what they are doing, and what improvements they must make, to contribute to the success of the organization.

The improvement system is built on the foundation of quality improvement and of the PDSA (plan–do–study–act) or PDCA (plan–do–check–act) cycle. The concept of the PDSA cycle is that of experimentation. Identify a problem, study the problem and develop a hypothesis for what is causing it, form an experiment and run it to see the effect it has on the problem, and then act on the results of that experiment. It also includes fundamental concepts such as the removal of waste, or non–value-added activities from processes, where waste is defined in terms of the customer or patient view of whether the activity is of value to them.

The Lean improvement system also has more technical aspects, most specifically around the flow, or sequence and timing, of work. Concepts like one-piece flow and pull systems are designed to optimize production while at the same time making it almost impossible to mask problems through excess inventory or resources.

All of these ideas regarding improvement were not invented at Toyota but were assembled from various organizations, practitioners, and thought leaders regarding quality improvement. The Ford Motor Company [5] represents one of the earliest and best examples of flow production through the establishment of the moving production line.

The breakthrough the Toyota Production System represents is largely around a systematic operational management system to support ongoing improvement. This management system has three main component parts: the strategy deployment system, value stream management, and active daily management.

Strategy deployment is a solution to the problem for how to gain organizational alignment. It is built around the idea of the establishment of a true north or fundamental direction that the organization will take, is set at the executive level of the organization, and includes the level of performance necessary to be successful. From there, that macro description is translated, level by level of organizational leadership, into meaningful terms and improvement ideas all the way to the frontline employees. In this way, improvement activities at the frontline are aligned with the broader organizational intent. The goal is that every member of the organization knows exactly what they are doing, and what improvements they must make, to contribute to the success of the organization. And because they are actively involved and engaged, both in the conversation regarding what the right goals and improvement activities should be and in the improvement activities themselves, their own level of engagement and sense of ownership in the organization are significantly increased.

> Value stream management is the answer to the question regarding how an organization optimizes its performance.

It is through active daily management that the connection is made to strategy deployment and value stream management, and it is at this level where the organization can transform itself through iterative, goal-directed, patient-centered improvements.

Value stream management is the answer to the question regarding how an organization optimizes its performance. The challenge with traditional forms of management is that it depends on the deconstruction of the organization into its component parts and then attempts to optimize those component parts. However, healthcare is by its nature not a deterministic and linear activity with significant interrelationships that exist between the component parts. It is therefore not possible to optimize the organization through the optimization of those component parts.

Everyone involved in the process knows at every moment what they should be doing, why they should be doing it, who they are in relationship to, and how to respond in the event of unusual conditions, including how to escalate.

Value stream management approaches this problem through the eyes of the patient. The value stream is the sum of the processes that define and deliver the patient's experience for a product or service. When a patient has an inpatient stay after an ED visit, the value stream looks at all of the component parts and experiences and defines that as the entity that should be optimized. For an inpatient stay, this might include the arrival and check-in at the ED, all of the clinical interactions that would occur there, the transport of the patient to and from various diagnostic modalities, the transport of the patient from the ED to a unit bed, and all the way through discharge and the transition ultimately back to the patient's house with appropriate follow-up care. That value stream traverses across multiple functions, but in value stream management, the aim is to optimize that set of experiences to achieve the maximum value for the patient.

Finally, there is active daily management, which is the process for checking the status of operations, for ensuring that standard work is being followed, for detecting abnormal conditions that require response, and for supporting ongoing improvement at the team level at the point of value. It is through active daily management that the connection is made to strategy deployment and value stream management, and it is at this level where the organization can transform itself through iterative, goal-directed, patient-centered improvements.

As the system of active daily management is used and matures, the knowledge of the process expands and capability and reliability are continually increased across all dimensions of measurement. And as the system matures, it becomes fundamentally more of a "real time" management system (see Figure 5.2).

At this stage, past performance is continually pulled forward through continuous improvement of the ability of the organization, and the ability to look forward and anticipate events and demands is enhanced through scheduling, forecasting, and prediction. Everyone involved in the process knows at every moment what they should be doing, why they should be doing it, who they are in relationship to, and how to respond in the event of unusual conditions, including how to escalate. This is the level of process knowledge in many organizations across several industries, but

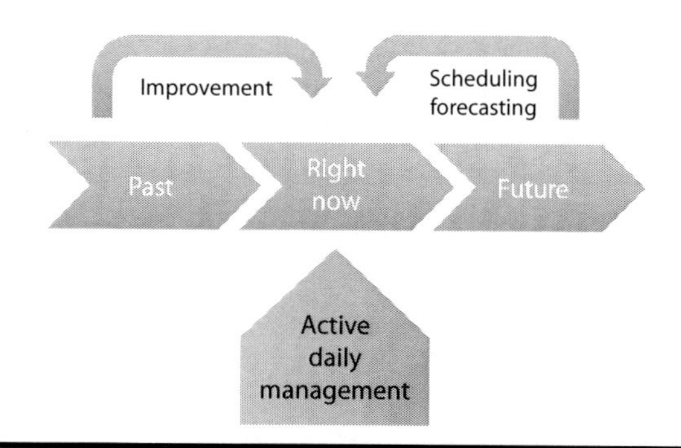

Figure 5.2 Real-time management.

it is rare in healthcare, even though the complexity of our operational environment is one of the most demanding in any industry.

Optimization Examples

Given that many of the readers of this text will have already implemented their EMR and have done so without the level of process knowledge that is described here, where is an organization to go to begin to optimize the use of their EMR in their operations?

Given the fact that so many organizations are now adopting Lean, the opportunity is to integrate EMR optimization as a significant part of improvement activities. One of the improvement methodologies often employed in Lean is that of the rapid process improvement workshop in which a team will come together for an intensive 4- or 5-day improvement effort focused around a specific process or problem. This is a tremendous opportunity to bring together operational and technology experts in a structured process to develop better process knowledge while examining how to best leverage the capabilities of the technology to improve process reliability and capability. Let me describe three different examples in three different organizations about how those are achieved.

Group Health Cooperative Case Study

The first example is from Group Health Cooperative. Group Health began its EMR implementation in 2003, well before it began its Lean journey. While we did not have the deep process knowledge that I describe here, we did start with the intent to use the EMR as a transformative tool operationally. Frankly, we were only partially successful, because of a lack of shared process knowledge across the 26 ambulatory care sites, multiple specialties, hundreds of physicians, and thousands of staff that were involved.

Once completed, we did not yet appreciate the need for a dedicated optimization phase, to push us from the level of capability that was attained during the implementation and to continue to develop our use of the EMR and to improve the processes that surround it. Instead, we opted for a traditional change request approach, where users could submit change requests, and those change requests would be prioritized and acted upon by the technical team.

The challenge was that the demand far outstripped capacity to deliver changes. Therefore, a very large inventory of change requests was held and continually prioritized and reprioritized. This system also failed because the change requests tended to be idiosyncratic to the requester, so what one person wanted to see was not shared by the rest of the users, and the changes happened slowly as the technical team went back to the users to clarify both the nature of the change and whether the change requested was really a change for the better. The slowness of the system to produce desired changes lead to dissatisfaction by the users, who felt the technologists were not responsive to their needs.

The difficulty was that we still lacked sufficient commonality across clinical settings and other sites to make implementation as impactful as it could have been.

This dynamic was changed first through the implementation of quality improvement support teams or QISTs, who would look at the change requests and aggregate them around common processes. They would then work with operational leadership to select a site at which to do an intensive improvement effort and obtain sponsorship that the changes that resulted from the dedicated improvement effort would be implemented system wide.

They would then spend, after a period of preparation, a dedicated week with a specific clinic with the members of the clinical team, informaticists, programmers, and other subject matter experts necessary to work through the optimization of the process and the technology. These initial efforts still did not have the level of process knowledge built in, but at least the work process carried equal footing with the technology changes that were being proposed. During the week, the changes would be worked through with the team, built into the system, and then tested immediately. In this way, the process resembled agile methodologies, where frequent build and testing iterations are used.

By the end of the week, a substantial series of changes both of the technology and of the process had been developed and tested and were ready for implementation. The result was a meaningful change that was quickly felt by the clinical teams, who also felt deeply engaged as owners of the change. The difficulty was that we still lacked sufficient commonality across clinical settings and other sites to make implementation as impactful as it could have been. This changed as we implemented our model line of the medical home in primary care.

As part of our Lean implementation efforts, we took advantage of the development of a medical home model developed at the Factoria Medical Center, in which the medical home model was specified in terms of enhanced staffing, staffing mix, panel size, and, most importantly, process knowledge. The team developed seven foundational work processes for the primary care medical home, and as part of that, through the partnership of the information technology function and medical informatics team, the EMR was optimized to support those foundational work processes.

The medical home model, including the technological enhancements, were then spread across all of the primary care sites at Group Health and resulted in significant improvements in operational performance for total cost of care management, patient experience, and positive impact to staff satisfaction [6].

The Impact on Population Health

> The key was to integrate population health activities into care processes and not to treat them as a separate set of actions taken outside of the work of the clinic.

One of the key impacts of the work that was done at Group Health was the impact on the capability of the population health performance of the delivery system. Group Health was a very early adopter of population health, including the creation of several registries, the creation of evidence-based guidelines, and comprehensive reporting regarding performance. While these improvements supported the performance of population health management, it wasn't until the adoption of the Lean-based model line that Group Health saw market-leading performance that led to its recognition as a Medicare five-star plan.

> The goal was to treat the patient as a unified whole, and to not segment them into independent members of various populations.

What explains this improvement? The explanations are consistent with a focus process supported through technology integration. The key was to integrate population health activities into care processes and not to treat them as a separate set of actions taken outside of the work of the clinic.

When population health was thought of as a separate endeavor, patients would be interacted within the context of the population they belong to, independent of their other interactions with the healthcare system. It was possible, even probable, that patients who needed to be followed up on from a population health perspective had recently visited the healthcare system and their primary care physician recently. If the patient happened to be a member of multiple populations, and therefore multiple registries, they would be managed independently, so they would often get multiple phone calls from different individuals reminding them to come to the clinic or to get lab tests done without any knowledge of either party to each other's actions.

The answer was to integrate the activities into the standard work of the clinic, leveraging health maintenance reminders that were triggered in the EMR in preparing for the visit processes to make sure that the clinical team knew everything that the patient needed, and that as much as possible could be addressed at the time of visit. The goal was to treat the patient as a unified whole, and to not segment them into independent members of various populations. This required that processes and standard work were developed for making sure that those additional care needs could be met before, during, or after the clinical visit.

That would help address the patients who were scheduled to be in the clinic but did not address the patients who had not proactively scheduled a visit. The second key was to develop team-specific reports regarding population health performance, prioritizing patients to be contacted. In addition, the team could see the number of patients needed to achieve their target for each element of the necessary prevention or treatment activities that were required. But knowing the information was not enough, standard work had to be built and visual systems put in place so that processes could be put in place to contact patients.

In the Group Health model, this was part of the medical assistants' work. They were responsible for making outreach calls, and they knew they needed to make five calls per day to patients with outstanding clinical needs. By making five calls per day, they knew they would shrink the number needed to achieve target to zero.

But what was most remarkable, though, was the feeling of contribution that the medical assistants had in terms of the success of the team and of the organization. They knew exactly how they were contributing to the success of the organization and its top tier metrics regarding HEDIS (Healthcare Effectiveness Data and Information Set) performance, as well as the success of the team. This created a level of engagement and pride that was palpable with the medical assistants and the team.

Palo Alto Medical Foundation Case Study

The second example of Lean-based process operational management and technology integration is from the Palo Alto Medical Foundation (PAMF), in Mountain View, California, which is a part of the Sutter Healthcare System. PAMF was a very early adopter of the EMR and had also been a leader in optimizing the EMR to achieve superior operational performance.

However, PAMF did not have deep process knowledge. As part of their Lean implementation, a model line was selected at the Fremont Medical Center in Fremont, California. A model line is essentially an existence proof, where the Lean management system is implemented along with focused process improvement. This technique of establishing a model line is often used in Lean implementations and forms the basis for spreading the Lean system to other sites.

As an evolution from the approach that we used at Group Health, and because of the more traditional fee-for-service component of the PAMF business model, the "flow manager" concept that was first used at Virginia Mason Medical Center in Seattle, Washington [7], was adopted at the Fremont facility.

The goal of the flow manager concept is to have the medical assistant become an integral part of the care team and strengthen their role to specifically help support the physicians flow through the course of the day. One of the key components of this flow management is the interaction of the flow manager and the physician's in-basket in the EMR. Part of the choreography of the day is that while the provider is with the patient in the exam room, the flow manager is teeing up the three most important things from the provider's in-basket for the provider to deal with in between the completion of the current visit and the start of the next.

If this can be done consistently, and the provider can complete their documentation and close the encounter before they leave the exam room, then by the end of the day, defined as 30 min after the last visit, the provider would be able to leave the clinic with a clean in-basket and all of their encounters closed. This is a powerful motivator for physicians who had become accustomed to having to go home and, after having dinner with their family and putting their kids to bed, put in another hour or two of work in the EMR.

In order to accomplish this, the informatics team and the process improvement specialists formed a tight partnership with the operational staff to design processes, make improvements in the EMR, and support skill building within the EMR. While publication of the results of these efforts is still in process, the improvement has been significant and has led to the spread of the model line processes throughout the primary care system and over the 500 primary care physicians within PAMF.

This is a good example of bringing together technology knowledge of the EMR and developing a deeper level of process knowledge concurrently, with the result being significant improvement in all dimensions of performance.

Stanford Health Care Case Study

A third example, and the next evolution of the integration of technology and process, is occurring at Stanford Health Care. There, we are attempting to fundamentally redesign primary care by challenging two fundamental assumptions. One is the exam room, which is a foundational element for ambulatory care. But what would primary care look like if the exam room is only one of many modalities from which the physician could choose? Other alternatives could include physical visits outside of the exam room, by the physician, by other clinical professionals, or even by nonlicensed individuals who could have the benefit of a live and virtual connection to a nurse or physician to support them. Other alternatives could also be virtual rather than physical and could be either synchronous or asynchronous text, audio and visual.

> This represents the next evolution in our thinking about how technology and process knowledge come together to form a more perfect union.

The second assumption is an acceptance of the lack of situational awareness of the patient's condition. But what if the flow of data could be significantly enhanced, and processed to make it readily available and actionable for the physician and the team? The concept of situational awareness is "the primary basis for subsequent decision making and performance in the operation of complex, dynamic systems…." At its lowest level, the operator needs to perceive relevant information (in the environment, system, self, etc.), next integrate the data in conjunction with task goals, and, at its highest level, predict future events and system states on the basis of this understanding [8].

The design team, made up of physicians, nurses, and administrators, along with supporting functions, is going through the process for Lean design known as the Production Preparation Process, or 3P. Typically, 3P is used to integrate operational knowledge with the design of space with a goal to optimize both the processes and the spaces in which they are enacted. In this case, we are adding to this a linked and concurrent process of technology development, including maximizing the use of the EMR, using an agile methodology of short development cycles. The agile team will be colocated with the three key design teams, with the activities deeply integrated to optimize the processes, the space, and the technology, with a goal of creating the enablers for situational awareness in the complex and dynamic system of primary care as the patient moves through their lives outside of the health care setting.

This represents the next evolution in our thinking about how technology and process knowledge come together to form a more perfect union. In this way, we believe that the process capability and reliability can be significantly enhanced, with a resulting significant improvement of operational performance.

Conclusion

We are still in our infancy in health care for developing deep process knowledge. As more organizations adopt and use state-of-the-art operational management techniques, and with time, they will continue to develop this level of knowledge, and with it be able to produce the enhanced operational performance that was initially thought possible at the introduction of EMRs. It will require a deep partnership between the technologists and the operational professionals, the use of a management system that promotes and supports ongoing improvement and knowledge development, and sufficient time for these factors to work. These are not simple approaches, but simple approaches to complex systems most often yield very little in the way of results.

References

1. Hillestad, R., Bigelow, J., Bower, A., Girosi, F., Meili, R., Scoville, R., and Taylor, R., Can electronic medical records transform health care? Potential health benefits, savings and costs. *Health Affairs*, 2005. **24**(5): 1103–1117.
2. Friedberg, M.W., Chen, P.G., Van Busum, K.R., Aunon, F., Pham, C., Caloyeras, J., Mattke, S. et al., *Factors Affecting Physician Professional Satisfaction and Their Implications For Patient Care, Health Systems, and Health Policy*. 2013, Santa Monica, CA: RAND. p. 1 online resource. xxv, 122 pages.
3. Thorp, J. and DMR Consulting Group Center for Strategic Leadership, *The Information Paradox: Realizing the Business Benefits of Information Technology*. Rev. ed. 2003, New York; London: McGraw-Hill. 336 pages.
4. Hammer, M. and J. Champy, *Reengineering the Corporation: A Manifesto for Business Revolution*. 1st ed. 1993, New York: HarperBusiness. vi, 223 pages.
5. Ford, H. and S. Crowther, *Today and Tomorrow*. 1926, Garden City, NY: Doubleday, Page & Company. 4 p. l., 281 pages.
6. Reid, R., Coleman, K., Johnson, E., Fishman, P., Hsu, C., Soman, M., Trescott, C., Erikson, M., and Larson, E., The group health medical home at year two: Cost savings, higher patient satisfaction, and less burnout for physicians. *Health Affairs*, 2010. **29**(5): 835–843.
7. Pittenger, K., *Flow in Primary Care*, in *Virginia Mason Blog*. 2012.
8. Endsley, M.R., Measurement of situation awareness in dynamic systems. *Human Factors*, 1995. **37**: 65–84.

Chapter 6

Platform for Innovation, Part I—Maximizing the EMR

Michael Blum, MD

"How quickly we forget struggling to decipher the handwriting of our peers and the hundreds of thousands of medication errors due to poor handwriting."

From that perspective, healthcare probably does stand alone in its pathetic use of technology.

I always chuckle when someone points out how technophobic healthcare providers are and how healthcare has failed to embrace the digital revolution that has brought such advances to almost every other industry and undertaking. The reality could not be further from the truth, but entirely true at the same time. Today's doctors and allied providers don't live in a bubble. They use computers, smartphones, tablets, wearables, and other connected devices just like everyone else. Sure, there is some stratification by age and trends driven by clinical specialization, but in general, providers are just as highly skilled users of technology as anyone else. The difference is in the quality of the tools that they have available to them in providing care to their patients and then documenting and attempting to get compensated for that care. From that perspective, healthcare probably does stand alone in its pathetic use of technology.

The systems that healthcare workers use to order, document, and charge for their services are indeed antiquated in comparison to the slick web apps and social media experiences that we use on a regular basis.

Certainly, it is not all bad—there are pockets of advanced computing throughout healthcare. Consider the advanced imaging of high-speed computed tomography (CT) scanners and magnetic resonance with three-dimensional reconstructions, digital pathology, real-time mapping of the electrical activity of the myocardium to detect and ablate malignant arrhythmias, and the robotic automation of medication management.

Think about it—we take their clothes away, we tell them when to come and when they can leave, we tie them up when they misbehave, and, when we let them eat, we generally feed them very bad food.

Still, the critics have a point. The systems that healthcare workers use to order, document, and charge for their services are indeed antiquated in comparison to the slick web apps and social media experiences that we use on a regular basis. The EMRs in particular, designed and built on decades-old technology, do not provide anything close to the experience that we seek. There is no Google-like information gathering, no Amazon-like suggestions based on our recent activity, no Facebook-like sharing and support from colleagues and friends, no Siri to answer our questions, and no Maps to get us from here to there. Worst of all, there is no context connecting any of our clinical activities that creates the richness, efficiency, and stickiness of today's consumer digital experience. Instead, there is incessant scrolling, clicking, typing, and dismissing dialog boxes that "remind" us with irrelevant, obvious, or dated warnings.

Still, healthcare is not standing still. In fact, change is happening at an unprecedented pace. Healthcare reform has added millions of insured patients to the system and created emphasis on primary and preventive care. Governments, regulators, and payers are rushing to gauge providers on the quality, safety, and efficiency of their care.

In a newer twist, they are now graded and increasingly paid based on the customer service they provide. The Meaningful Use program, initially designed with incentives to drive computing technology into healthcare, now penalizes providers whose patients do not sign up for their portals in sufficient numbers or communicate electronically often enough.

However, the two greatest forces of change are Medicare's move from fee-for-service to fee-for-value–based payment, and patients' changing expectations to be treated more like consumers and less like prisoners, think about it—we take their clothes away, we tell them when to come and when they can leave, we tie them up when they misbehave, and, when we let them eat, we generally feed them very bad food.

Despite these seemingly dire circumstances, we are seeing increasing penetration of digital innovation in healthcare that has the potential to massively affect the current delivery system. This chapter will describe how the EMR, with all of its warts, can and is being used in innovative ways to improve the quality, safety, and cost of healthcare delivery, and how contemporary technologies such as mobile, social, sensors, and apps are poised to make dramatic change in the way patients will experience the healthcare of tomorrow.

Part 1—The EMR

Let's start by getting it out of the way. EMRs have taken a significant beating recently. Once held out as the savior of healthcare with the promise to improve quality, consistency, and safety while reining in runaway costs, they are now vilified as electronic taskmasters that suck the life out of clinicians while causing new types of errors and facilitating fraud in billing and documentation. The market leaders' reliable, high-performing platforms are labeled "obsolete" and incapable of delivering a contemporary computing experience. The EMR has essentially been painted with most of the ills of the current healthcare system.

While I have no intention to be an apologist for the EMR industry, it is important to gain a more balanced perspective. It is undeniable that the EMR has changed the provider's clinical experience and the provider–patient interaction. Several studies have demonstrated the amount of time, some of it net-new, that providers now spend interacting with the EMR and some studies have suggested that a portion of that time would previously have been spent engaging with patients. Some of the numbers are disturbing—50% of a visit spent typing in the EMR, 30 seconds before interrupting the patient to enter data, 2 hours spent answering e-mails from the patient portal, completing clinic notes at 2:00 a.m., and so on.

Still, a reasonably successful implementation of an EMR typically brings powerful benefits to patient care that are typically not discussed, yet rarely denied. The elimination of handwriting is surely the most obvious, and the ubiquitous access to the chart is probably next. How quickly we forget struggling to decipher the handwriting of our peers and the hundreds of thousands of medication errors attributed to poor handwriting. How much time do we save by the ability to instantly access a patient's chart from most anywhere on the planet? How many errors and misdiagnoses have we avoided by simply having access to the patients' data? Even little things like immediate access to the medication list and recent labs while refilling medications is far more efficient than it was with the paper chart. Also, the timeliness of communications is greatly improved—when I complete a visit, my consultation note is instantly available to the patient's primary care physician (PCP) who they may be seeing later in the day. Previously, it took days to weeks for a letter to get to the PCP, if ever.

Still, while there is undeniable, significant benefit to the EMR, there are certainly significant issues as well. One of the areas where they continue to be criticized for failing to fulfill their promise is in the area of clinical decision support (CDS)—their ability to provide guidance to clinicians that enhances patient safety, clinical quality, and efficiency. From a parochial perspective, this criticism is fair. While the EMRs are technically capable of providing information and alerts in areas such as medication dose ranging, drug–drug and drug–disease interactions, and diagnostic support, the actual clinical usability of these promising capabilities has been a huge disappointment. Alert fatigue has proven to be such a powerful force that many critical safety opportunities are missed. Even at organizations with strong safety cultures, the mantra of "just ignore the alerts and keep going" is the M.O. The issues are complex, and, to be fair to the EMR vendors, in the medication alerting space, the blame can be shared with the third-party providers of the drug databases. Whether it is poor data, weak algorithms, or inadequate user interface (or all of the above), the EMRs are not delivering sufficiently usable medication ordering support to achieve the improvements in safety that we expect from them.

Having said that, there are several nontraditional forms of CDS and innovations within the EMR that are improving clinical practice, and I describe five of them below:

1. **Closed loop medication administration:** Several well-done studies have documented the frighteningly common occurrence of medication errors in both hospital and ambulatory settings. The literature suggests that between 1 in 5 and 1 in 10 patients experience a medication error and that 30% of these errors cause significant harm [1]. Those numbers quickly become staggering. As noted previously, the errors caused by illegible handwriting (estimated to be

10% of the total) disappear with implementation of the EMR. Unfortunately, because of the challenges with medication alerting mentioned above, many of the drug–drug interaction, allergy, and dose-range errors that could be caught (approximately 30% of the total) slip through because of poor user interface design and user experience. Still, the opportunity to eliminate 60% of the medication errors that are attributed to flaws in the administration process remains and can be dramatically affected with a closed loop medication administration process. The EMR is a key component of the strategy and provides the medication ordering, transmittal, and verification capabilities. The other key component is a robotic pharmacy that provides the fulfillment capabilities. At UCSF, in addition to computerized practitioner order entry (CPOE), we have implemented robotics for both oral and intravenous medications as well as bar code medication administration (BCMA). The combination of the three technologies has turned out to be incredibly powerful in reducing medication errors. The electronic order transmittal directly from the EMR eliminates transcription and faxing errors; the robots eliminate pharmacy technician fulfillment errors, as well as providing bar-coded, unit dose packaged medications for the nurses to administer. With BCMA, the nurses are assured that they are meeting the five rights of medication administration (right patient, right drug, right dose, right route, and right time).

Interestingly, while providers will tell you that they find little value in the medication CDS delivered by the EMR, nurses will tell you that they greatly appreciate the support of BCMA and commonly have stories of the system helping them avoid medication administration errors. In contrast to the ordering CDS, when the nurses are administering medications and BCMA in the EMR issues an alert, they pay attention and typically find that the system has detected an error in the making. On the basis of our clinical volume, medication administrations, and elimination of fulfillment and administration errors, at UCSF, we estimate that these technologies help prevent more than 100,000 potential medication errors annually, 15,000 of which could have caused significant harm.

This approach is not a one-trick pony—there are many scenarios where simply giving the ordering clinician the best options at the top of the list yields the best results.

---

2. **Improved imaging utilization:** High-end imaging is costly and, for CT and positron emission tomography, involves significant radiation exposure. Additionally, the use of contrast in imaging carries the risk of renal injury, anaphylaxis, and nephrogenic systemic sclerosis (associated with gadolinium contrast agents when used in patients with severe renal dysfunction). While most efforts, including the 2017 federal legislative mandate to implement radiology CDS in the ambulatory space, are directed at decreasing utilization on the assumption that many studies are unnecessary, we found another cause of overutilization—many studies that were necessary to evaluate a clinical issue were not being ordered correctly. For example, in obtaining a CT to evaluate an abdominal concern, providers were commonly ordering a CT of the abdomen, whereas a CT of the abdomen AND PELVIS is usually the correct study. If the radiology technician noted the error, they would page the provider to correct it, wasting valuable time and effort. If the error was not noted, the study often needed to be repeated, increasing waste and exposing the patient to further radiation and risk. While an elegant, well-constructed CDS rule could be expected to solve this problem, the reality is that they so

far have not done so. The problem was exacerbated by the fact that CT Abd and Pelvis was so low on the list of orderable studies that it did not appear on the first screen of orderables. As a result, there were no cognitive or visual triggers, and the correct selection was commonly missed. We trialed a very simple approach to the issue: by reordering the list of available studies, we placed CT Abd and Pelvis above CT Abd. Without any significant training effort to the providers, the number of incorrectly ordered studies and repeated cases fell by 35%. Interestingly, there was no increase in inappropriate use of pelvic CT when only abd was needed. Apparently, it is easier for the clinicians to say, "I don't need to include the pelvis" than to remember to include it in the study when it is necessary. Important elements of this success were both the ability of our radiology colleagues to identify the opportunity and our clinical EMR team to think creatively about a solution. Had the radiologists or the EMR programmers said "let's develop an alert" or a "hard stop" as a solution, we would have missed the opportunity. The ability to quickly develop a simple, timely, noninterruptive piece of decision support was the key. This approach is not a one-trick pony—there are many scenarios where simply giving the ordering clinician the best options at the top of the list yields the best results.

An entire sector of the healthcare IT industry has sprung up in the last 5 years peddling bolt-on BI tools and hype.

3. **Analytics to support guideline-based care:** Another common criticism of the enterprise EMRs, and Epic in particular, is the difficulty in extracting data for reporting and analytics. Certainly, the clinical data repository inside the EMR contains complex data structures that are optimized for transactional efficiency and are not easily usable reporting tools in their native state. Some of the EMR vendors have responded by partnering with reporting/analytic vendors to provide business intelligence (BI) and reporting packages, and an entire sector of the healthcare IT industry has sprung up in the last 5 years peddling bolt-on BI tools and hype. But these tools still require deep understanding of the complex underlying data structures in order to create reliable reports and analyses. We are seeing a next generation of solutions evolve as the vendors develop more contemporary, flexible clinical data stores and warehouses that do much of the data wrangling to create and expose greatly simplified views of the data that can be used to create timely reports and analyses.

   Still, even before these next-generation tools are implemented, there is ample opportunity to use the EMR data to improve clinical performance. A useful example is a project that we undertook to improve blood product utilization. The guidelines around blood products have been in flux recently, and, based on anecdotal evidence, we were suspecting that there was significant variation across the organization in adherence to the guidelines. The well-intentioned staff from the blood bank requested a set of ordering alerts for the providers to encourage proper ordering behavior that would comply with the guidelines. On the basis of our prior experience and data on ignored alerts, we discouraged this approach and joined forces with another organizational initiative pursuing improved red blood cell utilization. By extracting some relatively straightforward data elements from the database (hematocrit, attending provider, service, location, number of units ordered, etc.), we were able to provide the process improvement team with compelling data on variation across and within services. Those data allowed them to ask much more specific, probing questions in their interviews with providers and revealed several opportunities for targeted clinical intervention.

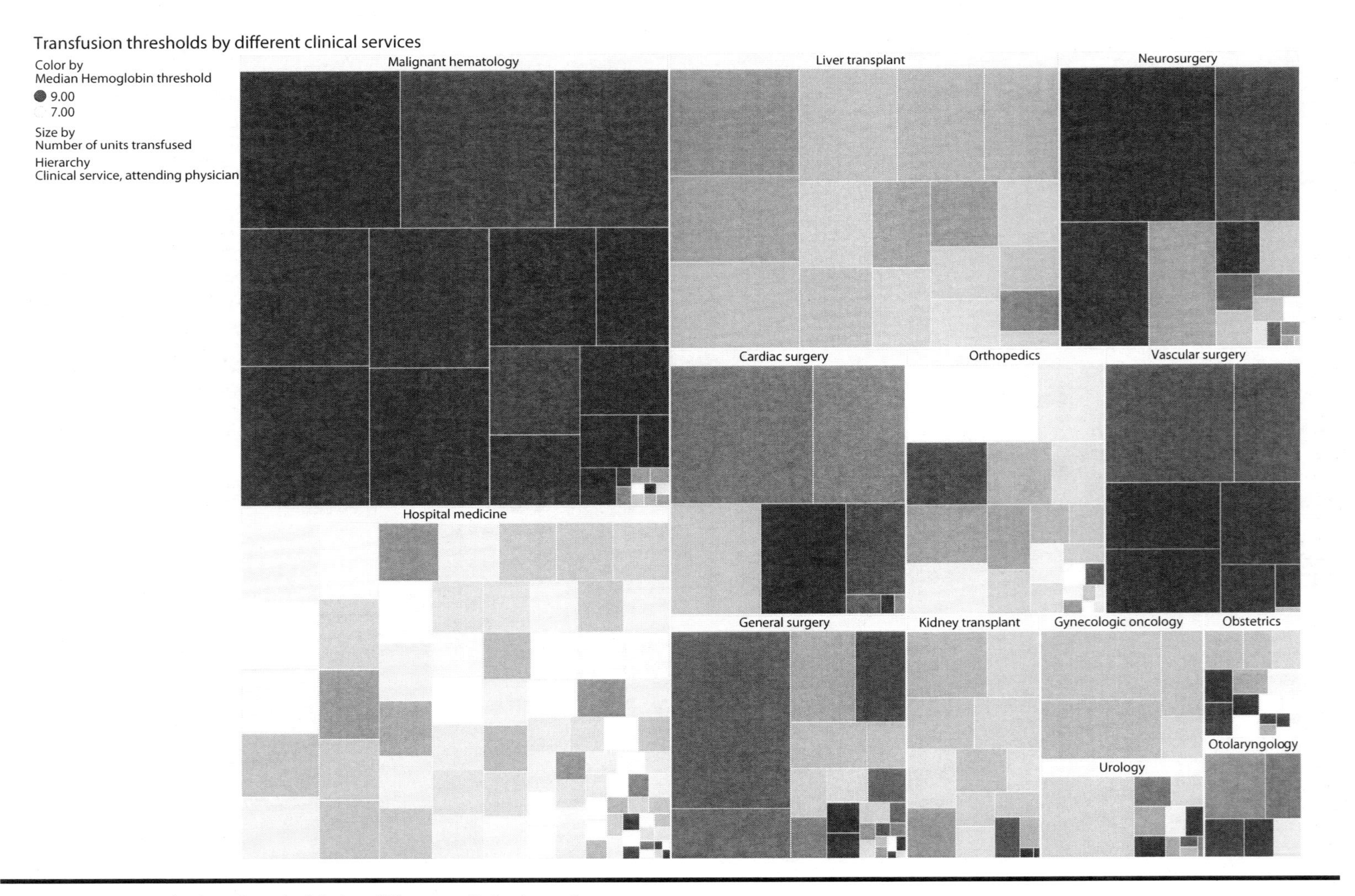

Figure 6.1 Transfusion thresholds by different clinical services.

Not surprisingly, some providers did not always warmly embrace the information regarding the current guidelines and believed they were already highly compliant. It was at this point that the data and a clever visualization became very powerful (Figure 6.1). In training sessions across the organization, providers were shown their data in comparison to their clinical peers and the entire organization (which were anonymized). The "heat map" visualization proved very impactful as the providers could easily see the volume and variance in the clinical activity compared to their peers. There was no dismissal of "bad" or "irrelevant" data. Providers want to be as good as or better than their peers in these types of metrics and it was easy for them to see that they were not. Particular outliers who were resistant to changing their practice were referred to their Service Chiefs who were shown unblinded data for their entire division. The program was very effective and guideline adherence increased significantly. More importantly, the variation within and between clinical groups decreased, demonstrating more consistent delivery of guideline-based care.

4. **eConsults:** One of the greatest sources of patient dissatisfaction is the referral process. Getting sent from a PCP to a specialist, scheduling appointments, waiting for insurance authorizations, hoping the records arrive, taking more time off of work, and getting to the appointment only to find that not all of the tests have been completed drive patients crazy. Frequently, the consultation centers on a fairly straightforward diagnostic question or management approach that might not even require another examination of the patient.

   In order to improve the patient experience and improve consultant availability, we created the eConsult process within the EMR. The eConsult process consists of a series of templates, designed by the specialists, that allow the referring provider to select a question for the specialist and walks the referring provider through the data set that the specialist is expecting in order to answer the question. The template gathers the available data and the referring provider fills in any missing information, orders any remaining studies, and electronically submits the eConsult. The consultant reviews the eConsult within 1 day of a completed request and messages the referring provider with either the answer to the question or a recommendation for a formal consultation. The process has worked beautifully, and more than 95% of the questions are answered without an office visit. Obviously, in a fee-for-service environment, a payment scheme for these eConsults must be in place, but as they have proven their value, insurance companies are beginning to cover them at a significant fraction of an office consultation. Patient satisfaction with the process is very high, and the process is well received by both referring providers and the specialists. The referring providers appreciate the efficiency of the process and the specialists can move through the consultations fairly efficiently, getting reasonable reimbursement for the time, while keeping their schedules clear for more complex referrals.

For a variety of clinical, technology, and computer science factors, we are not yet at a point where the EMR or other applications can help us make complex diagnoses.

---

5. **Decompensation prediction algorithms:** As noted, EMRs have had a poor track record in the area of diagnostic support and acuity assessment. For a variety of clinical, technology, and computer science factors, we are not yet at a point where the EMR or other applications can help us make complex diagnoses. Previously, the same could be said of algorithms and

applications that were designed to predict patient decompensation and provide an "early warning." While systems were demonstrated a decade ago that had reasonable sensitivity for patient decompensation, their specificity was poor and they simply announced the obvious—"your patient who is very old, is tachycardic and hypotensive, and has acute multi-organ failure and is at risk for serious complications."

Gee, thanks!

These systems typically ran on algorithms that included very limited data, mostly vital signs. Over the last few years, there has been a resurgence in the field. As EMRs are able to capture larger-structured data sets, scientists and vendors have developed more sophisticated decompensation prediction algorithms that show promise of predicting serious decompensation 24–48 h before it occurs. The Rothman index, a proprietary algorithm by PeraHealth, is an example of these new algorithms that combines physiologic measurements, nursing assessments, and laboratory data to create a composite risk score. The system integrates with the EMR and has demonstrated promising results compared with prior early warning systems [2]. An important hurdle that remains is for these systems to be integrated into a care process that results in better outcomes for these patients, not just earlier knowledge of pending deterioration. Deconstructing the composite score to help the clinicians identify the cause of the impending decompensation and effective treatments will be an exciting step forward. Additionally, other sites are developing even more sophisticated algorithms that incorporate streaming data and waveforms that they hope will further predict impending decompensation with higher predictive value or in cases that would otherwise be missed. This approach will require bringing big data techniques to bear that have not traditionally been used in EMR-based clinical analytics. It will be fascinating to watch the evolution of this field. Seeing whether additional data in the algorithms increases the predictive value, whether novel indicators with strong independent predictive value are discovered, or whether none of this truly helps us improve outcomes for our patients will be the work for these clinicians and scientists over the next several years.

So, as you can see from the case studies I just provided and the ones discussed in Chapter 4 by Les Reed, MD, the much maligned, costly EMR can have very significant value. The initial implementation of an EMR with CPOE, done reasonably well, intrinsically reduces a patient's risk of encountering a medication error, and more sophisticated implementations can reduce that risk even further.

Additionally, by viewing the EMR as part of the care team and process and not as a lone actor, organizations can create many further innovations in the space that leverage the capabilities of the EMR to create a safer, higher-quality, more efficient clinical environment. Hopefully, we will soon see these innovations delivered as "out of the box" competencies of the EMR so that all patients can benefit from them.

References

1. Bates DW, Cullen DJ, Laird N, Petersen LA, Small SD, Servi D, Laffel G et al. Incidence of adverse drug events and potential adverse drug events. Implications for prevention. ADE Prevention Study Group. *J Am Med Assoc* 1995; **274**:29–34.
2. Finlay GD, Rothman MJ and Smith RA. Measuring the modified early warning score and the Rothman Index: Advantages of utilizing the electronic medical record in an early warning system. *J Hosp Med* 2014; **9**:116–119.

Chapter 7

EMR Adoption Model Stage 7 Lessons

John Hoyt, MHA

"Organizations that strive to be among the best do not simply compare themselves to themselves; they compare themselves to others and set goals accordingly."

Welcome to the Starting Line

One of the most respected healthcare chief information officers (CIOs) in the United States, and an early Stage 7 recipient, taught me an important and easily remembered phrase: "Once you have gone live, welcome to the starting line." That is so true.

This chapter is about the HIMSS Analytics Electronic Medical Record Adoption Model (EMRAM) and what we've learned from hospitals and clinics that have traversed it in the first 10 years of its existence, from 2005, when Mike Davis and Dave Garets invented it, until 2015. The top tier of the model, Stage 7, has taken on a life of its own and has become an award for those hospitals and clinics that have achieved the highest level of EMR adoption and "meaningful use," in lower case, in their organizations.

Figure 7.1 shows the model and two periods—one is the third quarter of 2009 when the HITECH Act got passed by Congress, authorizing more than $20 billion of incentives to physician clinics and hospitals to encourage them to implement and meaningfully use EMRs, and the other is the second quarter of 2015 to see how much progress has been made.

It turns out, there's been a lot. The "Meaningful Use" program, in caps, has been a resounding success; look at the percentages on the right side of the graph. Those are the increases, or declines, in the various stages from 2009 to the present day.

Lessons from Stage 7 Recipients

One of the most important lessons is that achieving Stage 7 status is not about implementing systems, but rather about achieving benefits and value. And that takes three ingredients: planning,

US EMR Adoption Model

Stage	Cumulative Capabilities	Percent of Hospitals At Stage		
		Q3 2009	Q2 2015	
Stage 7	Complete EMR, CCD transactions to share data, Data warehousing, Data continuity with ED, ambulatory, OP	0.5%	3.7%	640.0%
Stage 6	Physician documentation (structured templates), full CDSS (variance & compliance), full R-PACS	1.2%	23.6%	1866.7%
Stage 5	Closed loop medication administration	4.8%	32.3%	572.9%
Stage 4	CPOE and clinical decision support (clinical protocols)	4.1%	13.2%	222.0%
Stage 3	Nursing/clinical documentation (flow sheets), CDSS (medication error checking), PACS available outside radiology	40.4%	18.2%	-55.0%
Stage 2	CDR, controlled medical vocabulary, CDS, may have document imaging; HIE capable	29.8%	3.6%	-87.9%
Stage 1	Ancillaries - Lab, Rad, Pharmacy - all installed	7.1%	1.9%	-73.2%
Stage 0	All three ancillaries not installed	12.1%	3.3%	-72.7%
		N=5172	N=5464	

Data from HIMSS Analytics™ Database, © 2015 HIMSS Analytics

Figure 7.1 The EMRAM, in 2009, and now.

persistent focus, and time. But time cannot be forever. Leading CIOs, along with their executive clinical leadership teammates, push their teams to adopt a continuous improvement mindset to achieve clinical quality improvements that exceed pre-live levels.

No stone goes unturned for these leaders. Stage 7 organizations must prove through at least three case studies that they have improved quality, safety, or efficiency since going live. Pre-live data can be used, but the evidence of positive benefit being derived from use of the EMR and its clinical systems must be clearly evident.

Much evidence of care delivery improvements have been delivered in Stage 7 visits. Some of those that stand out include the following:

- The beneficial use of 350 evidence-based order sets, developed by a multidisciplinary team and covering 80% of inpatient diagnoses, resulting in an 83% reduction in variation of antibiotic start time, and appropriate venous thromboembolism prophylaxis orders improved to 96% of candidate cases from 49% of candidate cases.
- The use of predictive alerting where a 40-variable algorithm is applied to each inpatient to predict the likelihood of readmission within 30 days, on the basis of their current condition and status, which has proven to be 80% accurate.
- The use of Bluetooth-enabled weight scales for CHF patients, whose weight was reported through a personal health record (PHR) to a case manager resulting in a 42% reduction in CHF readmissions in these initial trial patients.
- A comprehensive return-on-investment study showing the system benefits "paying off" 18 months ahead of plan.

Investing with a Purpose

Top tier organizations of all types invest with a purpose. Clearly, the Stage 7s have invested to the tune of billions of dollars. But the best of them clearly state the key performance indicators they intended to improve, up front. Further, these goals are not a secret from their employees, physician community, or patients. They are well known and built into everyone's expectations. They are part of the corporate communications plan. The goals are everywhere to be seen—on bulletin boards, in employee newsletters, and in middle management, executive management, and CEO performance goals.

One of the best examples of this was seen at an Ambulatory Stage 7 visit where each clinical service area had public bulletin boards with key performance indicators visible to employees and patients, and Stage 7 inspectors as well. Physician satisfaction, PHR use per primary care doctor, costs, and revenue per visit were all documented and visible. While this is somewhat unusual in its breadth, it is a clear indicator of a data-driven culture and is laudable in its magnitude and transparency. And no surprise, they were meeting the stated goals.

Holding Companies Do Not Work

Well, at least they do not seem to work for achieving Stage 7 on the HIMSS Analytics EMRAM. We all know that hospitals are assets that can be bought and sold to fit a need in a corporate portfolio. However, when it comes to delivering inpatient and ambulatory care across an enterprise, there is scant evidence to support the efficacy of a holding company, at least as it relates to the accrued benefits of enterprise EMRs.

For this discussion, we define a provider holding company in an IT–focused way: Organizations that acquire hospitals and leave the existing clinical systems in place so as not to cause disruption, or choose to not invest in centralizing or standardizing IT because it was excluded from due diligence or have more important capital needs, essentially never achieve Stage 7 across the enterprise. There are examples where some hospitals in a "holding company" earn Stage 7, but Stage 7 has never been achieved across an enterprise of mixed brand EMRs.

There are many multihospital systems that have earned Stage 7 across the enterprise with a common core clinical system. A common denominator in these organizations is a strong mission-driven vision that clearly articulates "this is the way we do business; this is the way we deliver patient care." This sets the stage for enterprise order sets and pathways, enterprise documentation tools, and enterprise standard ways of using technology to order, validate, and deliver medications at the point of care. It also provides the foundation, both technically and culturally, for significant clinical data analytics. Organizations that invest with a mission-driven purpose in underlying technologies to reinforce standards of practice also invest in the analytical capabilities to verify their chosen methods and constantly strive to improve upon them.

Holding companies do not appear to show this same diligence and level of success at standardization and consistency across the enterprise. Where would you rather receive your care?

A Corollary to "Holding Companies Don't Work"

"Best of breed" doesn't work, either. We've seen massive reduction of disparate best of breed applications in Stage 7 organizations. One highly respected academic medical center, with many Nobel Prize–winning department heads, was proud of its ability to rid the organization of dozens of standalone departmental or subdepartmental systems that did not communicate with each other or the main clinical data repository. Their stance was that department heads were corporate citizens of the health system and needed to do what was right for the interoperability of patient information, and that meant going on the main clinical information system or EMR.

This is not to say that you should expect the EMR vendor to have applications for every single need, but it is to say that a best practice is to minimize, to the best of your ability, the number of different vendor applications in your application portfolio. This is the path Stage 7 organizations consistently take.

Clinical Analytics

All the systems in the world will not deliver the value we need. Usage rates differ. Pathways are not always followed. Pathways may be outdated. Appropriate medications may not be available or covered by an insurance plan.

As stated above, Stage 7 organizations invest in the effort to analyze their care delivery and constantly compare themselves with others. They invest in an enterprise data warehouse, in analytical tools, and, very importantly, in data visualization tools. Interestingly, two Stage 7 organizations in 2010 showed that data visualization techniques helped them determine where the H1N1 virus was appearing in their catchment areas. Both were able to update state and local public health officials on a daily basis and direct vaccinations to appropriate local markets, thus improving public health.

Comparing yourself to others is more difficult than it seems on the surface. Of course, a provider can use a "printout" of some data source, but Stage 7 organizations are expected to go far beyond that. To obtain data from an outside source, process it using sophisticated extract, transfer, and load (ETL) methods, and then use it for internal comparisons is a complex task. Organizations that strive to be among the best do not simply compare themselves to themselves; they compare themselves to others and set goals accordingly.

The PHR as an ATM

Many providers offer a PHR to improve patient "stickiness" with their organization, and that is admirable. We look for that in our Stage 7 reviews and we expect to see proof that it results in improved chronic disease management.

However, there are two Stage 7 organizations that have gone beyond that single-provider focus and have offered their PHR as a multivendor, multiprovider PHR. As one CIO stated, "We want our PHR to be the ATM machine of personal health records." In addition, this positioned the organization to use the PHR as their downtime system. Hosted in a different data center miles away, it was the backup and mirror image of the comprehensive patient record.

Is this a trend of things to come? Or is simply the vision of the Community Health Information Networks of the 1990s finally coming to life?

Celebrate Your Successes

Why should an organization pursue Stage 7 recognition? Is it just an ego thing?

Clearly one of the values of Stage 7 recognition is the public acknowledgement and reward for everyone who worked hard and contributed to the accomplishment. These staff deserve the recognition that Stage 7 brings to the organization. People in organization after organization cheer, high-five, and have tears of joy when the Stage 7 validation is announced. Leading CEOs and CIOs encourage their teams to do the hard work and earn the recognition that is so well deserved.

Others in and outside the healthcare industry recognize the value of Stage 7 as well. For more than 5 years, we have heard Stage 6 and 7 organizations tell of bond rating due diligence processes that included preferential scoring for earning Stage 6 and Stage 7. Additionally, for a decade, we have seen evidence that EMRAM achievement beginning at Stage 4 has brought discounts in liability insurance. Another organization demonstrated increased employee satisfaction and reduction in staff turnover.

And in 2014, one Stage 7 client used an interesting 4-year data trend in their Magnet Nursing Journey. For 4 years, their "nursing satisfaction with staffing" increased year over year, but in fact, they never changed their nursing staffing ratios. Nurses perceived that they were better able to handle the patient load as they implemented additional IT tools. This is a strong testament to the value of IT investments in today's environment.

Medical Tourism

This may not sound like a "hot topic" in the United States, but it certainly is in Asia and the Middle East. Both of these geographies have health systems that intend to thrive on medical tourism. And interestingly, both of these markets have leading organizations that have partnerships of varying structures with leading US health systems such as Johns Hopkins, Partners of Boston, and Cleveland Clinic. These Asian and Middle Eastern health systems are striving aggressively to earn Stage 7 to help promote their medical tourism. For the Asian hospitals, that tourism is targeted at the West Coast of the United States and Canada as well as elsewhere in Asia. In the Middle East, the target is European markets as well as the significant population of "expats" in the Middle East. In crowded markets where an enterprise is striving to reach a focused area of the market and "prestige patients," the Stage 7 award is a clear differentiator.

The first international Stage 7, in October of 2010, was the Seoul National University Bundang Hospital. Since that time, in the Asian market, two Chinese hospitals earned Stage 7. As of this writing, there are four other Chinese and Korean facilities striving to earn Stage 7 and all state that their goal is to help them promote their medical tourism capabilities. One Chinese hospital is an English-speaking hospital intending to serve expats.

There are three hospitals in Europe that have earned the Stage 7 status, but medical tourism is not a major part of their marketing plan.

Fee for Value, ACO, and Capitation

While these terms are very familiar to the health economists in the United States and Canada, they are not often heard in the same conversations with Stage 7 status. That does not need to be the case.

The first Stage 7 in Europe is a hospital in Denia, Spain, called Marina Salud. This hospital is truly an Accountable Care Organization (ACO) without the official title. Marina Salud is paid by the Valencia government on a capitation basis for the population in a defined catchment area. Marina Salud is using the data generated from their EMR to drive down costs and help promote a healthy lifestyle for patients to reduce the days of care per 1000 population. This is a great example for organizations in the United States, Canada, and Europe that are striving to provide higher-quality care for less per-capita expense.

The first ACO without beds to earn Stage 7 is Atrius in Boston, Massachusetts. Atrius has superb analytics to monitor not only the care they provide but also the care consumed by their patients outside of the Atrius network. Atrius consistently shows that their costs per case are lower than other ACOs in the New England area. A great deal of that is attributed to their comprehensive ambulatory EMR and analytics that earned them a Stage 7 status, the first for an ACO without beds.

Editor's Note: The EMRAM as a Change Management Tool

The EMRAM is a highly successful model that guides HCOs through the EMR implementation process. It is so successful that it has become the international de facto standard by which most HCOs and countries measure their progress.

What is it about the EMRAM that resulted in it becoming the international de facto standard? Though most people would not think of it this way, the EMRAM is, in fact, an excellent example of an effective change management tool. Let's dissect the model to understand how the EMRAM exemplifies solid change management principles.

The EMRAM:

1. Paints a clear picture of the desired **future state**, an almost paper-free health care environment of clinician documentation, decision support, system integration, data sharing and patient safety.
2. Defines **sequential steps** to the future state (Stages 0–7).
3. Provides **feedback** to HCOs regarding their current EMRAM status so you know where you stand at any given point. **Measurement** and tracking progress provides **incentive** to continue. In addition, progress through the stages can be used inside the HCO to justify IT expense, demonstrate accomplishment, and engender broader **engagement** in the organization.
4. Enables **comparison** to other HCOs, sparking a competitive spirit.
5. Gives credit for capability demonstrated through limited use of a functionality, such as an HCO moves from Stage 2 to Stage 3 if one nursing unit is using automated nursing documentation. In Stages 1–6, credit is not dependent on house-wide use, making forward progress easier to obtain, which builds **momentum**.
6. Defines the pinnacle of accomplishment, Stage 7, and applies strict measures, including site visit verification, to achieve Stage 7 status. Reaching Stage 7 is a rigorous process that, to date, less than 300 hospitals worldwide have achieved. Stage 7 is not an easy accomplishment, which makes it all the more **coveted**.
7. The limited number of Stage 7s and the high standards for Stage 7 designation make the Stage 7 award a prestigious achievement and an internationally recognized symbol of **top tier status**. Stage 7 HCOs are part of a small but growing **elite** circle.

In other words, when the EMRAM was introduced, it made order out of chaos. The HITECH Act became law, putting desirable financial incentives into play. But where do you start? What is your current status? What are the steps? Are you on the right track? How will you know when you get there?

By providing HCOs with a target (Stage 7), and a roadmap for getting there (Stages 0–6), along with measurement and tracking, peer comparisons, incentives, and a coveted award for those who demonstrate successful achievement of the Stage 7 future state, the EMRAM enabled HCOs to begin a more organized and efficient journey. And the surprise bonus of Stage 7 status, it turned out to be a market differentiator, that as described earlier in this chapter, organizations are using to their advantage in unexpected ways (CEO version of "what's in it for me?"). The effort is worth it.

Claire McCarthy Garets
The EMRAM as a Change Tool

OTHER IT INFRASTRUCTURE REQUIREMENTS FOR FUTURE INITIATIVES

So you have an electronic medical record (EMR) implemented, and think, correctly, that you've now got a pretty good application infrastructure to manage clinical workflows in your organization. It's necessary but decidedly insufficient for capitalizing on the gains you've made in clinical documentation, clinical decision support, and reporting, not to mention protecting the security of your data.

This second section of the book addresses the technologies, applications, and human resources you need now that you've got all the structured and unstructured data coming from your EMR. Wes Rishel, retired vice president and research director and distinguished analyst at Gartner, Inc., does a masterful job of explaining interoperability and where healthcare is headed in its ability to share patient data.

Dick Gibson, MD, a research director at Gartner, and an affiliate assistant professor in the Department of Medical Informatics and Clinical Epidemiology at Oregon Health and Science University, does an equally masterful job of explaining the human and technology infrastructure a health system will need to do an effective job of delivering on the promise of business intelligence analytics and reporting.

Then, David Finn, chief health officer at Symantec Corporation, describes, in an entertaining and very informative way, what you need to know about cybersecurity. You will be afraid when you're done reading his chapter.

And finally, Scott Joslyn, SVP and CIO at MemorialCare in Long Beach, California, and Brian Malec, professor at California State University, Northridge, share their thoughts on the human resources you'll need going forward to support not only your EMR and the infrastructure cited above but also the technologies and applications described in Section III, including next-generation revenue cycle, population health initiatives, and patient engagement.

Chapter 8

Interoperability: Enabling Healthcare Data Sharing

Wes Rishel

"Interoperability is like sex: It's usually harder than you think to get some, it never lives up to your fantasies, and if you want a steady supply you have to invest a lot of time in maintaining the relationship."

Introduction

The fantasy is no-cost, standards-based, "plug-and-play" interoperability for all the data that would improve care, medical learning, and management within and downstream from the EMR. Indeed, learning developed using EMR output would complete the loop, flowing seamlessly back into EMRs to adjust cognitive assistance to incorporate evidence-based improvements into care. For some, the notion of a single EMR might become outmoded, replaced by a set of standardized modules bought freely from a robust, competitive "app store."

The reality is that standards are incomplete, are inconsistently implemented across software packages, and have been lagging rapid developments in technology and technological economics. However, even if the currently improving standards were to approach perfection, institutions feeding and drawing from EMRs will find barriers to interoperation in workflow, clinical culture, and legal and ethical risk.

Nonetheless, there has been some progress and there are some good prospects for the future.

A key theme in this chapter is setting realistic goals. This is not a new issue. In 1975, pediatrician and scholar John Gall published *Systemantics: How Systems Work and Especially How They Fail,** a pragmatic commentary on general theories of systems and semantics. One excerpt was so widely quoted that it ultimately became known as Gall's law:

* ISBN-10: 0812906748. The intent of the author is revealed by pronouncing the first word as "system-antics." Gall revised and expanded the book twice in subsequent years.

A complex system that works is invariably found to have evolved from a simple system that worked. A complex system designed from scratch never works and cannot be patched up to make it work. You have to start over with a working simple system.

This law argues for underspecification. It was prescient in that it explains the future success of systems like the World Wide Web and blogging, which grew from simple to complex systems incrementally, and the failure of systems like CORBA, which began with complex specifications. Gall's law has strong affinities to the practice of agile software development [1].

Gall's law is widely quoted and then widely ignored. It is highly applicable to healthcare interoperability and a basis for many of the conclusions in this chapter.

Gall's law is not a justification for building systems that are too simple to provide value and then "fixing it on bug reports." The relevant phrase is "found to have evolved from a simple system that worked" *[emphasis added].*

Health Data Sharing Arrangements

Many terms have been used for arrangements to share healthcare information such as health information exchange (where exchange is a noun), regional health information organization, and healthcare information services provider. Each of these terms is used to represent differences in the structure, participation, or subject matter of the arrangement. We use a Health Data Sharing Arrangement (HDSA) to avoid presuppositions about the nature of such an arrangement.

In this chapter, we primarily consider interoperability within an HDSA where at least one of the systems exchanging data is an EMR. Figure 8.1 illustrates the roles played by different entities that are joined together in a data sharing arrangement. The health data sharing organization provides the governance and is the channel through which funding is managed. The health data sharing organization usually chooses and maintains the relationship with technology providers that are used to implement data sharing. Healthcare data sharing participants include the institutions and practices that operate EMRs and other healthcare organizations that use data from or supply data to EMRs.

Table 8.1 provides examples of HDSAs. The first two columns describe the health data sharing organization and the rightmost column describes typical participants.

What stands out in Table 8.1 is the variety of forms of health data sharing organizations that are setting the governance and providing a trust framework for HDSAs. Examples include everything from regional nonprofits to EMR vendors to individual healthcare delivery organizations.

Individual healthcare delivery organizations operate their own HDSAs for different reasons. One typical reason is to exchange information with practices in their catchment areas. Another is to put off replacement of heterogeneous EMRs in their collected hospitals and practices.

Table 8.2 helps define HDSAs by listing kinds of organizations that are active parts of healthcare interoperability but are *not* health data sharing organizations or health data sharing participants (by our definition).

Most healthcare delivery organizations will usually participate in more than one HDSA. The multiplicity of arrangements may arise from geography or differences in purpose. Some scenarios that can lead to multiple participation include a healthcare delivery organization

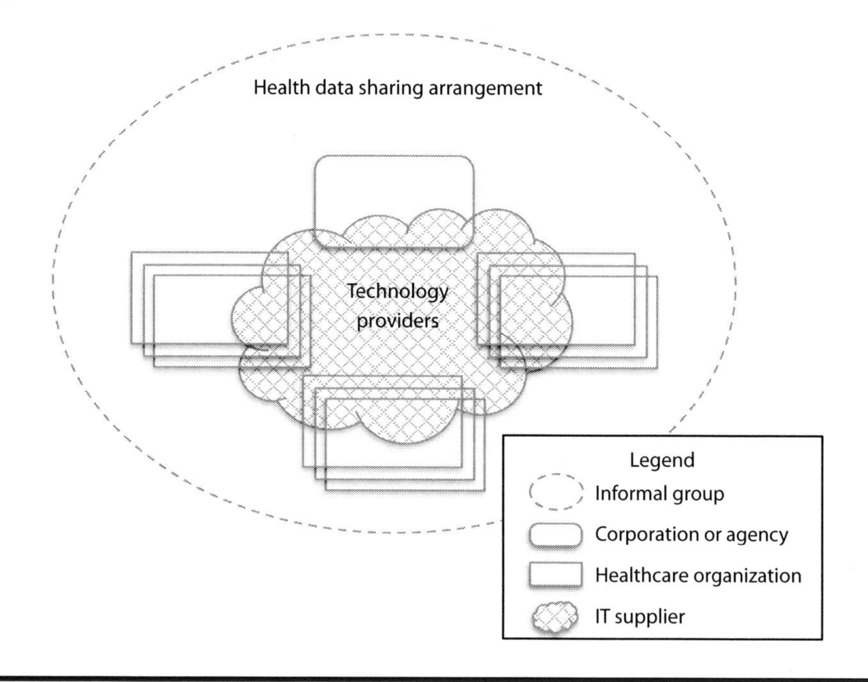

Figure 8.1 Roles in an HDSA.

Table 8.1 Examples of HDSAs

Form of Health Data Sharing Organization	*Examples of Health Data Sharing Organizations*	*Typical Health Data Sharing Participants*
Regional nonprofit	Rochester RHIO, North Coast Health Information Network	Hospitals, practices, health department, care managing organizations, immunization registries
National nonprofit	CommonWell Health Alliance	Clients of participating EMR vendors
EMR vendor	Epic (Care Everywhere)	Organizations that are clients of the vendor plus selected clients of other vendors
ePrescribing	Surescripts	Organizations that are clients of EMR vendors that have a relationship with Surescripts; prescription fulfillment businesses; pharmacy benefits managers
Individual healthcare delivery organizations	Capella Healthcare[a]	The same healthcare delivery organization and, perhaps, other such organizations

[a] See Chapter 13.

Table 8.2 Organizations That Are Not HDSAs

Type of Organization	*Examples*
Standards	HL7, NCPDP, IHTSDO
Standards profiles	IHE, Argonaut, HSPC, S&I Framework
Open source specifications	The Direct Project
Governance assistance and promotion	eHealthExchange[a]
Trust certification	DirectTrust, eHealthExchange
Facilitating internet HSDA connection	Carequality[b]

[a] Part of The Sequoia Project.
[b] Also part of The Sequoia Project.

- Serving several markets needing to work with local HDSAs in some of its markets
- Connecting to different HDSAs for function as when one HDSA supports direct transmission of messages across a national market, another provides retrieval of data from other sources within a market, and yet another has been established for collecting data for analytics
- Where specific business arrangements are predicated on data exchange

Setting Realistic Goals

Realistic interoperability starts with realistic goals. Table 8.3 identifies points along a spectrum of the degree of success achieved in most EMR interoperability efforts. Although no hospital executive will ever be quoted espousing a goal other than substantive interoperability, the reality is that

Table 8.3 Levels of Success for HDSAs

Substantive	Definite improvements in the efficiency or quality of care are being achieved on the basis of information exchanged via the HDSA. The operation is economically self-sustaining.
Perfunctory	There has been technical success but the only actual benefits participants achieve are the ability to "check the box" on grant applications, compliance requirements, or other proxy measures of success.
Technical	The interfaces to a number of EMRs and other healthcare applications are operational and data may be flowing in volume into repositories, but there is little usage.
Behind schedule	Most HDSA efforts become behind schedule at their first deadline and remain in that state until they succeed at least perfunctorily or are abandoned.
Abandoned	The healthcare data sharing organization has been shut down or is seeking to redefine its mission; there is a lack of ongoing grant funding, or many participating organizations have reassigned their people to other projects.

financial incentives/penalties and accreditation requirements often warp the real goals toward perfunctory compliance.

Realism on the Quantity and Fidelity of Information

> Until cognitive support from EMRs reaches the point that it can discern the data that is relevant to the tasks that a specific physician is or should be doing on behalf of a specific patient, care delivery is not ready for full availability of patient data.

It is not realistic to expect a "Vulcan mind meld" of EMRs within an HDSA where all patient data are shared with equal fidelity. Were it to be possible, it would create an intolerable burden on clinicians to be aware of a mass of irrelevant data and to judge the credibility of it all. Even the seemingly simple and potentially important process of sharing problem lists as coded data demands the time of a physician deciding whether to accept other physicians' perceptions of problems, guessing the clinical correlates of "billing diagnoses," weeding out entries that are redundant although not exact duplicates, and arranging them in priority for the conditions the receiving physician will validate or treat. Until cognitive support from EMRs reaches the point that it can discern the data that is relevant to the tasks that a specific physician is or should be doing on behalf of a specific patient, care delivery is not ready for full availability of patient data.

The need for physicians to perform the "sniff test" on data received from elsewhere is exacerbated by policies and practices with respect to patient identification in a given country. "Noise" is injected into patient identification processes in two forms: a lack of diligence when registering patients and the lack of a universal patient ID. While the United States is best known for the latter problem, experience has shown that it exists as well in other countries with indigenous populations or that have absorbed a large number of immigrants.

The latter issue leads to the common practice of linking patient records by matching the demographic information. Studies have shown that false positives can be reduced to less than 1% of the matches and false negatives, to less than 2% [2]. Furthermore, it is possible to tune the algorithms to reducing false positives by allowing for more false negatives. As the population within an HDSA grows larger, however, there is good reason to believe that both error rates would rise.

Shims versus Plug-and-Play Standardization

It is unrealistic to expect that desirable interoperability can be achieved entirely through the adoption of standards. A *shim* is a program function that alters data or the protocol by which data are transferred to match the behavior and expectations of two systems.

Where shims are employed, they often cause information to be lost. Some examples of loss of information include the following:

- Accepting diagnosis information in Systematized Nomenclature of Medicine (SNOMED) and outputting in ICD-9 or ICD-10
- Translating lab result codes from the lab's own code set to a limited subset of LOINC

- Accepting a time with a time zone and passing on a time with the zone unspecified
- Shortening patient names owing to limitations of source systems
- Omitting data fields that the receiving system cannot accept
- Omitting the posture and method portions of a blood pressure reading because these data elements are not stored in some specific EMR product
- Accepting only a single telephone number for a patient where the sending system included several

The shimming effect can occur without there being an intermediary program to perform the function because shimming functions are built into the interface software of EMRs and other IT products.

Shimming Enables Reasonable Goals

When shimming software is added to the toolset, some services become realistic and rise to the substantive level of value as defined in Table 8.3. These include delivering lab results either as structured data or as text reports and delivering other reports in PDF or text format within HL7 Version 2 messages. They have been the economic engine for many HDSAs.

Some HDSAs have responded to changes in financial incentives around readmissions by developing methods of notifying care managers when Registration and ADT (admit, discharge, and transfer) messages indicate that certain patients are in the process of being taken into hospitals and emergency departments.

Ideally, substantive value could also be received by sending Clinical Document Architecture (CDA) documents as well. Unfortunately, most EMRs currently generate CDA documents automatically with an indiscriminate, large bundle of data and most physicians see little value in perusing them. As of the time this chapter is being prepared in 2015, transmitting CDA documents is primarily being used to meet perfunctory requirements. Some EMR and HDSA technology providers have developed shims for one another so that they can extract problems, medications, and allergies from CDAs sent among heterogeneous EMR vendors. As discussed in the Alignment of Economic Incentives section, the person-time spent reconciling incoming data to EMR records limits the substantive value of this approach. Transmission of CDA documents is better suited to perfunctory value.

Instead of getting tangible buy-in for specific economic value, it is tempting to adopt a faith-based approach to HDSA using the theory "if you build it they will come." This is unlikely to rise beyond the level of technical success. Using this approach can only be considered realistic if the funders of the HDSA can support a new round of initiatives after it is built but before the participants actually come, and only then if the new round will be focused on specific perfunctory or substantive goals.

Alignment of Economic Incentives

The root cause of inability to reach beyond the perfunctory level of success is often a failure to realistically assess the economic benefits and burdens that determine the willingness of participants to sustain the joint effort. HDSAs often develop vague projections of benefits based on benefits "to the community." Whatever the value of such soft benefits, they do not serve well to predict project success.

Tangible benefits help predict and achieve success in several ways. They are more motivating in attracting participants and sustaining their support through inevitable project bumps and detours. They can help management rein in the focus of designers who might suffer project creep or over-elegant design. They can also help designers anticipate landmines to achieving benefits that would otherwise remain buried until late in project implementation.

Planners often overlook the need for reciprocity of benefits in a successful collaboration. Some participants are providers of data while others are users. The economic benefits are different. When participants are both providers and users, they must bear the economic burdens of playing both roles and will be accepted according to the benefits received in both roles. In other words, you can't share the sled with your little brother for long if you get it downhill and he gets it uphill.

Project planning should include an informal trade-off analysis showing the most tangible descriptions of benefits and negative impacts from a reciprocal point of view. Furthermore, these analyses should be performed from an organizational point of view and again from the point of view of the people who will use the data or whose work will be affected in making it available.

Personal-Level Analysis

In analyzing the impact on individuals, the economic costs and values are less likely to be measured in dollars than their time and the potential for distraction from information that informs their decisions.

One common scenario in health information exchanges is their creating access to a lot of health information for patients and finding that doctors don't request it while treating a patient. The technology is working, but the benefits are not accruing. It is instructive to examine the cost/value trade-off in physicians' minds, remembering that additional information has no value unless it changes a doctor's course of action to improve care or reduce unnecessary cost.

Many factors reduce the value or increase the cost from the physicians' point of view:

- Most of the individual diagnostic reports that are collected online are irrelevant to the current decisions being made.
- A long collection of prescriptions and problems for a patient contains mostly irrelevant data.
- For patients who have been seen recently or have relatively straightforward problems, it is hard to imagine a "zebra" situation where an outside bit of data might make a difference.

This is not to say that most physicians can't recall anecdotes where a nugget of outside information would have accelerated a decision or avoided a misstep. Their issue is with the expected value of the occasional data versus the expected cost of having to spend time seeking and reviewing a burdensome quantity of data in every case. The balance of expected value is highest in situations where physicians are confronted with new, complex patients such as in the emergency department, on the initial visit for a referral, or when a new or previously noncompliant patient visits a primary care physician. Even in these situations, however, the expected value may remain low if the physician finds that most searches don't provide relevant data or the relevant data are buried in a long and difficult-to-navigate document.

Unless the individual end users of an interface all receive benefits in proportion to the impact on their time, the prospects for project failure are very high. These failures can occur at many points in the life cycle of the interface. If the net incentive is small, one of the participants may simply prioritize the work so low it fails to happen. However, there is also a common failure mode where the technology works and is implemented but healthcare providers fail to make use of it.

In participants that send data to an HDSA, the economic impact on individual users is small. They usually have to do nothing extra to provide the data to an HDSA. The different burdens on senders and users of data often lead to failures of HDSAs. It is important to examine the economic incentives on both sides of an interface.

Personal-level burdens often appear as "unanticipated consequences" that limit the success of an HDSA. It is possible to anticipate many of these issues while planning an HDSA. For example, when evaluating other HDSAs built using the same EMR or the same HDSA technology provider, look closely to see whether their level of success is technological, perfunctory, or substantive. It may also be worth giving some attention to the naysayers that plague every project planning process. One would not accept their rants at face value, but look for some nuggets logic or accurate interpretation of previous experience.

Organization-Level Analysis

Evaluating economic incentives at the personal level is a new concept whereas the analysis of return on investment (ROI) at the organizational level is widely attempted. Indeed, the ROI for achieving the perfunctory level of value is often sufficient to justify a project.

Just as with analyzing economic incentives at the personal level, organizational-level economics must be reciprocal. An ROI analysis must consider the risk that other participants in an HDSA will fail to join or drop out because the economics do not work for them.

"Leveragability" as a Benefit

One of the rationales for soft benefits is that the resources of an HDSA can serve as a basis for a subsequent, more specifically targeted program to obtain more bankable benefits. The resources of an existing HDSA might be as simple as a community-wide cross-index of patients and documents, a healthcare data sharing agreement that could be expanded to cover sharing population information for analytics, or simply the interorganizational familiarity that comes from having participated together in a prior project. One resource that has proven easy to leverage for recent health information exchanges is a consolidated stream of ADT messages that indicate when a patient arrives at a clinic, hospital, or emergency department.

Absent such existing resources, the plan for a very specific network-enabled improvement in healthcare might involve years of planning, negotiating trust, and getting interfaces on the schedules of the vendors that support the participating healthcare organizations. For example, a care management program for recently discharged patients or those with a high, short-term propensity to high-cost interactions might be much easier to launch if there is an existing resource.

However, the "chicken and egg" question is how does there get to be a resource to leverage? Gall's law implies that the prior effort must itself have worked. At a minimum, project plans that call for leveraging existing HDSAs will carry a high degree of risk if the data in those arrangements are not being used.

Action Items for Setting Realistic Goals

In planning initial and evolving participation in HDSAs, get clear, if tacit, understanding about which services are expected to meet perfunctory requirements and which must rise to substantive success for the project to be sustained.

In seeking substantive value,

- Identify concrete economic benefits
- Have functional sponsorship on both the sending and receiving ends or the specific transactions

If your organization contemplates participation in an HDSA, you must develop your own appreciation of personal- and organizational-level economic burdens and benefits keeping in mind the following:

- Personal-level burdens are the most common unanticipated consequences.
- Realistically consider the level of success in other HDSAs and attempt to understand the root causes for failure to surpass mere technical success.
- Organizational-level burdens are usually financial and can sometimes be overcome by intangible benefits but vaguely conceived faith in future leveragability will not sustain a project.

Organize to participate in more than one HDSA recognizing that health data sharing agreements may be embedded in or associated with EMR vendor contracts and the agreements for business associates such as those that pool data for analytics.

Trust for Business Interoperability

In most countries, healthcare organizations may not transmit protected health information elsewhere except as explicitly permitted in laws and regulations. Generally, those mandates require due diligence to assure that the trading partner is a valid recipient. When information is sent via fax, the sending organization generally will have authenticated the recipient through pragmatic means.

Likewise, recipients have both business and legal requirements to assure that they recognize and accept the authority of the sending organization. For example, in the United States, a lab will not have performed the service without assurance that the ordering facility is valid. Authenticating the order is often accomplished simply by having a long-established business relationship with the ordering organization.

There are two aspects of trust: One is having a trusted business relationship with the other party. Since "on the Internet no one knows if you are really a dog," the second part is authenticating that each transmission is really with the intended organization. The first aspect is discussed extensively in this section.

Authentication of each transaction is a security topic not discussed here except to say that the security technologies employed depend on distributing digital certificates [3,4], files that uniquely identify an entity. The processes by which the identities of organizations receiving such certificates are assured, the certificates are securely distributed, and the certificates are authenticated when used require trusted third parties, some of which are shown in Table 8.2.

Data Sharing Agreements

HDSAs generally use a written data sharing agreement.* This is different from the HIPAA Business Associate agreement, which is required in the United States. A signatory to a data sharing agreement usually asserts at least the issues described in Figure 8.2.

Unlike most contracts and business associate agreements, the healthcare data sharing agreement generally is not subject to bilateral negotiation. In joining an HDSA, a participant agrees to be bound by the agreement as it stands and as modified through governance processes within it.

The most expansive and expensive data sharing agreement in the United States (and probably anywhere) is the Date Use and Reciprocal Services Agreement (DURSA) originally developed in support of the US Nationwide Health Information Network project. The agreement and the various governance committees it calls for are now maintained and operated by a private, nonprofit organization, The Sequoia Project [5]. The California Association of Health Information Exchanges maintains a version of the DURSA modified to recognize state-specific regulations. In some states, such as New York, there are efforts underway to create enforceable policies and procedures for a data sharing arrangement by state regulation [6].

Some of the complexity of the DURSA stems from the differing legal contexts in governmental and nongovernmental organizations. In the United States, federal agencies are regulated under the Federal Information Security Management Act of 2002† (FISMA). Many of them are also HIPAA-covered entities as are the nongovernmental entities with which they exchange data. The regulatory approaches under FISMA and HIPAA differ and a lot of lawyer hours were required to hammer out an agreement that would work for all parties. At the same time, even this effort did not deal with the more than 300 different permutations of exchanges among parties in different US states and territories and US areas governed by tribal law.

Multiway Business Trust

Most organizations that implement HDSAs use *transitive trust* and selective participation. Each of the "N" participating organizations that participate in the arrangement does not make $N - 1$ separate agreements on the conditions necessary to trust one another. Instead, each participant trusts the healthcare data sharing organization or some set of specialized service providers to accredit all participating organizations. At the same time, many HDSAs permit selective participation; they do not require that each participant interchange information with all the others.

Selective participation occurs when the transitive trust agreement is not sufficient for two participants to exchange data. Reasons for limiting participation are varied. Many laboratories interpret regulations as saying that they must be able to point to end-to-end testing that ensures that what the EMR users see is what they sent. Specific participants in the HDSA may not have

* Although in some jurisdictions attempts have been made to create regulations that cover all aspects of healthcare data sharing.

† "FISMA", 44 U.S.C. § 3541, et seq.

1. Acknowledges that it is receiving or sending protected health information.
2. Sends information and uses information it receives for a legally permitted purpose.
3. Obtains valid patient consent appropriate to the data being transmitted. This includes having assurance when receiving information that the sending organization has obtained appropriate consent.
4. Identifies technological specifications that enable interoperability to the level required for the business purpose.
5. Operates using procedures and technology that meet prevailing expectations for protecting the confidentiality of protected health information under its stewardship.
6. Onboards new participants in a manner that reasonably assures that the new organization is a legitimate participant and has implemented procedures and technologies to meet the requirements of topics 1–5.
7. Establishes a governance process to support evolution of the agreement itself, all technological specifications, and all operational procedures required for secure and reliable operation of the data sharing arrangement.

Figure 8.2 Topics of a data sharing agreement.

yet achieved bilateral testing with an end point. Participants may have issues of trust that extend beyond what has been included in the healthcare data sharing agreement. Unenlightened participants may have competitive concerns about sharing data with specific other participants.

There is general agreement that there is a net benefit to the patient and to population health costs if data are shared widely among qualified participants. However, the reality of day-to-day operations in HDSAs means that requiring all participants to play with all others is not often feasible.

Action Items for Trust for Business Interoperability

Consider the healthcare data sharing agreement early in the process of evaluating alternative healthcare data sharing agreements.

- Is one already in place? If not, allow many months to a few years for hammering one out.
- If there is a healthcare data sharing agreement, is it mature? Getting the necessary approval in your organization to accept an agreement without negotiating the terms is never easy. However, it may be easier if it has been accepted by comparable organizations in your catchment area. If nothing else, tweaks that were done for prior participants may answer objections within your own organization.
- Does the agreement address all the governance processes listed in Figure 8.2? If not, have the other processes been worked out? Does your organization understand the relatively low pace of change associated with the governance processes?
- If setting up an HDSA involves creating a healthcare data sharing agreement, consider the advice of Gall's law. The simplest agreement that suffices to achieve a self-sustaining enterprise is the best to get started.

Trends in Standards

Most organizations that purchase and implement EMRs have little direct control over the standards that their vendors choose. Very large health delivery organizations may have some opportunity to influence future directions, but the approach that is most valuable continues to be to use HDSA technology providers with a good catalog of shims and to live with the limitations in fidelity that arise from the use of shims.

Standards-Related Organizations

The mix of organizations that somehow purport to further health information interoperability is confusing and ever changing. In 2008, I used Figure 8.3 [7] to describe standards development and governance processes that were intended to facilitate interoperability of healthcare data.

The most important conceptual point is that standards must be combined to produce a full set of specifications for interoperability. The combined specifications are a lot more elaborate than simply a list of standards. The combination work product typically limits the options available in each of the bases. The need to narrow down the interpretations of standards is not unique to HL7. It is equally applicable to virtually every IT standard that exists. For example:

- Early attempts to apply the Digital Imaging and Communications in Medicine standard ran into disagreements on its interpretation and a choice of options. This stimulated the formation of Integrating the Healthcare Enterprise (IHE) to establish additional consensus agreement somehow to apply that standard. Nonetheless, many special-purpose technology products exist in diagnostic image networks to shim variances among modality vendors.
- Any enterprise that has made a systematic attempt to create interoperability through the use of Systematized Nomenclature of Medicine Clinical Terms (SNOMED CT) has found that it is necessary to create numerous systematic and specific rules on how to encode clinical events.
- In the United States, in 2008, the federally mandated X12 implementation guide for healthcare claims had at least 200 different payer-specific interpretations.
- Some uniformity exists for the use of X12 transactions in retail supply chains, not because the standard itself is airtight but because Wal-Mart has decreed that enterprises doing business with it will follow its interpretation of the standard.
- Even a venerable standard such as HTML has many options that are interpreted differently, ignored, or deliberately contravened by different browser developers. "Standard" use of

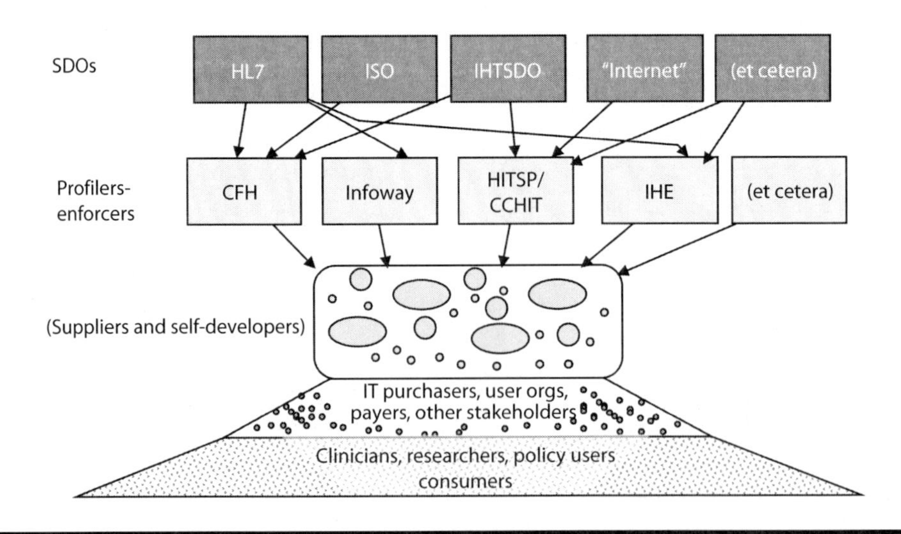

Figure 8.3 Organizations involved in standards.

HTML is only achieved by allowing for the peculiarities of several major browsers. Over time, the major browser products tend to converge, at least until the HTML standard is updated.

- When there is more than one way to employ standards for a specific problem, it is necessary for participants to agree on which standards to use and how to combine them. For example, applications that require secure file transfer may choose to use Secure FTP or may choose to use FTP over a virtual private network.
- Although certain technology standards such as universal serial bus (USB) and Bluetooth plug-and-play fairly well, each major upgrade of the standards starts with products certified to the new standards that do not work together smoothly if at all. It takes a period of 12–24 months for the rough edges to be worn off and upgraded products to make it into the supply chain. Even then, the specific aspects of the new standard releases that work well are those supported by the dominant hardware vendors. Other vendors scramble to get in line because they know that the major vendors will not update their product to interoperate with minor players in the market.

The term *profiler organization* in Figure 8.3 is an entity that produces the work products that at once narrow the optionality in the standards and described how they work together. Some profilers such as IHE have an excellent scheme of intervendor testing via "connectathons" and improving the profiles year by year.

An *enforcer* organization in the figure refers to one that would validate that the suppliers and self-developers followed the specifications so that their products would interoperate.

The diagram combines profilers with enforcers because the act of creating and using test scripts invariably uncovers ambiguities in the specifications that must be resolved into amendments to the specification. We thought then that a short amendment cycle would allow the detection and correction of problems where the standard was shown to need amendments to meet the intended use.

An updated version of Figure 8.3 would have only a few changes. The English National Health Service Connecting for Health program has been disbanded, Infoway is working to redefine its approach to standards, and the Healthcare Information Technology Standards Panel/Certification Commission for Health Information Technology (HITSP/CCHIT) box would be replaced by the Standards and Interoperability (S&I) Framework and the accredited testing laboratories and authorized certification bodies of the Office of the National Coordinator (ONC) for Health Information Technology.

Although this model has been widely used at national levels, it has generally failed to achieve plug-and-play interoperability at the substantive level (as defined in Table 8.3) in any venue. Two certified interoperable software products don't interoperate without substantial work configuring the software and the associated shims.

It is instructive to examine how interoperability has been achieved outside the field of healthcare. As a practical matter, it is feasible to design web pages (including the associated client- and server-side coding) to run with any of the major web browsers available to users today. However, this situation did not arise by any organization certifying web browsers to respond the same to HTML and JavaScript page content. Arguably, the major browser-writers work to achieve the same behaviors and to introduce new functionality in an identical fashion and the differences represent a very small percentage of the total behavior of a web browser.

Nonetheless, successfully creating applications that run with the major browsers in use today depends very much on shims that are created by web application developers in order to accommodate the different browsers. Most of the shim code is added value provided by toolmakers that sell their software to web developers. It is extremely difficult to introduce a new web browser into the market today because a new product has an insufficient user base to attract the attentions of the shim providers.

HDSA Evolution Requires Asynchronous Upgrades

The shims provided for web browsers not only adapt the applications to provide different HTML or JavaScript to different browsers but also provide shims for different versions of the browsers. This illustrates one of the most challenging aspects of plug-and-play interoperability. New products and software are introduced across an HDSA asynchronously generally tied to upgrades of EMRs or other clinical software or new versions of the software used by technology providers.

For in-hospital use of HL7, this has resulted in "frozen interface syndrome." The current versions of HL7 that are approved by the American National Standards Institute range from 2.2, approved February 8, 1996, to 2.8.1, approved August 27, 2014. If it were possible to average the versions of HL7 appearing in messages in hospitals today, most experts believe that the mean version number would be less than 2.3. Furthermore, the per-hospital variance would be high. Hospitals generally rely on interface engines to shim applications rather than expending the dollars and staff time necessary to update their application interfaces.

Frozen interface syndrome does not become a factor until a version of a standard is widely adopted and then it tends to lock down further progress.

This has been a concern in the standards community for some years. ONC and HL7 made a serious effort to address the issue in the specifications for Meaningful Use Stage 3. However, the people working on it discovered that standards really must be designed to work this way from the start. As a member of the HIT Standards Committee, I agreed not to introduce a systematic approach to asynchronous update to Stage 3 in the belief that most HDSAs will be able to put off updating to the Stage 3 standards for their substantive interfaces and will be able to meet the required thresholds for Stage 3 with perfunctory conformance.

Standards Maturity

In 2012, Dixie Baker led a workgroup of the HIT Standards Committee that produced a maturity model to serve as a basis for determining whether a proposed standard was ready for adoption in federal regulations on healthcare.* In the publication, the adoptability of standards was rated by the maturity of the standard and "adoptability," an assessment of the practicality of adopting a standard. Factors affecting adoptability included the degree to which the protocols that are in or underlie the standards are commonly understood in the developer community.

Figure 8.4 is a modified version of a diagram that has been used to explain the model. For this chapter, I changed the word *pilots* in the official version to *early production*. This is because the leap from pilot implementations to national adoption has turned out to be too broad. Of course, not all pilot tests are successful, although the reports issued by the pilot testers often gloss over significant issues. We are aware of a federally funded pilot test of transmitting healthcare data that was declared to be a success because it was possible to send the data, even though no system was found that was able to receive it.

A second concern is that many pilot tests do not measure end-to-end creation and usage of the data, so that the issues described in the Alignment of Economic Incentives section of this chapter are never

* A revised version was published in 2015 in *Journal of the American Medical Informatics Association*, 22(3): 738–743.

Maturity criteria:

- Maturity of specification
- Maturity of underlying technology components
- Market adoption

Adoptability criteria:

- Ease of implementation and deployment
- Ease of operations
- Intellectual property

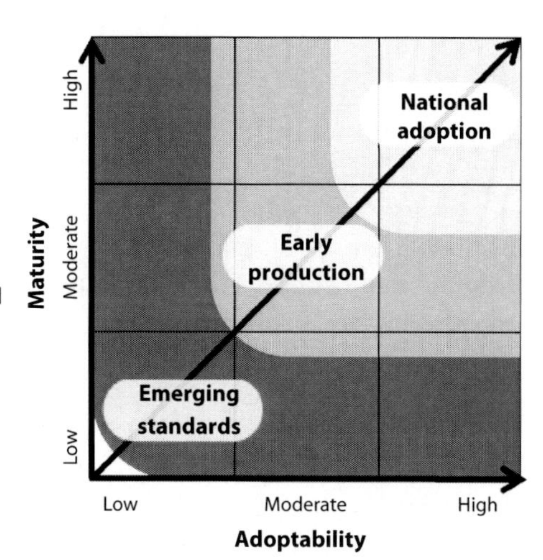

Figure 8.4 Modified healthcare standards maturity model.

explored. A final concern is that pilot tests are often conducted in academic settings where the specialized skills for adoption of new technologies are more available than in most EMR development shops.

Identifying early production use as a required stepping stone to national adoption helps address all the concerns listed above. It is reasonable to ask, however, if this is too high of a barrier. Who will adopt a standard that is not a national requirement? The answer to that critical question is also implicit in the Alignment of Economic Incentives section. If there are good economic incentives for all participants in an interface production, use will arise even before the standards are final.

In 2006, HL7 followed other standards organizations in adopting a methodology that includes draft standards for trial use (DSTUs). In theory, a new standard would not proceed to being a fully adopted standard until industry has implemented interfaces on the basis of a DSTU. HL7 does not guarantee that a final version of a standard will be backward compatible with a DSTU.

Although the intent of the US Meaningful Use policy was to keep to these guidelines, the program has been self-limiting in several ways. The underlying economics created a narrow focus in vendor and user organizations on perfunctory requirements and the schedule of the phases necessitated creating profiles and moving them to the national level without the feedback and hardening of the specifications that should have been attained through early adoption. On the other hand, the economics that might drive early adoption at the substantive level were not well served by most of the standards made mandatory for Meaningful Use so the early adoption phase would not have occurred even given more time.

In parallel with the Meaningful Use program, various public and private entities have launched initiatives to or to include a value component in payments. These programs may create economic pressure on user organizations to achieve substantive interoperability and this may drive early production adoption.

HL7

Although there are many important standards for health information transfer, HL7 has the widest impact and has been undergoing the most rapid development. We summarize here some important aspects of some HL7 standards.

Version 2

The HL7 Version 2 was developed "bottom up" in that chapters of the spec were created by groups of vendors and users that often had bespoke interfaces running for the topic of the chapter. The specifications for a chapter tended to be the union of the data elements and events used in the bespoke interfaces with the understanding that all but the most critical data elements and events were optional. For example, the ADT chapter included the events such as "admit," "discharge," "transfer," and "cancel admission," and the data that were described for each event consisting of all the data fields sent by any of the vendors are from hospitals that had written custom interfaces.

Version 2 interfaces are widely used within healthcare delivery organizations to connect the EMR with ancillary systems. Virtually all interfaces are shimmed by interface engines, and the specifications were adapted by individual organizations and application vendors. The all-too-true witticism is "if you have seen one HL7 v2 interface, you have seen one."

HDSAs have followed essentially the same approach, using shims as necessary to capture patient demographics, visit events, lab results, transcribed reports, and other data. A big area where shims have been necessary has to do with the codes that identify results in structured data. Virtually no lab uses LOINC codes internally, so the value-add of the HDSA technology is to maintain translation tables for each source. As a practical matter, it is difficult to get labs to include the HDSA in the workflow for adding new codes. Another HDSA value-add is to detect transactions with previously unknown codes, suspend its transfer, and call the lab to find out what the new code means so it can be translated into LOINC. Recently, a few large labs have begun sending LOINC codes.

Version 3

HL7 Version 3 was a serious attempt to break new ground in interoperability by establishing a reference information model (RIM) to describe all healthcare data. Messages would contain data elements derived from the model and software developers would build translations from their internal database schemas to the messages. Developing the RIM was a major challenge in large part because of the heterogeneity of clinical data. As the number of objects grew to hundreds, the RIM developers created abstractions lumping many different kinds of objects together and differentiating their use with esoteric codes such as for "mood." As the model was translated into XML representations, the abstract object names became used as tags in the actual messages and the use of codes obscured the structure of the data.

The HL7 CDA started as an independent effort to create some standardization around reports and to blend together textual information with structured data. After the effort joined HL7, it evolved as additional schemas that combined RIM-based representation of structured data with a document structure and text and the necessary metadata to deal with changes to documents and understanding the scope of signatures.

The HL7 Continuity of Care Document (CCD) is a specification that was developed using the CDA and is based on a paper form that was created by the Massachusetts Medical Society and an XML standard called the Continuity of Care Record. As a paper form, it was designed to be "right-sized," containing the necessary information for a patient transition without overburdening the sender in creating the document or the receiver in absorbing it.

The CCD and other documents derived from the CDA achieved the "early production" stage (as described in Figure 8.4) particularly in several profiles developed by HITSP and IHE. However, efforts to include a great deal of structured data with the text required substantial shimming or multi–person-year efforts to sort out different interpretations of the specification.

Overall, the specifications in the HL7 Version 3 family generally have been found to be very complex and difficult to understand by application programmers who know their application data well but haven't invested significant time in learning about the RIM.

Fast Healthcare Interoperability Resources (FHIR—An API-Based Approach)

In the past few years, FHIR (pronounced "fire") has achieved enormous effort and attention in HL7 and related organizations. HL7 adopted it as part of a "fresh look" initiative, addressing the question of how it could best serve its user community if not fettered by the requirement to evolve from previous versions.

FHIR is the brainchild of Australian Graham Grieve, and he has managed its development. He has built a coterie of participants in the effort that include many of the major drivers of previous HL7 versions, academic developers, and vendors. At least two profiling entities have been formed: The Argonaut Project and The Health Services Platform Consortium (HSPC). These organizations are notable for substantial commitment and funding from very large healthcare delivery organizations and major vendors of EMRs. It is safe to say that The Argonaut Project reflects the largest single focus of energy, personnel, and funding ever on profiling standards by the market-dominating vendors.

The fresh approach so far has shown several benefits:

- The specifications are developed to maximize the leverage of cross-industry web development tools and approaches.
- The specifications are purposefully developed bottom up defining "resources" (data structures) that are comprehensible to application programmers. This not only means that they can understand the specifications, it also means that they can understand the data in actual instances of a resource. The complexity and abstract nature of Version 3 XML created a barrier to developing and debugging programs.
- Complexity is limited by an "80/20 rule": FHIR only includes an element (in a resource) if 80% of systems implement it. This not only heads off exponential increases in complexity but also provides a rule to limit the time spent debating esoteric issues.
- The FHIR team has rigidly adopted the HL7 DSTU process. At this point, there is good reason to hope that DSTU implementations will reach the "early production" level as described in Figure 8.4.

A basic premise in the development of FHIR has been to follow the software architecture pattern known as Representational State Transfer (REST). One of the most important characteristics of REST is that it substantially decouples the business logic of applications from the specifications of the interface. This way, REST servers don't need to know much about the state of the client application. To the greatest extent possible, the transactions offered by servers are patterned around creating, reading, updating, and deleting (CRUD) resources.

This simplicity is necessary for large-scale cloud applications and ultracomplex networks. A by-product of this approach is that developers of applications that are clients to REST servers don't fall prey to hard-to-understand errors based on elaborate business rules.

A consequence of keeping the business logic in the client is that stands the prior approach to interoperability on its head. The old approach starts with use cases, developing data structures and choreography (the sequence of interactions among interfaced applications), and then produces standards specific to the use cases. The new approach says "Here is our data specification. Decide on your use cases and use them to sequence the CRUD calls, but the server does not have to change for each new use case or each step in learning the use cases."

The servers are often going to be EMRs, and the clients are going to be anything from adjunct, "sidecar applications" (see FHIR, SMART, and Sidecar Applications [8]) to other EMRs to agent software written to support HDSAs. FHIR enthusiasts foresee a time when innovators on the client side using CRUD services for established FHIR resources do not need to collaborate with EMR vendors to complete their applications.*

It remains to be seen if FHIR will rise to this ideal by the time Version 1 is released, which is currently planned for 2016. Early results look good, and the industry will be able to gauge the progress by the acceptance of the two draft standards for trial use released by HL7 in 2014 and 2015.

Action Items for Standards

Be very skeptical of proposals for HDSAs where the economics are based on plug-and-play (shimless) interoperability on the basis of current standards. Look for proof in HDSAs that have reached the substantive level of value.

In evaluating the potential for success in an HDSA or considering HDSA technology, look closely at

- Tools for creating and maintaining a catalog of shims
- The availability of predefined tools for adapting to existing EMRs and other clinical software

Monitor the development and rollout of early FHIR-based interfaces in HDSAs and the ongoing support of your EMR vendor. Consider initially using FHIR interfaces where a project failure or delays can be tolerated. Update your appraisal of the maturity of FHIR frequently.

Healthcare Consumer

In the long run, one of the biggest potential values of interoperability arises when EMRs interoperate with consumer-facing software in web browsers, smart device apps, and the growing collection of devices that interface directly with the consumer's body.

The possibilities are almost unlimited and very heterogeneous. The number one interoperability issue is establishing consumer identity and consent at a national scale. CommonWell is a nonprofit, national network that has formed with a primary focus on using the registration front end to EMRs to record consent, capture the most accurate demographic information for patients, and ensure a very high probability match. It is currently early in the stage described as early adoption

* By "collaborate" here, I mean negotiate the interface specification. Vendors of EMRs may require some sort of certification of applications to run against their products similar to the "app stores" run by Apple and Google to highlight potential issues of safety or the overall performance and integrity of the EMR.

in Table 8.3. Should it someday expand to include participation by patient-facing apps not associated with EMRs, it might provide a solution.

Proposals for the level of assurance of a consumer's identity run from every consumer going to the post office as if they were getting a passport to the procedures that consumers have long mastered to use their Facebook identities to connect to Spotify. Cross-industry authentication standards such as OAUTH2* are spreading and can be adapted to whatever level of identity assurance is established in policy.

We can hope that policy makers favor the "mutual login approach" used by financial institutions and consumer-facing applications such as Quicken online. A person logs into their own app and then requests connection to a provider's EMR using the credentials that they have to log into the EMR's portal. There is no universal ID for a healthcare consumer but they can extend their personal connectivity as far as they want.

Once EMR vendors are able to make use of an industry standard, web-based login procedure to interface to all independently developed consumer-facing apps, then the next question will be how to exchange data in standard form. Attempts to exchange CDA documents for textual rendering have been moderately successful. Attempts to use these same specifications for structured data continue to require shims that limit the ability of patient-facing app developers to collect data across many EMRs. The complexity of the CDA specifications has also been a barrier to getting them to try. A great deal of hope currently rides on the simplicity and logical decoupling that is available when EMRs become FHIR servers that offer CRUD services to any authorized application.

When consumer-facing interoperability is tied to EMR patients, an important value will be enhancing patient engagement in maintaining their health and their compliance with care protocols. The more complex the patient, the more likely that the application logic in the patient app will be tightly tied to the care protocols and events scheduled in the EMR. It may be a long time before the patient-facing portal of the EMR and any specific consumer-facing apps provided by EMR vendors are overtaken by generic apps relying on CRUD interfaces.

Action Items for Healthcare Consumer

Maintain perfunctory interoperability with patient-facing applications through interface software provided by EMR vendors or HDSA technology providers.

Look for substantive interaction with patient-facing apps on an opportunistic basis when organizational business needs drive incentives for EMR users to promote interoperability with the patient.

Reevaluate the challenge of substantive interoperability when (or if) FHIR passes through early-stage interoperability toward national acceptance. EMR user organizations with the technological skills, a culture that can evaluate and accept risk, and clinical users ready to promote patient-facing interoperability should consider using FHIR earlier on the basis of the DSTU.

* See http://oauth.net/2/.

Whither Interoperability?

> *"It is a paradoxical but profoundly true and important principle of life that the most likely way to reach a goal is to be aiming not at that goal itself but at some more ambitious goal beyond it."*
>
> **Arnold Toynbee**

This chapter paints a grim picture of interoperability today. To date, we have not even achieved a Toynbee-esque goal that is less ambitious than our hopes. The best we can claim is that the industry has learned a lot. Some of the findings that are clear now but weren't at the start of the Meaningful Use program are as follows:

- National interoperability will not be achieved by an orderly hierarchy of interconnected regional HDSAs but by individual EMR-operating organizations participating in more than one HDSA.
- The standards at hand in 2009, despite having undergone massive efforts to improve them, have only been successful to the extent that EMR vendors or HDSA technology providers offer shims.
- Patient identification remains a major challenge for achieving interoperability on a national scale.
- Interoperability challenges extend beyond the technological challenges of achieving high-fidelity data exchange. The biggest challenges are to ensure incentives to users on both sides of a data exchange, to find scalable ways to create business trust beyond individual healthcare markets, and to modify EMR user-facing functionality to minimize the burdens that are a consequence of interoperation.

I see no scenario on the horizon where interoperability would level the playing field between large healthcare delivery organizations and small, large EMR vendors and small and organizations that continue to use a variety of EMRs where patient transitions routinely cross among them.

Nonetheless, there is good reason not to give up. Changes in payment for healthcare are causing functional users to demand interoperability. This change leads to a change in user organization list of demands for changes that they present to EMR vendors. The largest EMR customers, those that have clout on a par with their vendors, are among the leaders in driving these demands. Interoperability is becoming a real priority. The level of support for FHIR from the community of vendors and large users is unprecedented in the history of HL7.

For its part, HL7 has aggressively adopted the major course correction being implemented in FHIR. There is good reason to hope that, in a few years, the decoupling of standards from use cases and business logic and the flexibility associated with CRUD interfaces will begin to support a rising level of innovation around and among the users of EMRs.

References

1. https://en.wikipedia.org/wiki/John_Gall_(author).
2. Grannis SJ, Overhage JM PhD, McDonald CJ. Analysis of identifier performance using a deterministic linkage algorithm. *Proc AMIA Symp* 2002: 305–309.

3. Parker C, Boone K, Brandt J. Standards, http://www.himss.org/ResourceLibrary/mHimssRoadmapContent.aspx?ItemNumber=30405, retrieved August 30, 2015.
4. Adams C, Lloyd S. *Understanding PKI: Concepts, Standards, and Deployment Considerations*, ISBN 0321743091.
5. http://sequoiaproject.org/ehealth-exchange/onboarding/dursa/. Retrieved July 8, 2015.
6. http://www.health.ny.gov/technology/regulations/shin-ny/docs/privacy_and_security_policies.pdf. Retrieved July 8, 2015.
7. Without Profiler-Enforcers Healthcare IT Standards Cannot Enable Interoperability, © Gartner, Inc., 2008.
8. http://fhirblog.com/2015/07/10/fhir-smart-and-sidecar-applications/.

Chapter 9

Business Intelligence Reporting and Analytics: Tools, Resources, and Governance

Richard F. Gibson, MD, PhD, MBA

"Most of the frenzy about Big Data in healthcare is unwarranted."

Introduction

Speech recognition, handwriting recognition, and natural language processing (NLP) may ultimately lead physicians to actually enjoy the interaction with the EMR.

For 20 years, informaticists have been trying to get physicians to use EMRs—first to look up labs and diagnostic imaging reports on the computer, then to enter orders on the computer, and then to document their visits on the computer. There were pros and cons to each of these steps. We argued that the computer made it easier to look up patient results than the old paper system. Computerized provider order entry was a harder sell. Doing postop orders from any PC in the hospital or from home was perhaps faster than on paper, but doing a la carte admitting orders for a patient with multiple problems could take 30 min or longer. Physician documentation was also a mixed bag; some surgeons liked the preformatted operative note where they could quickly fill in the important details. For physicians who couldn't type, doing even short visit notes was painful.

Like it or not, computers are ever present in patient care for the vast majority of currently practicing physicians. The task for vendors and informaticists is to create the most intuitive screens for display and data input and the smartest clinical decision support. Speech recognition, handwriting recognition, and natural language processing (NLP) may ultimately lead physicians to actually enjoy the interaction with the EMR.

The Ultimate Value of EMR Data

> In the future, linking all the patient's findings with all medical knowledge promises to take evidence-based medicine to the level of the unique patient.

Apart from the possibility of the EMR improving the enjoyment and efficiency of the patient care visit, the computer in healthcare also holds out promise to deliver value in the understanding of its data. The ultimate dream is that the computer could link every fact known about health and disease with every fact known about the patient. No diagnosis, however rare, would ever be missed by even the most rushed clinician. The computer can prompt the physician to inquire of the patient further pertinent details suggested by the already collected history. Rare diseases and uncommon presentations of common diseases are all fodder for the omnipotent medical database and reasoning system. Evidence-based medicine offers to improve the safety and reliability of medicine by laying out standardized approaches to common problems and eliminating practice variation not justified by the individual patient's presenting findings. The provider is expected to follow the data collection, diagnostic, and treatment protocol unless substantive aspects of the individual patient's case suggest otherwise. It makes sense to eliminate the potentially valueless non–patient-related variation in physician practice that has come with the apprenticing of allopathic physicians. In the future, linking all the patient's findings with all medical knowledge promises to take evidence-based medicine to the level of the unique patient.

EMRs and Clinical Trials

> Even with wide geographic dispersion, patients with uncommon illnesses can be characterized and grouped together for outcomes analysis.

One of the challenges of evidence-based medicine is assigning a given patient to a group of ostensibly similar patients and then subjecting that patient to the diagnostic and treatment protocols recommended for the overall group of patients. Patients are unique humans and their problems can also be unique. We need to trade off the protocol benefits of rigor and consistency with the disadvantage that protocols can be inappropriately applied to patients that differ from the target patient group. With computers, we now may be able to get more of those benefits with fewer of the disadvantages. As the EMR records more details of patient findings and more details of patient treatment in the electronic health record, we have the chance to collect larger cohorts of more specifically and narrowly described patients whose diagnostic and treatment patterns ought to be comparable. In addition to finding candidates for university-sponsored, randomized, controlled trials, we will soon be able to include nearly all patients in the country in a study of some sort. Even with wide geographic dispersion, patients with uncommon illnesses can be characterized and grouped together for outcomes analysis. By comparing each individual patient with a nationwide or worldwide database of patients, new outbreaks and new diseases can be detected and tracked earlier. It follows that evidence of effective treatment for new or rare diseases can be discovered sooner.

Building the Ultimate Medical Expert System

It has been established that the human mind can hold only five to seven items in active thought at any one time. As much of allopathic medicine is based on pattern recognition, if the patient's underlying disease is not among the top five to seven most likely presentation patterns, the correct diagnosis is likely to be missed on that visit. Such a delay is at best annoying for the patient and at worst life-threatening. Patients would be happy to spend hours entering data about themselves if they believed that it would lead to the correct diagnosis or best treatment. With the presence of increasing digital data about patients, exponentially growing literature of medical research, and the new methods of big data computer processing, we have the opportunity to create a cocoon of safety where a patient's diagnosis will never be missed, the patient will never receive an unwarranted intervention, and the patient will never fail to obtain indicated diagnostic or therapeutic actions. If we can show superior results using computers to match individual patients with a worldwide database of diagnostic and treatment facts, we can engage physicians in obtaining more thorough history and physical exams before launching potential diagnostic and therapeutic misadventures on the basis of convenient and speedy but incomplete rules of thumb. With the ideal in mind of computers as sage and omniscient companions, we can begin to build the data management systems of tomorrow with data from today's EMRs.

It has been suggested that we should have started to look at what data are needed to improve healthcare before we built our EMRs. Then, we could have optimized the EMRs based on the data we needed them to collect. That did not happen to the extent it should have. Although some have criticized the Meaningful Use EMR financial incentives as a huge waste, at least now we have the substrate with which we can electronically collect significant data about the patient's before-treatment state, their diagnostic and treatment details, and their after-treatment state. Learning health systems will be able to put this continuous feedback system to use in improving clinical and financial outcomes. Although EMRs have not yet delivered much benefit, the potential is increasing for a return on investment as a large multiple of their original cost (see Chapter 3, "EMR Benefits Don't Come in a Box: Why Structured Innovation Is Necessary to Realize Strategic EMR Value," by Doug Thompson).

Coded Data versus Free-Text Notes

We would do well at the outset to acknowledge the tension between collecting all significant patient facts as coded, digital elements and the extreme burden such a requirement would put on practicing clinicians. Right now, we don't yet have a use for encoding each historical finding or physical exam finding as a computable element, but we will in the future. The trick is to slow the clinician down only enough to capture the most important data elements that we believe can improve patient care—both care of an individual and care of populations of patients. Most clinicians prefer to learn about another clinician's experience with a patient from a free-text description, so we should endeavor to continue this tradition.

How can we get the best of both worlds? On the front end, we can improve the human–computer interface design to make it easier to collect coded data in front of the patient without detracting from the provider–patient interaction. On the back end, NLP will someday very soon be able to convert free-text dictation to computable, coded concepts.

Data Governance—Data Element Definitions

In order to derive full benefit from the data in an EMR, the organization needs to achieve consensus on the definitions of terms used in the EMR. For example, clinicians need to agree on the different types of sphygmomanometric and intravascular blood pressures they wish the EMR to collect and how to consistently assign those EMR terms to the various biomedical devices used. Administrative data are also important to understanding clinical outcomes. Is a "patient-day" 11 p.m. to 11 p.m. or midnight to midnight? What about a 26-h patient stay? How is a "catheter-day" defined to serve infection prevention? What is a "department"? Likely, the EMR will assign departments different from those assigned by the enterprise resource planning (ERP) system and which are different from the time and attendance system. In another example, there may be several useful definitions of "Physician FTE": one definition for an ambulatory office–based physician and another definition for a hospital procedure–based clinician. Multiple definitions are fine as long as they are all clearly named and have a precise definition that is consistently used for all reporting and analysis. In order to make sense of EMR data, organization-wide agreement on definitions is crucial. This consensus process is one of the most important functions of data governance.

Definitions need to be established for disease states of interest. For example, an organization could find many asthma patients based on ICD-10-CM codes in inpatient and office EMRs. They could find more asthma patients by including the results of diagnostic imaging, pulmonary function, and laboratory tests. Even more patients could be found by looking at medications used. In setting up registries, organizations will need to specify exactly how each patient population is defined.

Data Governance—Data Quality: Consistency

Another important aspect of data governance is data quality. For all intents and purposes, the quality of the data in the EMR reports derives from the quality of the data entered into the transactional EMR system at the point of care. For every module in the EMR, a data steward needs to be appointed. This data steward is a respected staff member from operations, meaning NOT someone in the information services department. The data steward is a clinical or business expert who spends most of his or her time in the transactional module in question.

Do you have clinician leaders who understand the challenge of collecting discrete data while preserving satisfactory workflow?

For example, patient safety starts with accurate patient identification. Duplicate EMR charts for the same patient invite a dangerous mistake. If an allergy is charted in one of the patient's charts but not in the other, a contraindication to a new medication can be missed. Or a second invasive diagnostic study is ordered because the original study was overlooked. A data steward from access services or the registration group should report the accuracy data back to his or her colleagues. The data steward convenes the committee and they decide that the maximum acceptable duplicate patient identity rate is, say, 2% or that the maximum null rate for the completion of the primary care provider field is 10%. The committee then takes responsibility for reviewing the performance of their staff so that the goal is reached. As performance improves, the data steward, with the authorization of the data quality committee, gradually takes on subsequent data elements in order of the greatest importance first. Similarly, data stewards in each clinical department launch a data quality feedback loop with a clinician committee.

Many organizations spend months or years installing their EMRs. It is a financially and emotionally exhausting project. Clinicians, administrators, and IT analysts are eager to declare the implementation "finished" and "a success." However, it is likely that compromises were made during implementation just so that the installation project could be completed. During the "optimization" phase, it is time to go back and check the details of what got charted where in the EMR so that the EMR report writers will be able to produce meaningful results.

It is also about this time where the culture of an organization takes center stage. Do you have clinician leaders who understand the challenge of collecting discrete data while preserving satisfactory workflow? Do those leaders understand the importance of definitions and charting conventions so that important patient details are charted just once and always in the same place? Are those leaders able to go to their peers and say, "This is why it is important that you document this finding in this way?"

Better yet, an effective culture will self-organize around the data. Clinicians will look at the outcomes reports and say, "Hey, a 68% completion rate for the time duration of the first stage of labor is unacceptable if we are going to understand our Cesarean section rate. Let's rally our nurse and physician colleagues to get 100% documentation on this important detail." It is not the responsibility of the EMR build analyst to get clinicians to chart adequately—it is the bailiwick of clinician leaders if not the rank-and-file clinicians themselves to commit to charting effectively.

Data Governance—Standardizing the EMR Process

In addition to agreement on definitions, the organization needs to come to consensus on the EMR process. Let's say that there is a single definition of what a "catheter day" is. What are the specific fields in the EMR that will be used to document the beginning of catheterization? The physician order for the catheter? A coded documentation element of insertion by a clinician? And what is considered evidence that the catheter continues to be in use? A daily description of the catheter site by the clinician? A measured output volume from that catheter? The continued listing of the catheter in the "Tubes, Lines, and Drains" section of the EMR? And what is the specific process for documenting the removal of the catheter? The order for removal? A clinician's chart entry? All of these details need to be specified before the first inquiry is made of EMR data in order for there to be a "single source of truth" for the organization.

More subtly, EMR builders need to be sure that there is only one place in the EMR for entering certain data, such as the Estimated Delivery Date in a pregnancy, regardless of the different specialties or caregiver roles that may chart on the patient. If one is looking to be sure that a beta-blocker is administered for heart failure, where will acceptable contraindications be displayed for the clinician? In the order set or in the documentation? Configuring the EMR to conform to data definitions is another important data governance process and it overlaps with the EMR build governance process.

Continuous Process Improvement—Modifying the EMR to Capture New Data

As clinicians individually and in committee begin to examine the EMR data collected, they will find missing data, inaccurate data, and conflicting data. Most of these data problems have their root in the EMR architecture and organizational culture. Although clinicians need to lead the charge on using the EMR consistently, there will always be a need for modifying the underlying EMR. The EMR build analyst needs to have a seat at the table when the committee examines their reports. At the discretion of the committee, the EMR build analyst needs to be able to demonstrate where the data element in question is collected in the EMR and what the surrounding EMR workflow looks like and what the potential effects of changing the EMR charting will be to collect the data element in a new or different way. It is the job of the EMR build analyst to present the options and the job of the clinician leader or committee to bring the committee to consensus on changing the EMR.

For example, if the clinicians want to look at the Cesarean section rate, they might want to capture the indications for C-section in the EMR. The EMR build analyst could turn that around quickly and the clinicians could evaluate the new data collected. Sometimes, the first time clinicians meet the EMR build analyst in their clinical area is when the outcome reports contain unexpected or inadequate data, and the clinicians request a change. Establish the relationship between the clinicians and the EMR build analysts early.

Getting the EMR Ready to Deliver Useful Data

At this point, we have an EMR with the following characteristics:

- Data Governance—Definitions: The important data elements have recognized definitions across the entire organization.
- Data Governance—Quality: An operations-based data steward and a committee are managing the quality and data capture rates of the data input to the EMR.
- Data Governance—Standardizing the EMR process: The important data elements are captured in exactly one EMR field and incorporated into the workflows of multiple administrative and clinician roles and specialties.
- Continuous Process Improvement and Readiness for Capturing New Data: An EMR build analyst is assigned to each group receiving reports so that incremental changes can be made to the EMR to improve the value of reporting.

Now let us turn to some more technical aspects of managing data.

Transaction System versus Analytical System

It is useful to distinguish transaction (source) systems from retrospective analytical (reporting) systems. The former are designed to provide minute-to-minute management of workflows at the point of care, whether it is at the registration desk, in the lab, or at the patient's bedside. The transaction system in healthcare, normally the clinical data repository in an EMR (Stage 2 in the HIMSS Analytics EMR Adoption Model), is optimized to receive lots of data input or display lots of data output on a single patient. Typically, the retrospective, analytical system is optimized to query and return several data elements across multiple patients, such as displaying the last anti-coagulation result for a group of atrial fibrillation patients. These differing use cases lead to different designs in terms of how the data are laid down in the permanent memory of the database for each system. At some point during the day, data need to be copied from the transactional system to the analytical system. Typically, this is done shortly after midnight when the operational use of the transaction system is at a minimum. A benefit of the two-system design is that computing-intense queries of the analytical system do not drag down performance of the transaction system as could be the case if the queries were made directly against the transactional system.

Definitions—Reports and Visualization Tools

A brief review of terminology may be helpful. The reader is forewarned that there is no consistent use of the following terms in the industry, so ideally the speaker will make clear to the listener the definitions chosen. *Reports* and *reporting* are terms used for a summary of data in a system. On one end of the reporting spectrum are the highly formatted, picture-perfect, scheduled documents that unit managers get every 2 weeks or so that allow them to manage their area of responsibility. Those reports may come with buttons or dropdown list options that allow the user to adjust the reporting period date, change the facility or facility unit, and so forth. These reports are predictable and answer questions of general value to the organization often with rows and columns of data.

For executives, reports are often graphical with minimal row and column data. "Visualization tools" are used to produce these visually attractive displays along with screen buttons that allow the executive to adjust the information content of the display. Typically, these graphical executive dashboards each cover a relatively narrow area of interest, such as number of EMR visits still open, or ICU length of stay, and so forth. Maybe 15 or 20 dashboards would be built for a given group of executives to cover the individual key performance indicators of greatest interest to them. Neither the scheduled biweekly operational reports nor the executive dashboards require much technical skill of the user—they just assume that the user knows their clinical or business area well so that they can make sense of the reports or displays.

Definitions—Ad Hoc Queries

An ad hoc query is where the user is not certain of exactly what data they want. They have a hunch and they want to look around in the data to explore possibilities.

On the other end of the reporting spectrum is the so-called ad hoc query or interactive reporting. An ad hoc query is where the user is not certain of exactly what data they want. They have a hunch and they want to look around in the data to explore possibilities. For example, a nurse manager or their clinical analyst may be faced with trying to understand why there have been so many falls recently on their unit. Are the patients sicker than usual? Have they been receiving more analgesics or sedatives? How is the nurse staffing ratio? The challenge for the analytics and reporting staff is figuring out what data the nurse manager or analyst may want to look at—not so much data as to overwhelm the user but enough data so that the manager or analyst feels their exploration is thorough.

One way to provide ad hoc query capability is to organize the data with clearly labeled "field" or "column" names. These labels are not the arcane number–letter combinations found in many transaction system databases but descriptive, plain English names that convey meaning to the experienced manager or analyst. Using the list of field names, the user can pull together a report "on the fly" by selecting what output fields they want to see, indicating what fields to filter or calculate on, and then pressing the "search" button.

Definitions—Data Mart

New database and visualization tools are blurring the distinction among the reporting, executive dashboard, and ad hoc query tools.

A data mart is a subset of all the tables in the retrospective analytical system or Enterprise Data Warehouse (discussed in a later section) that is prepared to answer queries in a given domain of organizational knowledge. By limiting the number of tables and the number of fields (columns) displayed, the reporting and analytics team can make it easier for the ad hoc query user to see their way around the data and get faster performance in their searches. The reporting team needs to be careful not to hide access to the data—sometimes small, specific, infrequently requested fields are very important to the knowledgeable user.

If the analytical system is snappy, the user can inspect the output and make small changes to the filter variables and rerun the report without a big time penalty. The user interacts with a "point and click" interface and does not need to know how to write code. A glossary of field names with explanations of how the data were collected by the transaction system is helpful. Use of an ad hoc query tool requires more technical training than scheduled reports or executive dashboards but allows the user to gain insight in an area where routine reports are not yet available or appropriate. Building an ad hoc query system is the job of the top performing reporting and analytics staff who have access to subject matter experts in operations to help them with deciding which data tables to make available in each subject area and how to name the fields (columns) in a manner that makes sense to the expected user.

New database and visualization tools are blurring the distinction among the reporting, executive dashboard, and ad hoc query tools. Some people also distinguish between reporting, which is a display of known information, versus analytics, which is a process that develops new knowledge for the organization. In this chapter, I have used these two terms interchangeably.

Direct Programming Access to Data

> Be sure that data governance is functioning well so that analysts in different departments come up with the same numbers when they run their own SQL code against the same database tables.

In addition to routine, scheduled reports, executive dashboards, and ad hoc query tools, there are some departments in healthcare, such as Finance, Pharmacy, Surgery, and Quality, that need their own data experts. These experts can write their own Structured Query Language (SQL) code, which is the standard language used for interacting with relational databases, the type of database most frequently used for analytical systems. They are given access directly to the data marts of the analytical reporting database. Best practice has the IT or the reporting and analytics database administrators building the databases and their tables and transferring data from the transaction system to the reporting database. The reporting and analytics team is responsible for the naming convention of the reporting database. Depending on the confidence in the database experts in the operations departments, the experts can be given Read Only access to the tables (meaning that they can view but not change the data) or they can be given Read/Write access to the tables.

Reasons for allowing certain high-intensity data users to have their own direct SQL programming access to the reporting database tables include high demand. If these high-volume users had to wait for the centralized reporting staff to build all their reports, ad hoc queries, or data marts, progress would be substantially slower. Also, it is unlikely that anyone on the centralized reporting team is going to have the business knowledge of the intense data-needy operational departments, and it is practical to give those departments direct access to the database. With that liberal access policy comes a duty to be sure that data governance is functioning well so that analysts in different departments come up with the same numbers when they run their own SQL code against the same database tables.*

Data Exporting

Another important function of the reporting and analytics team is data exporting. Instead of preparing reports and dashboard for internal users, the team receives requests to send data to outside organizations such as patient satisfaction survey vendors, national benchmarking firms, medical specialty societies, health plans, ACOs, and the like. Even though the data are going to outside organizations, it is still important that all the same practices that apply to internal reporting apply to the external data submissions because those data will describe the organization to outside stakeholders. The same care needs to be taken with data definitions (and new definitions may come from external sources), data quality, data completeness, and single source of truth. In addition to data going externally, some of those data will return to the organization after manipulation and standardization by the external agency. Dashboards would be able to show organizational performance relative to external benchmarks. Of course, any data sent to outside agencies would need to be stripped of patient-identifying information. If it is anticipated that external agency data when returned will need to be associated with internal data at the patient level, then individual patient

---

* This state of affairs is known as "one source of truth."

data can be labeled with a sequential, meaningless numeric identifier before sending out. This identifier can be linked to the internal data through a crosswalk table.

Outsourcing versus Insourcing

One of the current controversies in data management is outsourcing versus insourcing. Advantages of outsourcing data management include the following:

- Hardware infrastructure can be commissioned nearly instantly from the vendor.
- Hardware infrastructure can grow and shrink with the demand, with the organization paying only for what is used.
- Deployed hardware is usually refreshed frequently with the newest, fastest chipsets.
- External vendors have expertise in converting data to new hardware and software versions.
- External data management vendors may offer large comparison groups with similarly sized organizations.
- Online reporting is web based and performance ("screen flips") is usually very good.
- External vendors often have expertise mapping the organization's data fields to the vendor's data field library.
- The client organization typically needs to just provide an initial database upload, then periodic, incremental (such as daily) updates.
- External vendors typically have many different analyses already built for instant application to your organization's data once the data mapping has been completed.
- External vendors may have more experience combining claims and clinical data.
- Often the external vendor will offer the ability to send some data back to the organization for local storage and manipulation.
- External vendors typically can ingest new data from any new source such as a physician group that the organization is considering acquiring or partnering with, leading to a prompt analysis of the group's financial and clinical performance.
- External vendors may offer superior data security.
- Use of external vendors may provide contractual limits on demand so that the internal reporting team is not viewed unfavorably.

Some of the disadvantages of outsourcing include the following:

- Some organizations don't like all their data being offsite under someone else's control.
- The reports from the external vendor may not entirely match the organization's needs.
- There may be less opportunity to do ad hoc queries and explore the data.
- There may be less opportunity to join data across different source systems such as EMR and supply chain.
- Even though the data are managed externally, top performing organizations still need to manage cost and quality internally, where data are used to guide process interventions.

Advantages of insourcing data management include the following:

- The organization may be able to respond more nimbly to internal demands for a slightly changed report.
- Internal data management promotes internal departmental expertise, which can lead to exceptional performance gains by committed and knowledgeable individuals.
- It may be easier to trace reporting system data back to source transaction systems.
- It may be easier to build specific reports and ad hoc query systems to answer specific questions.
- It may be easier to export data to outside agencies because you already have those data under management.

Disadvantages of insourcing include the following:

- In large organizations with backlogs, it can take months to provision hardware.
- Purchased hardware decays in value over time.
- It is expensive to keep hardware and software updated to the newest versions.
- It may be hard to attract and retain capable staff members with sophisticated data skills.
- Internal demand may overwhelm supply and produce client dissatisfaction.

Reporting on Business Systems

So far, we have been discussing mostly the management of EMR data. But all of the same principles apply to the organization's other major source or transaction systems such as the ERP system (including the supply chain), the cost accounting system, the patient satisfaction system, and the time and attendance system, to name a few. Definitions of key fields are crucial, feedback to operations about accuracy and completeness is required, and attention to consistent workflow is still important. Data need to be moved from the source system to the retrospective analytical system. Field (column) names need to be intuitive and unambiguous. A variety of data tools need to serve a spectrum of users from casual users, to executives, to data gurus in some data-intense departments. For Lean/Six Sigma organizations, the ability to link clinical (EMR) and business data allows study of performance across the entire enterprise. For example, if bundling for total joint procedures is required by the marketplace, being able to use one data mart to compare clinical outcome with resource cost is fundamental.

Internal Performance Improvement versus Population Health Management

There is always value in optimizing internal performance regardless of whether one is part of an ACO or not. If an organization is receiving fee-for-service payments, then margins are greater if costs can be managed down. Whether in a fee-for-service environment or a value-based payment arena, using data to improve the safety, quality, and reliability of care is crucial. Comparison with national benchmarks may be useful at some point, but narrowing unnecessary variation and improving consistency can be done entirely internally, and such skill never goes out of style. Building a data-driven culture can start before ACO readiness is ever discussed. Such a culture means that frontline clinicians expect to see how they are doing with clinical and financial outcomes compared to their colleagues in the same clinic and to the best performing clinics in the organization. Data transparency tends to encourage sharing of best practice. Being able to join clinical outcomes with the resource use needed to achieve those clinical outcomes prepares a physician staff for the high-level performance needed to be successful in an ACO.

There is always value in optimizing internal performance regardless of whether one is part of an ACO or not.

Preparing the Data

Some reporting and analytics teams start out by reporting against a single important source (transaction) system. Within the source system, the database managing the transactions for the users is called the production database. Some source systems also make a copy of the production database (sometimes called the "shadow" database) and keep it synchronized up to the minute in case it is needed for backup or other tasks that might slow down the production database. Some transaction systems come with a reporting tool that works directly off of the source system (using either the production or shadow database). Such systems can be handy for responding to questions answerable by that source system alone because they avoid the need to move data to another database. Also, the analysts supporting the transaction system already know the column (field) names and preparing reports from that system is second nature to them.

A disadvantage already mentioned is that reporting off the transaction system can slow performance for staff seeing patients. Another disadvantage can be that the reporting or query tools provided by the vendor may not be as well known or may be more limited than standard industry database reporting tools. As an organization becomes more sophisticated with their analytics, there will likely come a time when they will want to combine data from two or more source systems, such as combining data from the supply chain and EMR systems as in the total joint replacement outcomes study. At that point, it is time to consider a more elaborate data management system than simply using the vendor's tools to report off of the transaction system.

The first step in building a powerful data management system is to move the important data off the transaction system to a separate, usually relational, database to support intense reporting and ad hoc queries. The set of receiving tables in the retrospective analytical system can be called the staging layer. This is done by data engineers using Extract, Transform, and Load (ETL) procedures. First, a copy is made of the entire source system's relevant tables and then a (usually) nightly procedure is set up to copy data that are new or changed during the previous 24 h. Management of this ETL process is complex and requires knowledge of the source database and the staging layer. Typically, the copy of the source system is made table by table into the staging layer without changing or transforming the source system data. One of the tasks of the reporting and analytics group is to decide which source tables need to be brought into the staging layer. That decision is based on the expected use of the source system data, a function of the business intelligence governance process.

Enterprise Data Warehouse

EDW refers to a database, group of databases, or staging layers and data marts used to store a copy of the crucial data from all of the organization's major transaction systems for purposes of reporting and analytics.

The term *EDW* has been used widely both in and out of healthcare and its definition is subject to argument. For purposes of this chapter, EDW refers to a database, group of databases, or staging layers and data marts used to store a copy of the crucial data from all of the organization's major transaction systems for purposes of reporting and analytics. Presumably, the same reporting, analytics, and data visualization tools can be used across any and all data in the EDW and one is not subject to the technical limits that might be placed on reporting directly from a vendor's transaction system. An EDW presents an opportunity to use powerful, cross-industry data tools on data from multiple healthcare transaction systems. An EDW also implies the ability to perform queries that span two or more source systems, such as "What is the cost of the hip implant and the total inpatient cost of hip replacement in patients 50–75 years old with American Society of Anesthesiologists (ASA) Class 1–2 rating sorted by orthopedic group and payer?"

Responding to the above query would require data from the EMR, the supply chain system, and the cost accounting or claims systems. Providing that data have been brought over from the three or four source systems into the EDW, there needs to be a way to link records from those source systems. We assume that a stock keeping unit (SKU) and serial number of the hip implant are obtained and stored in the EMR along with the demographic and clinical data elements of the patient. The query would take the EMR's implant SKU and look it up in the supply chain data tables to find its acquisition cost. Then, the query would need to obtain the calculated cost of the inpatient stay by looking up the EMR encounter number in the cost accounting system. The analytical system would then need to display a graph of the costs with onscreen buttons to select orthopedic groups, hospitals, dates, and so forth. Taking data from one table and looking it up in another table is computationally expensive, so sometimes data from different tables in the staging layer are combined in advance into a new set of data mart tables.

An EDW data model shows what tables and columns are brought over from what source systems and how the various tables can be linked to each other to respond to a user's query. In the past, organizations made efforts to move all the data from the important source systems into the EDW and build a comprehensive data model covering all possible queries. That process can work, but it is extraordinarily time consuming. Another less labor-intensive method is to build a data model for only those fields (columns) from the various source systems that will need to be combined to produce results of interest. In other words, determine how you are going to link the EMR tables with the supply chain tables, and the EMR tables with the cost accounting tables and diagram just that. The advantages of this method are that it is faster to yield results and calls for building data models and data marts only when there is a demonstrated need for the underlying data. Leave the source system data in the staging layer largely unchanged so that you can trace back from results in reports to the actual underlying data in the source tables. If the data in the two different systems cannot be reconciled, a bridging table may need to be built (see the Data Standardization/Data Normalization section). If a clinician challenges the veracity of the data, an analyst will be able to find and produce the original data in the source system. Such data management transparency will breed the organization's confidence in the analytics system.

Once freed of the constraints of the source system, the analytics team can name the columns (fields) in the staging layer and data marts with names that are intuitive as to the use of the data they contain. Many of the tables in the source system are likely used for logs and system maintenance and don't need to be brought into the EDW. Data marts can be built as needed to answer queries in a given domain.

Data Standardization/Data Normalization

Data normalization (not to be confused with database normalization) refers to the process of mapping or transforming organizational data to a chosen standard or canonical representation.

In general, the approach is to bring data from the source systems into the EDW staging layer with as little conversion or transformation as possible so as not to introduce corruption into the original data. Sometimes, new tables are built in the EDW for speed and convenience in reporting and analysis. For example, in the source EMR system, the physician's office address may be kept in a different table from the physician's personal identification information. In some instances, it may make sense to create a new table in the EDW that combines the physician's name with her office address so that there is less computation and faster performance at the time the user runs the query on physician names and addresses.

As we noted earlier in the section on Data Governance, sometimes source systems contain different data for the same organizational facts. For example, the listing of the hospital departments may be different in the EMR, the supply chain system, and the time and attendance system. If queries are to be run against "hospital department" and those queries involve data from more than one of the source systems, a new EDW table will need to be constructed that reconciles the three different department naming configurations. It is unlikely that any of the three source systems will be reconfigured to match the other two systems in granularity or in parent–child relationships. So, the only thing to do is to create in the EDW a new hierarchy of department names that is as finely grained as the most granular source system and then map that new naming convention back to the appropriate department names in each of the three source systems. This is an example of the opportunity that an EDW offers to fix things "on the back end" that cannot be fixed "on the front end."

Data normalization (not to be confused with database normalization) refers to the process of mapping or transforming organizational data to a chosen standard or canonical representation. For example, different EMRs may store blood pressures in separate systolic and diastolic fields or in a single field using a "/" mark. The inpatient EMR may have blood pressures taken with multiple different technologies (intra-arterial line vs. sphygmomanometric) from different anatomical locations whereas the office EMR may have blood pressures simply taken in different postures. Depending on the nature of the inquiry into the blood pressure data, these different representations need to be reconciled and possibly transformed into the same format. Diagnoses and "problems" can be free-text or represented with multiple different "standard" code sets. Gradually, the industry is converging on standard vocabularies for the different data types: LOINC for lab tests, RxNorm for medications, SNOMED or ICD-10-CM for diagnoses, and so forth. Commercial vendors offer products that automatically map EMR data to these standard vocabularies and code sets. Free-text data present a more challenging problem. NLP systems can convert free-text fields and transcription into standard code sets although there will always be some vagueness and need for human curation.

Business Intelligence Governance

> Data are an asset that require upfront investment and deliver downstream benefits just like brick-and-mortar assets.

Moving data and setting up reporting and analytics are expensive from both a capital and labor perspective. Data are an asset that require upfront investment and deliver downstream benefits just like brick-and-mortar assets. To build a useful asset for the organization, the business intelligence governance group needs to have a comprehensive view of the source systems important to the organization and how data from those systems can be used to manage the clinical and business affairs of the organization. It takes time to build an effective analytics team, so the governance committee also needs to make a priority list of which source systems shall be first to be copied into the staging layer. Analytics is ideally driven by the business and clinical needs of the organization, and it is the duty of the governance committee to assess the validity and urgency of the requests for reports. As with nearly any resource in an organization, the demand for reporting and analytics is likely to exceed the capacity of the team to fulfill the requests. Adjudicating the potential value (defined as benefit over cost) of the requests involves assessing some of the following characteristics:

- Is the intended use of the report tactical or strategic?
- Can the information be gleaned from an existing report or alternative system without the need to create a new report?
- How broad an audience will this report serve?
- Will proper use of the information result in greater
  - Patient safety?
  - Patient satisfaction?
  - Clinical quality outcome?
  - Process reliability?
  - Process efficiency?
  - Staff productivity?
  - Financial margin?
- What is the cost
  - To move the data initially?
  - To prepare the reporting?
  - To train the users?
  - To adjust the reports as users gain experience with them?

- To update the data transfer and reporting when the source system undergoes upgrade?
- To refresh the system hardware and software every several years?
- To acquire more storage capacity as data accrue over the years?

Considering all the other capital and operational dollar needs of the organization, the BI governance group needs to make a case why this data asset deserves investment versus say, acquiring a physician group, building a telemedicine program, constructing a parking garage, or buying a joint resurfacing machine for the operating room. Who is most qualified to assign a benefit-to-cost ratio or determine a return on investment for a data asset? Because such judgments require awareness of the entire organization, the BI governance committee is best composed of leaders from across the organization including those in roles managing clinical operations, revenue cycle, supply chain, human resources, marketing, strategic planning, and the like. Their business intelligence governance job is Why, What, and When. The job of the analytics team directors and managers is Who and How.

Big Data

Probably the largest store of big healthcare data for most organizations is their years' worth of transcribed free-text dictation from providers.

Big Data is a term used loosely in healthcare. In general, Big Data are data that challenge the previous crop of computers because of volume, velocity, and variety of data. New computing methods have been developed that allow computation to be distributed over massively parallel computers so that as the computing problem grows, more processors can be added to achieve adequate performance. Fortunately, this new computing platform comes at a time when the world is generating more data because so many previously manual processes have become digitized. Healthcare is generating massive amounts of digital data and the greatest single source of healthcare digital data is imaging. Apart from computer-aided image recognition and diagnosis, digital imaging data are currently difficult to bring into computation with the more important numbers and text that describe human health and disease. Another source of big healthcare data is the continuous recording of vital signs and waveforms, mostly cardiovascular, generated in ICUs and step-down units. Early research indicates that subtle changes in the electrocardiograph waveforms of premature infants may portend significant clinical events. Probably the largest store of big healthcare data for most organizations is their years' worth of transcribed free-text dictation from providers. NLP is beginning to process free-text into coded, computable concepts. These concepts are valuable especially when combined with structured EMR data to describe more nuanced patient status and outcomes than diagnosis codes used in billing.

Most of the frenzy about Big Data in healthcare is unwarranted. Healthcare has a long way to go before it exhausts the insights and management potential of regular data. We don't need Big Data to tell us that one antibiotic is preferred over another, that a diabetic patient needs a screening eye exam, or that there is unjustifiable variation in physicians' treatment of common diseases. We need to get serious about the quality of the data we currently collect and feed it back to the clinician teams that can make a difference and then track the improvement in clinical and financial outcomes. That represents at least a decade of work for most organizations. Don't let Big Data take the organization's eye off of what is really important to do right now.

One approach to healthcare Big Data is that you will know it when you need a big data computing platform. If your current reporting and analytics functions are not running fast enough and you have upgraded to new hardware and software and database experts have constructed adequate indexes within the database to help it run faster, then you may need a Big Data computing platform. Another reason you might need a Big Data computing platform is because you need more insight into a domain where true big data may be helpful to you. Big Data processing is good for detecting trends and associations that may have missed human perception. Once an area of interest has been discovered, the problem can be further analyzed using conventional data techniques.

There are some Big Data opportunities that may have increasing healthcare value in the future, such as the following:

- Clothes with embedded biosensors given to at-risk patients discharged from the emergency department may signal early worsening before it is apparent to family or providers.
- Genomic, proteomic, microbiomic, and metabolomic data will radically change our disease diagnosis and treatment.
- Social media posts, search engine entries, and sales of over-the-counter data will signal the onset of epidemics before it is apparent to healthcare providers.
- Location tracking data of patients, staff, and equipment can signal imminent catastrophic events in the hospital.
- Tracking movements and activities of seniors in their homes will indicate both acute and chronic worsening of disease.
- Credit card purchases, credit scores, census tract data, and mobile phone activity and location data may indicate risk for disease or unfavorable status of known disease.
- Traffic patterns, weather data, air pollution data, and pollen counts will help in managing chronic respiratory disease.

If your organization has already mastered Lean, Six Sigma, and continuous process improvement with regular data and if you cannot further improve the safety, quality, and reliability of the care you deliver, then perhaps you need the insights that the above Big Data opportunities can afford. In any case, it is not a question of regular data OR Big Data, it is regular data AND Big Data.

Descriptive, Predictive, and Prescriptive Analytics

Most of the reporting and analytics we see after EMRs have been installed are descriptive—the reports tell us what happened (past tense—a look in the rear-view mirror) with our patients or with our processes. Descriptive analytics are essential for getting on top of your organization's quality and cost of care.

As organizations get more analytically sophisticated, their thoughts naturally turn toward whether they could use their data to prepare for what's ahead (predictive analytics). If they knew who was most likely to be readmitted, could they do something different with the patient and the family before the patient leaves the hospital? Which of their ACO patients or Medicare Shared Savings Plan patients are most likely to have an expensive or risky emergency department or hospital stay that could be avoided if providers intervened? Community-based care could benefit even more from predictive analytics by looking at geographic hot spots with high pediatric lead levels, high asthma emergency department visits, and low vaccination rates.

Few organizations are routinely doing prescriptive analytics, a nascent technology with application in optimizing processes. This might involve using data to help care management decide how and in what order to manage complex patients with multiple chronic diseases. It's not important what label an organization applies to its analytic efforts—what counts is that it sees the value of data as an asset that can guide the investment in and management of clinical and business problems.

Reporting and Analytics Team Roles

There are many names applied to the various roles on a business intelligence or reporting and analytics team. The names aren't as important as being sure that the important tasks are addressed by someone. Also, some organizations seem to be more centralized in their reporting approach and some more decentralized and that will influence who does what and what the roles' names are.

Business Analysts: these people know the working of the reporting and analytics department and are skilled in interviewing clients and documenting their need for data. Even in an agile development shop, it is still important to have a knowledgeable person evaluate the multiple incoming requests by connecting with the client, analyzing the problem to be solved, and proposing a response. Then, the business intelligence governance committee can begin to make a priority list of new reports based on organizational benefit versus cost.

ETL Engineers: these engineers are expert at moving data from the source system to the EDW staging layer and from the staging layer to a data mart. Not only are they expected to know routine databases and SQL programming, they also will need to learn the eccentricities of the source system and how to extract data from it without impairing its transactional performance.

Database Administrators: these engineers are responsible for setting up the EDW databases and running routine maintenance to be sure that the databases are running fast enough and have enough hardware space to accommodate incoming data. These folks may stay in the IT department instead of residing on the reporting and analytics team.

Report Writers: often these staff members have no special content knowledge of the domain for which they are writing reports. Using requirements written by the business analysts, they prepare the routine, scheduled, highly formatted documents that managers throughout the organization use to run their units.

Visualization Analysts: working with the business analysts, these wizards prepare focused data marts and graphical front ends to support users in specific clinical and business domains to help answer the questions posed by those users.

Data Architects: people in this role might be described by multiple names. Their job is to create larger data marts for more sophisticated and trained users to run their own ad hoc queries or SQL code. They decide how much detail of the entire EDW to expose to data experts in the operational departments—enough to get the questions answered without overwhelming the user.

Trainers: whether it is helping a nurse manager to look at a scheduled, biweekly report or training a business analyst in the finance department to run an ad hoc query, trainers serve a wide range of user roles. Trainers can build computer-based training modules and teach classes. As there will always be turnover in the user ranks, training and support are ongoing functions. Training can be thought of as the initial education of a user before they use the system and support as the ongoing help provided to users indefinitely.

Data Scientists: typically, these analysts have training in quantitative areas such as physics, mathematics, or statistics as opposed to the clinical or business training of experts in healthcare. The attraction of hiring a data scientist is that presumably they do not come with a bias as to what healthcare data should reveal. They apply rigorous quantitative methods to the existing data and faithfully represent what the data show even if the assessment is contrary to orthodox healthcare thinking. Data scientists are particularly helpful in searching for trends in Big Data where associations may be unpredictable but potentially valuable.

Conclusion

US healthcare spends $3 trillion a year, the greatest per capita cost in the world, yet the clinical and service satisfaction outcomes are generally unexceptional. Its practitioners have largely been trained in a cottage industry, apprentice model where independent thinking has been highly valued and variance in approach to the patient is ascribed to professional judgment. Continuous performance improvement where data tie outcomes to process is not practiced widely. Precisely describing patient states before and after treatment is somewhat subjective and difficult to quantify in discrete terms. Electronic record keeping has only recently been adopted widely and outcome measurements are not yet standardized.

In short, healthcare presents an outstanding opportunity for business intelligence to deliver results. Healthcare delivery organizations need to carefully define terms, consistently use their EMRs to collect data, continuously improve the quality of those data, feed those data back to the clinicians in a learning healthcare system, and display how incremental improvements in diagnostic and therapeutic interventions can yield superior clinical and financial outcomes. Although the effort to implement EMRs was enormous, the business intelligence effort will be larger still and will deliver on EMRs' decades-old promise of better, safer, and more cost-effective care.

Chapter 10

The Future of Information Security in Healthcare

David Finn, MA

"In the age of Meaningful Use and the Affordable Care Act, security is not just an IT issue."

It shouldn't seem strange to start a chapter on the future of anything with a brief history of that topic, but when you are talking about data security in healthcare, your first thought may be, "There is no history of data security in healthcare—it is just starting." And you'd be, for the most part, correct.

Protecting a patient's information, like medicine itself, goes back to Hippocrates (see Figure 10.1): "What I may see or hear in the course of the treatment or even outside of the treatment in regard to the life of men, which on no account one must spread abroad, I will keep to myself, holding such things shameful to be spoken about."*

From Hippocrates (roughly 400 BC) until HIPAA (the Privacy and Security rules were not effective until 2003 and 2005, respectively), not a lot happened. When healthcare was predominantly "documented" in conversations and on paper, the issue was less one of security than of privacy and confidentiality. These issues were primarily addressed as ethical issues, not security. Section 4 of the American Medical Association's Principles of Medical Ethics (1920 edition) said this: "A physician shall respect the rights of patients... and shall safeguard patient confidences within the constraints of the law."

Many state medical boards also incorporated professional ethics related to confidentiality into their medical practice acts and regulations. This extended beyond physicians to other licensed and/or credentialed medical professionals. Hospital policy and procedure, as well as medical staff by-laws, also frequently spoke to the issues of the confidentiality of patient information and the critical nature of trust in the relationship between a patient and a caregiver, be it a physician, a physical therapist, nurse, or an entire HCO.

* The classical version of the Hippocratic Oath is from the translation from the Greek by Ludwig Edelstein. From *The Hippocratic Oath: Text, Translation, and Interpretation*, by Ludwig Edelstein. Baltimore: Johns Hopkins Press, 1943.

Figure 10.1 Hippocrates' privacy lectures. (Copyright ©2015 David S. Finn. Illustrations by Katy Huggins.)

Then Came Computers

Then came computers… not centralized IT departments and integrated enterprise resource planning or EMR systems, but rather departmental systems such as LIS (laboratory information system) or RIS (radiology information system) systems that were used within the department to track and store departmental information on scheduling, orders, and results. Security typically meant that anyone working in the department could get to anything in the system. These systems were not professionally managed, and security concepts around systems and networks that were just beginning to arise in other industries were still completely unheard of in healthcare.

Soon, other caregivers became aware of the information in these systems and they wanted access to it. The fact that the information was available anywhere in the facility created even more demand for access. This led to situations where the 800 users of the lab system may all have had the same user ID (doctor) and password (123). This approach was high on convenience, not so much on security. Still, because of limited usage, a network confined to the physical facility, and the fact that everyone knew every other user, made headlines about breaches rare. It also helped that there were no laws or regulations around computer access or who could look at clinical information—outside of the ethical standards and internal policies.

Financial and clinical information systems continued to expand and evolve. Network technology improved and became more widely available, and industry started automating. "Green screens" and "terminals" were appearing on desks in a wide variety of industries. While healthcare lagged in these trends, it was not uncommon to see IT departments in hospitals—focused on the business functions of healthcare, registration, and billing—along with departmental (clinical) systems that operated independently from "central" IT.

In the early 1980s, the personal computer (PC) exploded onto the scene and all bets would soon be off. IT would become the purview of any person who could find a budget and a *little* bit of IT knowledge. Budgets and bed control were done on spreadsheets. A PC could collect information on a nursing floor and upload batch charges to the central billing system. Information could be sent from one system to another and the ability to share information in an automated way came to healthcare.

Sharing within a facility was one thing, but sharing between facilities or organizations was a game changer. The problem was data could be shared, but because there were no data standards, one often couldn't tell what was being shared. One hospital's Universal Billing Code became another hospital's "appropriate code should be verified with insurer" warning message.

And Then Came HIPAA

> We soon learned that HIPAA was more a lifestyle suggestion than a prescription.

Then came HIPAA. It was August of 1996 and lest you want to blame legislators for another "bad law," the HIPAA Privacy Rule was not legislated by Congress but rather by the failure of Congress to enact legislation!

When HIPAA was passed, it required the Secretary of Health and Human Services (HHS) to propose standards protecting the privacy of individually identifiable health information by August of 1997. The Secretary submitted a report to Congress recommending and urging comprehensive privacy legislation by August 21, 1999. If Congress failed to act by that date, the Secretary was directed to finalize regulations containing proposed standards relating to the electronic transfer of medical information by February 21, 2000.

Shockingly, Congress was unable to reach consensus on comprehensive privacy legislation. The Secretary of HHS finalized the regulations. Today, most of us think of HIPAA as the Privacy and Security Rules but privacy and security were really an afterthought. HIPAA's initial purpose was to set standards for transmitting electronic health data (transactions and code sets) and to allow people to transfer and continue healthcare coverage with an insurer after they changed or lost a job. Until 2003, there were no national privacy standards for medical information under HIPAA. All protections were based on state laws.

Privacy and security emerged into the vernacular of healthcare in 2003 and 2005, respectively, as each of those rules' effective dates passed. Unfortunately, from the very beginning, the focus for implementing these rules fell to the IT department and the fun—and the problems—really began. Even in facilities that had not started to adopt an EMR and were completely paper bound, the Health Information Management (HIM) department, then known as Medical Records, wrote the policies but looked to information technology (spreadsheets) or physical security (locks) for tracking and controlling access.

We soon learned that HIPAA was more a lifestyle suggestion than a prescription. Many elements of the Security Rule were identified as "addressable." Addressable, of course, meant they weren't required but you were supposed to explain why you didn't adopt those elements in your risk assessment. So, in fact, until 2013, addressable meant that you could ignore them.

Enforcement was unclear, inconsistent, and rarely carried out. Healthcare providers actually did a fairly good job on the privacy side in the paper world. Charts were locked up every night and even when clinicians took them out of the facility for review or sign-off, it was a limited number, they had little value, and marketing or selling them was extremely difficult. That would all change very soon.

By 2009, we were well into President George W. Bush's "Decade of the Electronic Medical Record." In 2004, the president laid out a 10-year initiative for transforming health information technology and highlighted this by saying: "By computerizing health records, we can avoid dangerous medical mistakes, reduce costs, and improve care."* The Health Information Technology for Economic and Clinical Health Act, enacted as part of the American Recovery and Reinvestment Act of 2009, was signed into law by President Obama on February 17, 2009, to promote the adoption and meaningful use of health information technology. The Patient Protection and Affordable Care Act became law about a year later in March of 2010.

> In the age of Meaningful Use and the Affordable Care Act, security is not just an IT issue.

HIPAA recognized that a one- or two-doctor practice would not have the same needs as a large academic medical center with international research, and this was why so much was addressable. Everyone understood the idea that HIPAA was a "floor," but the floor was never leveled nor was the material for the floor ever defined. That lack of definition coupled with a lack of firm, consistent enforcement and often conflicting state law led to an extended period of very little progress in terms of privacy and security across the healthcare industry. Some covered entities put a lot of time and effort into improving security and privacy, but many did nothing. Most business associates didn't know they were one and, if they did, didn't think they actually had to do anything except sign the Business Associate Agreement. This has only started to change since the HIPAA Omnibus Bill Final Rule became law in 2013 and the definition, as well as the responsibilities, of business associates and contractors were expanded.

The growing adoption of EMRs was the underlying engines of both of these pieces of legislation. Now, with large amounts of clinical data and related billing information, these laws aimed at driving the sharing of massive amounts of clinical data. In addition to the data collection and sharing required under Meaningful Use, these laws drove fundamental changes to both the care delivery and the reimbursement models for healthcare.

> Health information and the required information technology are now strategic functions of the delivery and business of healthcare.

We saw the creation of HIEs and ACOs. Sharing of and access to these data will only grow as patient engagement initiatives move the continuum of these data into the hands of the data

* President George W. Bush, State of the Union Address, January 20, 2004.

owners, the patients. Payers are now embedded into the flow of information far beyond claims and payments. We are faced with what seems like an ever-increasing number of business associates ranging from state registries to researchers and from home health services and durable medical equipment providers to software vendors. That will drive more accountability deeper and more broadly into the "continuum of data" that will reflect this expanding continuum of care.

Finally, and frankly, the reason we are doing all these other things (enterprise EMRs, the shift in care reimbursement, HIE, accountable care, etc.) is outcomes. You can pick a name—Clinically Integrated Networks, population health, patient engagement, and bundled payments—but it is about providing value-based services to the patient, provider, and payer. It is all about collecting an astounding amount of data and organizing them into useful information that allows your business and clinical users to turn them into insights, improvements, better care, and better clinical, financial, and patient satisfaction outcomes.

The stage is now set from the healthcare side. Payers and providers have large amounts of protected health information in digital formats (ePHI). They are being required to share much of these data (from both a regulatory and market perspective). Finally, this is an industry where, historically, the job of information protection has fallen to the CIO and the IT department. In the age of Meaningful Use and the Affordable Care Act, security is not just an IT issue. The information, appropriate access to it, and its availability and protection are strategic to the clinical and business operations of the organization. Indeed, with ACOs, HIEs, and Patient Engagement (a Meaningful Use requirement for Stage 2), information and the technology used to collect, store, maintain, share, and protect information are the operations. Health information and the required information technology are now strategic functions of the delivery and business of healthcare. So, as healthcare was evolving, what was been happening in the strange and mysterious world of technology? Especially out in the ether—the Internet? The changes in healthcare privacy and security may be easier to track and understand, but without the hyperconnectivity, the consumerization of IT, and the commercialization of data, we would not find healthcare in the situation it is in today—a highly targeted, data-rich industry with only a rudimentary control over the security of its data. This situation must change quickly and dramatically.

Technology Has Been Evolving as Well, and So Has Cybercrime

While healthcare was struggling to catch up with changes in technology, delivery models, and changing reimbursement models, the world of technology was undergoing its own staggering evolution, and it had a remarkable dark side to it. Initially, it was things like "phone phreaking" and putting the little picture of the bomb on someone's computer and wiping their hard drive. It must have been fun for someone, but they didn't even know if the "bomb" ever went off. Perpetrators were kids on summer vacation and then Eastern European soldiers who "hacked" when they were bored or their government stopped paying them. We had the people who wanted cable TV but didn't want to pay for it. People hacked for fun and for services they could get without paying.

Then, we experienced the convergence of some remarkable technologies and social behaviors: smartphones and social media, texting, and social apps. The Facebooks and Amazons of the world had massive amounts of data that they could "harvest" from their users who visited their sites, used their apps, or bought things from them. The data became valuable and a target for cybercriminals.

There have been many types of cybercrime, but what really drove the crime is an underlying change in Western philosophy. Yes, in 1637, when René Descartes wrote "I think, therefore I am,"* he defined what made us human. By 1998, however, that was no longer true. You didn't have to think to be; you simply had to "surf" to be—or just be connected. Your "virtual self" was more valuable than your real self; if someone were to rob the real you, maybe they get some cash and credit cards. You probably don't carry much cash and you can cancel a credit card (if you know it's been stolen). In cyberspace, they can steal "you."

It is easier to get away with cybercrime than "traditional crime" (see Figure 10.2). After all, you don't have to worry about driving to (or from) a crime scene. You don't have to worry about guards, homeowners with guns, or vicious dogs. In fact, to commit a cybercrime, you can be just about anywhere—and appear to be anywhere else while you are committing the crime. All you need is an Internet connection, and they are easy to find nowadays. The best criminals don't even have to "do the crime," they simply send a link in a compelling e-mail and the poor innocent user can become the victim of his own crime by clicking "unknown" links. Cybercrime is easier to hide from and easier to do.

Since we first swung out of the trees and walked upright, the quest for personal gain (money or power) has been a major (maybe *the* major) motivator of human activity. The largest single driver of positive growth in human endeavor is the creation of marketplaces—and the largest negative drivers have been those aimed at undermining those markets through violence (bank robbery) or theft (data breaches). Security exists, for the most part, because people buy things or need to share information to "buy" things (including healthcare; "wellness" is something you achieve more than buy, but you may use apps that share information to see if you are getting or staying "well"). And then people started collecting data that they didn't really need and couldn't obtain in legitimate ways. Things like the metadata in the pictures you post on Facebook or Twitter, the websites you visit, what you shop for, and what you use search engines to look at. Individually, a single element may not provide a lot of information or be worth much, but start correlating it and searching across a variety of databases and suddenly you can know an awful lot about a person.

Cybercriminals have no "physical" presence and can almost totally obliterate any evidence of the crime having been committed. What is left is almost never enough to tie it to an individual. That's why we blame "groups" for all that is going on.

Without a "physical" presence, we don't even know which countries', states', or other jurisdictions' laws are being violated. The cyber world, in fact, doesn't have to be in a country or state. They can operate virtually—appearing to be or come from wherever they want—and change their base of operation almost at will. Because we don't know where they are, what they are doing may not even be against the law there. Even if we could find them, bringing them back may not be easy. They also don't have to follow programming standards or change control, so the "bad guys" can move much faster than organizations trying to do things the right way.

But it isn't just a few "bad guys" anymore. It has moved well beyond cops and robbers to include highly organized, politically or idealistically motivated groups, some unofficial and some "government sponsored." These attacks by nation states for apparent intelligence gathering or theft

* His best known philosophical statement is *Cogito ergo sum* (French: *Je pense, donc je suis*; "I think, therefore I am"), found in part IV of *Discourse on the Method* (1637—written in French but with inclusion of *Cogito ergo sum*), and §7 of part I of *Principles of Philosophy* (1644—written in Latin).

Figure 10.2 Robbing Mr. Mouse. (Copyright ©2015 David S. Finn. Illustrations by Katy Huggins.)

of intellectual property and the waves of "hactivism"* sweeping the globe add to the complexity around preventing cybercrimes and tracking down cybercriminals.

> In healthcare, these data are not only the currency that the industry will run on; they are also the most important asset of all the stakeholders.

Information security is unique in that threats (and unaddressed vulnerabilities) are cumulative. Physical locks may improve but once you've got a lock on the door, adding layers of locks is probably not going to significantly improve security. Layered information security is a requirement. Old threats don't disappear just because there are now new ones. Until the technology is removed, the existing threats are still there and new ones are continually being added. This is one of the issues around biomedical devices (from medication cabinets to pacemakers) and the concept of "collateral damage."

For healthcare (not just providers, here, but the entire continuum of healthcare), the next wave of growth and innovation will involve intelligent analytics, rich mobile experiences, and one-tap processes that reduce or eliminate interventions or interactions with other human beings. Healthcare has always "run on trust." This will become more critical as patients (consumers) will demand that their caregivers protect their data. Physicians must believe that the data they are getting is not only

* **Hacktivism** or **hactivism** (a portmanteau of *hack* and *activism*) is the subversive use of computers and computer networks to promote a political agenda. With roots in hacker culture and hacker ethics, its ends are often related to the free speech, human rights, or freedom of information. From *Wikipedia*, the free encyclopedia.

the most current and accurate available but is 100% reliable. As the continuum of care expands (HIEs, ACOs, payers, pharmaceuticals, DME, etc.), the companies exchanging the data will only engage with others they know are providing appropriate protection for this highly sensitive data in this hyperconnected continuum. In healthcare, these data are not only the currency that the industry will run on; they are also the most important asset of all the stakeholders.

Healthcare now finds itself with huge volumes of very valuable and marketable data. It also finds itself woefully lacking in understanding the responsibility for, and the techniques of, securing those data. What will the future of information security in healthcare require? How will it happen? What do providers need to do now?

Asking the Right Question

When HCOs talk about cybersecurity today, the question is usually, "How do we protect ourselves and comply with all these regulations, and how do we keep from being the next headline?" The question should be, "How can we make good, rational decisions (business and clinical) given the risks we face?" You will always get the wrong answer if you ask the wrong question, and the results have borne that out, consistently and repeatedly. Far too often security is relegated to the IT department rather than making it a strategic function of the business.

The Key Principles of Compliance and Security

One book would not be enough to explain the myriad of technologies and approaches to cybersecurity now and in the future. One chapter will allow me to paint a very high level picture of the key areas that need to be addressed to begin to provide appropriate security and compliance, both strategically and tactically. I will not focus on technologies and I will start at the highest level (least technical) and work down the ladder from there.

The five key principles of compliance and security are as follows:

1. Governance
2. Secure information access
3. Information protection
4. Infrastructure management
5. Infrastructure security and protection

The words may be different depending on who you are talking to, but the general principles and areas or functions that need to be addressed will not.

Information Governance

Information governance shifts the focus from technology to the people and the policies that generate, use, and manage the data and information required for care as well as related processes.

It all starts with governance, in this case, information governance. Like any other critical asset (people, capital, or inventory), information is a strategic asset that requires high-level oversight in order to be able to use it effectively for decision-making, for performance improvement, for cost management, and for risk management. This can't be done in a bottom-up model. Information governance ensures that information is trustworthy, that it can be used to align with organizational strategy and to engage leadership and critical stakeholders across the enterprise. In the future world of healthcare, this will extend beyond the "four walls" of your organization (it is already happening) to make sure the right information is available in the right place at the right time to the right people in order to provide and support health and healthcare.

While it would be nice to just hand out a project charter, a list of members for your information governance committee, and the policies and procedures you should address, it won't work that way. Even if you have a "traditional" information management process, it is likely not going to be effective given the expansion and growth of IT including EMRs, specific clinical systems, mobile health, cloud computing, and other new sources of data. No one questions the need for timely, accurate information to provide safe, quality health care, but the complexity of processes and workflows makes it much more difficult to address the issues. Information governance shifts the focus from technology to the people and the policies that generate, use, and manage the data and information required for care as well as related processes.

Changes in the delivery of health care, in payment systems, and in the delivery of IT have brought new kinds of information from new sources. Regulatory requirements also complicate the use of that information and the documentation of that use.

Meeting the challenges of improving care and reducing per capita costs will require the effective and efficient management of all HCOs' information. For most HCOs, that will require investment in ways to understand, manage, share, control, and dispose of all that information. It will require an information governance strategy, the focus and organizational wherewithal to implement and enforce it, and the tools to assure that the right information is in the right places and that only the right people are getting access to it.

Successfully implementing information governance will produce high-quality data (data integrity), better capacity to share the information, and predictive analysis across the organization—not only in clinical areas but also in staffing, supply chain, and financial modeling. Not doing information governance may result in the following:

1. Incomplete medical records
2. Inability to access and use information or the wrong people gaining access
3. Increased breaches
4. Issues in exchanging information beyond your own organization
5. Inability to document/verify appropriate access

Perhaps the most important thing that governance will be charged with is creating a culture of compliance around information—who uses it, how, where, who it can be shared with and how, and how users access which data (remember that users include your employees, workforce, volunteers, business associates, patients, parents, guardians, and so on).

Finally, governance will include stakeholders (information collectors and users from across the organization, and beyond) who will determine strategy, create policy, review procedures, and make sure these are enforced. It isn't just about people in a room. Once the policies are in place, for example, around who may access what information in your EMR, there will need to be tools to see if policy is being implemented (maybe the policy needs to change based on what you are seeing). There will need to be reporting and dashboards to see where governance is being effective and if not, where and why. Governance will need to develop the risk management framework and the processes around information and determine the acceptable level of risk around various classifications of data or information (assuming, of course, it was "classified" when they started).

This information governance committee will look at the personnel, technology, and policies and procedures necessary to ensure the preservation, availability, security, confidentiality, usability, and disposal of the company's data. This should encourage strategic thinking (it is your most important asset!) about the use of the data within the organization.

Like any governance body, it starts with establishing roles and objectives for the group. These should be clearly communicated in a governance charter and should be well understood by its members. This group should focus on establishing data standards for privacy and information security, records management, employee data, trade secret and intellectual property protection, e-discovery and litigation readiness, and vendor management. Those focus areas should tell you who needs to be involved as members of the committee: IT, HIM, HR, Research, Legal, Risk Management, and Purchasing. The standards will include a comprehensive set of rules, policies, and procedures governing the proper use and disposal of the company's data. Not only will this group be the decision-makers when issues arise related to data use, they will also consider the appropriate level of risk allocation, assuring insurance and contractual risk transfer in connection with data risks.

Perhaps the most important thing that governance will be charged with is creating a culture of compliance around information—who uses it, how, where, who it can be shared with and how, and how users access which data (remember that users include your employees, workforce, volunteers, business associates, patients, parents, guardians, and so on).

Information Access Is Next

Once you've got governance in place (wasn't that easy?), one of the first issues that will need to be addressed is information access. This includes access management processes—who authorizes users to which systems or locations (not everything is digital, yet). Done correctly, this requires an organization mapping of what roles/departments/units get what information and at what level (read, write, change, delete). What is the process for getting access? Is access for the new employee, John, really "just like Jane's?" Will some access require that a higher level of assurance is required for certain functions?* While identity management and authentication typically fall to IT, that may not be the best place for it. Who oversees the people "issuing" access? And after the people, there are issues of digital trust† and e-authentication.‡

* Authentication focuses on verifying a person's identity based on the reliability of a credential offered, typically a password. Assurance answers the question, "How sure am I that you are who you say you are?"

† *Informally*: characteristic of a computerized environment that has benefits of trust equivalent to that of a paper-based world. Unlike in the paper-based world, concluding transactions online cannot rely on handwritten signatures and human instincts of trust. From Digital Trust: Goals and Obstacles by Rafal Lukawiecki.

‡ Electronic authentication (e-authentication) is the process of establishing confidence in user identities electronically presented to an information system. From http://nvlpubs.nist.gov/nistpubs/SpecialPublications/NIST.SP.800-63-2.pdf.

I'm going to attempt to remain nontechnical, but moving from a strategy and governance perspective to that of ongoing security operations, information access will address the following:

1. The principles and policy of access management
2. Roles and responsibilities, accountability, and digital trust
3. At the operations level, identity management, authentication, and activity review

As with governance, you will need the staff and tools to monitor and report on access. Are you following policy and procedure? Are you achieving the goals you set out for secure information access—why or why not and where? How will you adjust either operations or policy?

Information Protection

The IT department is a custodian or protector of all the digital data, but that should not be confused with a data owner.

Now that you've covered information access—who gets what and when and how they get it—it is time to address information protection. Information protection at the highest level is about classifying data (public, private psych notes, which have protections in excess of ePHI) and determining ownership of the data. While we all recognize that the patient "owns" their data, while it is in your possession, there must be a designated organizational owner—the person, group, or department that will be responsible for making decisions about the data.

Historically, that has fallen to the IT department—if the data are electronic—but that is a mistake. The only information that the IT department needs is network diagrams, inventories of devices, and other IT information, which almost no one else cares about. The financial data, EMR, other clinical information, research, employee information, and other information are used by some primary owner or a group of owners who collect, maintain, and use that data; they should be the owners. The IT department is a custodian or protector of all the digital data, but that should not be confused with a data owner.

Information protection should include data criticality, or defining which data are most important and must be protected at all costs, such as the following:

1. Multiple backups, for example; or not even backups, but
2. Redundant live "images"
3. What is most important and what you could afford to lose (the spreadsheets with 12 years of March Madness office pool, which you have been backing up and storing for, well, 12 years)

Protecting information involves cost, and because of that, these are business decisions, not IT decisions.

In the olden days, we used to get the staff attorney to write retention policies about letters, memos, audits, and financial statements. Today, we save everything, not just "final" documents, and all those data can be used to recreate or create new "versions" of official documents, so don't forget the data life cycle issues—what do you keep, for how long, does its storage status change (online, off-line, microfiche, yes, it still exists)? IT can't make those decisions; only data owners can decide when to get rid of data. In healthcare, many specific types of data have legal retention periods as well.

Just like the tricky part of governance was building culture, the tricky part of information protection is people. Security is ultimately a "people problem" not a technology issue.

Information protection is not only about protecting data but also about understanding data and their usage. Where did the information come into your organization from, who is using it, and how fast is it growing? If you don't understand the data—and who needs them when and how—you cannot apply the appropriate protection to them. You may be overprotecting data that aren't important (remember the March Madness pool spreadsheets?) or worse, you are not protecting data that requires it.

Frequently, people think that information protection is pretty straightforward. That was never really true, but it was certainly truer than it is today. Protection of information has become increasingly complex with the changes in storage and use of data. Information is not just stored in your data center anymore, it is in the cloud and it may not even be your cloud. The consumerization of IT has increased the number of mobile endpoints that you don't own or control but you still have to protect "your" data when they wind up on them or to assure that the information doesn't get to those devices. E-mail contains an enormous amount of ePHI not to mention other critical personal and personnel information and financial data. Those e-mails are often sent to or from noncorporate accounts and wind up stored not only on the end-users' device but also perhaps on servers around the globe.

What data will you encrypt? Encryption represents safe harbor from breach notification in most cases, but at what point do you encrypt it? All mobile media (backup tapes, jump drives, laptops, cell phones, and tablets) should be encrypted, but if it is sent in clear text, how much protection are you getting? Then, there are those SMS or text messages* that now abound between caregivers, employees, and patients.

A huge part of information protection is educating and training the people who collect, use, store, and share that information.

And don't forget that data now live on your fax machines and copiers. So make sure you are eliminating those data before you sell or give the machine away. In April of 2010, the US Department of Health and Human Services settled with Affinity Health Plan, a New York–based managed care plan, for HIPAA violations to the tune of $1,215,780 after a photocopier containing patient information was compromised [1].

* Short Message Service (SMS) is a text messaging service component of phone, Web, or mobile communication systems. It uses standardized communications protocol to allow fixed line or mobile phone devices to exchange short text messages.

Just like the tricky part of governance was building culture, the tricky part of information protection is people. Security is ultimately a "people problem" not a technology issue. No one leaves their house unlocked when they go to work, but they'll leave screens up with information on them. You don't leave your car unlocked in the parking lot, but every day people e-mail to the wrong address, fax to the wrong number, or share passwords. Why do they lock their house and car but don't worry about the information they are responsible for? Well, they don't understand the value of those data and they know exactly what they paid for their car. A huge part of information protection is educating and training the people who collect, use, store, and share that information.

Infrastructure Management and Infrastructure Security and Protection

If you think any technology or number of technologies will "fix" security, you are wrong.

The last two topics in this chapter are infrastructure management and infrastructure security and protection. These are clearly focused on the IT component, but if the organization hasn't addressed governance, secure access, and information protection, frankly, it doesn't matter that much what the IT department is doing. Conversely, if IT is not well managed and doing what they need to do to support the organization's security infrastructure, there is little the organization can do to fix IT except to start over.

Infrastructure management is just what it sounds like—in the vernacular, for IT, that means doing the basic blocking and tackling of managing the technology infrastructure. In this space, not putting the right resources on it is a much larger and more dangerous problem than other sectors of IT. If you think buying an e-mail gateway will keep out all the bad stuff, you are wrong. If you think any antimalware product will catch every piece of malware, you are wrong. If you think any technology or number of technologies will "fix" security, you are wrong.

We all know that our cars will become more expensive to maintain than to replace at some time, so why are CFOs still surprised when you tell them you have to replace the 8-year-old hardware that your EMR is running on?

First, remember that security is a people problem. No PC has ever social engineered its way into a data center. No tablet locked in a drawer has ever clicked on phishing e-mail that compromised the network that it wasn't connected to. People cause security problems—using hardware and software. So the place to start is making sure you understand your hardware and software. That is infrastructure management.

Infrastructure management, from a business strategy perspective, will address life cycle management for both hardware and software. Hardware and software "wear out" or go out of date. This typically happens on some known schedule or window. We all know that our cars will become more expensive to maintain than to replace at some time, so why are CFOs still surprised when you tell them you have to replace the 8-year-old hardware that your EMR is running on? And the operating system on that 8-year-old hardware won't run on the new hardware. And the utility software (backup, fail-over) running on that 8-year-old operating system won't run on the new operating system. Oh, and that 8-year-old EMR application isn't supported anymore and doesn't do what it needs to do anyhow so you need to replace that, too. This can all be planned for from a staffing perspective, from a financial perspective, and from an operational impact and a risk management perspective.

The solution: inventory and track your assets—hardware, software (and remember your information governance group is "inventorying" the data). The data are the most important asset but not an IT infrastructure issue. IT just needs to make sure that they have the data safely stored on some hardware and are providing secure access to them for the appropriate users.

Change management (the IT system management kind, not the people changing their behavior kind) is part of this process, too. You can't upgrade or replace systems or parts of systems (applications, hardware, databases, and storage devices) without planning the changes, scheduling the changes, and working through the implications of those changes and plans to address things if they go wrong through the process. There are still organizations making changes in the production system on Monday morning. Not typically a good time to do that, particularly in healthcare. I won't go into a lot of details here, but if your CIO or his responsible designee can't explain the Change Management process in a way you understand when you ask what it is... find someone who can.

The IT department should have policies around maintenance; yes, even digital, nonmechanical devices need maintenance. Some require more policies than others. Biomedical or clinical engineering does a great job (they are mandated to) monitoring maintenance schedules and "mean time between failures" on medical devices, something that many IT departments could learn from.

We talked about understanding your data, but the same thing applies to devices and software. Remember, you don't usually own the software; you are only licensing it, and if you have more software "deployed" than licensed, it can lead very quickly to an unhappy day and a big bill. You have to know what you have, where it is, and who is using it.

It isn't just the devices—it is the media, too. Where are your tapes going? Are you sure? How long do they stay there, and what happens when you don't need them anymore (or can't mount or read them)?

HIPAA and the Final Omnibus Rule have created an entirely new area for IT to oversee—contracts and business associate management. While IT always had to oversee the IT contracts, they now need to keep an eye on contracts that may not have gone through IT but exist through "shadow IT." Shadow IT may include users or departments that are using cloud-based services or apps to do their work. It may well include sharing data with others regardless of their status as a covered entity, business associate, or just a plain old "contract." Business associates are not new, but the definitions have changed and rules have become stricter, so most covered entities now have more business associates. The stakes for business associates are also steeper. Not only will they be treated as a covered entity in the event of a breach, they will be included in the audit program of the Office of Civil Rights going forward.

Finally, as we move toward ongoing IT operations, we get to things like build, deploy, and maintain procedures. How do you decide to "buy or build," and what are the rules for in-house development of software? How do you know when to unplug a project? That will likely mean you have a project management program or office, and that it is applied to infrastructure projects. How do you measure success and failure, and to whom is that reported? Is there a continuous improvement plan around project management? How are new systems, upgrades, and patches deployed? Is it based on need, on requirements? How do you prioritize which systems get patched and in what order, which get upgraded and why, which are replaced based on new functionality or regulatory requirements? Are maintenance procedures documented to the appropriate level?

Two key areas in infrastructure management are most directly related to security: (1) patch management and (2) log and event management. Even if you don't know what patch management is, you have no doubt heard of it—Microsoft made it famous through its Patch Tuesday.*

Patch Management

Patch management is an area of systems management that involves acquiring, testing, and installing multiple patches (code changes) to a computer system. Patch management tasks include the following:

1. Maintaining current knowledge of available patches
2. Deciding what patches are appropriate for particular systems
3. Ensuring that patches are installed properly
4. Testing systems after installation
5. Documenting all associated procedures, such as specific configurations required

If you don't understand all that, you need to make sure someone who is responsible for patching in IT does.

If you thought patch management was fun, just wait for log and event management! I borrow heavily here from my friends at the National Institute of Standards and Technology. And so should your IT department [2].

Log and Event Management

A log is a record of the events occurring within a computer system or network. A log may be made up of many (hundreds of thousands or even millions) of entries; each entry contains information related to a specific event that has occurred within that system or network. Most logs contain records related to computer security. These logs may be generated by many sources, including security software, firewalls, and intrusion detection and prevention systems, operating systems on servers, workstations, and networking equipment and even the applications themselves.

The number and volume of computer logs have increased greatly, creating the need for log management. Log management is the process for generating, transmitting, storing, analyzing, and disposing of log data—unfortunately, these logs cannot be burned in your fireplace. Log analysis can be beneficial for identifying security incidents, policy violations, fraudulent activity, and operational problems. Logs are also essential when performing audits and forensic analysis. Organizations also may store and use certain logs to assure compliance with Federal laws and regulations, including the Health Insurance Portability and Accountability Act of 1996, the

* Patch Tuesday is an unofficial term used to refer to when Microsoft regularly releases security patches for its software products. It is widely referred to in this way by the industry. Microsoft formalized Patch Tuesday in October of 2003.

Sarbanes–Oxley Act of 2002, the Gramm–Leach–Bliley Act, and the Payment Card Industry Data Security Standard.

A fundamental problem with log management is balancing a limited quantity of storage, analysts, and changing needs with a continuous supply of log data. Log management also involves protecting the confidentiality, integrity, and availability of logs. Probably the biggest issue around log management is making sure that regular analysis of the log data is performed. Lots of organizations have lots of logs and do nothing with them except delete them when they hit their expiration date.

Infrastructure Security and Protection

> Healthcare flows at the speed of trust. Once someone has taken all your information, who is going to trust you? You will cease to exist.

Last but not least is infrastructure security and protection. This is the part of security that is supposed to be "sexy." It is the threat intelligence and security analytics—the tools you see in movies that track down the bad guys and show where they are.

That is in the movies.

There is nothing sexy about security management and infrastructure protection except that if you don't do these things in the future world, your business will simply cease to exist. That's not hyperbole. The bad guys will have all your information, which is not only the currency healthcare runs on but your primary asset. Healthcare flows at the speed of trust. Once someone has taken all your information, who is going to trust you? You will cease to exist.

Threat Landscape Getting Worse

Everyone agrees that the threat landscape in the cyber world is getting worse. Attacks are moving faster, and defenses don't seem to be keeping up. In 2014, targeted attacks increased by 40% over the previous year [3]. In 2015, criminal attacks became, for the first time, the number one root cause of data breaches in healthcare [4]. While healthcare is specifically targeted, the increases are across all business sectors and all business sizes. If you think being small and rural is going to help you avoid being a target, it won't.

You can't hide, and in fact, no defensive technologies can adapt as quickly as the constantly mutating threat landscape. We are faced by highly skilled, well-funded, organized cybercriminals who freely deploy an array of ever-changing tools and tactics to steal your data. The simple, hard truth is that it is not a matter of if but when you will experience an attack. Attacks lead to breaches. What is critical is that your organization knows about it quickly, stops it immediately, and remediates it so it cannot happen again. In order to do that, you need to have the right monitoring tools in place to detect the breach early, but more importantly, these tools need to support the right processes and skilled staff to handle incident management and forensics.

IT and security are now busy trying to manage all that infrastructure (PC, laptops, tablets, cell phone, servers, storage, biomedical devices, software, etc.), and now they've got this ever-changing world of threats. It is too big, too fast, and too dynamic to allow for "informed decisions." Like in the practice of nursing or medicine, there is too much to know in a real-time setting. Clinicians have order sets and clinical decision support. We need to have standing orders for certain "threat diagnoses" and big data sets that help us make decisions about anomalous or previously unknown situations.

Automated Security Risk Management

Continuous monitoring and mitigation allows companies to observe the behavior of networks, systems, applications, and people, and take rapid action to stop problems.

Continuous diagnostics and monitoring was originally a term used in security circles in the federal government. The government is now calling it *discovery and remediation*. Because decision-making around security and compliance should be risk based, maybe a better description is automated security risk management.

This approach uses the built-in ability of computers to monitor and log performance and then use those data against specific standards and known vulnerabilities. It is the digital version of using outcomes measurement to improve outcomes. Measure outcomes to improve care—what a novel idea—it is population health for your data!

The goal is to move away from approaches that are not dynamic, or that are simply reactive and don't provide enough information to make decisions on risk mitigation. Continuous monitoring and mitigation allows companies to observe the behavior of networks, systems, applications, and people, and take rapid action to stop problems.

Healthcare does a great job practicing for emergency situations (plane crashes, chemical spills, even terrorist actions), but we don't "practice" for the cyber emergencies that are, frankly, much more likely to happen (unplanned outages, cyber-attacks, and breaches). It is time to start.

In combination, continuous monitoring and mitigation strategies provide the basis for guiding and shaping cybersecurity strategy and tactics. It can identify, for example, where users need more training on phishing. The approach combines constant automated diagnostic monitoring for anomalous behavior with mitigation strategies that address the most frequently exploited vulnerabilities. In addition to reducing costs associated with manual verification, continuous monitoring will highlight security deficiencies before they can be exploited and more rapidly identify ongoing threats to the environment so they can be stopped before achieving their goals.

Continuous monitoring can help automate cybersecurity functions. It allows organizations to automatically collect data on the behavior of their networks, systems, applications, and people and generate quantifiable data that allow them to identify risks. It lets security verify that their security measures are working—and report that to management. If they are not working, it allows security to "change directions."

> The combination of automated, continuous monitoring and mitigation strategies can reduce costs.

That also means incident response and contingency planning. Healthcare does a great job practicing for emergency situations (plane crashes, chemical spills, even terrorist actions), but we don't "practice" for the cyber emergencies that are, frankly, much more likely to happen (unplanned outages, cyber-attacks, and breaches). It is time to start.

Effective security requires continuous automated monitoring for security problems, immediate access to threat intelligence and other sources of data to be able to identify problems and immediately mitigate them when they are found, and continuous refinement of defenses. While many organizations try to do this in-house, they are only seeing the "bad" stuff coming at *them*. Services that actually gather data from around the globe and from multiple sources have a better perspective on what is really "out in the wild" and its impacts across a broad mixture of hardware,

Figure 10.3 Dr. Mouse gets brave. (Copyright ©2015 David S. Finn. Illustrations by Katy Huggins.)

software, industries, and geographies. These services can screen false positives freeing your own security people to focus on remediation and mitigation rather than on figuring out what is a real virus and what is a new, unrecognized piece of software (see Figure 10.3). The combination of automated, continuous monitoring and mitigation strategies can reduce costs.

Now, if you picked up on those last few words in the preceding paragraph ("reduce costs"), I do have some cautions for you. First, I have made infrastructure security sound fairly simple. It is not. It is incredibly complicated. It cannot be done quickly, cheaply, or without the right skills and a lot of governance, planning, and forethought. This is a new world, especially for healthcare, and no one today has solved all the issues or even knows all the things they should be looking at and correlating it to.

You will still need all the things you have today, such as antimalware and technical audit support, but you will need to start integrating those tools and correlating the information from them. The threat intelligence may come from multiple sources, and what most companies will find is that they cannot staff all these functions on a round-the-clock basis with adequate staffing levels and skill sets. This is not just a healthcare problem; this is a national issue for us. The expertise simply doesn't exist in the workforce today or for the foreseeable future—we must automate threat intelligence, collection, and analysis, and share it broadly. This is where we all must move, personally and professionally, as we enter the post-EMR cyber world.

References

1. http://www.healthcareitnews.com/news/12m-photocopy-breach-proves-costly.
2. NIST Special Publications 800-92: http://csrc.nist.gov/publications/nistpubs/800-92/SP800-92.pdf.
3. 2015 Internet Security Threat Report (ISTR), volume 20. http://www.symantec.com/security_response/publications/threatreport.jsp.
4. "What was the root cause of the healthcare organizations' data breach." Fifth Annual Benchmark Study on Privacy & Security of Healthcare Data, The Ponemon Institute, May 2015.

Chapter 11

Staffing IT for a Post-Live EMR World

J. Scott Joslyn, PharmD, MBA and Brian T. Malec, PhD

"CIOs must face the fact that the HIT workforce of the present is perhaps not ready to be the workforce of the post-EMR implementation future."

The Environment of Today

The world of healthcare IT after widespread rollouts of EMRs is dramatically different from when the huge wave of rollouts began in the wake of Stark Law relaxation, the Affordable Care Act, and Meaningful Use. Understanding staffing IT in a post-live EMR world requires one to first understand the dramatic changes in technology, business, and the workforce that have occurred in parallel with EMR rollouts. These changes markedly affect the current and future work environment and the strategies to staff and manage the IT function. That they happen to coincide with the equally dramatic changes of healthcare transformation only confounds the situation. All of it together creates truly unprecedented disruption. Attracting, retaining, and developing IT talent will most assuredly be a critical component of professional and organizational success for IT leaders and for the success of healthcare delivery organizations.

Business and Technology Drivers in the Post-Live EMR World

Businesses of all types are under continuing and seemingly endless economic pressure in the relentless pursuit of growth, profits, and organizational relevance that are all vital to surviving in a hypercompetitive world. Today, no one can relax or take their eye off the ball. While that has always generally been true, the intensity and pace of business continue to increase as efficiencies and scale are sought to remain competitive and grow. It's a very Darwinian world.

Andy Grove may have said it best. In the title of his book, *Only the Paranoid Survive*,[1] he clearly didn't mean a form of clinical psychoses. He was referring to a mentality required of organizations to survive and thrive beyond *inflection points* that naturally occur in organizations and industry at various points in time. These are periods of perceived stability and comfort that often follow great achievement where there is temptation to rest and reap the rewards of efforts and investment. One could easily argue a successful EMR rollout is such a situation. An inflection point in an organization that has just gone through an EMR rollout would indeed look like the period of stabilization and celebration that ensues right after activation. The world doesn't stand still, however; certainly not healthcare. The business of business is intensely serious in this century. One can expect with each day greater speed, greater complexity, and more competition. Not just in healthcare, but everywhere.

We also happen to live in a "digital economy" today where everyone and everything is connected. The "Internet of Things" (IoT) is happening before our very eyes to ends that can only be imagined. View your home, control its temperature, and water the lawn while vacationing overseas. Jog a few miles and automatically track your heart rate, distance covered, calories burned, and trend the data over time. These everyday capabilities are already enabling interesting healthcare applications when it comes to wellness or extending care of patients to the home. Where this all goes can only be imagined.

Rapidly advancing technology is both enabling and threatening. "Enabling" in that it provides a key ingredient to innovation. "Disruptive" as innovations intrude upon and potentially displace established players. Such is now understood by all as *disruptive innovation*, a term coined by Clayton Christensen, which describes a process whereby a product or service takes root at the bottom of a market and then moves "up market," threatening the status quo of established players. Or simply, but dramatically, changing the way things have always been done.[2] A new paradigm, "eVisits" are a perfect example in healthcare where a virtual patient visit can be accomplished via computers and the Internet, or smartphones and cellular service.

The confluence of social media, mobile technology, and cloud computing is cited by Gartner as a "nexus of forces" that fundamentally change how nearly everything is done in society, how people work together, and the expectations of what's possible.[3] These forces are affecting organizations as they affect individuals and society. They are the key ingredients of disruption that stem from the *creative application* of technology in various forms, and it all flows from and to the IT function to create and support these capabilities in partnership with the business.

A lot of new C-suite titles and roles are emerging in the digital economy: Chief Digital Officer, Chief Data Officer, Chief Transformation Officer, Chief Privacy Officer, Chief Strategy Officer, Chief Innovation Officer, and so on. These positions may report to the CIO or work alongside that person. Either way, they change the nature of the "traditional" CIO role. They may make the job bigger and create competitive roles with potentially overlapping functions. These roles are also possible career paths for both IT and business leaders. They are real functions regardless of label and reporting, and they reflect the complexity of business and its interactions with technology.

Technology is also changing today's workforce in and outside of IT. People are becoming more knowledgeable of technology and competent and comfortable with its use. They see it as increasingly relevant in their personal lives, if not a necessity to everyday living. Individuals expect to see and use technology in their organizations. For example, a "bring your own device" (BYOD) movement (and the associated operational challenges it brings to IT) springs from an increasing penetration of smartphones in society. Things such as BYOD and the like continuously and insidiously emerge on the scene. As a result, the view and expectations of the IT function change and, by implication, the skills necessary in IT for the support that is expected. All of these forces affect healthcare, itself in the midst of transformation, as shown in Figure 11.1.

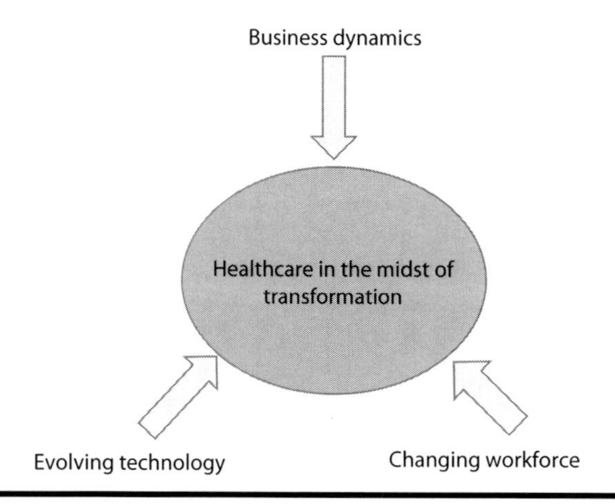

Figure 11.1 The forces impinging on healthcare.

A Labor Supply in Flux

The size and makeup of the workforce are changing, in and outside healthcare, in and outside technology. A perennial concern is the number of workers, their educational levels, and attitudes toward work. Various data point to a coming labor shortage as a result of a broad demographic shift. People are retiring; the oldest of the Baby Boomers are now 69 and leaving the workforce. Roughly 10,000 Baby Boomers will turn 65 today, and approximately 10,000 more will cross that threshold every day for the next 19 years.[4] The Census Bureau estimates that in the next 10 years, the population of people 65 and older will increase by 37.8%. The population of those aged 18 to 64 will rise by only 3.2%, and those aged 18 to 24 will actually decrease in number.[5]

The emergence of Millennials will also factor into IT staffing. Older generations have tended to glorify hard work as a virtue in and of itself. Millennials tend to only value work insofar as it creates results or fosters personal growth. Millennials want to see the impact of and enjoy a return for their efforts. Millennials also leave jobs more easily to pursue other ones and have different expectations about "climbing the career ladder." However, who can blame them? Any loyalty to the worker has all but disappeared in this century as businesses seek all means of agility and flexibility as it concerns labor along with virtually all other aspects of the business, for example, supply chain.

That Millennials tend to be more interested in finding meaning and purpose in their work is quite relevant. Large numbers of them want to work for a socially responsible or ethical company, potentially favoring the healthcare sector. They tend to be self-confident, creative, optimistic, energetic, social minded, and highly innovative. These characteristics can reap huge rewards for IT leaders who can attract and retain such individuals.

On another front, the foreign-born population of the United States has changed dramatically in the last 50 years. This population accounted for 1 in 20 in 1960; today, it is approximately 1 in 8.[6] The educational and cultural backgrounds of these individuals are different from those born and raised in the United States. This diversity is a good thing in a world where ideas and creativity matter, and where education and experiences span a broader range. At the same time, IT and other managers will need to be mindful of how this diversity might affect the culture and interaction among a very different workforce.

The Forces within Healthcare

Healthcare is in the midst of a massive transformation that will depend heavily on IT and IT leadership. The largest driving force in healthcare is payment reform as a result of the passage of the Patient Protection and Affordable Care Act (ACA). Fundamentally, it is a transition from volume-based to value-based reimbursement that broadly links reimbursement to outcomes. Along with the ACA came the advancement by the Institute for Healthcare Improvement of the "Triple Aim," which it expresses as a goal to simultaneously improving the health of populations, enhancing the experience and outcomes of the patient, and reducing per capita cost of care for the benefit of communities.

Think about ACA and the Triple Aim as it concerns IT. So much effort has gone into legacy revenue cycle programs to perfect billing and ensure reimbursement in a fee-for-service world. To be sure, those systems and support structures will still be needed. But in a world headed toward forms of global capitation, the tilt is toward activities and costs (see Michael W. Davis' Chapter 12, "The Brave New World of Fee-for-Value Reimbursement"). That will change processes, systems, and what needs to be tallied. Whole new systems will be needed to measure outcomes while the definition and depth of what outcomes actually mean evolve. Such things significantly affect workforce skills, for example, the mid-career IT worker who may need to reskill and match technology and business needs in completely new ways.

It was the HITECH Act of 2009 and the Triple Aim that really spurred increased adoption of EMRs, but their value had long been recognized. EMRs and CPOE were rightly touted as key solutions to patient safety issues.[7] The transformation from paper-based toward paperless medicine was deemed both safer and necessary if an individual's medical information was to be available and essentially complete as to content regardless of time or venue.[8–10] The EMR was the foundation technology of this transformation. Many organizations either have finished or are midstream with first-time EMR rollouts or replacements of older systems. Certainly, a critical mass of healthcare organizations has accomplished successful EMR rollouts and is exchanging healthcare information with other organizations on behalf of patients, and this large bolus of work has been completed in a relatively short period—effectively all at once as it affects, for example, educational curriculums.

The Fallout of EMR Implementations and Changed Expectations

EMRs themselves have changed the environment as they have been developed, promoted, and rolled out. Governance and senior leaders often set expectations for a return on an EMR investment. That typically meant specific goals or targets with tangible or intangible financial benefits. In turn, that meant a need to capture and measure results. Also, along with the HITECH Act of 2009 came billions of dollars of incentives to install EMRs—the reason for the crescendo of rollouts. With those incentives came great expectations known as *Meaningful Use*. EMRs could not just be bought. They had to be used in meaningful ways, which meant achieving certain results.

Meaningful Use was and continues to be a set of moving targets, or *Stages*. Besides moving through the Stages of Meaningful Use, there is as with any IT system investment always the function of maintenance. That runs the gamut of fixes, new modules, new releases, and wholesale upgrades. Meaningful Use is making that maintenance very prescriptive. Thus, implementing an EMR turned out not be a matter of just getting the EMR "slammed in," as this book title highlights. It was get it in and start moving down a path of expanded and prescribed use, a process that has come to be known as "optimization" (see Doug Eastman's Chapter 1, "The User Experience:

An Underexploited Opportunity"). All at a pace set by Meaningful Use regulations that both EMR vendors and customers alike find daunting. More speed.

Apart from Meaningful Use, it is a fact that current-generation EMRs generally cover a broader scope of functions, are more complex to support, and are far more capable. They have much greater functional depth than earlier generations of the EMR. As a result, they create a whole new set of opportunities to affect healthcare in positive ways when fully exploited and adopted. More can and should be done with a never-ending series of new features and functions that spew forth from EMR vendors through periodic upgrades. The result is that expectations expand. What was required of IT to successfully implement an EMR is very different in terms of skills and organization than what is required to operate, exploit, and optimize it. More pressure.

So Much Less Clarity Ahead in Healthcare

> Many organizations slammed in an EMR system, in part to get some incentive funds prescribed under Meaningful Use and partly to look like they knew what they were doing to support the future of healthcare reform.

A somewhat less obvious business and IT challenge looking forward doesn't really stem from the EMR, but rather the contrast with what it was to accomplish an EMR rollout versus what now needs to be done in healthcare.

The aspirations of the EMR implementation initiative might have wanted to mirror the moon landing that President Kennedy proposed, to land a man on the moon and return. However, the circumstances were very different. For the EMR initiative, while there were clear goals, these were not supported by precise trajectory and mathematics for a moon landing. There was not the single leadership managing the process from beginning to end. The workforce for the moon landing was committed and supportive of technology. The workforce charged with implementing the EMR was and is fragmented at best in terms of knowledge of what to do. Many organizations slammed in an EMR system, in part to get some incentive funds prescribed under Meaningful Use and partly to look like they knew what they were doing to support the future of healthcare reform. If we need a better analogy, then EMR implementation is like sending off a rocket with limited fuel to try to reach the moon and now trying to figure how to build a rescue rocket to save the day before it crashes into the sun.

> The healthcare industry is generally labeling the "how" of transformation as "population health," but it is translating it in the short run to grossly mean "intense efforts to lower costs by any and all means."

The technologies used to build EMRs have been around since the late 1960s and early 1970s. They have existed since the days Lockheed developed the Technicon System that was piloted in the 1970s at El Camino Hospital in Mountain View, California. Notably, the Technicon System was predicated on CPOE, direct entry of orders by physicians—40 years ago. Today's EMRs are eminently more capable and complex, but the principles and goals are the same.

The key success factors in both going to the moon and installing EMRs required disciplined execution devoted to an explicit set of unambiguous goals. In strong contrast, we simply do not have that clarity on the road ahead in healthcare.

To be clear, the comparison here is about goals, not execution. Payment reform is unclear beyond its implied goal of more out and less in, better value as it is often expressed. In fact, the term *value* shows up all over in discussions of healthcare payment reform and transformation.

The healthcare industry is generally labeling the "how" of transformation as "population health," but it is translating it in the short run to grossly mean "intense efforts to lower costs by any and all means." Externally, the market is simply lowering prices through brute force—lower reimbursement by government and commercial payers. The challenges lie in the response that is inherently varied by the multitude, variety, and interaction among all the players in the healthcare space. It happens to also be a highly regulated and very personal place once the tables are turned, and one becomes not a player, but a consumer of healthcare services that may have life or death consequences. The challenges to creativity and innovation could not be higher, and IT will be critical and central to all of it.

The bottom line is that the work ahead is difficult and not as clear as an EMR implementation with all its dysfunction and ambiguity. Services need to be redesigned and processes need to be refined and reorganized, if not eliminated altogether. In the long run, a completely different model of healthcare delivery is needed. New skills and new leadership strategies are needed in and outside the IT function to move toward that aspiration. The culture and expected competencies of the present and future healthcare workforce will need to include the skills and tools to formulate strategies, propose solutions, implement new systems, and ensure their effective use and adoption while maintaining or improving productivity, all the while continually measuring and reporting results.

The Convergence of Forces on IT

IT leaders will most certainly need to think differently, act differently, manage differently, and staff differently.

The reality of the foregoing is that forces of business, technology, workforce, healthcare, government, politics, and society all converge upon IT. IT leaders will most certainly need to think differently, act differently, manage differently, and staff differently.

A great example of the result of converged forces is "Big Data." IT resources will need to be expanded to accommodate the sheer volume of new data from systems such as EMRs, devices such as Fitbits, and that which literally spews from the IoT. Healthcare organizations now sit atop new, vast stores of structured and unstructured medical information with their EMRs. The informational content of such stores is a vital asset, relevant well beyond its transactional value. These data can be "mined" to understand the health of populations (recall Triple Aim), what works and what doesn't when it comes to treatment, disease processes such as diabetes, risk profiles of a population or disease cohort, and the understanding necessary to survive the world of "population health."

The analytics necessary to pursue population health represents a whole new set of skills and roles that are vital to the healthcare enterprise that must take on additional risk of value-based healthcare services delivery. Those services span not only treatment but also health and wellness, disease prevention and delay, managing disease and mitigating its ravages, maintaining the quality of life as long as possible, and ultimately the passage of life. This pursuit takes the contemporary, forward-looking healthcare organization out of traditional venues of treatment and into mobile spaces and the home—and IT along with it.

Population health could be subdivided into two broad capabilities. One is devoted to groups of patients—populations. Within that, various cohorts exist, such as those with diabetes or chronic kidney disease. For populations, it is necessary to understand an overall risk profile as to their forecasted aggregate healthcare costs. That comes from understanding the risk profiles of the various cohorts such as diabetics along with overall demographics. It is also necessary to understand among possible treatment regimens, for example, medication therapy, what works and to what degree. It is also vital to know what doesn't work and therefore represents waste. With that understanding comes insights into best practices and the information necessary to power clinical decision support tools.

The second category is all that pertains to a single patient. The ability to assemble the essence of what is known about a patient regardless of data source into a virtual record is important to care management. It is most effectively done in the native workflow of the caregiver, for example, the EMR of the primary care physician, at the point of care. In fact, if not in the native workflow, for example, the physician's EMR, the extra effort to gather information via other tools at the time of need simply won't be done.

The two functions of population health are shown in Figure 11.2. The whole subject of population health is addressed in Chapter 14. However population is defined, the functions listed in the figure in the two general intelligence pursuits require IT support. They go beyond the EMR; some are actually enabled by the EMR. To the extent these are new and different functions, they mean new, more, and different IT roles and skills.

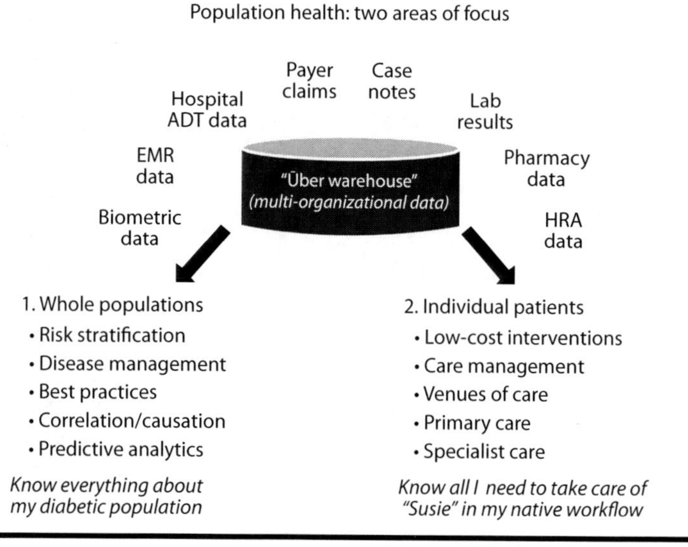

Figure 11.2 The new world of population health.

IT Staffing and Management Strategies

> The future workforce will have to be competent and comfortable working in an environment of population health that is only just beginning to be defined and will reach well beyond the "four walls" of hospitals and clinics to populations in the community.

CIOs must face the fact that the HIT workforce of the present is perhaps not ready to be the workforce of the post-EMR implementation future. The HIT job descriptions 10 years from now will be very different from those we have today. Retraining the current IT workforce to take on new or expanded tasks and responsibilities must be done. Expanding the IT workforce with individuals from other industries or new graduates from academic institutions will help forestall talent shortages.

The future workforce will have to be competent and comfortable working in an environment of population health that is only just beginning to be defined and will reach well beyond the "four walls" of hospitals and clinics to populations in the community. These populations will be connected to providers by home-based and mobile wearable devices that transmit information back to the care team. A whole new orientation to what healthcare IT means will be required.

Organizations will need IT professionals with skills in process reengineering, Lean manufacturing techniques, change management (the human kind), and workflow expertise among other skills to adapt healthcare delivery services to new models of business and get caregivers and other employees to adapt to those models. As an example, data analytics will emerge as a specialized profession with quantitative and statistical knowledge and skills to transform and understand the vast amount of information generated by EMRs[11] and other systems in the care delivery or ACO environment.

Management Imperatives

> CIOs will need to inspire and foster IT innovations to drive breakthroughs in care coordination, disease management, patient engagement, clinician productivity, and overall organizational effectiveness.

IT leaders will have as many opportunities as challenges in the years ahead. Greater value will be sought from IT investments. IT leaders will need to strongly link their recommendations to value propositions, and in business terms. Commodity IT services, infrastructure, and basic support services will need to be driven to the lowest possible cost levels to reduce operating costs and direct spending to that which is more closely linked to revenue. Cost-saving sourcing strategies will need to be pursued.

Innovation will be an increasing differentiator for organizations. CIOs will need to inspire and foster IT innovations to drive breakthroughs in care coordination, disease management, patient engagement, clinician productivity, and overall organizational effectiveness. They will need to ensure that IT understands the needs of individuals and how they work together all across the organization. IT is, in fact, in the perfect position to facilitate mobility, social interaction, and teamwork through innovative work practices. IT can and should help surmount barriers between business and IT, bringing business knowledge into IT, while simultaneously supporting IT activities outside the domain of the IT department.

IT leaders will need to:

- Possess an in-depth knowledge of the business beyond IT
- Collaborate with business to a far greater degree, oversee multifunctional teams, and facilitate change
- Understand key business drivers for IT decisions in areas such as finance, clinical practice, marketing, business development, and customer relationship management
- Elucidate and redraw the evolving boundaries between IT and business, and tolerate a much blurrier line between IT and functions outside of IT
- Screen, sort, and select from among a multitude of technologies those that are relevant and differentiating for the organization
- Organize and lead innovation efforts
- Revamp and revitalize analytical jobs and incorporate skills such as Lean
- Add new jobs such as the data scientist
- Bring more clinicians into IT and also add staff with nontechnical degrees and skills

Basic Staffing Strategies

Healthcare will have to compete with technology employers like Google and Silicon Valley that provide innovative environments for a talented IT workforce.

Healthcare organizations have traditionally been volume-centric, fee-for-service entities. While ambulatory care and physicians in private practice have always existed, the face of healthcare up until recently has been the hospital. As the view and perception of healthcare has changed, so must the strategies to staff the IT function of a changing healthcare industry.

First and foremost, IT leaders will need to create an environment and culture where people want to work. That is generally a place where teamwork is valued and collaboration is the norm, and not just within IT but between IT and the business. The various strategies of creating a "great place to work" environment are well articulated in books, articles, and meetings on the subject. They are beyond the scope of this chapter and all that need be said is that there will be no long-term successful staffing strategy without an enticing environment conducive to collaboration and teamwork. Healthcare will have to compete with technology employers like Google and Silicon Valley that provide innovative environments for a talented IT workforce. A solid work environment and culture must be established and maintained by IT and, for that matter, the business. It is one of the surest ways IT managers can attract, engage, and retain talent that will be in short supply.

Softer skills matter as much if not more than technical skills, and it is vital to imbue staff with soft skills to accompany technical skills.

A major step in a strategy to staff the IT function for the future of healthcare is to invest in the existing workforce through education and training. Talented people have exited EMR rollouts. In many cases, staffing gaps can be filled by augmenting the skills of those in place or who had EMR implementation-related roles.

Keeping up with the IT field in general and with healthcare transformation will be essential, either through advanced education, certification, or in-service training. Most likely, it will require a combination of all three. CIOs must invest more time and resources into workforce development and set a strategic direction for that workforce. At the same time, IT leaders must continuously reinforce the need to be comfortable with change and quickly changing environments.

Softer skills matter as much if not more than technical skills, and it is vital to imbue staff with soft skills to accompany technical skills. IT projects typically fail because of lack of leadership, participation, change, and collaboration—the "soft" skills—more than outright failure attributed to technical skills. These tactics are important for both staff and managers, and all team members will appreciate the attention and investment in them by the organization.

Investing in staff does, of course, risk their departure for other organizations. That is no argument to avoid the effort. It is one good reason to have a solid partnership with the human resources function to ensure that:

- Individuals are adequately compensated and that their salaries keep pace with their accumulated skills
- Job descriptions are revised and expanded in accordance with new roles and responsibilities
- Recruitment efforts are effectively and adequately supported to fill vacancies and new jobs
- Salary, benefits, and other comparative data are sought and analyzed to establish and maintain a competitive pay and benefit structure
- Managers are supported in addressing ineffective and poorly performing people who otherwise put a drag on productivity and the performance of teams
- Programs are developed to entice older folks to postpone retirement
- Mechanisms exist to outsource labor via consultants, contract labor forces, or through vendors of various services, for example, SaaS or Cloud computing
- Citizens of other countries can be employed though special visa programs

---

"Bright empty heads" in the right environment, given the right training and opportunities, can be a tremendous source of talent.

Another way to boost staff capacity short of just adding positions is augment IT by leveraging the staff outside of IT. IT leaders can and should extend the experience and precedent of EMR rollouts and continue to get work done through others. It's often possible to retain at least part-time dedication of resources external to IT that joined the EMR project. Their knowledge and ongoing connection to the business are vital ingredients of collaboration and effectiveness—a clear focus on what is needed and how something might be done.

IT managers must get more comfortable with growing talent rather than chasing experience when filling new positions. For one thing, experience is hard to find. For another, it is expensive, and for the sake of the greater good, robbing staff from another organization is a vicious cycle. It is wise and, to a degree, unavoidable to grow talent from the ground up, so to speak. This is true in recruiting staff from within the business that may require training with a specific system or basic analytical skills.

A big talent pool is new graduates, and not necessarily those with technical degrees or skills. "Bright empty heads" in the right environment, given the right training and opportunities, can be a tremendous source of talent. To be sure, it takes time, patience, and mentorship by others. Time passes quickly, however, and an ongoing influx of newly minted graduates into the right talent-growing infrastructure will soon produce needed staff on a continuous basis.

Help from Educational Institutions

Professional association certification and credentialing as well as vendor certification are a valuable resource for individuals to advance in their careers and for organizations to be confident in the skills and knowledge levels of their employees. While some have sprung up in the wake of EMR rollouts, HIMSS, American Health Information Management Association (AHIMA), Epic, Cerner, and many other associations and vendors have a long track record of providing a wide range of educational and professional opportunities.[12]

Academic institutions are expanding HIT and health informatics programs at many levels. Community colleges have traditionally offered job-ready programs in a wide range of IT-related areas. Some of these programs were supported by the HITECH Act of 2009, which provided resources to develop educational modules related to EMR adoption and implementation. The goals were to provide a job-ready workforce to assist in the expansion of EMR adoption. The modules commissioned by the ONC, are currently managed by American Medical Informatics Association (AMIA) and can be accessed at http://knowledge.amia.org/onc-ntdc.

Growth in bachelors and masters programs in health informatics and HIT is adding to the IT talent pool, acknowledging and addressing the HIT workforce needs of the industry. It can hardly be fast enough. A related strategy that is emerging is the partnership between academia and the healthcare industry to provide internships for students and also to recruit current employees back to school to pursue advanced degrees. Internships are a terrific way to "try" new people, that is, for both the individual and the organization to try each other to ensure good fit. The AUPHA received grant funding from HIMSS and Siemens US Healthcare to develop graduate-level modules in HIT education. These modules, in part, elevated the HITECH-related ONC modules from entry-level knowledge and skills to graduate level. These modules are free to download and can be found at http://network.aupha.org/himsta.

In-house training programs are an emerging organizational strategy as they concern HIT to advance the skills and knowledge of their current workforce. Such programs can be accelerated through partnership with academia and professional associations. The ONC and Health Information Management Systems Technology and Analysis (HIMSTA) modules are potentially a very useful resource for institutional in-service training.

Basic Skills and Roles That Will Evolve into the Future

While programming and technical skills will continue to be at the base of many HIT workers, (not all) advances in these areas will be supplemented with a clearer connection to the end product, the consumer, and the public as a whole.

HIT workers will need to be more collaborative in their approach to solving problems and working with other individuals with vastly different backgrounds.

It is important to realize that a number of IT roles remain unchanged and essential to IT service delivery. They represent a core set of skills that have stood the test of time as to need and applicability. As we move into the era of post-EMR implementation, it is important to understand to what extent the skills, knowledge, and soft skills of these traditional roles and functions remain the same and where and how they change in the future. Regardless, keeping up with the IT field will be essential through advanced education, certification, or in-service training, most likely a combination of all three. Organizations will be investing more time and resources into workforce development and strategic directions *for* that workforce. The HIT workers of the future will have to be comfortable with change and quickly changing environments. While programming and technical skills will continue to be at the base of many HIT workers, (not all) advances in these areas will be supplemented with a clearer connection to the end product, the consumer, and the public as a whole. In other words, why we do what we do.

HIT workers will need to be more collaborative in their approach to solving problems and working with other individuals with vastly different backgrounds. The HIT worker will be a team player, and fostering those skills will be the job of in-service education or perhaps external degrees and advanced certifications. Strategic workforce development plans will be essential to foster communication skills at all levels in the organization and build a workforce that is comfortable with new roles. Personal attributes are sometimes the hardest to enhance, but curiosity and engagement in the mission of the organization will help achieve the goals of the post-EMR world.

IT will always need strong analysts with good communication skills, both written and verbal, as well as good people skills.

Other attributes of the future HIT worker, according to Dave Garets and John Glaser,[11] include the following:

- Understanding the expansion of the reach of the care provider into home health and population health via the use of telemedicine and other mobile technologies.
- Incorporating data analytics and outcome assessment into all aspects of HIT.
- Concerted focus on process improvement at all levels of the HIT workforce.

- Having a focus on connectivity and interoperability; connecting to the community, the patient, and other care providers.
- "For individuals interested in tech fields who also have a desire to give back to their community, healthcare information technology will offer great fulfillment."

The following are some examples of skills that will continue to be needed and enhanced: **Systems analysts** are needed to solve problems, untangle issues, and improve ideas with systems thinking that lead to potential solutions—the familiar role of healthcare IT in automating and improving the flow of work. Systems analysts can help identify and define solutions that will maximize the value delivered by an organization to its stakeholders. Continuing to exploit and derive greater value from technology investments will always be a key goal.

Good analysts also occupy the role of change agents who can help identify and articulate the needs and opportunities, and the necessary changes to address them. Clearly, a leading role as change agent is fundamental to what is happening in healthcare.

Systems analysts also work across all levels of an organization. They have an opportunity to be involved with everything from defining strategy, to creating the enterprise architecture, to taking a leadership role by defining the goals and requirements for programs and projects. In many ways, analysts are the face and ambassadors of IT that bring strong logic and thinking skills to new or intractable problems. IT will always need strong analysts with good communication skills, both written and verbal, as well as good people skills.

PMOs present an incredible way for IT staff to partner with the organization beyond IT in various areas of the business.

Project management absolutely endures as a critical skill and service. In fact, organizations can be somewhat abstractly viewed as a series and combination of projects—in perpetuity. Thus, project management will remain an ongoing need.

A key reason project management is so important is that projects bring monetary and strategic risk to the organization. The EMR could not be a better example. EMR rollouts are big and complex. They involve staff of all educational backgrounds and responsibilities and impose large amounts of change on the organization. That such skills will be needed for follow-on business initiatives with an IT component is without question. Experience is showing that rollouts of modern EMRs are followed by an ongoing series of projects related to expansion, optimization, and maintenance efforts. That which emanates from population health is sure to be also complex and risky, if not big. Thus, a solid and ongoing project management foundation must remain in place.

Large-scale EMR efforts bring a staffing dividend. These projects conclude—to the extent they truly conclude—with a professional team that can operate at the scale of the organization, and IT often has the deepest skills when it comes to project management. Further, with projects all over the organization, there is a strong argument for establishment of a project management office (PMO). Often they already exist, some as the result of the EMR rollout. They are arguably a vital function for the organization and a service that can naturally flow from IT.

PMOs present an incredible way for IT staff to partner with the organization beyond IT in various areas of the business. PMOs build relationships that grow when subsequent projects emerge. Project teams often include people who don't usually work together—sometimes from different organizations and across multiple geographies. Such is the genesis of teams, teamwork, and new relationships. Leadership by IT staff in business projects broaden IT's understanding of the business with opportunities to learn and share knowledge. That increases the ability of IT staff to add value, provides critical visibility to the spectrum of IT talent, and can only increase overall collaboration with the business over time.

New Jobs and Roles

> The next professional skill set hill to climb, at least for some systems analysts with the right interest and aptitude, is one of deep skills associated with **workflow**.

Some specific new skills are needed going forward. For example, cost pressures have led to a growing incorporation of **Lean thinking and Lean principles** into healthcare organizations. Addressed in detail in Chapter 5, Lean is essentially about removing waste in various forms such as queues, inventories, and non–value-added process steps. Lean is about developing and introducing *standard work* that makes production repeatable. It is about relentlessly examining and improving processes.

Lean is as much a mentality as it is a set of techniques that is most effective when it is embedded into the culture of the organization. Lean invariably involves the IT organization, and for the sake of this chapter, it affects the expectations, functions, and skill mix of IT staff. Not far from traditional systems analysis, "Lean Fellows" now make up part of the IT and business team.

Interestingly, systems analysis might be one of those things at an inflection point. The next professional skill set hill to climb, at least for some systems analysts with the right interest and aptitude, is one of deep skills associated with **workflow**. Hardly any function or skill could be more important to healthcare transformation. Lean and workflow are inherently related. Training staff in the Lean methods and workflow tools is a perfect example of growing staff as discussed above.

Taking workflow a step further, combining technical understanding and management principles, the role of management engineer has reemerged in healthcare. Formal undergraduate and graduate degrees in management engineering deliver professionals that integrate the skills of analysis, workflow, technology, and project management. This is a high value-added role to tackle the thorny and complex workflows of today's healthcare system that has way too much friction and wasted energy.

It nearly goes without saying that the future includes an increasing role for **medical, nursing, and other clinicians** involved with the use and application of technology. The combination of clinical and technological expertise within individuals gained real momentum with the rollout of EMRs. While some clinicians returned to traditional practice roles, others remained in an IT function to support the maintenance, growth, and adoption of the EMR. As the footprint of the EMR widens and as healthcare services transcend the home and other venues, more of these "informaticists" will be needed. They will come from clinical, medical records, administration, public health, and epidemiological backgrounds to bring an intimate knowledge of medicine—treatment, diagnosis, and follow-up as example elements of population health programs.

In the fast-moving world of HIT adoption and implementation, the workforce will be faced with the time-consuming realities of actually **measuring the expected future economic and**

noneconomic benefits of IT implementations, managing those expectations, and continuing to evaluate the achievement of what was the original expectation of the IT investment. The workforce will need to be trained and have special skills to measure, evaluate, and manage EMRs. These systems are by their nature expensive and the selection and implementation alone is a long process with many dimensions and perhaps competing expectations.

From the initial business plan to a fully functional EMR integrated into the workflow of the organization, there is a need to measure achievement of goals and to hold administration accountable to managing the outcomes. A workforce that can see outside the box will recognize that EMRs can improve organizational efficiency, reduce redundant cost, reduce errors, reduce readmissions, increase provider and patient satisfaction, perhaps increase revenue and market share, and provide the necessary structure for population health strategies. The skill set for these positions will require financial knowledge, process and systems workflow skills, Lean and Six Sigma tools, and communication skills to validate the return on investment in EMRs. These individuals will probably come internally but will need to develop the perspective and credibility to achieve their goals.

Integrated delivery systems, with multiple hospital facilities, are no longer going to be in the business of running a hospital; they will be population health organizations that need the revenue of the facility side of the organization to manage populations of people who never come to the hospital. The workforce that will be needed in IT departments and other areas of the organization will have to have the knowledge and skills to work with vast amounts of data that will be gathered and stored in large databases. Professionals with skills and knowledge of "Big Data" and "Data Analytics" are, and will be, in short supply. These individuals may come with backgrounds in public health and epidemiology or evolve from systems analysts or other quantitative disciplines, but they will need to understand context of the healthcare environment and political and social pressures to meet community needs. The role of these analysts will be to extract from the databases meaningful outcomes, both clinical and administrative, to achieve organizational and community goals.

Such is the **data scientist**, a role that has gained considerable notoriety and press in and outside of healthcare[13] (see Richard F. Gibson's Chapter 9, "Business Intelligence Reporting and Analytics: Tools, Resources, and Governance"). Roles in this space have emerged to gain a better understanding of your business, from supply chain to operations to customers that are possible from either massively large datasets or simply streams of data from transaction systems.

Although the title may be new, the role has existed in some fashion. Today, it is more about the scale of the role, the deep skills that are needed, and its increasingly vital role to the business. Also, new technologies like Hadoop provide orders of magnitude more powerful statistical and reporting capabilities. In many cases, highly specialized skills are not required to explore and manipulate data sets. However, installation, training, and support of various analytics tools are often the domain of IT and another area of key partnership with the business in a continuum of skills from highly technical to end-user business specialists working with visualization tools.

Conclusions

The bottom line is that new skills are needed, and IT management must organize, recruit, and lead in new ways.

Converging forces are at work that are dramatically changing the way business operates, the nature of work, the sources and supply of labor, and the impact of increasingly powerful and mobile technology on the lives of everyone in and outside of work. These forces and the responses to them are at work in all industries. At the same time, the business of healthcare is transforming under incredible economic and regulatory pressures. This environmental milieu ultimately drives and determines the need for IT and the roles IT staff must play.

The IT function is as much on the receiving end of these rapidly evolving business dynamics as much of IT and technology helps drive and enable the responses of business to its customers and competitors. The bottom line is that new skills are needed, and IT management must organize, recruit, and lead in new ways. As daunting as these challenges are, there has never been a better time for IT to partner with business for all that needs to be done to transform healthcare. For those with the aptitude and desire, there has never been a better time to enter the workforce or change one's career in the direction of healthcare IT.

Finally, IT must begin and end with the business. IT leaders must ensure that IT be seen as a means, and not an end. It's no silver bullet; it never will be. That said, there are very few areas where there is success without its application.

Appendix

Four Examples of Emerging Skill Sets You'll Require in Your Future HIT Workforce

Health care executives and organizations, if they have not learned, need to learn that you can't just buy HIT and plug it in and expect it to produce the expected results. It was an explicit element of Meaningful Use to actually use the EMRs meaningfully to the end goal of improving health care and not just buying a system and turning it on. Now, with many having gone through the challenges of not having the workforce skills to actually create a meaningful use of the data, a new vista has emerged, and it is the morass of data that collects within these systems as a by-product of their use and, now obvious to most, in an era of population health.

The chapters in this book have expertly discussed the initiatives and innovation that are emerging and will continue to emerge. The workforce characteristics needed to advance those initiatives are also emerging but are in short supply. For example, some current job descriptions for a Big Data Analyst requires 5 to 7 years of experience performing data analytics and reports, perhaps an SQL certificate, advanced Excel skills, experience creating complex data mining algorithms, leadership skills, and perhaps a masters or more advanced certification. Not too many around that meet those qualifications.

Planning for the future healthcare world and the various initiatives discussed in the book will require workforce development strategies. As already indicated in this chapter, those skills will come from partnerships with academic institutions, in-house focused development programs, and hiring from the consulting world. IT leaders will need to understand the challenges of finding the future HIT workforce and they need to focus on how their organization develops and attracts the skills required.

To help put healthcare workforce HIT needs in perspective, the following is a futuristic look at a few emerging career paths and the job skills, education, experience, and other attributes employers expect to be performed effectively in these positions. The perspective is an extrapolation of trends and job descriptions found in *Careers in Health Information Technology* by Brian Malec (Springer Publishing, 2014).

Business Intelligence and Analytics

In the BI and Data Analytics future space, we will find a great need for individuals with the following attributes: proven ability working with complex data to create analytical insight and deliver business value; an undergraduate degree in a technical field but also a master in business or health administration: certifications are probably a part of the professional development of a BI professional; and evidence of leadership and people management skills and communication skills. The following are two current certificates that will enhance the resume of an individual seeking a future position in business intelligence:

- An example: Certified Business Intelligence Professional (CBIP) from http://www.tdwi.org
  - http://tdwi.org/pages/education/cbip-certification/cbip-home.aspx
- Also an entry-level IBM Certified Associate Business Process Analyst
  - http://www-03.ibm.com/certify/certs/58000203.shtml

In this analytical space, the role of business intelligence will be to create structured information from a variety of data warehouses to create predictive and perhaps, most importantly, prescriptive modeling to support both strategic and operational management of healthcare organizations.

We will also see professional career development for the range of skills that support the BI leader, such as database administrators, report writers, visualization analysts, data architects, trainers, and data scientists. Upward career mobility in this space will be very important to develop individuals who understand where the data are coming from and what is important to the organization to achieve its organizational mission and strategic goals.

Data Analytics or Big Data Analyst

IT Data Analytics or Big Data Analyst is probably more entry level than the BI professional. They will have to have a lot of analytical experience and to not just be comfortable with computer software but to master analytical tools such as SQL and Excel as well. These individuals might have degrees in biostatistics or IT, but most likely it will be beneficial to also have a degree in a health-related field so that they understand what they do as an analyst benefits the management and mission of an organization. The individuals in this analytics role will be responsible for making sense of data that one would think is complete and comprehensive, but in reality perhaps is riddled with garbage, thus the old saying "GIGO" or garbage-in, garbage-out. These individuals will have to augment their clinical and analytical skills with interpersonal and communication skills to present complex analytics to organizational leadership who will not be as comfortable with analytics.

For more details on BI and Data Analytics, please refer to Richard F. Gibson's Chapter 9, "Business Intelligence Reporting and Analytics: Tools, Resources, and Governance."

Population Health Management

With the political and economic pressures to develop organizations that manage populations, the HIT workforce demands will only continue to grow in the future. According to the Center for Medicare & Medicaid Services, "Accountable Care Organizations are groups of doctors, hospitals and other healthcare providers, who come together voluntarily to give coordinate high quality care to their Medicare patients."[14] The technology and workforce necessary for ACOs to understand the needs of their communities, and at the same time have the technology to coordinate the care, is daunting.

Besides the ACO movement, community and population needs assessment will require a workforce that understands a world where not-profits are being challenged by state governments to continue to demonstrate that they serve the needs of their community and populations in order to maintain tax exempt status. Understanding the targeted service area and the community needs and the lack or adequacy of healthcare delivery is essential for all healthcare organizations. Basic economics tell us that we need to know and understand the needs of our clients so that we can match the service that we deliver that is consistent with our organization's mission and the service and product needs of our community.

Understanding and managing population health will require a wide variety of IT functions according to Scott Joslyn (CIO Forum, Nixon Presidential Library, November 18, 2014). Organizational relationships and contractual agreements between the elements of an ACO alone will need strategic and innovative thinkers. The IT components to make it work will need a workforce that can identify populations, map and track care, coordinate a continuum of care, monitor the delivery of care, engage patient, and monitor and report results (The Advisory Board Company). The world of ACOs, and the continuing need to understand the health needs of our communities, will require organizations to seek and develop professional expertise such as:

- Knowledge of and experience with ACOs and care coordination would be desirable
- Academic backgrounds in public health, epidemiology, social work, strategic planning, business, or health administration
- The workforce needed to address population and community health needs probably requires the following attributes:
  - Experience with provider network management
  - Bundled payments
  - Quality measures like HEDIS
  - Team building and external relations capabilities
  - Analytics and epidemiology skills
  - Strong verbal and communication skills
  - Knowledge and experience in care coordination
  - Strategic thinker
  - Collaborative leadership style

Revenue Cycle Management

The challenging initiatives we will see in the future will have a significant impact on an organization's financial position and the need to manage the revenue cycle (see Michael W. Davis' Chapter 12, "The Brave New World of Fee-for-Value Reimbursement"). Perhaps the best way to look at the revenue cycle is it starts with contracting with health plans, followed by the initial patient engagement with the healthcare organization, and continues through various points of contact to the payment process. The workforce to support this complex after EMR and ICD-10 implementation will require some new skills and knowledge. The revenue cycle workforce will require a higher level of clinical understanding. Basic terminology will not be sufficient because of the necessity to work with an increasing amount of clinical and financial data that the EMRs will be producing. Data analytics skills will become very important.

The revenue cycle workforce will, in the future, still require MBAs or MHAs at the higher levels. We will see at the midlevel staff positions individuals with specialized certification like the Certified Health Financial Professional through Healthcare Financial Management Association or perhaps new specialization like a Certified Revenue Cycle Professional. The workforce will have very advanced skills in SQL, Excel, and Data Base Applications. Evolving payment methods such as full-risk models, bundled single-payment models, or quality performance–based models will only succeed if the EMR and financial data are standardized across facilities to aid management decision-making. Also, as the complexity of healthcare continues to evolve, even staff-level workers, such as business office staff in registration and financial counselors, will need to be trained and tested regularly in compliance payment models and privacy and security.

References

1. Grove, Andrew S. *Only the Paranoid Survive: How to Exploit the Crisis Points that Challenge Every Company and Career*. Currency Doubleday; 1996.
2. Christensen, Clayton M. *The Innovator's Dilemma: When New Technologies Cause Great Companies* to Fail. Harvard Business Review Press; 1997.
3. Gartner reference TBD.
4. *Baby Boomers Retire*, Daily Number, Pew Research Center, posted December 29, 2010. http://www.pewresearch.org/daily-number/baby-boomers-retire/. Accessed June 5, 2015.
5. *Beyond Jobs Numbers, Labor Shortage Looms: Our View*, USA Today, May 7, 2015. http://www.usatoday.com/story/opinion/2015/05/07/jobs-numbers-labor-shortage-baby-boomers-inflation-editorials-debates/70973518/. Accessed June 5, 2015.
6. *How Do We Know?* America's Foreign Born in the Last 50 Years. U.S. Census Bureau, February 13, 2013. http://www.census.gov/library/infographics/foreign_born.html. Accessed June 5, 2015.
7. Kohn, Linda T., Corrigan, Janet M., and Donaldson, Molla S. (Editors). *To Err Is Human: Building a Safer Health System.* Institute of Medicine; 2000.
8. Dick, Richard S., Steen, Elaine B., and Detmer, Don E. (Editors). *The Computer-Based Patient Record. An Essential Technology for Health Care.* Institute of Medicine; 1997.
9. Merritt, David (Editor). *Paper Kills—Transforming Health and Healthcare with Information Technology.* The Center for Healthcare Transformation; 2007.
10. Merritt, David (Editor). *Paper Kills 2.0—How Health IT Can Help Save Your Life and Your Money.* The Center for Healthcare Transformation; 2010.
11. Garets, Dave and Glaser, John, in *Careers in Health Information Technology*, Chapter 5, Springer Publishing; 2014.
12. Wyant, Dave, in *Careers in Health Information Technology*, Chapter 3, Springer Publishing; 2014.
13. Davenport, Thomas H. and Patil, D.J., Data Scientist: The Sexiest Job of the 21st Century. *Harvard Business Review*, October 2012.
14. http://www.cms.gov/Medicare/Medicare-Fee-for-Service-Payment/ACO/index.html.

III

SPENDING MORE ON IT: GOING BEYOND THE SCOPE OF YOUR EMR

Board member: "Didn't we just spend $300 million on our EMR? Surely, we don't need to spend much more on IT for a while!"

CIO: "Since healthcare is finally catching up to other industries in automating its core business processes, which are those related to patient care, using IT to support the future business process needs is now the way work gets done around here. Get out the checkbook, and don't call me Shirley!" [*Ed. Note—Apologies to Leslie Nielson*]

Most HCOs in the United States, and a fair number internationally, have spent millions of dollars implementing their EMRs in the last dozen years, and now are facing the fact that it was necessary, but insufficient, for competing in a value-based reimbursement, population health, patient engagement environment. As we move from the historical "mom and pop" fee-for-service health care delivery model, many other things, in addition to the electronic medical record, are required if we are to truly transform into modern healthcare organizations. Those are some of the initiatives that this third section of the book addresses.

First, Mike Davis, co-inventor of the EMR Adoption Model and ex-Gartner and Advisory Board analyst, takes on the difficult task of explaining what HCOs will need to measure and report to be successful in competing in a fee-for-value reimbursement world. Then, Alan Smith, SVP and CIO at Capella Healthcare, and Jeff Cobb, principal security consultant at World Wide Technology, describe Capella's money-saving strategy of standardized exchange of patient information with other provider organizations in their hospitals' geographies without having to replace all their EMRs.

We asked a team of clinicians from Bellin Health in Green Bay, Wisconsin, led by Pete Knox, Bellin's EVP/chief learning and innovation officer, and Jacquelyn Hunt, former CIO at Bellin, now chief population health officer at Enli Health Intelligence, to share Bellin's industry-leading work on population health management. It's a compelling account and sure to be one of the most-read chapters in the book.

Jan Oldenburg, an industry expert and multiple-book author on the topic of patient engagement, then explains the major IT component that enables participatory medicine and patient portals and gives the reader some guidance on revamping the portal your HCO has if you're not seeing the patient engagement you expect. And finally, Mike Blum is back with the second act of his chapter on the Platform for Innovation, explaining some hot technologies he's betting on in his additional role as director of the UCSF Center for Digital Health Innovation.

Chapter 12

The Brave New World of Fee-for-Value Reimbursement

Michael W. Davis, MS, MBA

Healthcare organizations (HCOs) understand that FFV is not an option.

The US healthcare market is on the downside of the EMR implementation cycle driven first by the Health Information Technology for Economic and Clinical Health Act followed by the Patient Protection and Affordable Care Act [1]. Taxpayers have spent approximately $32 billion supporting the implementation of EMRs by providers to digitize health information that is designed to improve care quality and patient experience while driving down cost. Other chapters in this book assess the impacts that EMRs could have on healthcare delivery and health maintenance as we move from a fee-for-service (FFS) model to a new model for reimbursing healthcare services—fee for value (FFV). FFV becomes the reimbursement model that supports the Institute of Health Improvement's Triple Aim—improving the patient experience of care (including quality and satisfaction), improving the health of populations, and reducing the per capita cost of healthcare [2].

Relative to RCM discussions in this chapter, RCM will include patient access, patient scheduling, referral management, patient billing, claims processing, and the charge description master (CDM).

Healthcare organizations (HCOs) understand that FFV is not an option, but is increasingly becoming a requirement of all providers in the near term. An announcement by the Department of HHS on January 26, 2015, stated the following: "HHS has set a goal of tying 30 percent of traditional, or fee-for-service, Medicare payments to quality or value through alternative payment models, such as ACOs, patient centered medical homes (PCMHs) or bundled payment arrangements by the end of 2016, and tying 50 percent of payments to these models by the end of 2018. HHS also set a goal of tying 85 percent of all traditional Medicare payments to quality or value by 2016 and 90 percent by 2018 through programs such as the Hospital Value Based Purchasing and the Hospital Readmissions Reduction Programs." Therefore, all providers should be in some state of assessment of their current revenue cycle management (RCM) applications environment relative to their ability to comply with the rapidly evolving FFV reimbursement models. Relative to RCM discussions in this chapter, RCM will include patient access, patient scheduling, referral management, patient billing, claims processing, and the charge description master (CDM).

The basis of FFV reimbursement models is managing populations of patients against benchmarks of care quality, outcomes, and patient satisfaction as defined by the payer contracts. The providers are "at risk" for meeting contractual thresholds for achieving those benchmarks. If they meet them, they will be given incentives/rewards to share across their providers. If they miss the benchmarks, they will suffer payment penalties, which could be devastating for low-margin provider operations. Also, capturing clinical data from EMRs to support FFV contracts is a key requirement for success. Investments made in Meaningful Use–compliant EMR systems will be justified in the new FFV reimbursement environment. The need to effectively manage patients, especially high-risk patients with real-time clinical, operational, and financial data, generates new and significant challenges for all healthcare providers in the FFV environment.

FFV Business Challenges

The biggest challenge healthcare providers face in the new reimbursement environment is the need to support both FFS and FFV models simultaneously. A provider may have several patient populations who have FFS payer plans that will need to create claims for capturing their service fees as defined by payer contracts. Over time, the percentage of FFS claims will decline, but at this time, FFS is still the predominant reimbursement methodology for most providers. The challenge for implementing and managing FFV while also maintaining the support needed for FFS revolves around the transition of staffing and skill sets for supporting FFV, while also implementing FFV application modules that can be integrated into the existing RCM application environment. The ability to make this transition with as little disruption to operations as possible is the ideal goal. Figure 12.1 represents

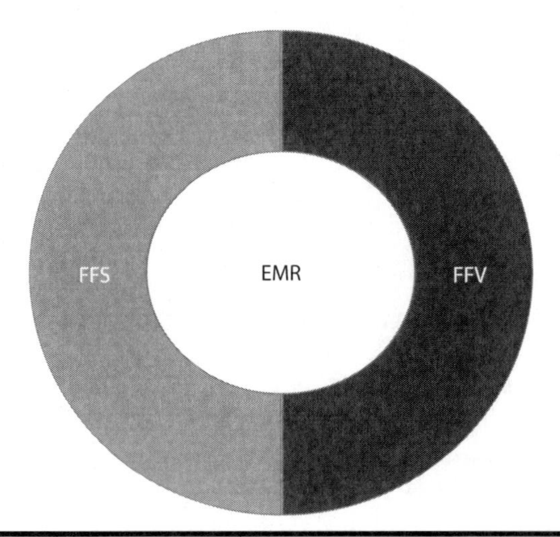

Figure 12.1 The hybrid RCM environment of the 21st century. (© 2015 Davis Business Advisory, LLC.)

the hybrid RCM environment that will need to be created by provider organizations to successful FFS and FFV contracts. Note the inclusion of the EMR as a key component of the RCM hybrid environment.

An Overview of the Hybrid RCM Environment

The FFS RCM application environment is the foundation for establishing a successful FFV RCM application environment. Table 12.1 provides a high-level matrix of what RCM applications support the FFS and FFV RCM environments, as well as the RCM applications that are specific to each hybrid RCM component.

All provider organizations should acquire an NLP solution that supports their coding and analytics environments.

Table 12.1 RCM Applications Supporting the Hybrid RCM Environment

RCM Application	*FFS Required*	*FFV Required*
Patient access/registration	X	X
EMPI	X	X
Benefits/eligibility/authorization EDI	X	X
Enterprise scheduling/referral management	X	X
EMR	X	X
Care management/HIE interoperability		X
Encoding/ICD-10	X	X
Patient billing/charge description master	X	X
Claims/remittance EDI	X	X
EFT/ERA EDI	X	X
Contracts management	X	
Contracts management with performance monitoring		X
Retrospective BI/analytics/EDW	X	
Predictive and prescriptive BI/analytics/EDW		X
Cost accounting/budgeting	X	
RVU cost accounting/flexible budgeting		X
Population health care management		X

Source: Davis Business Advisory, LLC, © 2015.

Let's examine the RCM application overlaps and specific applications that support either FFS or FFV. For example, both the FFS and FFV application environments require a Meaningful Use–certified EMR, but the FFV application environment requires additional capability such as care management/registry applications managing populations of patients, as well as tight integration with Health Information Exchanges or directly with EMRs from other provider organizations (e.g., direct exchange transitioning to Fast Healthcare Interoperability Resources [3]).

Knowing the true costs of care for each modality of care and being able to track budgeted costs relative to services performed become the highest priority business function as organizations transition to FFV contracts.

A current focus of most acute care organizations that must be continued is the conversion to ICD-10 coding with the supporting clinical documentation improvement and standardization processes. FFV will require not only more specific codified data but also supporting physician documentation that further clarifies or supports the codified data. A key technology for turning the unstructured clinical documentation into valuable information and data is NLP. All provider organizations should acquire an NLP solution that supports their coding and analytics environments.

The cost accounting system used in the FFS environment is most likely based on ratio of cost to charges. For the FFV environment, costing will need to be much more accurate and based on relative value units (RVUs) or activity-based costing (ABC). Budgeting in many organizations is performed using Excel spreadsheets. In the FFV world, a flexible budgeting system will become a requirement, and the budgeting application should be tightly coupled with the cost accounting system. Knowing the true costs of care for each modality of care and being able to track budgeted costs relative to services performed become the highest priority business function as organizations transition to FFV contracts. The ability to shift service resources and costs related to care delivery skill sets to meet care delivery demands in different care settings in the ACO in a timely manner will define an organization's success with risk contracts for populations of patients. Payroll data will become more important for managing the costs of clinical resources across various care settings and should be scrutinized after each payroll run.

A key challenge for PHM will be creating the interoperable data flows between the care management applications and the EMR.

Business intelligence (BI)/analytics/EDW applications are a keystone application suite in the FFV environment. Most of the BI/analytics applications in the FFS environment are focused on retrospective analytics. With FFV, the BI/analytics focus will be on predictive and prescriptive analytics. At some point in time, an EDW solution will need to be implemented to incorporate and support the data from the BI/analytics applications that have been implemented to address key business needs. Analytics becomes the key driver in predicting healthcare delivery costs, population risk, and new treatment protocols/processes that continue to drive higher-quality outcomes. The EDW becomes the great melting pot of normalized data that drives analytics to accomplish breakthroughs for achieving the Triple Aim.

Population health management (PHM) is a keystone application suite for FFV environments as well. For the purposes of this chapter, the analytics component of PHM will be addressed as part of the BI/analytics applications.

The care management component of PHM becomes a necessary application for managing high-risk patients with registry and care plan functions that also support secure, direct patient communications (e.g., messaging, Face Time, etc.). A key challenge for PHM will be creating the interoperable data flows between the care management applications and the EMR. Care management is discussed further in the Key Components of the FFV RCM Environment section. The acquisition of PHM applications must be evaluated to ensure that it can be integrated into existing RCM and EMR environments and that it optimizes the performance of clinicians who will be monitoring and managing healthcare services to populations of patients on risk-based contracts.

Contract management applications will also need to be upgraded to support real-time performance monitoring of contract revenues and costs to support the FFV environment. Contract management applications in the FFS environment track key contract requirements but rarely have performance monitoring capabilities that are needed to support risk-based contracts. Contract management systems will need to define key performance metrics for PHM risk contracts and then provide the ability to monitor those metrics. These metrics will be important for managing contract performance related to expected reimbursement and in assisting with the negotiations for extending or creating new population risk contracts.

Finally, the patient billing and accounts receivable (AR) component of the core FFS revenue cycle application must be able to account for payment withholds and incentive payments and clearly differentiate it from under- and overpayments for each risk-based contract transaction. This will be very important for bundled payment services and will be a necessary function for evaluating expected reimbursements for population risk contracts during their "true up" negotiations with payers.

Key Components of the FFV RCM Environment

PHM also contains an environment of BI/analytics that will include retrospective, predictive, and prescriptive methodologies; key performance indicator (KPI) monitors; and population health care plans that focus on higher-risk patients.

The key components of the FFV reimbursement environment are composed of applications that capture detailed net revenue, cost, operations, and patient data, which can be combined to provide real-time insights into service line performance—including physician performance. In this environment, variations in performance metrics can be identified and resolved to minimize the risk of missing potential bonus payments or meeting the baseline requirements of the risk contracts. The EMR will provide a significant amount of these data, but the ICD-10 CM/PCS encoding applications will also be an important contributor to the data needed to monitor and manage the populations of patients. Providers will go at risk for delivering payer requirements for clinical performance, outcomes, quality, and patient satisfaction threshold metrics. FFV will now provide a new component of return on investment for EMRs.

PHM also contains an environment of BI/analytics that will include retrospective, predictive, and prescriptive methodologies; key performance indicator (KPI) monitors; and population health care plans that focus on higher-risk patients. One challenge related to PHM is extending the analytics from this environment with data from other service environments (e.g., EMRs, supply chain management, and national data sets, such as Hospital Compare [4]) to provide more complete insights across all care modalities within the ACO. As FFV BI/analytics capabilities are built out, **it is important to implement an EDW that supports the BI/analytics applications that have been selected by the business and clinical departments, versus implementing an EDW and then trying to find BI/analytics applications that can support the EDW.** EDW solutions are very expensive, so it will be important to choose an EDW solution that can be implemented in an incremental fashion that supports the business strategies of the HCO.

Another challenge is the ability of PHM care management applications (e.g., registry/care plans) to interoperate with acute care and ambulatory EMRs for sharing patient care data to ensure that clinical performance, outcomes, and quality metrics targets are met or exceeded for high-risk patients across all modalities of care. In provider environments with a large number of disparate clinical applications and EMRs, the use of HIE solutions can provide an effective integration of disparate data that will produce more effective operational and analytics data.

The ability to manage budget variances in a timely manner by monitoring key costs (e.g., variable direct labor costs) for service lines will bring a requirement for service oversight to ensure contract metrics are met or exceeded. Budgeting and cost accounting will become key components not only for monitoring service performance but also for creating and maintaining an accurate CDM that will be used for both FFS and FFV. If you are not familiar with the issues around the CDM, an excellent article by Steven Brill was published in *Time* magazine, "Bitter Pill: Why Medical Bills Are Killing Us," on April 4, 2013. The Brill article provides an excellent insight into how inaccurate and poorly maintained CDMs have corrupted the FFS reimbursement model.

Lack of attention to timely healthcare delivery performance will be an impediment to achieving or exceeding risk-based contract metrics.

Many organizations have contract management systems that support their current creation, review, and management/oversight needs. **The challenge for contract management in the FFV world will be the ability to review and monitor FFV contracts in a timely basis against cost, clinical performance, quality, outcomes, and patient satisfaction criteria for each FFV**

contract. Contract management will need to get aggregate data feeds from the patient accounting (FFS) and BI/analytics (FFV) to perform these services, or BI solutions will need to have analytics and reporting functions established for monitoring each contract.

In the FFV world, data from the EMR for clinical performance metrics, outcomes, and quality will need to be fed to BI/analytics for aggregation and reporting to support the monitoring of contract performance daily. Evaluating any variances from expected or projected metric thresholds will allow HCOs to more quickly detect and correct performance issues that are generating negative variances. Lack of attention to timely healthcare delivery performance will be an impediment to achieving or exceeding risk-based contract metrics.

One of the most difficult challenges for provider organizations moving to FFV will be the need to significantly upgrade their cost accounting solutions and skills, and tightly couple the cost accounting environment with both the CDM and a flexible budgeting system. Most provider organizations are still using ratio of cost to charge costing approaches. This approach is simply not detailed or specific enough to provide the level of costing accuracy needed to support risk-based payer contracts. Moving to resource-based relative value scale (RBRVS)/RVU-based costing or ABC will be necessary to achieve the level of cost accounting needed to support FFV. Budgeting systems will need to be tightly coupled with the costing systems, and budgets based on spreadsheet will not be feasible for the increasingly complex ACO. Many post–acute care processes have not been appropriately mapped or costed to ensure high performance with FFV reimbursements.

Patient access applications will be challenged to correctly identify patients and to determine if their service is covered by FFS or FFV payers. When the patient presents, the patient access environment should also be able to initiate real-time electronic data interchange (EDI) transactions to determine the explanation of benefits, eligibility, and authorization of service at point of access. AR for patient-responsible payments is growing, and the ability to identify outstanding balances and collect them at point of service or via web services will become an increasing need for the provider organizations.

The last area of focus for the hybrid RCM environment is using financial EDI transactions to optimize cash flow. Provider organizations have implemented claims and remittance EDI transactions, in many cases with claims clearinghouse services, and have established processes to monitor these environments with denial management applications. FFV may not use claims/remittance EDIs, but should use electronic funds transfer (EFT) and electronic remittance advice (ERA) transactions to handle all FFV payments. Bundled payments will be handled on a per-case basis, but risk contracts for populations of health will be paid in most cases by the payer on a monthly basis and "trued up" at the end of the contract with final performance metrics to establish bonus or penalty payments (another requirement of contract management systems in FFV environments).

The Hybrid RCM Application Market Challenges

New companies are emerging to provide some of the FFV modules that will be connected with an organization's current FFS environment. Some examples of companies (this is not an inclusive list and listing does not imply endorsement) that are emerging to fulfill the evolving FFV needs are as follows:

- BI/Analytics/EDW: Health Catalyst, The Advisory Board Company, Health Fidelity, IBM Watson, Caradigm, Inovalon

- Population Health Management: Phytel (acquired by IBM in 2015), Orion Health, Vree Health, ZeOmega/HealthUnity, Optum, Aetna, Enli Health Intelligence
- Cost Accounting and Budgeting: Organizational Intelligence, Ormed, Kaufman Hall, Allscripts/EPSi
- Contract Management: Rycan, Experian Health, iContracts

EMRs will need to create data feeds to the BI/analytics solutions to create the ability to aggregate, display, and create alerts around clinical thresholds that will affect the outcomes of FFV contracts.

The history of healthcare IT shows us that when new markets emerge, new companies are formed to provide innovative solutions for new market needs. Niche/point solution vendors emerge that connect to legacy systems to support the new operations functions of the HCO. As the market matures, many of these niche/point solution vendors will be acquired by larger enterprise vendors when they achieve a market position that validates their value to the industry. Enterprise vendors may also decide to develop FFV solutions on their architectures to extend their product portfolios. Enterprise vendors have a large client base that allows them to more efficiently market and sell their products. When this happens, it tends to begin the consolidation of vendors and products that are in the market. Some of the key enterprise vendors that will affect the FFV market are Epic, Cerner, Allscripts, McKesson, and Meditech.

HCOs need to determine their level of risk tolerance as the RCM application market moves to a higher percentage of FFV reimbursements. Many of the new and emerging vendors/solutions for FFV may not be well capitalized or possess an executive team that can steer the company to business stability and sustained success, but in some cases, it may be necessary to take on the higher risk of emerging vendors if the HCO's enterprise vendors are not responding to the market in the time frames required to take on and manage FFV contracts.

The role of the EMR environment to support FFV should be apparent to all financial executives. The Medicare Shared Savings Program [5] requires the tracking and reporting of several clinical performance, outcomes metrics, quality, and patient satisfaction data to derive the formula for determining if benchmark metrics were achieved, exceeded, or not met. **Finance executives, directors, managers, and supervisors will now be required to monitor and manage key performance initiatives relative to clinical care delivery operations.** EMRs will need to create data feeds to the BI/analytics solutions to create the ability to aggregate, display, and create alerts around clinical thresholds that will affect the outcomes of FFV contracts. The EMR feeds should be at a minimum of 24 h, when feasible, to ensure that negative variances in clinical performance can be identified and quickly corrected. A few outlier patient cases could jeopardize an HCO's ability to achieve or exceed FFV contract requirements.

Many HCOs may be at risk with their current EMR vendor capabilities for capturing, reporting, and sharing clinical data with FFV modules. This is a more acute risk problem for ambulatory EMR vendors, as the ambulatory EMR market is consolidating. As mentioned earlier, the use of an HIE may facilitate more efficient data linkages, integration, and sharing.

FFS, EMR, and FFV Data Linkages—The Critical Success Factor

> The ability to effectively create timely data exchanges between FFS and FFV applications is the critical path for achieving success in the hybrid RCM environment.

The key FFV modules that HCOs will need to add to their RCM application portfolios are as follows:

- Contract management
- BI/analytics/EDW
- Budgeting and cost accounting
- Population health care management

While many people consider PHM to include analytics and care management, for the purpose of this model, the analytics may be achieved via the BI/analytics environment that many HCOs have or are in the process of implementing.

The ability to effectively create timely data exchanges between FFS and FFV applications is the critical path for achieving success in the hybrid RCM environment. Figure 12.2 depicts key data flow exchanges that must be established in the hybrid RCM environment.

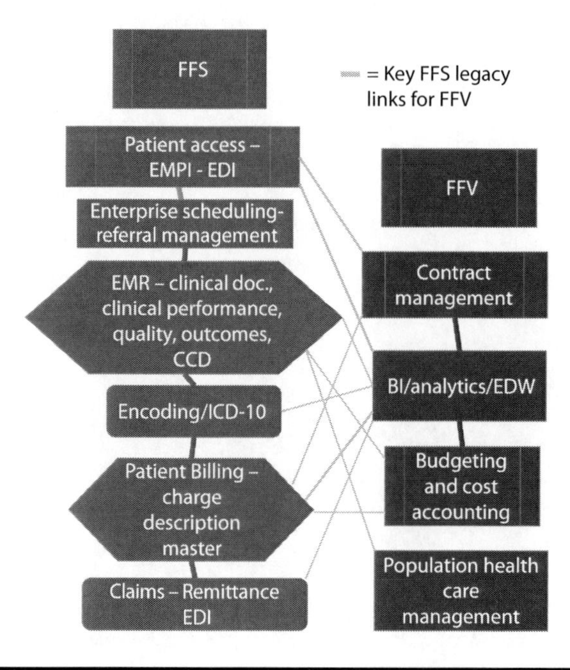

Figure 12.2 The hybrid RCM environment data linkages. (© 2015 Davis Business Advisory, LLC.)

The majority of HCOs have interface engines that can be used to create the linkages between these systems. In many cases, existing interfaces can be modified with minimal work to create new data exchanges between the FFS and FFV applications, but there will also be new work required to create some of these linkages. As the industry moves to "interoperability" requirements that are being planned by ONC, the data exchanges may be accomplished with application program interfaces using RESTful web services, which may be more efficient than using older Health Level 7 (HL7) interface transaction protocols (see Wes Rishel's Chapter 8, "Interoperability: Enabling Healthcare Data Sharing," for a comprehensive discussion of the emerging interoperability requirements). The approaches used will be decided by the IT departments in the ACO.

For HCOs that have multiple EMRs across acute care and ambulatory environments, the creation of data feeds from these EMRs into a BI/analytics solution will require a more complex design and implementation effort. Not only will the interfaces need to be created to feed data from the EMRs, but the data will, in most cases, require a level of normalization to ensure that the data represent the same clinical context. If different master person indexes are used in the EMR environments, then a process to accurately associate patient data collected across different modalities of care by disparate EMR systems will also need to be developed.

Excel spreadsheets will no longer suffice to support the complex budgets that will be needed to track the costs of patient care services across the various modalities of care in an ACO.

Another key component of the EMR environment will be the need to exchange data between the EMRs and the PHM care management care plans to ensure that all care is being managed and tracked efficiently. The PHM care management application will also need to create and exchange orders created in that environment with the patient accounting system. Fees generated by the care management system may result in FFS patient bills/claims, or they will be captured for tracking the patient care costs for FFV contracts. Figure 12.3 provides a high-level representation of how the data from an environment of disparate EMRs will need to be processed to support FFV.

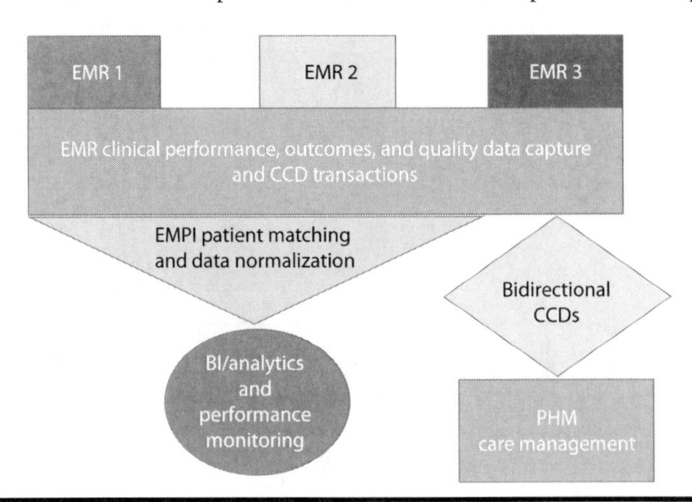

Figure 12.3 EMR data feeds for FFV. (© 2015 Davis Business Advisory, LLC.)

The use of lower-level clinical skill sets to monitor and initially interact with patients in home health or telehealth services will allow the higher-skilled clinicians to focus on the high-risk patients to improve the chances of meeting or exceeding FFV contract thresholds.

Budgeting and cost accounting applications become a significant factor for establishing accurate service costs for all modalities of care and for implementing flexible budgeting packages that can be monitored on a daily basis by executives, directors, managers, and supervisors responsible for care delivery services. Cost accounting will need to move to a more advanced methodology such as the use or RVUs/RBRVS or ABC. ABC is probably not within the purview of most HCOs today, as it requires the use of industrial engineers to create and maintain cost units based on workflow/processes used for care delivery. Therefore, the RVU approach will probably be the most valid at this time as organizations move to more closely evaluate their service costs. The costing systems must be tightly coupled with budgeting applications that can support flexible budgeting and also provide real-time budget performance views for financial and clinical managers. Excel spreadsheets will no longer suffice to support the complex budgets that will be needed to track the costs of patient care services across the various modalities of care in an ACO.

The ability to reallocate clinical resource labor between services as volumes increase or decrease will become a major contributing factor for meeting or exceeding ACO FFV contracts.

A process for the timely review of service costs and updating the CDM as these costs change will be critical for supporting both FFS and FFV. The key cost components that will need to be monitored will be labor costs by skill levels (e.g., RN, LPN, Nursing Assistant, etc.), medication costs (average wholesale prices change weekly), diagnostic testing costs, and material supply costs (review of group purchasing organization contracts and performance should be included). The use of lower-level clinical skill sets to monitor and initially interact with patients in home health or telehealth services will allow the higher-skilled clinicians to focus on the high-risk patients to improve the chances of meeting or exceeding FFV contract thresholds.

Budgeting is another critical application for supporting FFV and will move beyond spreadsheets or simple rollups of departmental budgets to clinical service–focused budgets. **Budgets will need to be available for real-time monitoring on a daily basis and driven down to the managers and supervisors of the clinical services**. Daily monitoring of budget variances will need to become an operational task to ensure that negative variances are corrected and documented. The ability to reallocate clinical resource labor between services as volumes increase or decrease will become a major contributing factor for meeting or exceeding ACO FFV contracts. It will also be important to have any updates of the cost accounting system update the budgeting system to ensure the most accurate budget actuals reports and forecasts.

This environment moves beyond patient registries for disease management and becomes a care record environment used by several types of clinicians to manage patients as a team.

Population health care management is the environment where clinicians will monitor high-risk or at-risk patients using patient monitoring devices and telehealth services. The care plans for this environment will not be as complex as acute care plans but will need to be able to upload the most current medication records, diagnostic testing results, and physician notes from acute and ambulatory EMR systems (e.g., transition of care records). Plus, the care management solution will need to be able to capture and send service charges for therapies, medication orders, and diagnostic orders to the patient billing application of the FFS, which may update the contract management system for FFV contracts, depending upon the patient's insurance. This environment moves beyond patient registries for disease management and becomes a care record environment used by several types of clinicians to manage patients as a team.

Data captured in this care management environment must also update the associated EMRs within the ACO. Therefore, the current focus on EMR interoperability and data sharing that is the focus of ONC [6] is a critical path for implementing a useful care management solution. While there are niche/point solutions that are emerging for care management that sits on top of the ACO EMRs, the enterprise EMR vendors are building out their environments to accommodate care management. The ACO's approach to care management will be dictated by their current enterprise vendors and degree of risk tolerance. Niche/point solution vendors will always have a higher risk factor but may also provide the best innovations and functionality for addressing ACO needs. The enterprise vendors may be slower to deliver the required functionality in the time needed by the ACOs to respond to their markets. If the enterprise vendors acquire population health care management functionality, it will create the same interoperability challenges in most cases, as those found with niche/point solutions.

Legacy FFS RCM—The Foundation of the Hybrid RCM Environment

The FFS applications that are implemented in most HCOs today include patient access (with explanation of benefits, eligibility, and authorization EDI transactions) and enterprise patient scheduling with referral management support. Their EMRs produce the clinical documentation that is needed to supply the encoding applications (including computer automated coding) that support ICD-10 coding, patient billing/CDM, and the claims/remittance/electronic cash flow EDI transactions.

Patient Access

The patient access environment is an often overlooked component of both FFS and FFV solutions. The patient access system includes the patient registration and master patient index applications. The patient access application must be tightly coupled with an enterprise master person index (EMPI) to ensure that you are establishing services for the right patient. If an HCO has master person indexes that are used with several different patient accounting or practice management systems, these systems may be capturing different information to identify the same patient. One system may have Michael W. Davis, whereas another has Michael William Davis as an index record. Are these the same patient? EMPIs are designed to use several identification schemes to identify patients with greater accuracy. All patient registration systems should be connected to an EMPI to ensure correct patient identification in an HCO, and especially in ACOs where there are several different modalities of care that could include several disparate master patient index and patient registration systems.

The patient registration systems should also accommodate real-time EDI transactions for determining a patient's eligibility and benefits, and authorization for treatments as required by the payer. All organizations should be following the Council for Advancing Quality Health (CAQH)/CORE guidelines for establishing these EDI transactions [7]. A recent report by the CAQH identified significant savings by using EDI transactions [8].

At point of registration, the patient access system must be able to identify which reimbursement model will be used by the patient, FFS or FFV. For both FFS and FFV, service costs (via encoding), medication costs, and diagnostic service costs will be captured in the patient accounting system. Details on how patient accounting is used in the hybrid RCM environment are discussed in the section that follows.

A new critical component of the patient access environment will be extending the ability to preregister to patients via web services as provided by secure patient portals. Wouldn't it be great if you could report to the hospital, outpatient clinic, or diagnostic department without stopping to fill out registration data that have most likely not changed, or if it has changed, could be captured in the preregistration system and verified via EDI? In some forward-thinking HCOs, the registration process is confirmed/verified at the point of care with tablets. Mothers and millennials will expect these capabilities, which will affect patient satisfaction scores—another element of most FFV reimbursement models.

Enterprise Scheduling and Referral Management

Enterprise scheduling has become an important resource control and management application for HCOs. The ability to use costly resources (facility, equipment, and human) efficiently has a direct impact on margins and profitability. The ability to expand enterprise scheduling to all care modalities used for FFV services has the same necessities as FFS but also provides the ability to improve patient satisfaction. As with preregistration, enterprise scheduling should allow web access for patients to request the scheduling of services that best fits their work and family calendars.

Referral management has become an important component of tracking specialty care for patients who receive the majority of their primary care within an HCO. HCOs want to control where patients receive their specialty care to maintain good business relationships with specialty physician providers whom they have contracts with. Patients who go to other specialists may expose the FFV providers to higher encounter or episode care costs, or a complete loss of service revenue. This is referred to as "leakage." This becomes a significant risk factor for patients in FFV contracts, as contract performance is projected for services defined in the ACO, including specialty services. If there is too much leakage in the FFV patient populations, contract performance will most likely not be met, and the organization will incur a penalty. This is one factor that prohibits more active participation in ACO reimbursement models for many HCOs—an ACO cannot restrict a patient to its services.

One way to track services patients are receiving outside of the ACO is to track CCD transactions (from clinics or organizations outside of the ACO) that are received by the primary care providers; another way is to monitor medication transactions on the patient's medication record, where the prescribing physician is not affiliated with the ACO.

The EMR

EMRs provide billing data for the FFS RCM system via order/charge capture and clinical documentation applications. The order/charge capture systems generate billing entries for patients for diagnostic testing, supplies used, and medications. Clinical documentation from structured physician documentation templates, transcribed reports interpreted by coding staff, or a combination of both is used by coders to generate international classification of diseases (ICD) codes (transitioning from ICD-9 to ICD-10), which are then used by the encoding systems to generate DRGs that FFS payers use to determine payments. For outpatient services, a combination of ICD and Current Procedural Terminology, 4th Revision (CPT4) codes are used to submit bills/claims to FFS payers. FFV will require the same level of order/charge capture and clinical documentation capabilities, but as stated previously, in the FFV environment, the EMRs will use standard care protocols supported by evidence-based medicine that will standardize the orders, care plans, medications, and diagnostic testing performed on the patients. This greatly reduces the cost of care variation seen in FFS. EMR data will be fed to the BI/analytics systems to use for performance analysis, future care cost projections (forecasting), and prescriptive analytics (e.g., giving an antibiotic 30 min before surgery reduces hospital-acquired infections).

Other chapters in this book delve into more detail relative to the current and evolving capabilities of the EMR environment to improve healthcare cost, quality, outcomes, and patient satisfaction (see H. Lester Reed's Chapter 4, "Using EMR Data to Improve Clinical Protocols, Outcomes, and Patient Safety").

Encoding/ICD-10

FFS systems use encoding applications to generate the DRGs that are used by payers, along with ICD and CPT4 codes to assess the payments for the patient services that have been rendered. It was very important that our industry moved to adopt ICD-10 codes as the standard in 2015. ICD-10 codes provide an additional level of specificity that will help track both FFS and FFV costs at levels that will be required to generate accurate service consumption and costs. DRGs, ICD-10, CPT4, and Healthcare Common Procedural Coding System codes are important data sets for populating the BI/analytics system for evaluating service performance within and across care modalities. As stated earlier in the chapter, the importance of efficient and standardized (as much as possible) clinical documentation processes will support ICD-10 coding specificity and will also provide additional clinical information to support predictive and prescriptive analytics.

A new application that provides a higher level of automation for the coding environment is called computer-assisted coding (CAC). As CAC systems evolve and prove their coding accuracy, the backlog of coding cases will decrease, and coding information will be available on a timelier basis for the BI/analytics operations that support FFV.

Patient Accounting/Patient Billing/CDM

> The comparison of profit margins between FFS and FFV services will enable HCOs to evaluate their healthcare and diagnostic service costs from different operating perspectives, which should help them effectively evaluate their risk tolerance for FFV contracts.

For FFS patients, the system will work as usual and generate a patient bill that will then generate a claim to the FFS payer. If the patient is covered via an FFV contract, the same process will follow, and a patient bill will be created with the patient accounting or billing data uploaded to the BI/analytics system with charge detail data. In some cases, the claim may be processed and paid by the payer for FFV services and then become part of the aggregate population bill that is trued up at specified times. The total patient bill amount will be uploaded to the contract management system to aggregate patient service costs for the FFV contract. For bundled payments, the organization will bill the payer for the contracted amount, and then create a comparison of the billed amount versus the true cost generated in the patient accounting system in the BI/analytics system. The comparison of profit margins between FFS and FFV services will enable HCOs to evaluate their healthcare and diagnostic service costs from different operating perspectives, which should help them effectively evaluate their risk tolerance for FFV contracts. A recent study from UCLA revealed that one procedure had a cost variation of 400% between providers with no significant impact to outcomes [9]. This example shows why the industry must move away from FFS and toward FFV, which supports adoption of standardized care protocols based on evidence-based medicine.

The management of the CDM to ensure accurate billing for patient types and payer accounts will take on a new level of significance. Accurate charging for services will be an imperative to track expenses associated with FFV services. Remember, the service budgets should be created with the same costs that are used in the CDM to ensure consistency between these environments. If the CDM gets out of sync with what has been used in the budgets, the organization will not have an accurate view of what costs are actually being generated. The BI/analytics system will not be able to generate accurate forecasts or comparative analytics. Inaccurate reports from BI/analytics systems result in a loss of credibility for those systems with the clinicians. HCOs will need to assign dedicated resources to manage the costing, CDM, and budgeting functions if they have not already done so. In conservative provider organizations, the service budgets will be created with historic Medicare payments as a base, to provide a lower operational budget baseline for assessing FFV contracts.

Patient Satisfaction Data

Now, for the really hard act within FFV—the need to track and improve patient satisfaction for the ACO services rendered. ACOs will need to design effective patient touch points to excel in this area. The following are key points to consider:

- Web services for preregistration, scheduling, and bill payment (there still may be copays for some FFV services such as diagnostic testing) that can be executed on a tablet or smartphone (as form factors allow—small smartphone screens cannot accommodate long forms in most cases).
- A patient portal for accessing diagnostic test results accessible by tablet or smartphone and accessing clinician-approved content on diseases, medications, and treatments.
- The ability to message physicians and care managers for instructions and guidance.
- Web service alerts for medication refills and upcoming appointments; links in the alerts would provide the ability to complete a medication refill for the physician to execute or to verify ability to attend the scheduled appointment.
- The ability to capture patient data from medical devices easily connected to smartphones and uploaded to an EMR for review by clinicians.
- The ability to survey patients on recent services or to determine the clinical status of a patient (e.g., postsurgical follow-up on condition of the wound).
- Providing multiple patient interaction access points—phone, e-mail, Facebook, and so on. Remember, you have to design the patient touch points relative to the generation of patients you are trying to interact with (e.g., Baby Boomers, Gen X, Gen Y, Millennials, etc.).

Many HCOs are capturing patient satisfaction via Press Ganey survey tools, but these surveys must now comply with the Hospital Consumer Assessment of Healthcare Providers and Systems survey standards for acute care patient surveys. Data from these surveys should be used to populate the BI/analytics systems and potentially the contract management system, as these data will be used in some FFV contracts (e.g., Medicare Shared Savings Program and Value-Based Purchasing) to determine contract compliance, penalties, or bonuses.

The Requirement for Treatment Protocol Standardization

> Putting this in perspective—HCOs will not be successful in the FFV environment unless they standardize their care delivery protocols.

Standardization is not a dirty word, even though we treat it like one in healthcare. As HCOs move to FFV contracts, it will be vitally important to standardize treatment protocols across all modalities of care. Performing this task helps standardize care costs associated with labor costs, medication costs, diagnostic testing costs, and administrative costs. As previously mentioned in the Patient Accounting/Patient Billing/CDM section, the UCLA study perfectly frames why we need to work on standardizing protocols with evidence-based medicine guidelines. A 400% variance in the treatment process for any disease with no statistical significance in outcomes begs the industry to resolve this fiasco quickly. Can you imagine trying to manage a risk contract using treatment protocols with high variations between physician treatment approaches? Putting this in perspective—HCOs will not be successful in the FFV environment unless they standardize their care delivery protocols.

Remember, it only takes a few cases with cost, quality, or performance failures to expose the organization to penalties in risk contracts.

Part of the cost accounting evaluation and update must include the ability to review treatment protocols and determine where they can be standardized based on evidence-based medicine. These protocols should identify the care plans, clinical skill sets required, and tasks they perform with time allotments for the care paths, standard medications, standard diagnostic testing (clinical and imaging), standard supply kits (e.g., surgery, catheters, etc.), and the expected coding (e.g., DRG, ICD-10, CPT4, etc.) outcomes.

Once the standard protocols are created for healthcare services across all care modalities, variances from the protocol components need to be closely monitored. All variances from protocols need to be reviewed by a team of selected clinicians. In some cases, the variances may point out improvements or corrections that need to be made to the protocols. In other cases, the variances need to be reviewed with the clinicians in violation of the protocol for an education session. If reviews with clinicians are required, they need to happen on a timely basis—such as weekly. Policies for handling frequent violators of protocols need to be defined by the executive team. Remember, it only takes a few cases with cost, quality, or performance failures to expose the organization to penalties in risk contracts.

If you want to be successful in FFV, your selected team of clinicians must review all services and standardize the treatment protocols.

Once protocols are defined, care plans and order sets that support the protocols need to be created. Once created, the charge capture from these protocols needs to be tested to ensure accurate charging is taking place across the care modalities. The IT department should have a test system where this testing can be accommodated, or if the clinical and financial applications are Software as a Service (SaaS) solutions, the vendor should be able to provide a testing environment.

If you want to be successful in FFV, your selected team of clinicians must review all services and standardize the treatment protocols. If you can't find evidence-based medicine protocols, use this team of clinicians to negotiate protocols that will be acceptable to the other clinicians in the organization.

RCM Outsourcing Considerations

Many HCOs are beginning to outsource some or all of their RCM functions. This is more predominant in the ambulatory market than in the acute care market. In most cases, outsourcing for RCM is pursued because the provider is having problems finding the necessary skill sets required to manage and operate the RCM solutions. **The challenge of finding the skill sets necessary to support RCM will only intensify as providers move to FFV reimbursement models.**

All FFV components could be outsourced, and in many cases, these emerging applications are architected as web services that are offered as SaaS solutions (e.g., remote hosted over the web). Contract management, BI/analytics/EDW, budgeting and cost accounting, and PHM care management could all be evaluated for outsourcing if an organization has limited FFV skill sets or hiring capabilities for these skill sets. RCM service companies that will provide outsourcing services are emerging, but most of these services are still focused on FFS support.

Healthcare providers will need to evaluate the skill sets and experience of FFV outsourcing services to ensure these resources can meet the service level agreements (SLAs) that will need to be established. SLAs need to identify KPIs that outsourcing agents need to meet, in order to ensure that FFV contract expectations are met. The SLAs also need to include the requirements for data linkages needed between FFS and FFV applications, with appropriate data normalization.

A key requirement of these SaaS solutions is that data be encrypted at rest and during transactions. That will provide the highest level of security to ensure that personal health information used in the FFV applications is not compromised. Another security requirement is that no data shared with any outsourcing vendor is to leave the United States. Companies can use offshore resources to facilitate their outsourcing solutions, but resources not residing in the United States need to access US-based RCM applications via secure tunneling applications with terminals that have no disk drives or USB ports. Tunneling with this configuration will provide access to the applications for processing and management, but it will prevent any patient data from being downloaded. Even with these safeguards in place, many provider organizations will hesitate to outsource their RCM functions. In some organizations, this would be synonymous with giving the keys of the kingdom to a stranger (see David Finn's Chapter 10, "The Future of Information Security in Healthcare," for a comprehensive discussion of security).

General Financial Workflow Model for FFV

The general financial system will also be affected by moving to new FFV reimbursement models. A model for the workflow components for the general financial applications and the data flows are defined with the following steps:

1. The FFS applications generate a bill/claim for FFV patient services, as identified when the patient presents for registration. Either the claims from the FFV patient bills can be sent to the payer, who will aggregate them for review against the contract, or claims can be sent to a special account set up in the EDW or contract management system. Alternatively, claims could be sent to both environments. Detailed claims data should be sent to the EDW, while summary claim data are most feasible for the contract management system. It is important that FFV claims can be indexed by service date, service type, service facility, and service providers (e.g., physicians, physician extenders, etc.) for evaluation and analysis in the BI/analytics applications. Claims data for both FFS and FFV should be used for predictive analytics relative to determining which FFV contracts and patient populations have the lowest risk.
2. The contracting entity (ACO, health system) generates monthly invoices for the FFV contract(s) that are sent to the payer with the negotiated amount that may or may not include performance withhold amounts designated in the FFV contract. In most cases, the FFV payments will not include the performance withhold amounts. Recent changes to

CMS FFV models may allow billing/payment for FFV services, at time of service, that are trued up at later dates, as specified in the contracts.

3. FFV payments are made to HCOs and captured in AR. The payments from the payers should be set up to accommodate EFT transactions directly to the provider organization's bank, with a corresponding ERA transaction to the organization for uploading to the AR.
4. The general ledger (GL) will need to be set up with chart of accounts for each FFV contract. The GL will capture the monthly patient claims AR amount, the monthly payer FFV payment, and an amount associated with the monthly performance withhold. The difference between the FFV claims and the sum of the payer FFV monthly payment and monthly performance withhold should be a zero balance. If the difference in these numbers is a positive number, the organization is delivering FFV services at a cost that will provide a positive margin. If the difference is a negative number, the organization needs to quickly access their performance metrics to determine where costs are driving the negative margin.
5. The accounts payable (AP) system creates monthly payments to the participating FFV service providers and physicians. Again, in most cases, these monthly payments will not include any FFV contract performance withholds.
6. The GL system is updated with the AP transactions.
7. The FFV contract is evaluated at Year End to determine contract performance relative to KPIs (e.g., clinical performance, quality metrics, and outcomes). If the KPI metrics are met, the performance withhold monies are paid to the HCO. If the KPIs are exceeded, the HCO may have negotiated a bonus payment, but if the KPIs are not met, the performance withhold monies will not be paid and will most likely result in a negative margin for the FFV contract. If the FFV contract KPIs are not met, the GL accruals for the contract performance withholds will need to be adjusted to reflect a debit versus a credit, to show the appropriate contract loss.

A diagram of the general financial environment FFV data flows is shown in Figure 12.4.

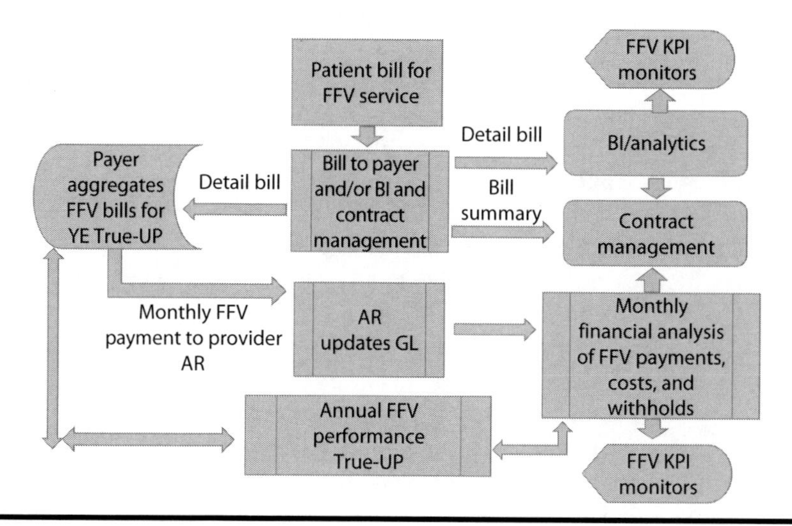

Figure 12.4 Hybrid RCM—general financial workflow. (© 2015 Davis Business Advisory, LLC.)

HCOs can seek the outsourcing services of a third-party administrator to provide the general financial services identified above, if they do not have the general financial systems to implement these capabilities.

Conclusion: Key Action Checklist

- ☐ **Conduct Review of the Current FFS Environment.** The FFS environment is not going away anytime soon. However, it is important to review the FFS applications and architecture to ensure that it can create timely data linkages with FFV applications. The FFS environment should also be enabled to provide real-time EDI transactions for eligibility and benefits, and treatment authorizations. Collection of patient-responsible payments is becoming the third largest AR in many organizations, and providing point-of-service capabilities to identify patients with outstanding balances when they present for services should be a key consideration.
- ☐ **All claims/remittance/claims status functions should be conducted via EDI transactions**. If smaller practice management systems can't accommodate this capability, determine if the acute care RCM can take on these functions for the practice(s). If not, look for billing services to assist the organization until a longer-term solution can be implemented.
- ☐ **EMPI functions are now a requirement for all ACO organizations**. Positive patient identification will reduce significant rework, embarrassment, and revenue loss. In many cases, an organization will need to implement an EMPI that can integrate with the patient access/registration applications.
- ☐ **The FFS environment should be web enabled to support web services for preregistration, scheduling, and bill payment.** These are key functions that will enhance patient satisfaction ratings that affect FFV. If the current FFS environment is lacking in these capabilities, it may be time to evaluate a replacement. This will make the CFO (chief financial officer) very nervous, as this could be a career-limiting move for that person. Spikes in AR days during RCM replacements have cost many CFOs their jobs. Most RCM implementations today include a rollover date where the new RCM system becomes operational and the old RCM system is taken offline but remains operational, to work the AR in that system to zero balance. This mitigates the risk for implementing new RCM systems to some degree.
- ☐ **Complete the FFV Application Gap Analysis.** Organizations must begin to evaluate their FFV application environments relative to cost accounting/budgeting, BI/analytics, contract management, and population health care management. HCOs that have these applications in place must begin to evaluate the ability to integrate the existing FFS and FFV applications with timely data flows that provide KPIs for optimal management of patient populations under risk contracts.

  Interface engine applications that are in place at the majority of hospitals and integrated delivery systems should be able to establish the data flow linkages between the FFS and FFV applications. In some cases, it may be necessary to add more staffing for the interface engine departments to create the necessary focus and timely delivery of these data flows.
- ☐ **Initiate Board Review/Discussions.** It is imperative that HCO executives initiate the FFV reimbursement transition discussion with the board. As FFV adds a new risk factor for financial stability, the board should be made aware of an organization's current status for

adopting FFV risk contracts. If FFV risk contracts are being undertaken by market competitors of the HCO, the status of these discussions takes on a higher level of priority—especially if the organization has not entered into FFV contracts or participated in early pioneer programs from CMS. It may be wise to allot a designated period for FFV discussion at every board meeting, which should also include executives who manage clinical operations and physician services.

☐ **Create Capital and Operating Plan for FFV.** A key challenge for the HCO will be to create both a capital and operating plan for establishing the hybrid RCM environment to accommodate the transition to higher levels of FFV reimbursement versus FFS.

Capital budgets may or may not be affected depending on the approach for acquiring FFV applications or replacing legacy FFS applications needed to support FFV. If the HCO moves toward SaaS application models, operating budgets will need to be increased versus the capital budgets if the RCM applications are acquired and operated in-house.

Operating budgets will be affected as HCOs begin to evaluate the skill sets of their current FFS staffs for supporting the transition to FFV reimbursement. Staffing for cost accounting/budgeting, contract management, and BI/analytics may need to be added to support FFV. In some cases, the BI/analytics operations and staffing may reside in other departments, such as IT. If so, then the IT operating budget will need to be increased. This also applies for the PHM care management component. An evaluation of the clinical staff needed to support the care management services for FFV contracts will need to be reviewed relative to the operating costs of the clinical services supporting this environment.

In many cases, the HCO will rely on outsourcing services to help supplement the staffing for the transition to higher levels of FFV reimbursements. HCOs in markets with good access to prospective employees with required FFV skill sets have the option of hiring these skill sets versus using outsourced services, but this will be the exception and not the rule for most of the HCO markets.

☐ **Review Legacy RCM Applications Annually.** An ongoing process for HCOs will be the need to review the legacy RCM applications that currently support FFS reimbursement relative to the ability of the FFS applications and architectures to support FFV services.

Any legacy RCM application that cannot create or accept data feeds from other applications should be prioritized for replacement relative to its impact for supporting the FFV strategy of the organization.

Key starting points would be the patient access, contracts management, patient accounting, and EMPI capabilities with the current RCM environment. Identifying the right patient with the right service (FFS or FFV) is a critical capability for deriving success in the hybrid RCM environment. The next highest priority would be for implementing EDI transactions to optimize operational efficiency for eligibility/benefits, authorization, claims/remittance, and EFT/ERA transactions with payers. Improving these capabilities improves the FFS efficiencies while also establishing a good foundation to support FFV.

☐ **Continue to Build the BI/Analytics/EDW Environment.** BI/analytics/EDW environments will continue to grow in importance as HCOs move to higher levels of FFV reimbursement. Many organizations are already conducting patient population analytics to evaluate patient populations for risk-based contracts or to evaluate risk-based contracts. Prudent HCOs have implemented BI/analytics solutions that focus on current needs and priorities. At some point in time, these organizations will need to implement an EDW solution that can incorporate the data from their disparate BI/analytics applications.

The BI/analytics approach we are seeing in the market today mimics the implementation of clinical departmental systems in the 80s and 90s. Most organizations selected best-of-breed laboratory, pharmacy, and radiology systems to support departmental organizations. As the market evolved to need more sophisticated EMR systems, these organizations began to implement the integrated lab, pharmacy, and radiology systems of the EMR vendor to improve data flows and decrease operating costs associated with interfaces to connect the clinical systems. At some point in time in the next 5 to 10 years, the market will again see the transition toward BI/analytics/EDW solutions designed from a common architecture from a singular vendor that will challenge the operational and integration costs of best-of-breed solutions related to BI/analytics and EDW solutions.

Final Note: Just Starting? You're Behind!

If your organization is just now starting the discussions and discovery related to transitioning to FFV reimbursement models, you are behind! However, that doesn't mean you won't be successful in creating a hybrid RCM environment that maintains the financial viability of the organization as the market transitions to higher levels of FFV reimbursements. Participating in the new HHS program, Health Care Payment Learning and Action Network [10], is a good place to monitor emerging FFV government programs and participation rates in these programs by payers and providers.

HCOs can also gain insights for transitioning to support FFV reimbursement through consulting services that are emerging. A key point is that these services are emerging, but proven methodologies have not emerged to help HCOs transition to FFV reimbursements without some level of financial risk. In some cases, consultants or advisory service firms have acquired or built applications that they provide to help HCOs evaluate FFV risk or manage FFV contracts. When evaluating consulting firms with applications and products they promote as part of their service, make sure they are a good fit for the organization relative to workflow, integration, customer base, and customer service. Bad choices made regarding FFV services and applications can be very expensive, especially when evaluated on the impact on opportunity costs.

HCOs already have a start on transitioning to the FFV reimbursement environment with their current legacy FFS application foundation. If the FFS foundation is weak, the HCO should focus on implementing a new FFS environment, which can support the transition to support FFV reimbursements, to increase their success in implementing a hybrid RCM system for the 21st century.

Acknowledgment

The author would like to acknowledge Ajit Sett, CEO, Sett Healthcare Advisors, LLC, for debating and discussing the hybrid RCM model. Ajit's advice was extremely insightful in helping to craft this chapter.

References

1. http://www.hhs.gov/healthcare/rights/.
2. http://www.ihi.org/Engage/Initiatives/TripleAim/pages/default.aspx.
3. http://hl7.org/fhir.

4. http://www.medicare.gov/hospitalcompare/search.html?AspxAutoDetectCookieSupport=1.
5. http://www.cms.gov/medicare/medicare-fee-for-service-payment/sharedsavingsprogram/.
6. http://www.healthit.gov/sites/default/files/ONC10yearInteroperabilityConceptPaper.pdf.
7. http://www.caqh.org/CORE_operat_rules.php.
8. http://www.beckershospitalreview.com/finance/study-switch-from-manual-to-electronic-transactions-could-save-healthcare-8b.html.
9. http://www.healthdatamanagement.com/news/UCLA-Clinicians-Map-Entire-BPH-Care-Process-Cost-50018-1.html?utm_campaign=daily-mar%2019%202015&utm_medium=email&utm_source=newsletter&ET=healthdatamanagement%3Ae4032837%3A3713610a%3A&st=email.
10. http://www.hhs.gov/healthcare/facts/blog/2015/02/participate-healthcare-payment-learning-action-network.html#PAGE_4.

Chapter 13

Health Information Exchange Case Study: Implementing a Multicommunity Hospital Set of Solutions on a Budget

Alan Smith, MPH and Jeff Cobb

"EMR replacement is one of the most incredibly disruptive projects a hospital can undertake."

Questions to Answer

- What approaches are out there for health information exchange?
- What did Capella pick and why?
- What is the role of the Patient Portal?

This chapter will seek to discuss the role of data exchange between different systems in different health systems and how one community-based hospital health system is attempting to tackle this challenge within a limited budget.

Data exchange is an evolving space in health information technology, and completely understanding the interfaces between different care settings is not a perfect science at this time (see Figure 13.1). There will be much learned in the coming years as we move to a truly interoperable future where patient data can flow to the appropriate care setting at the appropriate time for high-quality care to be given. Meaningful Use (MU) Stage 3, risk-based contracting, consumerism, and evolving advanced standards such as FHIR will all play a role in shaping the future of system and data interoperability and making this dream a true reality in the future. (For a comprehensive review of interoperability and the technologies being applied to it, see Wes Rishel's Chapter 8, "Interoperability: Enabling Healthcare Data Sharing.")

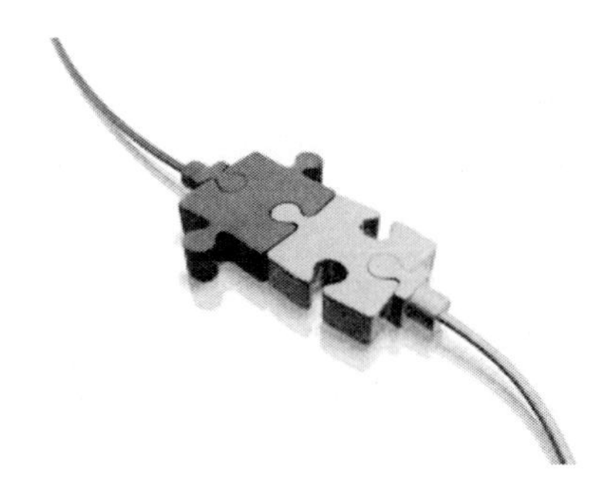

Figure 13.1 The puzzle of connection.

We acknowledge that there are still plenty of data exchange challenges within the walls of the hospital (e.g., bio med device integration with the hospital's EMR, proprietary clinical data formats), but we will leave that discussion for another day.

Background

Capella Healthcare is a for-profit healthcare system that specializes in acquiring and operating community-based hospitals throughout the country. A typical Capella hospital is located in a non-urban setting having somewhere between 75 and 350 licensed beds. As an acquirer of hospitals, our geographic reach is not regional but rather is based on finding hospitals that fit nicely into the Capella portfolio and could be located anywhere in the country regardless of their proximity to another Capella facility. Our current 12 hospitals are located in six different states, which quite literally represent a coast-to-coast reach. This geographic spread represents a unique challenge when it comes to data exchange that we needed to address within our Information Services strategy (see Figure 13.2). Some items that were considered include the following:

- Multiple data trading partners. Most Capella facilities are not in proximity to other Capella facilities, so our primary data trading partners have a strong local flavor and are varied dependent on the local marketplace dynamics.
- Multiple partnerships to integrate into in terms of ACOs. Each of our markets is at a different place in terms of ACOs, at-risk contracts, and PHM, so we need to be flexible in how we hook into different strategies, platforms, and vendors for sharing clinical data. Each market is unique in sophistication and approach to data exchange and will demand us to partner with different larger players who ask us to join with them on these types of initiatives. Since we are community hospital based, we are not the market mover in terms of ACOs and we seek partnerships with tertiary providers in the local or regional area. This will require us to exchange data with a variety of ACO partners and fit into their IS infrastructure required by their ACO and PHM support systems.
- State-specific requirements in terms of Public Health reporting as well as HIEs. Each state is unique in how they approach these initiatives as is the maturity level of the data exchange infrastructure. We needed flexible solutions that can work with the state readiness and data architecture that is in place now and as it evolves in the future.
- EMR-agnostic. We run several different EMR vendor applications, so solutions need to work with multiple EMR vendors and provide functionality outside of the EMR application itself.

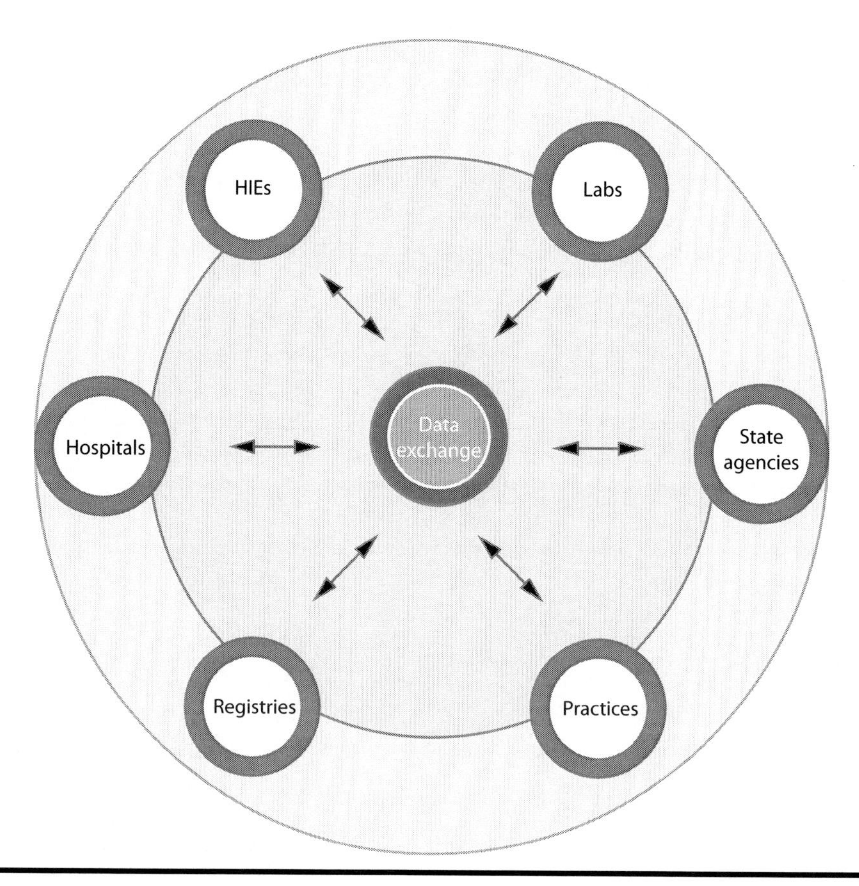

Figure 13.2 Data exchange platform.

As an acquisition company, we inherit whatever EMR the hospital is running and then have to decide what to do. One obvious approach to this challenge of multiple EMRs is to collapse newly acquired facilities onto a standard common EMR. However, in our culture it is not always possible to collapse each newly acquired hospital, at least initially, onto one EMR platform for the following reasons:

> If a new hospital has spent a significant amount of time installing and optimizing their EMR, they usually do not want to replace it just because they have been acquired.

- Cost. With the MU incentives tapering off or even drying up in the next few years, we are no longer able to "hide" the true capital and operating costs required to completely replace the entire EMR at each hospital. Like many organization over the past few years, EMR replacement had become our biggest capital expenditure for a newly acquired hospital, often requiring a delay in other needed investments until after the EMR was deployed. This in turn caused frustration to some of our business owners as they wanted to divert the capital required for EMR conversion to other needed areas such as in market acquisitions, service line expansion, building projects, medical equipment investment, and so on. Also complicating the cost equation is the thin margins for community hospitals in the current era of health reform, so strategies that reduce the overall capital and operating requirements were needed in order for the overall organization to meet its financial goals.

- Revenue Cycle Challenge. Another barrier to moving all of our employed physicians over to one EMR (along with our hospitals) was the role our incumbent ambulatory EMR vendor played in our revenue cycle. We not only would have had to do a conversion of all of our owned physicians, we would have had to hire and build out a business office where we had relied on a vendor partner to do a large part of that function for us. It's less of a technical issue, but nonetheless another challenge to overcome while still trying to meet tight MU deadlines.
- Politics.
  - If a new hospital has spent a significant amount of time installing and optimizing their EMR, they usually do not want to replace it just because they have been acquired. This is especially challenging if the physicians at the newly acquired hospital are reasonably satisfied with the EMR. While there are many advantages to an organization being on a single EMR, the cost of a "rip and replace" strategy solely does not work well in our environment and we believe will be harder and harder to sell in the coming days of shrinking margins and no MU incentives.
  - In the community hospital marketplace, we are unlikely to "own" all the different parts of the care continuum. Since those nonowned entities are unlikely to want to convert onto our systems but are still critical to our success, as care partners and data trading partners, we would be living in a world that would demand a flexible, non–EMR-based solution to HIE.
- Business disruption. EMR replacement is one of the most incredibly disruptive projects a hospital can undertake. The amount of resource time it takes to build, train, and then implement a new EMR is massive. With many hospitals having just undertaken this in preparation for MU, the appetite and enthusiasm for another project of this magnitude are often just not there.
- Lack of referral patterns. Since our hospitals are geographically distributed, some of the inherent benefits of a single EMR platform are muted. Benefits like one patient record across multiple hospitals within a geography especially where there are strong referral patterns do not apply to our hospitals today.

Like many other health systems, our first foray into the land of data exchange was wrapped up under the ability to meet MU guidelines for 2014. With the MU Stage 2014 edition, we were called upon to implement a Patient Portal, comply with state Public Health Agency desire to gather data, and begin to send data outbound via a CCD as part of our routine discharge process. Each of these required us to implement strategies designed to move data from Capella facilities to other non-Capella facilities.

Patient Portal and Data Aggregation Strategy

Since it was not going to be feasible to convert all of our hospitals and physician clinics to one EMR, we knew we needed a more flexible non-EMR solution to data aggregation and data exchange with the outside world. At the same time, as part of the MU program, we were called upon to enter into the world of patient engagement by implementing a Patient Portal. As we began looking at Patient Portals, the vendor we chose allowed us to tackle multiple needs with one set of solutions.

First, we believed that we needed to focus on what was best for our patients and have a Patient Portal vendor that was EMR-agnostic and was cloud based for ease of access and use. This would allow us to not only place our hospital data into the Patient Portal but also in successive waves move our employed physician patient data and then affiliated community provider's data into one portal. This in turn would allow us to present a community-wide patient portal and allow patients one-stop shopping versus letting each community provider put up their own portal and have islands of information that confuse and alienate our patients.

> Since it was not going to be feasible to convert all of our hospitals and physician clinics to one EMR, we knew we needed a more flexible non-EMR solution to data aggregation and data exchange with the outside world.

Second, we believe that a patient portal over time becomes a community-wide mini-HIE if you can get a number of external providers on board. As the richness of data grows, the portal will represent a longitudinal data picture for the patients for all care provided in the community. This in turn would give us a platform for supporting the analytics that we would need within the community to drive quality improvement initiatives whether as part of a risk-based contract or not. Since we did not already have a clinical analytics solution in place, this became a logical engine to drive a solution in that area as well, as much of the needed data were already in the portal.

Public Health Agencies

In the current Capella environment, there are six different states (and more to come in the future) to work with for the successful ongoing transmission of the public health–required interfaces, which are electronic lab results, immunization data, and syndromic data. While the MU guidelines did a decent job of trying to prescribe the data format for each of these required submissions, we have found wide variation in the actual implementation of the standard, each state's ability to stay abreast and current with changing data format standards, and the transmission requirements (e.g., batch, real time, and data transport protocol). Knowing that our base EMRs all have to have the ability to produce the required files is a great first step but we needed some ability to be flexible in the transmission of data and reduce the underlying complexity of data transmission and the tracking of the successful transmission of the data (in case of an MU audit). To that end, we partnered with one of our EMR vendors who had developed a solution that is essentially an "interface engine in the cloud" application to meet these needs. Since they have a large number of community hospitals throughout the country, they were already familiar with the unique requirements of all the states that we are in, so that allowed us to not have to learn from scratch and take advantage of their knowledge and lessons learned. They also understood that a typical community hospital has a small IS department and does not necessarily have the skills/expertise or the bandwidth to take on this initiative, and then to continually monitor the successful data transmission going forward.

This approach has allowed us to connect our different EMR instances via one virtual private network (VPN) tunnel to our vendor and provide them the certified data feeds for all EMRs across all six states and let them deal with the complexity of each state on our behalf. It is important to note that Capella has a long history of outsourcing most our technical infrastructure work and that includes security like VPN tunnels as well as traditional interface engine work. This interface engine in the cloud approach allowed us to minimize the work and complexity of the work with our normal outsource partner and push this work to our public health interface vendor that in turn isolated us from having to work directly with each public health entity that we needed to work with. While this does require another vendor outsource relationship to monitor, we feel this approach has the following advantages for us:

- Speed to market. Allowed us to leverage expertise from an outside source and not have to build up our own team. Also, it gave us the ability to leverage resources already skilled in public health interfaces and individual state requirements, which shortened our learning curve and ability to comply with MU requirements.
- Cost. Avoided having to purchase our own interface engine as well as having to build and pay for the management of multiple secure data transmission mechanisms.

CCD Transmission

The last area of data exchange we have addressed to date is with the CCD transmission to our referral sources. In this scenario, we need to send patient clinical data from our hospitals to community providers where our patients are discharged to and potentially to HIEs on a community or statewide basis.

For CCD exchange with community physicians that patients are discharged to, we leverage the Direct messaging protocol and route messages through our Health Information Service Provider or HISP. The MU regulations called for the use of such technologies, and so we have followed a fairly standard path and let our EMR vendors guide us to the best HISP with which to partner. After a few technical challenges, we have begun to successfully send data out to community-based physicians. The biggest challenge we have faced is really less about technology and more about new workflows within the physician practice and eventually within the hospital as we begin to accept inbound CCDs of who will look at the data, how will it be incorporated into the medical record, what should be incorporated into the medical record, and how these data will be reconciled with what we know already about the patient. Again, we see the challenge as more operational than technical at this point. One point of note is that we have found the current CCD standards to be a first start but the feedback from our clinicians has been that the data being exchanged can be voluminous at times, so more work should be done from a standards perspective to further refine the data itself and make sure that only the data that are truly useful should be exchanged in order to be efficient.

In the case of HIE data exchanges, our plan is to leverage our investment and data already in our patient portal. Our patient portal vendor has the ability to forward CCD transactions to any HIE that we would choose to enter into a relationship with which allows us once again to leverage a single vendor for more than one purpose. This will isolate the number of connections (security and interfaces) that we need to manage and put the burden on a vendor who has more expertise, resources, and experience in building these interfaces (see Figure 13.3).

You will also notice that our patient portal vendor not only will serve as another interface engine in the cloud for us in terms of CCD records but also will serve the same function for us for outpatient radiology and laboratory results. These capabilities will serve our outpatient business lines within our hospital well and help us provide timely results electronically back to our community physicians for inclusion into their EMRs. Leveraging one vendor for multiple purposes (patient portal, HIE interface engine, and results distribution) allows us to rationalize our product portfolio as well as keep costs down.

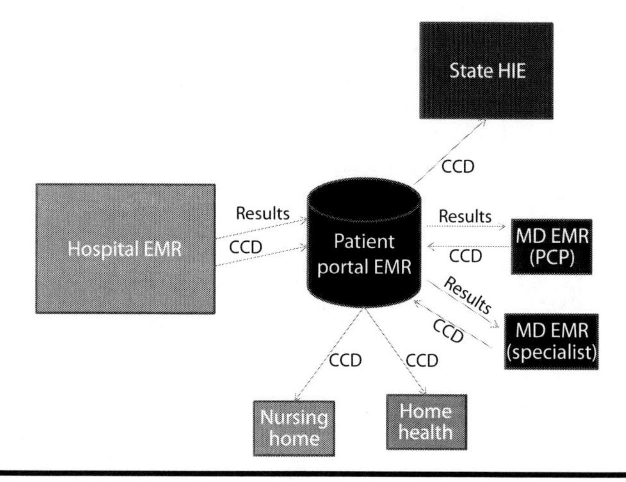

Figure 13.3 CCD exchange through the Patient Portal.

Conclusion

> Change is always difficult, but for those who persist and push through, there are benefits to reap.

As the saying goes, patience is a virtue. And a little luck never hurts, either. When we embarked on our data exchange journey more than 2 years ago, it was very painful. These initiatives were new for everyone. Health systems weren't quite ready nor were the vendors certified to play in this space. Change is always difficult, but for those who persist and push through, there are benefits to reap.

> Ultimately, we will all benefit from progressively more sophisticated data exchange and interoperability.

- **Technology is improving.** It is nice to see how our vendor platforms, particularly our patient portal platform, not only have evolved to meet today's needs but also are positioning to meet the demands of the future. New interface technologies (e.g., FHIR) and approaches to data exchange and analytics will change the way we work with data today.
- **Clinicians and care providers are seeing the light.** Before, it looked like a Mack truck coming at you at a hundred miles an hour. Today, it is a possibility. As processes solidify and technology becomes second nature, the value of having information available to view and share becomes exciting. Situations where we simply could not share data or were cumbersome to do so are becoming a thing of the past. Now that robust data exchange is more tangible to the end users, the brainstorming and what-if scenarios start to drive conversations that will lead to new and improved ways to use data and improve care.

- **Patients are benefiting from our work.** Patient portals and all the health information that is now readily available can be likened to the banking industry more than 10 years ago. No one really wanted to have their banking information "out in the unknown Internet" let alone pay bills, deposit checks, and transfer money without physically going to the bank to do so. Now look at us. Healthcare is facing this same transition. Ultimately, we will all benefit from progressively more sophisticated data exchange and interoperability. We will have more access to information to make better decisions. Care providers will have not only more data but also more frequent data that can change and improve care plans and approaches. And more data will be available to analyze and see trends and outcomes that have the potential to aid in improving services and approaches to caring for patients.

There were no guarantees of success when we started and no promises that the future will be completely free of frustration. We had a vision simply based on flexibility and trying not to get trapped or hardcoded into one way of doing things, and to create a scenario where we could partner and work with virtually anyone along the way. All that and a little luck along the way have us excited about the future of healthcare and interoperability of data.

Chapter 14

Bellin Health: A Model for Population Health

Pete Knox, MS, BS; Jacquelyn Hunt, PharmD, MS;
Brad Wozney, MD; James Jerzak, MD; and Kathy Kerscher

"The people in our region will be the healthiest in the nation."

To the casual observer, Bellin Health appears to be just another Midwest healthcare delivery system. Bellin's marquee 167-bed hospital pales in size compared to large metropolitan academic medical centers. The location of Bellin's corporate headquarters in Green Bay, Wisconsin, inspires mixed feelings among football fans. Mention of Green Bay more likely conjures an image of beer, brats, and curds than a breakthrough model for population health design. However, anyone looking beyond corporate size and Monday Night Football will find an organization in steadfast, relentless pursuit of the highest-quality health and lowest-cost outcomes in the country—and we are showing dramatic results.

Our vision is simple yet expansive: "The people in our region will be the healthiest in the nation." To achieve this audacious goal, we've spent the past 15 years building an innovative population health framework and IT strategy guided by the needs of both patients and care providers. We've proven our processes internally and have sold our PHM solution to more than 115 external companies in our region.

Like many organizations across the country, we have successfully implemented a top EMR. However, we now recognize that these investments have left Bellin and our customers far short of needed population health capabilities. Now, we're looking beyond the boundaries of our existing healthcare delivery system and EMR to a system that is designed to deliver true Triple Aim [1] results.

The Journey Begins with a Vision

Bellin Health is led by CEO George Kerwin, a 43-year employee who moved up through the ranks of this century-old healthcare system. Bellin has a long history of investing in system design and improvements to support our goal of providing quality, affordable healthcare to all members of Northern Wisconsin and Upper Michigan communities. Our commitment to improvement has been exemplified by our status as a charter member and active ongoing participant with the IHI [2], as well as Wisconsin's statewide quality and transparency activities [3].

We needed to produce a better product, at a lower price, packaged conveniently for potential customers.

Despite our long-term commitment to quality, it was an organizational crisis that spurned our population health awakening. Our crisis initiated in 2000 when a large multistate hospital system made significant investments in moving into Green Bay. Suddenly, there were three large integrated health systems along with regional hospitals competing for 630,000 lives in an area that covers 200 miles north to south and 60 miles east to west. Even the local newspaper speculated that Bellin Health System would experience significant negative market share impact because of the competition. Some predicted that Bellin Health would not survive the anticipated loss of volume and revenue. Like any business that finds itself in a hypercompetitive environment, Bellin needed to innovate in order to survive. We needed to produce a better product, at a lower price, packaged conveniently for potential customers.

While analyzing options for controlling expenses, the Bellin executive team uncovered a significant liability that would ultimately turn to opportunity. Without intervention, the already sizeable expense for our self-funded employee health benefit was expected to rise by an unsustainable 30% in the next year. Additionally, we could not identify the value of our multimillion-dollar health benefit expense. Where was the investment going? Did it produce results? How healthy were our employees?

We set our strategic sights on controlling healthcare benefit costs while helping our employees and their dependents improve their overall health. For example, we sought data about the health of our population, implemented a system to improve access to appropriate services, changed the benefit structure, and focused on a culture of health among employees. Over the next couple of years, Bellin's continuous focus resulted in dramatic improvements in measures of cost, health, and employee engagement. Within 2 years, we reduced the cost of our employee

BELLIN HEALTH

- Integrated healthcare delivery system founded in 1907
- Located in Green Bay, Wisconsin
- Vision statement: "The people in our region will be the healthiest in the nation, resulting in improved economic vitality in the regions we serve."
- 2500 employees
- Hospital services: 167 bed acute care, multispecialty hospital, critical access hospital, 80-bed psychiatric facility
- Medical group: 300 multispecialty providers operating in 40 locations of care

health benefit by 33%, while increasing the features in our benefits design. Within 8 years, we saved an estimated $13 million while simultaneously improving the measurable health scores of our employees [4].

We soon realized that our internal experience in lowering employee benefit cost while improving health could be extrapolated to employers in our community who were plagued with similar issues. We refined our approach and invested in a new line of wellness services called Business Health Solutions that targeted self-funded employers. Bellin's Business Health Solutions focused on three key components to achieve results: medical care, leadership, and culture. Medical management integrated customized onsite services into a medical home care team that was capable of managing risk and utilization, along with chronic illness management and prevention. Going further, Bellin's Business Health Solutions team engaged company leadership and employees to develop a culture of wellness. More than a decade later, we continue to innovate and grow Business Health Solutions. Bellin has worked with more than 2500 companies with onsite services at 74 locations, achieving improved health risk assessment scores and lower employee health benefit costs.

With the experience of managing the health, quality, and cost of employee populations, Bellin joined IHI's first Triple Aim Collaborative in 2007, along with 14 other organizations from the United States, England, and Sweden [5]. IHI's initial Triple Aim community rapidly swelled to 40, including organizations from various healthcare sectors and other countries. During this time, we refined our approach to PHM through interactions with thought-leaders, collaborative learning, and a focus on drivers of health and Triple Aim measurement [6]. As we refined our views on population health, however, we realized the need to redesign care delivery across our continuum with a robust IT platform to support the change.

iVision Establishes an EMR Foundation

Bellin's IT environment has evolved and adapted with the organization's changing needs and as improved solutions became available. Through the late 1990s, application system support for the hospital was provided through internally developed AS/400 applications. Beginning in 1998, we adopted vendor-developed applications that included Meditech in the hospital and MEDIC practice management in ambulatory clinics. These systems were supplemented with function-specific applications as needed, such as Picture Archiving and Communication System and an emergency department management system. Eventually, we initiated a system-wide search to replace Meditech's LSS ambulatory EMR. In 2009, Bellin's Board of Directors approved a strategy to implement the Epic system starting in the ambulatory environment and then expanding across the system.

The shift to a wholesale EMR conversion dictated significant financial, operational, and political investments. As a result, our executive team was determined to leverage the transition as an opportunity to hardwire a better delivery system with a more connected experience of care. We took several key steps to ensure that our investment returned our desired results.

First, we created an organizational vision to guide Bellin's IT-related decisions, referred to as our iVision. Rather than basing Bellin's iVision on the latest technology architecture, it was founded on the desires of patients and families (see Figure 14.1). We credit Dave Underriner, James Harker, and leaders at Providence Health & Services for sharing what they learned in delivering an experience where patients and families feel that everyone on their care team knows them, cares for them, and eases their way [7].

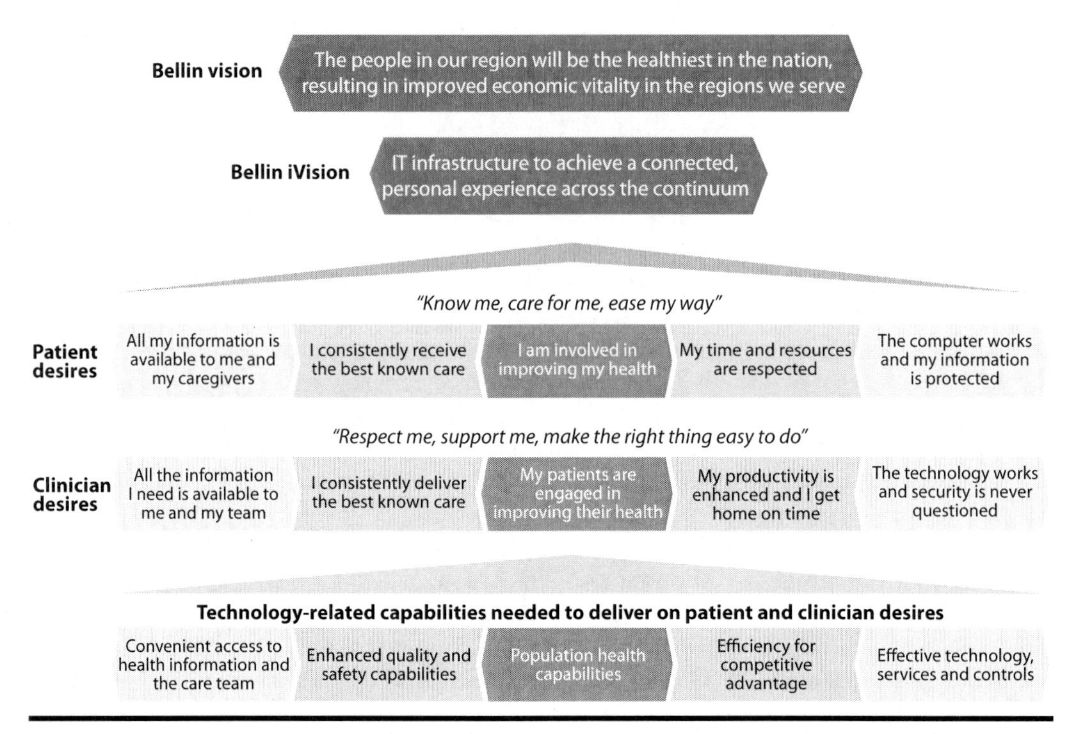

Figure 14.1 The iVision aligns patient and clinician desires with the technology, people, and process investment required to support the Bellin Vision.

The iVision framework also aligned the desires of patients and families with the desires of providers. By aligning these needs, we defined a technology capability roadmap aimed at the customer while considering the desires of the frontline care provider. This concept—of designing better systems by deeply understanding the needs of the customer and the challenges of the frontline caregiver—became a fundamental theme for our success and served as the basis for our future, broader population health IT platform.

The iVision framework was used to specify the technology capabilities needed to create the desired patient and clinician experience. This clear understanding of capabilities helped align stakeholders and prioritize investment. Beyond technology investment, we also expanded the iVision framework to specify the organizational investments in people and processes required to leverage the technology investment and create value.

Next, we shared the iVision with each department across the system. Department leaders worked with their executive leaders to cascade the concepts and create metrics for how their area would contribute to the new desired state. Department leaders then shared their plans with the rest of the organization to gain a cross-system perspective, eliminate waste, and create a more connected experience across the continuum of care.

Lastly, we applied two principles we learned from IHI. The principles include engaging the hearts and minds of providers and staff [8] and scaling learnings from an individual to the population. In this case, we learned about Betty, an 81-year-old practicing tax accountant who had been frank in expressing her disappointment about how the well-intentioned care across our system fell short of her expectations [9]. Instead of filing her complaints away, we embraced Betty's fearless desire to help us improve her care experience. Our admiration for Betty's honest observations led to her becoming the namesake for Bellin's EMR conversion, both in person and in spirit. With a

Figure 14.2 Betty, a Bellin patient who was candid and inspirational in her feedback, became the iconic representation of the multiyear patient-centered EMR conversion.

playful image that kept the individual front and center (see Figure 14.2), the Betty project helped staff members personalize the EMR transition and inspire the pursuit of more than just an IT implementation [10].

By 2012, Bellin had converted its hospitals and primary care clinics, as well as many of our employed and community-affiliated specialty partners. The single-minded focus of the Bellin executive leadership team and the efforts of all providers and staff paid off. The Betty project was deemed a success, having delivered on time, 17% under budget, associated with positive spikes in employee engagement and patient satisfaction scores, and achieving all other predefined measures of project success.

Bellin Population Health System Design

> Our aim was to create a system that would improve the health and well-being of individuals, improve the health of populations while lowering costs and improving the overall experience, and create sustainable results for communities and our country.

Like many organizations across the country, we had successfully implemented a top EMR, met the Meaningful Use Incentive requirements, and were investing in optimization. However, Pete Knox, Executive Vice President and Chief Learning and Innovation Officer, recognized that these investments still left Bellin and its customers far short of the healthcare design and technology needed to produce breakthrough results. Pete pressed for a new healthcare system design that would reliably deliver on Bellin's Triple Aim promise. To design the new healthcare system, we started with the end in mind. Our aim was to create a system that would improve the health and well-being of individuals, improve the health of populations while lowering costs and improving the overall experience, and create sustainable results for communities and our country.

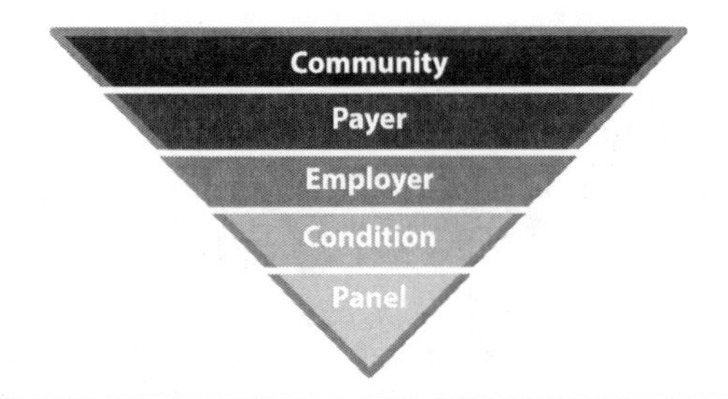

Figure 14.3 Segmented views of a population to guide system design and spread strategies.

We identified major tension points that we would need to overcome in order to deliver on our Triple Aim promise. We knew that healthcare accounted for approximately 20% of individuals' health and that the majority of health determinants were located outside of traditional healthcare delivery. That led to the first and possibly most difficult challenge we faced—our own preconceived notion of our span of responsibility and control. To achieve our desired results, we would need to push outside of the boundaries of our existing hospital and clinic walls. We would need to develop new partners, access different information, and find new business models to engage individuals and populations where they learn, work, and live.

We have learned that our healthcare design needs to scale, regardless of the size or characteristics of the population segment we are serving. To assist in developing design requirements that deliver at scale, we segment our population in several ways, including a provider's panel of patients, patients with a common disease or condition, employees within a place of employment, members attributed to a payer, and whole communities (see Figure 14.3).

Segmenting the population allows us to consider the unique characteristics and opportunities of different groups so that we could configure our system to meet their needs. Table 14.1 summarizes examples of population segments we are working with to improve health and lower cost. We leverage available sources of data to drive insights and guide system design.

The second major tension point we faced was the continued fragmentation of services within and across primary, specialty, hospital, and community services that persisted despite our "successful" EMR conversion. We continued to see the patient more through the eyes of the services we were trained to provide than as individual customers. Regardless of the population segment, our approach to understanding a population, designing solutions, and producing results needed to leverage a single consistent production system. Our work led us to a new system design with deeply integrated components, each harmoniously connected and necessary to drive Triple Aim results (see Figure 14.4).

Population Insights to Solutions for Individuals

The initial requirements of the population health system design focus on knowledge of the individual and the population. These new insights stem from new sources of information, including the individual. We have thought deeply about the challenge from Maureen Bisognano, President and CEO of the IHI. Ms. Bisognano has spread the words of Susan Edgman-Levitan and Michael Barry, who encouraged health systems and care givers to ask "what matters to you?" in addition to asking "what's the matter?" in all interactions with patients and families [11].

We gathered information to define the needs of a population with as much detail as possible, including an understanding of the clinical and socioeconomic risk within the population.

Table 14.1 Example Population Segments Engaged with Bellin in Health Improvement

Population Segments	*Example*	*Population Size*	*Data Source Leveraged*
Panel	Dr. Jerzak's primary care panel	2400	EMR
Condition	Diabetes	8000	EMR
	Heart failure	3000	EMR
Employer	Bellin Health	2500	HRA, EMR, insurance broker report
	Green Bay School District	1000	Insurance broker report
	North Wisconsin Technical College	1500	HRA, partial EMR
Payer	Anthem commercial population	8000	Claims, EMR
	Wisconsin Medicaid Disabled	5000	Claims, member functional screening
	CMS Medicare Pioneer	6950	Claims, EMR
Community	Bellin Run	20,000	Online registration
	Algoma County	4000	Claims, BRFSS, community assessments, focus groups
	Packer fans	Too many to count	BRFSS

Note: BRFSS, Behavioral Risk Factor Surveillance System; HRA, health risk assessment.

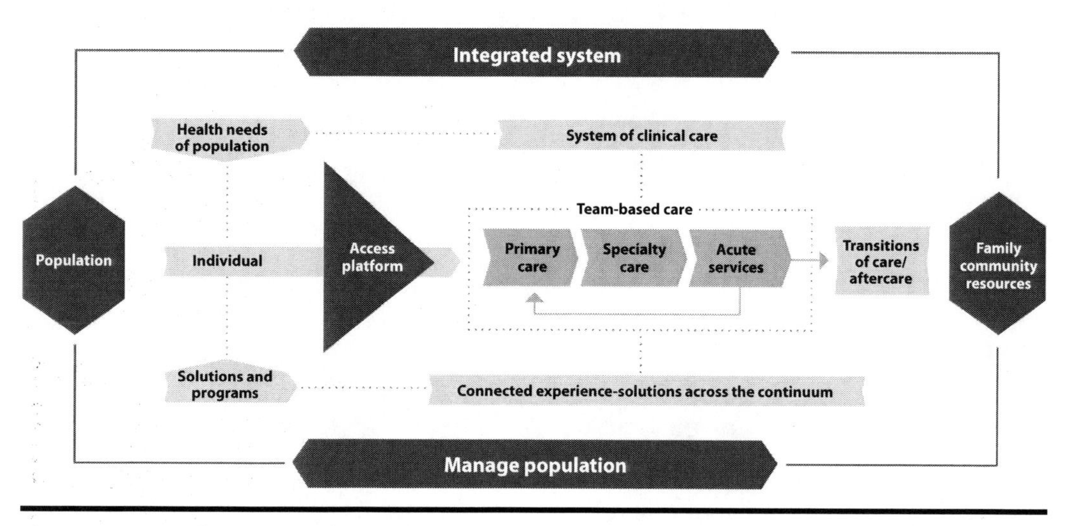

Figure 14.4 Bellin's population health system design leverages an integrated, consistent platform to drive Triple Aim results.

This information is used to strategically design solutions to deliver Triple Aim results for a specific population. This high-level strategic activity also supported resource planning and contracting.

Access Platform

The Access Platform guarantees convenient and timely access to support individuals as they navigate the healthcare system and receive the needed, desired level of care [12]. We have expanded our Access Platform beyond the initial 24/7 nurse triage and scheduling with traditional primary and specialty services to also include online virtual visits, onsite employer services, telemedicine, and linkages to community services and resources.

Connected, Team-Based Care

Our population health system design is grounded in the principles of team-based care. We are redesigning primary care using top-of-credential principles and leveraging an extended team of healthcare professionals, integrated with the core primary care provider/medical assistant teamlet, to meet the complexity and diversity of the individuals being served.

We are focused on eliminating unwarranted clinical and workflow variation to guarantee that every patient receives world-class, evidence-based care at every encounter with any member of the team. We have an aim to reliably translate evidence into practice within 90 days of publication.

Additional support and resources for high-need population cohorts are accommodated through customized programs that consider the plight of patients as they journey across the care continuum.

Transitions of Care/After Care

We learned from our Medicare risk experience that a significant portion of healthcare-related expenses goes to skilled nursing home and other services, particularly following hospital discharge. Based on that experience, we are risk-stratifying patients to match resources to needs, developing new community partners, redesigning our care systems, and incorporating best practices related to safe and reliable care transitions [13].

Family and Community Resources

A prevailing requirement of the population health system design is the ability to align patients and family (as defined by the individual) with community resources in support of the individual's unique needs. We are focused on asset mapping to leverage the strengths of each community [14]. Community assets include such resource as agencies, churches, food banks, libraries, schools, and parks.

Infrastructure and Competencies

As we moved from pilot to spreading proven components of our population health design, we recognized the need to develop new infrastructure and support. Our new design requires a different alignment across the organization. Employed and partner physicians must share in the aim, purpose, and incentives of the new value-based system. We have engaged physicians in changes from care practices to culture. Implementing the new design requires competency development for every member of the care team.

We have been testing and improving each interrelated component in our population health framework in order to achieve results at scale for any population segment (see Figure 14.5). This is important because it speaks to building a single proven system versus starting from scratch for each unique population and risk contract. For each of these population segments, we use a nine-step process to understand and configure the system.

1. Understand the population
2. Define goals for the population
3. Create a high-level design—match demand and capacity
4. Activate the team
5. Engage the individual
6. Measure outcomes
7. Provide feedback
8. Thirty-day improvement plans
9. Recalibrate goals

This approach not only allows us to take advantage of the new system platform but also creates designs that are unique to the population segment we are working with.

New Information and Analytics Platform Takes iVision a Step Further

With specification on population health design requirements came clarity on the technology and analytics we needed to power the system. In addition to new perspectives, new partners, and a new healthcare production system, this maturation would require investment in additional technology. We came to understand that our iVision aim of creating a "connected experience across the continuum" was necessary but insufficient to deliver on our promise of Triple Aim results. The realization that what got us here with an EMR would not get us to our ultimate goal was followed by a period of confusion, as we found hundreds of PHM vendors with big promises and apparently overlapping product capabilities.

We updated our iVision thinking by revisiting the needs of patients and the care team in the new production system. We used Clay Christensen's jobs-to-be-done (JTBD) framework [15] to clarify the high-level needs of each stakeholder in the expanded care team. In this case, the JTBD specifies the PHM problems that must be solved (i.e., jobs to be hired) by IT to efficiently and effectively deliver Triple Aim outcomes across population segments. When constructing the JTBD categories, we found it helpful to focus on the needs of the primary stakeholders responsible for each PHM job. Table 14.2 delineates our view of the four categories of PHM stakeholders, along with their potential roles and perspectives [16].

With an understanding of the PHM stakeholder perspectives and their high-level JTBD, we developed detailed business requirements to support each job. Investing the time to create ideal future state requirements enabled us to assess current capabilities, consider build-versus-buy IT alternatives, communicate future direction to vendors, and seek innovative new solutions

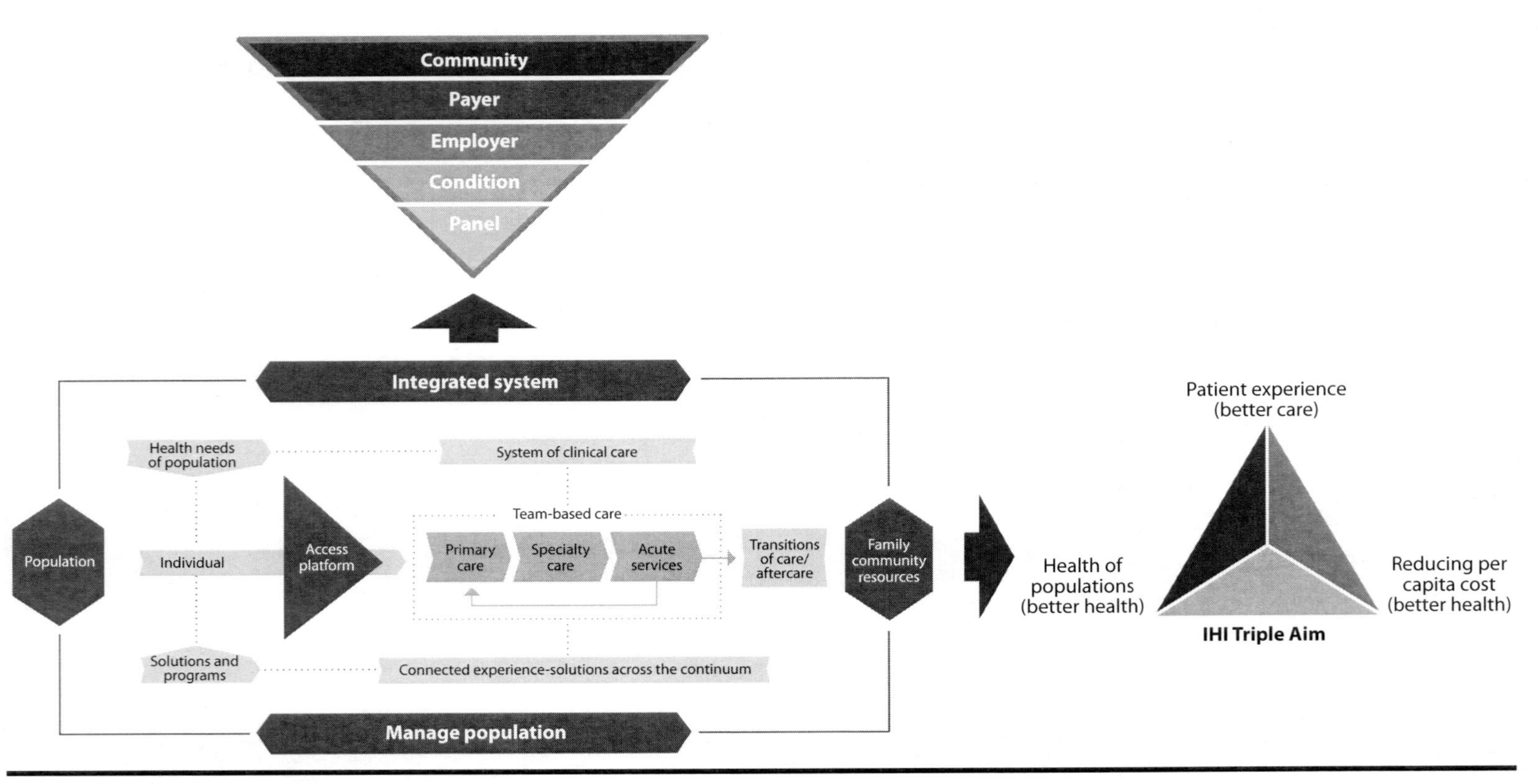

Figure 14.5 Healthcare design components to manage any population segment to achieve Triple Aim results.

Table 14.2 PHM Stakeholders—Roles, Perspectives, and JTBD

Stakeholder (Typical Roles)	Ideal Perspective	Needs	Jobs-to-Be-Done
Strategic **(ACO, strategy, clinical, operations, quality and/or finance leader)**	Executive roles are responsible for the strategy, business and network development, budget development, operations, personnel management, resource allocation and performance associated with transition from fee-for-service to at risk population health contracting.	Access to information that will align their investment in resources and internal performance improvement with external population risk contracts.	**Population-based data:** access new sources of data to drive new, timely insights **Cost-of-care insights:** understand cost drivers within a population to support contracting, program development and resource investment geared toward improvement **Performance feedback:** understand performance to drive improvement and estimate financial returns **Financial management:** project financial return, understand impact of benefit design and disperse payments

Stakeholder (Typical Roles)	Ideal Perspective	Needs	Jobs-to-Be-Done
Mezzanine **(care consultant, case manager, case navigator, disease management coordinator, clinical pharmacist, nutritionist, behavioral coach, community worker, housing specialist)**	Mezzanine roles are responsible for specific activities for defined population segments with higher need of care coordination (e.g., hospital discharge), medical attention (e.g., medication management), or nonmedical attention (e.g., housing). A mezzanine role is defined as one that spans more than one provider/-care team panel. Ideally, they are considered an extension of the frontline care team.	Access to data from across a patient's care continuum. Increasingly, they may be documenting outside any single organization's EMR because they may cross organizations and/or be based in the community.	**Population-based data:** access new sources of data to continually identify patients who will benefit from mezzanine-level roles **Case finding:** identify individuals within segments who would benefit from additional attention and care coordination **Case management:** efficient, standardized workflows and tools to manage high needs or complex individuals with specific needs **Care management:** provide wellness and disease prevention and management services for high-need or complex patients across provider panels

(Continued)

Table 14.2 (Continued) PHM Stakeholders—Roles, Perspectives, and JTBD

Stakeholder (Typical Roles)	Ideal Perspective	Needs	Jobs-to-Be-Done
Frontline **(physician, nurse practitioner, physician assistant, nurses, medical assistant, front desk and back office staff)**	Frontline roles are the patient's primary partners in a continuous, connected care relationship. They are responsible for the care and well-being of patients. Frontline roles are transitioning from a solo-practice, visit-focused perspective to one that increasingly involves care teams attending to today's clinic appointments while simultaneously minding the care needs across their entire panel.	Should seamlessly integrate with patients and families and their affiliated mezzanine roles to create the ideal care team—in and outside their own organization.	**Actionable data:** integrate new sources of data into the daily workflow to drive new insights and action **Decision support:** provide current, evidence-based disease prevention and management services for every patient at every encounter without lag in translation of evidence or alert fatigue **Workflow support:** support top-of-license standard role activities across expanded care team to reliably drive new levels of performance more efficiently a lower cost **Patient outreach:** conduct individual and mass-customized communication with patients

Stakeholder (Typical Roles)	Ideal Perspective	Needs	Jobs-to-Be-Done
Patient and family **(patient, caregiver, family, consumer)**	Patient and family roles are responsible for their own health and often the well-being of family and loved ones. They are interested in navigating the complexities of healthcare delivery with as few impediments and little cost as possible.	Increasingly technically savvy and hungry for knowledge about their own or a loved one's health. However, they may not be accustomed to consuming health information in the manner historically provided by the healthcare system.	**Individual-based data:** access all relevant health, medical and cost data related to oneself **Informed consumer:** access data to support selection of healthcare services based on cost and quality **Care map:** have a single, living, coordinated care map that includes life/health goals, along with a plan to achieve those goals, across a care team as defined by the patient **Self management:** understand and monitor one's health, update the care plan, make informed health-related decision and access the care team when needed

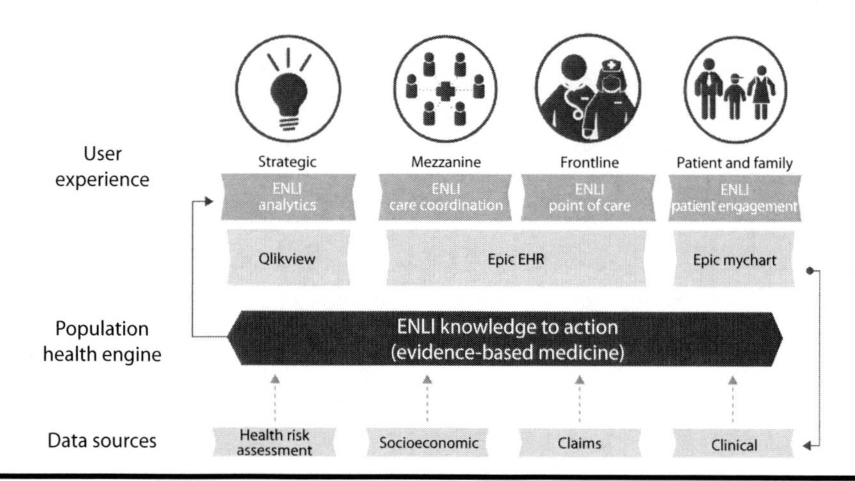

Figure 14.6 Bellin population health technology stack.

and partners for solving our gaps. Given limited resources, we created a subset list of minimum or must-have requirements to assist us in allocating IT investment across short- and long-term priorities.

Figure 14.6 depicts Bellin's population health technology stack following years of discovery, evaluation, testing, and learning. We continue to focus on EMR implementation and optimization with our partner, ThedaCare. However, we have also invested in technologies that integrate with our EMR, leverage multiple data sources, promote evidence-based decision support, enable more efficient workflows, and support population health activities across community partners.

We believe that organizations have approximately 2% of their overall resource and energy, at best, to focus on innovation. We have thought deeply about where to place our bets with Bellin's limited energy and technology investment.

Outcomes Prove the Approach

Our confidence in the population health design increases as we experience favorable results. Our first positive outcomes materialized with our own self-insured employee health benefit. As we implemented elements of the population health model, we observed improved health and lower cost outcomes among our employees and their dependents.

The design was further reinforced based on our experience as a Pioneer ACO [17]. The Pioneer program is the first ACO pilot administered by Centers for Medicare & Medicaid (CMS) and the first to report results. Figure 14.7 displays CMS composite clinical quality scores [18] for all Pioneer and Medicare Shared Savings Program participants and shows that Bellin-ThedaCare Healthcare Partners (BTHP) achieved the top clinical quality score.

Although all Pioneer participants showed improvements in quality and patient satisfaction, not all garnered financial savings. Figure 14.8 displays the annual cost of care per Medicare enrollee for BTHP as compared to the national Medicare trend at baseline and during the first 2 years of the Pioneer ACO demonstration project. Baseline data established that the cost of care for a Medicare patent at Bellin and ThedaCare is far lower than the national average. During years 1 and 2 of Pioneer, BTHP reduced Medicare spending beyond the expected target, despite starting with the lowest annual cost per enrollee.

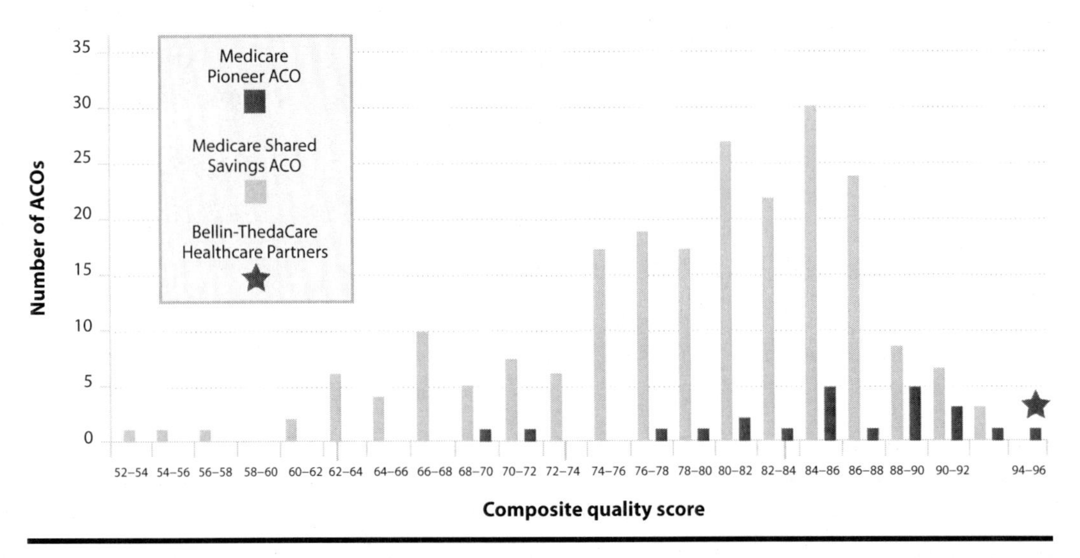

Figure 14.7 Composite quality scores for BTHP, along with all Medicare Pioneer and Shared Savings Program participants.

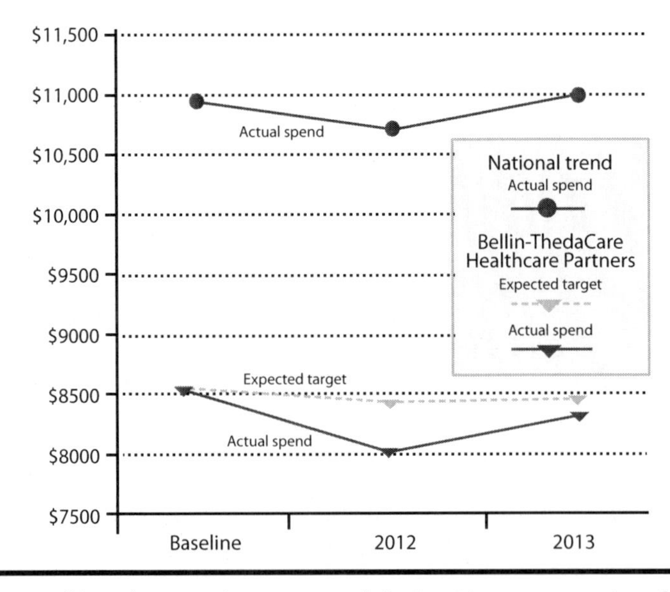

Figure 14.8 BTHP achieved a negative cost trend during Pioneer years 1 and 2.

The Road Ahead

Our work will continue to evolve as we learn, experiment, and innovate. The Bellin Vision has set a high bar in terms of the impact we want to have in the world. The Vision challenges the boundaries of our current healthcare system. The answer to the question of "challenges and opportunities in a post-EMR world" hinges for us on design of a system that will remain relevant into the future and create sustainable communities where we live and work. This will certainly require new insights driven from diverse sources of data displayed in ways that drive integrated actions across a broader set of stakeholders beyond the boundaries of today's healthcare system.

References

1. Berwick DM, Nolan TW, Wittington J. The Triple Aim: Care, health, and cost. *Health Aff.* 2008; 27:759–769.
2. http://www.ihi.org/about/Pages/default.aspx [Accessed August 12, 2015].
3. http://www.wchq.org/about/ [Accessed August 12, 2015].
4. *Pursuing the Triple Aim: Seven Innovators Show the Way to Better Care, Better Health and Lower Costs.* Bisognano M, Kenney C. San Francisco: John Wiley & Sons, Inc., 2012.
5. IHI Triple Aim Prototyping Partners. http://www.ihi.org/Engage/Initiatives/TripleAim/Pages/Participants.aspx [Accessed August 3, 2015].
6. http://www.ihi.org/engage/initiatives/TripleAim/Documents/BeasleyTripleAim_ACHEJan09.pdf [Accessed August 3, 2015].
7. Dave Underriner, personal communication, August 4, 2015.
8. Balik B, Conway J, Zipperer L, Watson J. Achieving an Exceptional Patient and Family Experience of Inpatient Hospital Care. IHI Innovation Series white paper. Cambridge, MA: Institute for Healthcare Improvement, 2011.
9. Bellin Health—Betty Video. https://www.youtube.com/watch?v=R54Cv1nYoz0 [Accessed August 3, 2015].
10. Bellin Betty Whiteboard. https://www.youtube.com/watch?v=vT0jEwL4HWs [Accessed August 3, 2015].
11. Barry MJ, Edgman-Levitan S. Shared decision making—The pinnacle of patient-centered care. *N Engl J Med.* 2012; 366:780–781.
12. Feder JL. Charting a life-and-health cycle and expanded primary care options for patients in Wisconsin. *Health Aff.* 2011; 30:387–389.
13. Sevin C, Evdokimoff M, Sobolewski S, Taylor J, Rutherford P, Coleman EA. How-to Guide: Improving Transitions from the Hospital to Home Health Care to Reduce Avoidable Rehospitalizations. Cambridge, MA: Institute for Healthcare Improvement, June 2013.
14. What is asset mapping and how can it be helpful to a health care organization? https://www.youtube.com/watch?v=8ArQNlnF2XY [Accessed August 3, 2015].
15. *The Innovator's Solution: Creating and Sustaining Successful Growth.* Christensen CM, Raynor ME. Boston: Harvard Business School Press, 2003: p. 73.
16. Hunt JS, Gibson RF, Whittington J, Powell K, Wozney B, Knudson S. *Population Health Manage.* 2015; 18:159–171.
17. Pioneer ACO Model. http://innovation.cms.gov/initiatives/Pioneer-ACO-Model/ [Accessed August 3, 2015].
18. Accountable Care Organization 2014 Program Analysis Quality Performance Standards Narrative Measure Specifications. https://www.cms.gov/Medicare/Medicare-Fee-for-Service-Payment/sharedsavingsprogram/Downloads/ACO-NarrativeMeasures-Specs.pdf [Accessed August 3, 2015].

Chapter 15

Patient Portals: Enabling Participatory Medicine

Jan Oldenburg

"...patients' lives may depend on understanding what their medical record says about them."

Despite all the advances in medical treatment and despite all the new scanners, lasers, and genomic medicine treatments, we often still ask our patients to interact with us primarily through pen and paper or via telephone. Not only is this an anachronism for many of our patients, who use digital tools to accomplish almost everything in their lives, it makes healthcare operations less efficient and more expensive for everyone involved.

July 4, 2015, was declared a "Day of Action" for healthcare data and "Data Independence Day." Patient advocates and organizations concerned for public health launched a movement to help patients and consumers get access to their records electronically at getmyhealthdata.org/. The principle behind this movement is that patients' lives may depend on understanding what their medical record says about them. Asking a patient to understand his or her medical history without the opportunity to view and correct it is like having someone write an unauthorized biography of their lives from overheard conversations—but the consequences of inaccurate information can be far more severe.

It's time to provide our patients with easy access to their medical records in ways that allow them to correct and update the information—and it is time to reengineer our operations around convenience for patients, better and more participatory care, and anytime–anywhere digital tools. Patients will be more satisfied, healthcare operations will be more efficient, and we will be better able to work together with patients in ways that are both leading edge and empowering.

Launching a patient portal is certainly a great step toward this goal, but achieving it also requires updating internal procedures to work for patients and caregivers rather than just physicians and staff. It requires changing healthcare culture from "doctor knows best" and "how dare you challenge me?" to a collaborative, partnership-oriented culture that takes into account the needs, feelings, and lifestyles of the patients we serve. Sustaining the changes requires listening to patients and caregivers and involving them in the way we design everything from clinics and wards to software and procedures.

Implementing a patient portal on web and mobile devices can be a lever for transforming your operations and organization to be more patient centric as well as more efficient.

Engaging More Fully and Deeply with Consumers, Patients, and Families

> Consumers want the same seamless, convenient connectivity from their healthcare experiences as they have in the rest of their lives.

Consumer expectations of healthcare are changing. More and more, consumers use mobile and digital tools to manage all aspects of their lives. Between the web, smartphones, connected devices, and ordinary cell phones, much of day-to-day activity has been transformed. From a phone, tablet, or PC, consumers can schedule a meeting at a moment's notice; plan and book travel; comparison shop, check reviews, and purchase consumer goods and services; handle almost every financial transaction except getting "real" cash; engage with friends, family, and a broader community. All of these tasks are available in real time, many of them from any device. Often it's possible to start a task on one device and seamlessly pick it up on another.

Consumers want the same seamless, convenient connectivity from their healthcare experiences as they have in the rest of their lives. They are no longer willing to wait patiently for callbacks from their doctors, take appointments that are scheduled around physician's availability without considering their own, and cope with 9-to-5 telephone-based services. A series of studies have shown that consumers say they would switch doctors to have access to more digital services or to have direct access to their medical records.[1–3] Consumers are voting with their feet, as demonstrated by the increase in membership in concierge practices, and loyalty to integrated delivery systems that serve their needs online and offline.[4]

> In this age of information democracy, some consumers are as knowledgeable as their doctors about aspects of their disease.

Consumers' changing expectations are not limited to the desire for convenient digital services. They have also experienced the democratization of information and expertise in their lifetimes. Now, anyone can be a critic or reporter, as illustrated by the way that social tools such as Twitter and Instagram have enabled "the person on the street" observations to provide in-the-moment reporting of news, and consumer ratings from Angie's List to HealthGrades have changed how people find personal service providers. Anyone can now self-publish and market his or her writing, set up shop as an hotelier through Airbnb, or be their own travel agent. We have moved from a world in which medical information was kept in the hands of a few to a world where it is both searchable and accessible by consumers with the inclination and drive to learn more about their diseases. In this age of information democracy, some consumers are as knowledgeable as their doctors about aspects of their disease.

While consumers and patients are looking for self-service convenience from the healthcare system, perhaps more importantly, they are looking for evidence that their doctors and health system have changed their thinking and will treat them as partners in their own care. Your patient portal can provide a way to signal that you "get it."

This chapter provides tools and approaches to help you either implement or relaunch your portals, focusing on the way the process can help you shift both culture and behaviors. Note that in this chapter, *portal* is used as a short-hand term to refer to both web and mobile capabilities.

Defining "Patient Engagement"

In 2012, Leonard Kish famously called an engaged patient "the blockbuster drug of the century"[5] because of the potential for engaged patients, working together with their physicians, to change the course of their health.

The Healthcare Information and Management Systems Society published a report last year called *The State of Patient Engagement and Health IT*, which also highlights the importance of engaged patients. The report defines patient engagement as

> The relationship between patients and healthcare providers working together to promote and support active patient and public involvement in health and healthcare and to strengthen their influence on healthcare decisions, at both the individual and collective levels.[6]

In a similar vein, the Center for Advancing Health defines patient engagement as

> Actions individuals must take to obtain the greatest benefit from the health care services available to them.
>
> This definition focuses on behaviors of individuals relative to their health care that are critical and proximal to health outcomes, rather than the actions of professionals or policies of institutions.
>
> Engagement is not synonymous with compliance. Compliance means an individual obeys a directive from a health care provider. Engagement signifies that a person is involved in a process through which he or she harmonizes robust information and professional advice with his or her own needs, preferences and abilities in order to prevent, manage and cure disease.[7]

In this more current perspective, engagement is no longer something bestowed on individuals by the healthcare system but something that emerges from within the person, encouraged, supported, and enabled by the healthcare system.

You'll notice that there's a similar theme in both of these definitions—both represent a move away from the paternalistic attitude in healthcare that a "good" patient is one who follows the doctors' orders without questioning them and is adherent to or compliant with the treatment option that his or her doctor recommends. Instead, these definitions focus on engagement as action people take on their own behalf or in partnership with their providers. In this more current perspective, engagement is no longer something bestowed on individuals by the healthcare system but something that emerges from within the person, encouraged, supported, and enabled by the healthcare system.

There are a great many documented benefits to implementing a patient portal and providing easy access to clinical records and personalized health information. Emmi Solutions, an organization that provides structured education, especially about clinical procedures, found that patients who viewed at least one of their interactive programs were more satisfied than patients who did not. While this is a vendor-driven study, the impact of higher Consumer Assessment of Healthcare Providers and Systems (CAHPS) and Hospital Consumer Assessment of Healthcare Providers and Systems (HCAHPS) scores is significant for providers.[8] A recent study in the *Journal of Medical Internet Research*,[9] "The Effect of Patient Portals on Quality Outcomes and Its Implications to Meaningful Use: A Systematic Review," looked at 26 studies and 1 review published between 2011 and 2014. This meta-study found a range of benefits associated with portal use, ranging from "the perception of high-quality care, better patient-to-provider communication, greater levels of patient education, and a high level of patient engagement/empowerment" to an "association of patient portal use with medication adherence, disease control, self-maintenance of health, and including the patient in the medical decision." The study also found correlations to increased patient retention and loyalty.

The original OpenNotes study found positive outcomes attributable to patients viewing their physicians' notes:

> Of 5219 patients who opened at least 1 note and completed a post intervention survey, 77% to 87% across the 3 sites reported that open notes helped them feel more in control of their care; 60% to 78% of those taking medications reported increased medication adherence; 26% to 36% had privacy concerns; 1% to 8% reported that the notes caused confusion, worry, or offense; and 20% to 42% reported sharing notes with others. The volume of electronic messages from patients did not change.[10]

It seems clear that the use of patient portals has significant positive impacts on patients' sense of empowerment, relationship with physicians, and understanding of their own conditions—all positive impacts to the patients and the healthcare system overall.

The Basics

Many organizations have had a hard time getting to the level of patient engagement that they desire with their portals. For some, even meeting the engagement levels required by Meaningful Use Stage 2 has been hard. Meaningful Use Stage 2 requires providers to show that portal capabilities are available to 50% of patients and that for each evaluation period, 5% of patients view, download, or transmit their records, and 5% send a secure message to their providers. Some providers argue that they shouldn't be held accountable for actions taken by their patients as Meaningful Use 2 currently requires. Records of Stage 2 Meaningful Use attestation show low levels, attributable in part to these patient-facing requirements. Some provider organizations have lobbied for reduction in these patient activity measures so that they only have to show that they have the capability for patients to view, download, and transmit their records and accept a secure message, and ONC is considering this approach.

On the other hand, some small providers as well as larger organizations like Group Health Cooperative where 75% of members are enrolled in the portal;[11] Kaiser Permanente where 4.89 million members are enrolled in the portal out of 9.6 million total members;[12] Virginia Mason, where 67% of patients are enrolled in the portal[13]; and MD Anderson Cancer Center, where 57% of patients access their portal an average of 3.3 times a week[14] show significant levels of adoption and use of portals.

This chapter provides insights into what successful organizations are doing to be more engaging—and how those results can be replicated in your practice and across the healthcare system as a whole.

Clues to what makes an organization successful in engaging patients online start with understanding that engagement is a whole system effort, rather than the responsibility of a few people charged with "achieving Meaningful Use" or "raising our portal usage rates." This has implications such as the following:

- Portal implementation and use is not an IT project. Rather, it involves rethinking and redesigning workflow, communications, processes, and attitudes from both clinical and administrative standpoints.
- Engagement is a team sport, which means that each person in the clinic or hospital understands his or her role in engaging patients and showcasing its benefits.
- Asking doctors and staff to invite participation with the portal is significant in increasing usage. People are very influenced by their providers and feel better about using the portal when they are clear that their doctor supports their usage.
- Engaging with the portal can be framed as part of a broader mission of the organization to be more patient centric and offer more convenient and empathetic care.

Although it is ideal to make these changes before you initially implement a portal, if you have already launched, you can also be successful by taking a step back, redesigning aspects of your organization (together with the patients, caregivers, consumers, and healthcare workers who you hope will use them), and then renewing or relaunching the portal as a signal of your organizational change.

Taking Stock of Where You Are Today

> Be fearless in your exploration of the current state, like someone in a 12-step program taking a moral inventory: sugar-coating reporting about the current state doesn't help anyone.

The first step is to understand what is currently happening in your organization: How patient centered is your operation? What proportion of your patient population has registered for your portal? What capabilities are you considering or do you have in place? What's being used, and by whom? What attitudes do your physicians and staff have about the portal?

If you don't know the answers to these questions, it is time to take inventory to understand your starting point(s). Be fearless in your exploration of the current state, like someone in a 12-step program taking a moral inventory: sugar-coating reporting about the current state doesn't help anyone. Leadership requires having both a vision for where you want to go and a clear sight about the distance you need to travel to get there. Only when you can demonstrate that you have both of these in place is your staff likely to climb on board the bandwagon.

Inventory Questions

Of course, you can't tackle everything at once, but understanding—and framing for your community—that you are on a long-term journey to be more inclusive, patient centric, and empowering can have a significant impact.

You may not have the answers to all of these questions. Some of these data may not be tracked by your vendor and your vendor may not have all of these features. Don't let the lack of data hold you back from getting started—you can certainly get access to lots of relevant data and can hypothesize about the rest.

PORTAL STATUS WORKSHEET

____ What proportion of your patient population is registered for your portal? MU requires at least 50% registration rates but consider that the floor, not the ceiling.

____ What features are you offering? How many are "basics," required to meet meaningful use requirements and how many are from the more advanced list?

Basic informational features *(check all that you have launched)*:

- ☐ Conditions
- ☐ Immunizations
- ☐ Allergies
- ☐ Medications
- ☐ Procedures
- ☐ Hospitalizations
- ☐ Results of laboratory tests
- ☐ After-visit summaries (outpatient)
- ☐ Discharge summaries (inpatient)
- ☐ Find a doctor (name, credentials, specialty, location)

Basic transactional features *(check all that you have launched)*:

- ☐ Request an appointment
- ☐ Request a prescription refill
- ☐ Send/receive secure messages with doctor or care team
- ☐ Download your data using blue button
- ☐ Send your data using the direct protocol

Advanced features ***(check all that you have launched)*****:**

- ☐ Schedule an appointment (the consumer actually books the time)
- ☐ "Proxy" access for caregivers and parents
- ☐ Secure text messaging
- ☐ Open notes
- ☐ View pathology reports
- ☐ Clinical outcomes (such as lab tests or procedures) are linked to education
- ☐ Registration forms can be reviewed and revised online before the visit
- ☐ Cost estimation
- ☐ Online bill payment
- ☐ View features can be correlated by conditions
- ☐ Downloads can be regularly scheduled using Blue Button Plus
- ☐ Surveys are provided online, just after the visit
- ☐ Patient-generated data can be uploaded to the medical record with the users' permission
- ☐ Mobile tools are "prescribed" as part of care management programs
- ☐ Find a doctor using additional information about beliefs, practice approaches, interest areas, and so on
- ☐ Follow up reminders and alerts for overdue preventive care or unfilled prescriptions

What is your registration process like?

- Y/N Is registration only available in person? Allowing remote registration can increase registration rates.
- Y/N Is your registration process one step? If the person has to wait for a password in the mail, it complicates things.
- Y/N Is the process itself so daunting that it limits engagement or discourages people from getting registered when they have a need?

How are patients and caregivers using your portal?

- ☐ How many people use the portal more than 2 times a year? More than 5 times a year? More than 12 times a year? ____________________
- ☐ What percentage of your usage is mobile versus web? ____________________
- ☐ What are the three most popular features? ____________________
- Y/N Do you have a way to handle questions?

Do you have a patient and caregiver council? If yes, ask yourself:

- ☐ How high do they report into the organization?
- ☐ How are their insights made visible to leadership? To the board?
- ☐ Are patients and caregivers incorporated into other practices in the organization? Systems implementations? Process redesign? New physical features? Please comment below.

How well trained are physicians and staff on portal use?

Y/N Are physicians trained to encourage portal use?
Y/N Are physicians trained and measured on e-mail responsiveness?
Y/N Do nurses have a responsibility to encourage portal use?
Y/N Do all staff members have scripts to use?
Y/N Have you changed compensation and incentives to reflect goals for portal use?

How do your physicians and staff feel about the portal?

Y/N Do they consider it a hassle?
Y/N Do they embrace it as the wave of the future?
Y/N Do they understand the benefits?
Y/N Do they love the ability to touch their patients more frequently?
Y/N Do they wish you were providing more and different features?

What do your CAHPS and HCAHPS scores or other satisfaction measures tell you about how patient centered you are? What key areas of service would you like to improve? Please comment below.

The results of your inventory will say a lot about both the challenges and opportunities ahead of you. Use it as a self-reflection tool to consider whether or not you are pushing your organization to continue to adapt and change. Of course, you can't tackle everything at once, but understanding—and framing for your community—that you are on a long-term journey to be more inclusive, patient centric, and empowering can have a significant impact. Showcasing the way portal use contributes to those outcomes can help bring people on board.

Attitudes and Goals

Staff members either can be supporters and cheerleaders for portal access or can convey their own irritation with the process and the requirement.

The attitude of your physicians and staff members may be the biggest determinant of the success of your portal. If their overwhelming feeling is that it is another hoop to jump through, something being imposed on them by management or the government, a ridiculous intrusion on their procedures, or an unnecessary step for patients who probably won't understand what they're seeing, you are highly unlikely to have a successful portal launch.

Attitudes matter. Patients can tell when doctors resent receiving secure messages or roll their eyes when asked about digital access to clinical data. Staff members either can be supporters and cheerleaders for portal access or can convey their own irritation with the process and the requirement. Consumers and patients are experts in discerning when procedures are designed more for the convenience of doctors and staff than for them.

These attitudes don't just affect adoption of your portal; they likely affect your reputation and standing in the community because of the overall impression they create about your organization.

While attitudes are hard to change, it is not impossible to do so. An example is the change in physicians' perceptions of whether opening their notes would be appropriate. The results showed otherwise, as the study found that "despite initial resistance, not a single doctor opted out of OpenNotes after the study was concluded despite the offer to do so." "To us, that was the real test," Delbanco says. "One doctor's comment best summarizes the collective experience: 'My fears were longer notes, more questions, and messages from patients. In reality, it was not a big deal.'"[15] There are entire books written on change management, and I'll not try to capture their essence here. Some specific techniques that work for portals, however, are discussed below.

Start with your goals. If you are getting resistance, it may be because you have framed your goals in limited and short-term ways, for example, by focusing only on meaningful use measures rather than accomplishing broader clinical goals. You may not have included a broad enough coalition of physicians and staff in forming your goals.

Myron Rogers, an expert in how living systems change, has five maxims that are deeply useful for understanding how to implement change in systems and cultures. Three of the five maxims are especially applicable to implementing a system change such as access to the portal:

- People own what they help create.
- Real change happens in real work.
- People who do the work do the change.

Leadership is required to make sure that goals are more than empty promises that sit on the shelf.

These principles reveal how impossible it is to "make change happen"—instead, it is important to create a culture where change can happen by involving the people who are doing the work in planning the change.[16]

Goals need to be both big enough to capture the imagination and realistic enough to give people a sense that they can actively contribute to their attainment. It's also important to ensure that it is clear who is accountable for attaining specific goals and reinforce the goals by cascading them into performance measures and assessments. Leadership is required to make sure that goals are more than empty promises that sit on the shelf. They need to be reinforced with action, behaviors, and measurement.

Make sure that the goals you establish for the patient portal are big and visible and have the noticeable support of leaders at each level of the organization. To engage leaders at every level of the organization, designate those who are willing to "live the values" that you are espousing and demonstrate leadership side by side with your staff as "champions."

Internal Communication

Every program needs a communication plan, and launching a portal is no exception. Your communication to staff and physicians needs to incorporate a focus on the benefits and "what's in it for me." Key things to consider in establishing the communication program are as follows:

- Find the people who are protesting the loudest about the change. These are your negative opinion leaders. Find out what most concerns them. Discuss what they would need to see to believe differently. Address those concerns in your materials.
- Consider bringing in representatives from other organizations that have made this type of change to speak with physicians and staff. Make sure they are honest about both the challenges and the rewards of making the change.
- Find your champions. Consider the people who are well respected by their peers as opinion leaders. Find the people who already believe in this change and work with them to promote the concept.
- Communicate early and often, even before you feel as if everything is "baked" enough to communicate. Explain what you are wrestling with so your staff doesn't feel that you are being secretive.
- Bring people into the planning process for the communication and test your messages on others.

In planning the process, think through what you want staff and physicians to say to patients and customers. Consider creating "scripts" for each role. To do this well, you must have planned the appropriate workflow. The following are some aspects to consider:

- Registration staff can ask people if they are signed up for the portal at registration and, if needed, direct them to a kiosk in the reception area to sign up.
- Nurses who room patients can support the process by mentioning the portal and noting what a good opportunity it offers to communicate with doctors and review test results.
- Physicians can invite patients to e-mail them with results from a test or encourage them to sign up to better understand their own health and enable easy communication about questions. It can also be effective to send patients you know are registered for the portal after-visit e-mails from the doctor inviting them to check in to let the physician know how a new medication is working or ask whether a treatment has been effective.
- Phlebotomists can help adoption by telling people when they are taking blood that signing up for the portal will give them early access to results.
- Discharge is another opportunity to recommend the portal and help people sign up. Some offices have volunteers who can help people with the process either when they are waiting for their visit or on the way out after the visit has occurred.

These moments of personal contact can be key to helping people understand the benefits of the portal and motivate them to take action. eVisit.com suggests this approach, saying:

> Script your messages to stress patient convenience and access to avoid any inference that the portal is a self-service tool designed to reduce health system workload.

> Look at every patient interaction as an opportunity to promote the patient portal. If a patient calls in to schedule an appointment, have the receptionist explain that next time they can schedule an appointment online, and even receive appointment reminders by email. When patients are checking out, make sure staff say they'll be able to pay their bills online. And, before you leave the exam room, remind them that they'll be able to access any lab results and a clinical summary (or other materials, relevant to your practice) through the portal.[17]

Script your messages to stress patient convenience and access to avoid any inference that the portal is a self-service tool designed to reduce health system workload.

External Communication and Marketing

Getting the rates of registration up is a combination of raising awareness that the capability exists, helping people—both your customers and your internal staff members—understand the value, making it easy to register, preferably as a straightforward part of another activity, and helping people take the next step.

The first part is raising the awareness among your patients and their caregivers that the capability exists and showcasing the value of doing so. The best way to achieve this is with an integrated communication plan that identifies key messages and identifies how you will convey them through multiple types of media. Integrating promotion of the portal into staff workflows, as described above, is one of the most important approaches.

Some organizations have taken a distinctly humorous approach to conveying the benefits. Group Health Cooperative, which has one of the highest rates of portal registration and use in the country, used a humorous advertising campaign in the early days of its portal launch to showcase the benefits. The campaign showed people trying to have a phone conversation with their doctor about uncomfortable health topics in places like the pool or their work cubicle—the alternative was a secure message. BetterHealthTogether Canada has created a series of ads that highlight various benefits of digital health records in a humorous, engaging way. Each ad ends with "Think digital health isn't making a difference? Think again."

- https://www.youtube.com/watch?v=owzS0F7At6g
- https://www.youtube.com/watch?v=YImpBGHoc9Y
- https://www.youtube.com/watch?v=iSxycBkYVyQ
- https://www.youtube.com/watch?v=i85SK5N86Mo

You don't have to have a big budget for an ad campaign to remind patients and caregivers that the portal exists and has useful features.

Kaiser Permanente used humor and an upbeat style to highlight benefits to members and the community in their Thrive ad campaign. Once they had built credibility with the campaign, they introduced ads that highlighted electronic connection with your doctor.[18] Lessons learned from the Kaiser Permanente Thrive campaign are described in an article on Five Lessons Learned from Kaiser Permanente's Thrive campaign.[19]

You don't have to have a big budget for an ad campaign to remind patients and caregivers that the portal exists and has useful features. Posters in physician offices, flyers at registration desks, and newsletters showcasing individual patients who benefited can be helpful, low-budget ways to increase awareness of your portal.

As you can see, there are a number of ways of incorporating the portal into the way you market your organization both in humorous and serious ways. When building a communication plan, however, it is also important to remember that you need to reinforce key messages at every turn, as discussed below.

Registration

Place information about the portal and a link to it in all of your communication materials. That includes your newsletters, instructional materials, and even your bills. Make sure that information about your electronic features is highlighted on your phone answering messages, especially if patients are on hold waiting to refill prescriptions or make appointments—remind them at the moment when they might be frustrated from waiting that there's a faster way to accomplish the same task. We noted above the way that reminders can be placed around your clinic or hospital.

In addition, since staff members who use the system are the best ambassadors for it, some organizations have created competitions for the clinics or hospitals that succeed in getting the highest percentage of staff members registered for the portal. Others have focused attention on consumer registration during "surf the web" days where staff members dress up in Hawaii-themed clothing and focus on increasing end-of-day registrations.

Don't forget to stress the benefits of the portal rather than the features. Focus on issues like increased convenience, less hassle for making appointments, getting immunization lists for camp, and taking lab test results to other physicians. Stress how helpful it can be to have your medical record at your fingertips if you are in an emergency away from home. Don't forget caregivers when you are stressing the benefits. Studies show that women are generally the "family health managers" and marketing the convenience of being able to make appointments or refill prescriptions for the whole family can be a significant driver of enrollment and use.

Simple techniques can also help increase awareness. Adding portal registration instructions to the back of physician business cards highlights the fact that physicians are actively involved in the process. Putting registration instructions or just reminders that online appointments are available on the back of appointment reminder cards also signals alternative approaches to the same things.[20]

Many portals still require in-person registration. If that's one of the requirements of your system, make it convenient for people to do so while in the office. More and more organizations and vendors, however, are initiating remote registration capabilities using the "one stop" approach pioneered by the banking system. In this system, the person validates his or her identity and authenticity by information only he or she would be likely to know. If your vendor is not already offering this kind of capability, advocate for it at user groups and in priority setting, as it eliminates hassles for patients and can improve registration rates.

A recent study in the *Annals of Family Medicine* showed that a coherent approach to promoting the portal across the clinic, involving not only clinicians but also every staff member, increased portal registration significantly over mailings or clinician promotion alone as shown in Table 15.1.[21]

Table 15.1 Comparison of IPHR Use with Mailed Invitation (Prior Efficacy Trial) versus Practice-Level Customized Implementation Strategy (Current Study)

	Mailed Invitation, 18 months, Prior Trial		*Integrated into Care, 31 months, Current Study*	
Practice	*Patients Mailed Invitation*	*Patients Who Created IPHR Account, n (%)*	*Patients with Office Visit*	*Patients Who Created IPHR Account, n (%)*
1	550	69 (12.6)	26,659	6668 (25.0)
2	50	4 (8.0)	5418	1254 (23.2)
3	504	75 (14.9)	23,712	6336 (26.7)
4	46	5 (10.9)	5181	1205 (23.3)
5	500	35 (7.0)	11,546	3225 (27.9)
6	100	7 (7.0)	6742	1493 (22.1)
7	500	70 (14.0)	12,697	3218 (25.3)
8	500	77 (15.4)	20,938	5511 (26.3)
	2750	342 (12.4)	112,893	28,910 (25.6)

Note: A total of three invitations to use the IPHR were mailed to a randomly selected sample of 2750 patients, and IPHR use was prospectively tracked for 18 months. IPHR, interactive prevention health record.

The same study found that registration rates were highest among patients aged 60–69 years and among those with more than one condition, perhaps because they had more office visits and more opportunity for reminders to use the portal.

Ongoing Use

For you and your staff, this means an ongoing effort to change the messages about why to use the portal, add new features, encourage those who haven't used it much, and, generally, continue to tout its benefits and make it clear that usage is welcomed and encouraged.

It isn't enough to get people registered for the portal, however. For patients, caregivers, and the organization to reap the benefits of registration, the portal needs to be used in consistent and ongoing ways. Often, organizations place the emphasis on registration rather than seeing registration as the first step in a program of getting people to form the habit of using the portal. For you and your staff, this means an ongoing effort to change the messages about why to use the portal, add new features, encourage those who haven't used it much, and, generally, continue to tout its benefits and make it clear that usage is welcomed and encouraged.

Some organizations have physicians write "prescriptions" for registering for and using the portal.

Here again, it's important to remember that engaging individuals is a team sport. It isn't just the responsibility of one person or one "role" in the organization. We mentioned creating scripts for different members of the care team—it matters to have those scripts reference benefits that are relevant at each point. The people scheduling appointments can remind patients that online appointment scheduling is an option; the phlebotomist doing a blood draw can mention that lab test results are available online and faster than waiting to get them in the mail or through a phone call; both nurses and doctors can mention that a summary of the visit will be available online. Some organizations have physicians write "prescriptions" for registering for and using the portal.

A key incentive for patients to sign in to look at their data is to alert them when something in their record is updated. Ensure your portal vendor is capable of sending patients an e-mail (to their regular mailbox) with a link to the portal when data are changed. If you do this when the doctor sends a message, when lab results are posted or updated, or when it is time for preventive care appointments, you remind patients that the portal is available as a resource. It is also helpful to set up standard after-visit e-mails that doctors can initiate several days after a visit, inquiring whether symptoms have dissipated or whether a change in medications is working. The same thing can help when the doctor has recommended that the patient begin an exercise program or cut down on drinking—a simple secure message, inquiring about success not only builds trust that the physician cares about the patient but often initiates an e-mail response that is clinically useful.

One of the things that best predicts ongoing portal use is whether patients perceive the features to be more convenient than alternatives.

Listening to Patients; Designing for Them

Advanced organizations incorporate patients and caregivers into every process and systems design project in the organization to make sure insights from "real people," rather than health system insiders, guide the development.

The process of launching a portal can be a great opportunity to evaluate how convenient and patient centered your overall operation is, as a patient portal often reflects your commitment to the overall patient experience. Review your procedures and policies to ensure that they don't inadvertently make simple processes much less convenient for patients and their families.

If you don't have one already, set up a patient council reporting to a senior leader in the organization or even to the board. A patient council gives you a way to hear and promote patient experiences by giving them a voice in policies you are designing or new services you are contemplating, things like changes to the cafeteria menu or patient gowns, and, of course, patient portal features. The Beryl Institute (www.theberylinstitute.org/) and the Planetree Institute (www.planetree.org)

have consolidated and codified advice on how to be more patient centered if you want further guidance.

Advanced organizations incorporate patients and caregivers into every process and systems design project in the organization to make sure insights from "real people," rather than health system insiders, guide the development.

Some healthcare organizations employ "secret shoppers" to understand the experience of patients from the moment they call, through parking, to the care they receive. These programs can open your eyes to inadvertent roadblocks and conflicts between your intentions and the actual experience of patients.

Setting up "listening" without a way to respond to people and resolve the problem or improve the service—both in the short term and the long term—can make things worse rather than better.

Healthcare organizations often have a corporate Facebook page or Twitter account that allows them to broadcast messages about the organization. Consider using these forums for listening as well. Listening in these "immediate" mediums also gives you the opportunity for service recovery—to contact the person and invite a phone or in-person conversation to address their complaint or issue. While this is an area that is just beginning to be studied, there are indications that an immediate response from someone who is caring and empathetic can significantly change a person's perception of the interaction.[22] Sophisticated organizations are beginning to establish social media listening "command centers" so that social media issues as well as individual complaints or kudos about experiences can be handled in real time.

In an effort to get insight into patient experience, practices are making use of surveys ranging from mailed surveys to text-messaged surveys to online surveys. The more "in the moment" your survey is, the more likely you will get an accurate understanding of the patient's perception of any service problems, making it easier to fix the situation. It may also be possible to add in-the-moment surveys to your patient portal to better understand how the tool is working for people.

To be effective, listening has to have a response component. Setting up "listening" without a way to respond to people and resolve the problem or improve the service—both in the short term and the long term—can make things worse rather than better. Patient-centered programs need to have enough authority to actually make changes and showcase that the involvement of patients and caregivers is making a difference in how the organization operates. Surveys need to be followed by action—and it's best if you highlight the actions you're taking in newsletters and on your website, especially if you note that you're specifically taking action in response to surveys or patient council activities, as it builds trust.

Reporting and Analytics

Reporting and analytics are another way to understand how effective your online tools are and what works best for your patients. Start by looking at registration and usage: are your patients registering for your portal? Are they using it once and never coming back or are they returning time and again, indicating that it is a convenience they have incorporated into their daily lives? Track as many aspects of your portal as you can:

- How many people are registered for your portal and what percentage is that of the people you see? Successful organizations are seeing registration rates above 60%, when the national average is approximately 30%.[23]
- How often do registered users actually sign on to the portal? When they do, what features do they use? Popular capabilities are sending your doctor a secure message, viewing lab test results, refilling prescriptions, and scheduling appointments.
- How satisfied are people with your portal? Although you can get some hints about satisfaction from usage rates, to answer this question you need to dig in a little. Perform focus groups, send out surveys, and ask your patients what they like and what they don't like and why. It may be that your portal works fine, but doctors aren't responding to secure messages in a timely fashion. Or you may need to work with your vendor to fix some problems with usability.

Are some physicians doing much better enrolling patients? Find out how they are accomplishing it and broadcast it to everyone.

Before you make the assumption that people don't want to use your portal or don't like electronic capabilities, make sure you're looking at the way portal use interacts with your policies and procedures. For example, if you are trying to encourage use of online appointments but the rate isn't rising, it could be that you aren't offering enough early morning or late afternoon appointments online.

The use of analytic tools in healthcare, combined with the wealth of data currently available, has led to a great deal of enthusiasm about the potential for "big data" to transform how we understand the health of populations and tailor interactions with patients on the basis of their conditions and behaviors. This can also help you extend the use of your portal by analyzing the demographics and illness profiles of your population and comparing them with an analysis of portal use. The results may surprise you and may help you tailor both marketing and some of the ways you configure the tool.

Don't forget to share your analytic insights with your doctors and staff. Are some physicians doing much better enrolling patients? Find out how they are accomplishing it and broadcast it to everyone. How long is it taking physicians and nurses to respond to secure messages from patients? Does actual response time match patient expectations? Doctors who have really embraced digital methods of interacting with their patients may need a break on how many patients they see during the day. You may need to look at new policies on how quickly physicians will respond to e-mail messages or prescription refill requests, or how many appointment slots will be available online.

The advent of new capabilities almost always creates these kinds of gaps between the policies of the organization, which were designed for a different era, and the way the organization actually works. If you are not careful, patients can get caught in the middle, and it will negatively affect your rates of portal use.

New and Emerging Features

> One of the most frustrating things for patients is the lack of interoperability between the different providers they see.

First-generation portals, though useful for engaging patients, are more static records of past care than lively interactions that extend the relationship between physician and patient outside the four walls of the clinic or hospital. Increasingly sophisticated capabilities are possible, and patients expect access to those capabilities because, as we noted earlier, they experience sophisticated technologies for interaction in other areas of their daily life.

To some degree, we are still stuck in an era where most portals are primarily list based: showing people their medical records through discrete lists of things like medications, procedures, lab tests, hospitalizations, immunizations, and conditions. Increasingly, portals also offer transactional features, most commonly the ability to schedule an appointment, refill a prescription, or update forms online. Although many portals include health education features, few organizations connect the information to the specifics of an individual's health, despite the usefulness of contextual education about your condition, lab test, or procedure. Secure messaging functionality that enables online communication between patient and doctor continues to be a key value.

One of the most frustrating things for patients is the lack of interoperability between the different providers they see. In a 2010 study, Practice Fusion found that the average person sees 18.7 doctors in their lives; that increases to 28.4 doctors for people older than 65 years and decreases to 8.3 for 18- to 24-year-olds.[24] The number is likely higher for people with chronic conditions as well. Because there is little interoperability, the average person has multiple portals to log into, each with a different logon approach and different features—and different parts of their medical record. Patients' frustrations with this situation can lead them to stop participating in any portals. While you can't fix this problem from within a single organization, you can alleviate it by participating in community or vendor health information networks (HIE) or community data stores. Encourage patients to sign up and release their data to the community portal, as it increases their safety by giving all of the physicians in the community more comprehensive data and can reduce the frustration of dealing with multiple portals. It also helps you meet Meaningful Use Stage 2 goals, as you can take credit when a patient views data from a community portal to which you contributed. Making "Blue Button" downloads of patient data available can also help patients take charge of building a consolidated patient record of their own.

One of the most exciting new features that vendors and health systems are adding is access to physician notes. This is an outgrowth of the OpenNotes project, mentioned earlier, in which patients are enabled to see their doctor's notes in the record. The website for this initiative, www.opennotes.org, indicates that more than 5 million people currently have access to their records, with a list of 23 major institutions that are already sharing notes. The list includes organizations like Beth Israel Deaconess, The Vancouver Clinic, the University of Washington Medical Center, and the Department of Veterans Affairs.[25]

From an administrative standpoint, forms completion or verification and preregistration simplify interactions with the health system and save time. Cost estimation and online bill payment are increasingly important capabilities as consumers are responsible for more of their medical bills because of the prevalence of high deductible plans. These features make it simpler for health systems to collect the growing patient portion of their revenue. American Health Insurance Plans recently estimated that out-of-pocket payments for insured patients are expected to grow from $250 billion in 2009 to $420 billion in 2015, a 68% increase in 5 years.[26] A McKinsey study noted that consumers now pay more in healthcare costs than employers and that consumer bad debt for medical expenses were $65 billion in 2010; a McKinsey study noted that consumers would pay more if they had up-front cost estimates and clearer payment options.[27]

Some of the most promising work is being done with the integration of apps and sensors with portals and electronic medical records. Patients are buying or being provided with intelligent blood pressure cuffs, connected scales, continuous blood glucose trackers, and exercise monitors that also track heart rate and blood pressure. Information generated from these devices, with patient permission, is being incorporated into their medical record. This continuous trending from patient-generated data sheds light on treatment efficacy and allows for more real-time modifications when indicated. In February of 2015, Reuters reported that 14 major hospital systems were experimenting with using Apple's HealthKit to aggregate and incorporate patient-generated data into their records.[28] Propeller Health is but one example of a startup that is tracking patients' use—and the location of use—with a new, connected inhaler/app combination that allows patients and physicians to understand not only the frequency of use but also the context of use.[29] Diabetic patients are hacking their blood glucose meters—and those of their children—to enable in-the-moment interventions.[30] See Michael Blum's Chapter 16 for more examples of innovative products and services in this arena.

Further sophistication in analytics can also help doctors and care managers appeal to patients with behavior change programs that fit their lifestyles and personalities. There is a significant opportunity to incorporate real-time exchanges of data with analytic and graphing options to make the data relevant and useful for things such as

- Managing chronic disease
- Empowering patients with more and better information
- Providing physicians with the ability to work more collaboratively with patients through interactions based on their data and powered by algorithms and visualizations

When you are struggling with getting the basics right, these may seem like remote, futuristic capabilities, but they are starting to be used today. Talk to your vendor about your interest in these improvements in the portal. Be vocal at vendor meetings, and experiment today. You may not have a portal that fully enables linkage to apps and trackers, but you can probably begin experimenting with off-the-shelf applications that may help your patients.

In Closing

The patient portal contributes an important channel for improving communication with patients around their health while also demonstrating your organization's focus on patient-centered care.

The patient portal contributes an important channel for improving communication with patients around their health while also demonstrating your organization's focus on patient-centered care. Although it takes time to make active use of the portal as a patient engagement and education tool—and how we do business for both patients and staff, the effort can result in significant rewards. The following are key things to remember when launching your portal:

- Make it a team sport, involving your entire organization in planning for it and promoting, encouraging use.
- Measure what people are using and how much, as well as their satisfaction with your portal—and use the results to shift policies and lobby for better usability from your vendor.
- Push yourself to add new functionality, encourage experimentation with mobile applications, and explore new ways to engage with patients around their data.

Portals are a leading indicator of the way healthcare will work in the future, and consumers expect it today.

References

1. *Accenture Consumer Survey on Patient Engagement: US Research Recap;* September 2013; Available from: https://www.accenture.com/us-en/insight-accenture-consumer-survey-patient-engagement-summary.aspx (Accessed August 2015).
2. Health Care Check-Up Survey; *Intuit Health Survey: Americans Worried About Costs; Want Greater Access to Physicians*; March 2011; Available from: http://www.bloomberg.com/apps/news?pid=newsarchive&sid=avjexfl6izhc (Accessed August 2015).
3. Deloitte Center for Health Solutions; *2011 Survey of Health Care Consumers in the United States Key Findings, Strategic Implications*; 2011; Available from: www.deloitte.com (Accessed August 2015).
4. http://www.power2practice.com/concierge-medicine-gains-momentum-increases-practice-revenue/.
5. http://www.hl7standards.com/blog/2012/08/28/drug-of-the-century/.
6. http://www.himss.org/ResourceLibrary/genResourceDetailPDF.aspx?ItemNumber=32950.
7. http://www.cfah.org/pdfs/CFAH_Engagement_Behavior_Framework_current.pdf.
8. http://www.govhealthit.com/news/want-boost-hcahps-engage-patients?utm_content=18243872&utm_medium=social&utm_source=twitter.
9. http://www.jmir.org/2015/2/e44/.
10. http://annals.org/article.aspx?articleid=1363511.
11. Tweet 9/30/14 from @grouphealth.
12. http://share.kaiserpermanente.org/static/kp_annualreport_2014/.
13. https://www.virginiamason.org/body.cfm?id=158&action=detail&ref=3920.
14. http://www.healthcareitnews.com/news/patients-referring-docs-md-anderson-making-good-use-web-portal.
15. http://library.ahima.org/xpedio/groups/public/documents/ahima/bok1_050172.hcsp?dDocName=bok1_050172.
16. https://www.rcseng.ac.uk/surgeons/supporting-surgeons/regional/events/documents/innvation-and-surgery-myron-e.-rogers-presentation.
17. http://evisit.com/10-secrets-to-engage-patients-with-patient-portals/.
18. https://www.youtube.com/watch?v=Cv_w0TZ84OI.
19. https://archive.ama.org/archive/ResourceLibrary/MarketingHealthServices/Documents/Five%20lessons.pdf.
20. http://tsihealthcare.com/news-and-blog/patient-portal-registration/.
21. http://annfammed.org/content/12/5/418.full.pdf+html.

22. http://atc3.bentley.edu/conferences/service2013/files/22.pdf.
23. https://www.virginiamason.org/body.cfm?id=158&action=detail&ref=3920.
24. http://www.practicefusion.com/pages/pr/survey-patients-see-over-18-different-doctors-on-average.html.
25. http://www.myopennotes.org/who-is-sharing-notes/.
26. AHIP Center for Policy and Research 2005-2011 hsa/hdhp census reports.
27. McKinsey Quarterly, "Next Wave of Change for US Healthcare Payments" http://www.mckinsey.com/insights/health_systems_and_services/the_next_wave_of_change_for_us_health_care_payments.
28. http://www.reuters.com/article/2015/02/05/us-apple-hospitals-exclusive-idUSKBN0L90G920150205.
29. http://propellerhealth.com/solutions/.
30. http://www.wsj.com/articles/citizen-hackers-concoct-upgrades-for-medical-devices-1411762843.

Chapter 16

Platform for Innovation, Part II—New Technology and Applications

Michael Blum, MD

> *"Providers are already awash in data—you never hear a provider saying 'I could provide higher quality, more efficient care if I only had more data.'"*

Given the tremendous amount of time that providers spend interacting with the EMR and the increasing penetration of patient portals, it is not surprising that, to many, the EMR seems to be the entire universe of clinical computing. Add to that the huge investment that practices and enterprises have made to license and implement the EMRs, and it becomes easy to appreciate their desire for these systems to be all encompassing. However, the reality is that a great deal of innovation is occurring outside of the EMR, and it is critically important for providers and health care organizations to understand the opportunities that this innovation presents, the challenges of implementation, and implications for support.

The way I like to think about the evolving landscape is that the EMR is a foundational platform for clinical care delivery. It is a critically important tool to the organization, but it is not itself strategic. A reasonable analogy is that the EMR is to healthcare as ERP systems are to traditional large corporations—they are critical in managing the business' processes, and they force (and enforce) standardization during their implementation that drives business efficiency. Still, just as ERP systems are not a complete picture of the business IT landscape, EMRs are not the only important clinical IT tools in healthcare. Indeed, many experts argue that newer technologies that are being developed outside the EMR will eventually supplant it, just as cloud-based systems such as Salesforce ate away at the traditional ERP market and enabled powerful innovations for business that were not feasible in the traditional server-based ERP world. However, just as healthcare is far more complex than most businesses (despite the incessant comparisons to the banks and airlines), the EMRs manage core clinical and business processes that are highly complex and sometimes life-critical. The decades spent developing and honing the EMR content, clinical workflows, and workflow engines create a very significant barrier to entry into the enterprise EMR space. Still, regardless of whether the "peri-EMR" innovation that we are currently seeing eventually disrupts the EMR market, there are many valuable opportunities evolving, and I will discuss several of them below.

Patient-Reported Data

One of the earlier disruptions that occur with an EMR implementation is the enabling of digital communications between patients and providers. In many cases, those communications are handled by office staff, but, in other organizations, the messages are delivered directly to providers. While these digital communications clearly lead to improved customer satisfaction and, the literature suggests, improved care compliance and efficiency, they have added significant workload to the providers. Many tasks previously handled by office staff are now landing directly on the providers as a result of implementation decisions (or lack thereof), regulatory requirements that were previously ignored or finessed, or bona fide attempts to improve patient engagement. While providers may be distressed by this new workload, it is only the tip of the iceberg.

A dizzying array of app, device, and sensor vendors are chomping at the bit to connect to provider organizations to improve the value of their offering by inserting their data into the patient–provider interaction. There are more than 1000 healthcare-related apps in Apple's App Store, and an increasing number are focused on true clinical data beyond "steps." Vendors would like to send everything from blood pressure, heart rate, weight, and glucose values to electrocardiogram waveforms and arrhythmia information to stress indicators to genetic sequences, patient symptom and risk surveys, patient-reported outcomes and satisfaction metrics, medication compliance data, and much more. From the vendors' perspective, simply getting these data into the EMR is a success.

Unfortunately, life in the EMR is much more complicated, and while delivery of data to the record is necessary, it is not sufficient. Data delivered without context or workflow integration are nearly useless and create the opportunity not only for dissatisfied patients but also for adverse outcomes if a patient believes that a provider is aware of data that they have not seen. Additionally, the state of the art is such that many of these devices simply provide data without any significant analytics. Providers are already awash in data—you never hear a provider saying "I could provide higher-quality, more efficient care if I only had more data." What providers need is *actionable information* delivered within an appropriate workflow—which frequently means **not** delivering it to the provider but to their staff who will manage the issue.

Patient-reported data is a fairly broad category and includes survey and risk assessment data that may be completed as part of an encounter with a provider or separately. For example, most EMRs have functionality that supports patient intake questionnaires and allows patients to report symptoms or to complete a history or review of system data. There is typically little programming logic required to support these tools and the data are typically incorporated directly into the record after review by a clinician. Going beyond these simple data entry interactions, however, requires more robust programming and branching logic capabilities that most EMRs do not easily support.

To meet this need, third-party vendors have developed some fairly elegant tools to engage and educate patients on a variety of fronts. An excellent example is the Athena Breast Health Questionnaire (http://athenacarenetwork.org) that allows patients to enter personal and family history data and then provides a personalized risk profile based on the data, using evidence-based breast cancer risk models. A report is then generated and can be imported into the EMR.

VisionTree, another vendor of a cloud-based patient engagement system, provides sophisticated tools that help practices engage with their patients through customizable, user-friendly survey and data entry tools that are more elegant and powerful than those native to most EMRs. In addition to traditional patient engagement and data entry, the software has been proven useful for patient-reported data in clinical research.

Sensors, Devices, and Apps

Wearable sensors are the white hot space in patient-reported data these days. Initially the domain of the Fitbit, Nike Fuel, and the Quantified Self crowd, the space has grown exponentially over the last few years, with wearable sensors that can seemingly monitor every physiologic process in the human body. While sensors that monitor heart rate, rhythm, and blood pressure are certainly not novel, devices that can continuously monitor blood pressure noninvasively may soon be available. Also on the horizon are noninvasive sensors that can determine blood glucose. Sensors that help optimize the chances for becoming pregnant and sensors that warn of preterm labor are in testing. Today, sensors that report a person's relative stress level via galvanic skin response as well as devices that monitor sleep quality are available. If you can measure it (or even imagine measuring it), chances are there is a wearable sensor that is available or in development.

Wearable sensors are the white hot space in patient-reported data these days.

However, before we get too excited about these next-generation sensing devices, we need to figure out how to take advantage of the devices that are currently (or soon to be) available. There are two main areas that need to be dealt with in order for these devices to have the clinical impact that they promise—the devices need clinical validation (even beyond Food and Drug Administration [FDA] approval) and they need to be thoughtfully integrated into clinical workflow. The validation is critically important. We need to understand it on three levels:

Without a reasonable level of confidence that the sensors not only measure accurately and reliably, but that knowing the data will truly help our patients, providers will not generally adopt the new technology.

1. Does the device accurately measure and report what the manufacturer says it does? While seemingly answered with FDA approval, remember that if there is a "predicate device," the manufacturer only needs to demonstrate that the new device performs similarly in lab testing.
2. Does the device accurately measure and report in the real-world setting for which it is intended? In our Digital Health Innovation Lab, we have found blood pressure sensors that work well when subjects are seated and resting but fail when the subjects are moving around

or exercising. Similarly, there are many reports of skin tone reducing the accuracy of measurements that are derived from colored light-emitting diodes, which is a common signal acquisition approach. Additionally, clinical disease states may affect accuracy and reliability; thus, the devices should have demonstrated capability in patients suffering from the disease for which the device or sensor is intended. Understanding when the measurements are reliable will be critical to the data's clinical acceptance.

3. Finally, there needs to be a demonstration that the data can be effectively incorporated into a reasonable clinical workflow and that having the data leads to better health outcomes at lower cost. Without a reasonable level of confidence that the sensors not only measure accurately and reliably, but that knowing the data will truly help our patients, providers will not generally adopt the new technology. Also, without that provider engagement, retention and persistence will continue to be as poor as they are for the current generation of activity tracking devices.

   Bringing the new data or information into a usable clinical workflow often requires integration with an EMR. While device vendors and entrepreneurs hawking a startup to investors are convinced that patients and providers will be more than happy to log into a vendor's newly launched site that is complete with the latest whiz-bang analytics and stellar visualization, the reality is that clinicians will not leave their existing EMR-based workflows to navigate and log into third-party sites with any frequency or consistency. Again, if patients don't believe that their provider is gaining insights and making decisions based on the data, they will stop using the device.

Apple has pushed the ball down the field in this area with the launch of HealthKit, but even that falls short of what is truly required. While HealthKit can indeed upload device and app data into several EMRs, it is not currently capable of embedding the data into a workflow that ensures that it is seen and actionable. For example, while glucose and blood pressure values can be uploaded to an Epic EMR, it is simply stored in a flow sheet and requires a provider or staff to know that data have been uploaded, go find the data, and then decide whether the data need any response or follow-up. While there is capability to notify providers of a data upload, the thought of hundreds of in-basket messages notifying me of individual glucose values or blood pressure readings is enough to cause me to become hypertensive and hypoglycemic. Similarly, a heart rhythm monitoring patch that simply passes rhythm strips or reports to a flow sheet but is incapable of alerting to relevant (even if not immediately dangerous) heart rhythms will quickly lose its appeal. A more compelling vision is that while the data are uploaded to flow sheets, they are also analyzed and triaged by the app, and the app messages the appropriate staff with relevant, actionable *information* relating to clinical condition, trends, compliance, and even lack of device reporting. A provider would only be notified in the event of a more urgent situation that requires their attention. At the time of a visit, the provider would be able to view a summary report of the data with drill-down and temporal alignment capabilities that would facilitate a meaningful discussion with the patient.

An additional aspect of these new apps is that they are commonly built with more elegant, sophisticated visualization tools than are supported in the EMRs. For example, Tidepool's open source Blip app (http://tidepool.org/products/blip/) (Figure 16.1) allows users and providers to see time-aligned diabetes data from insulin pumps (including basal and supplemental insulin), continuous glucose meters, spot glucometers, carbohydrate intake, and activity trackers. With this visualization, it is far easier to see trends and spot concerning patterns than in reviewing the raw data.

Sophisticated visualization such as Blip has not been achievable in the EMRs; hence, we are building the capability to link directly to these apps with user and patient context so that the providers can remain in their workflows, yet have access to the power of these new tools. Given that

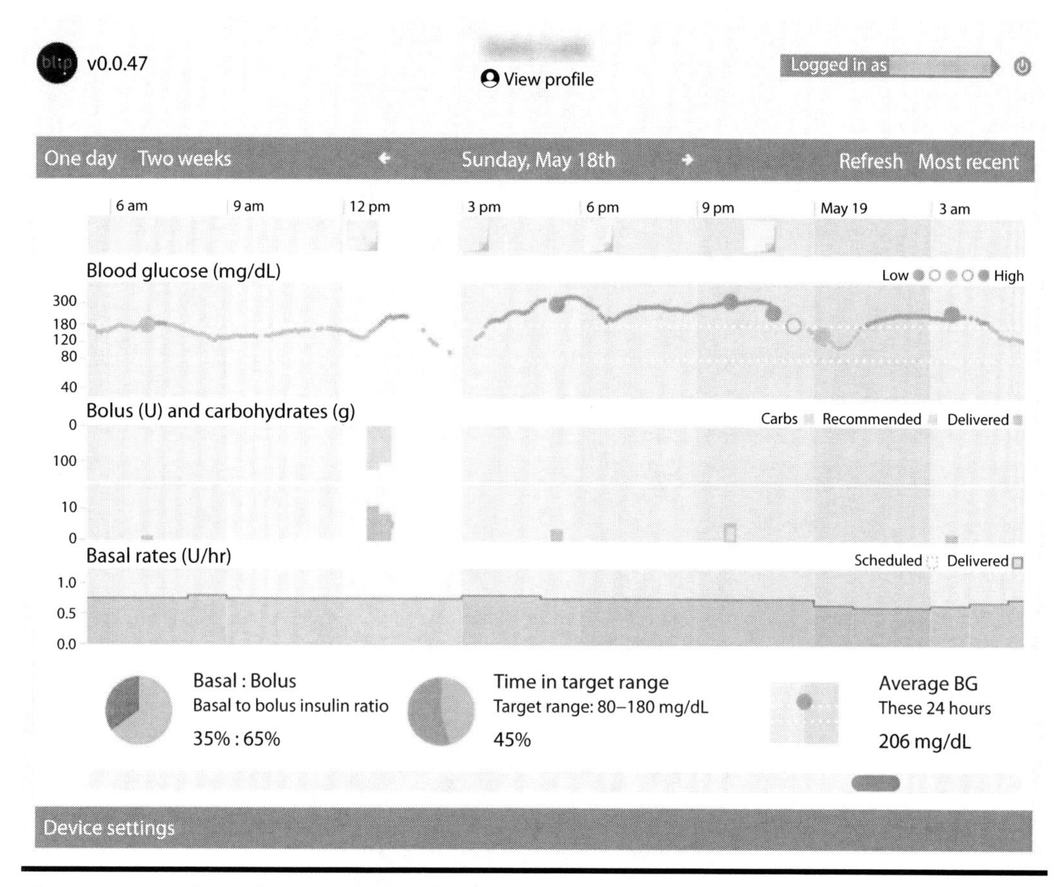

Figure 16.1 Tidepool's open source Blip app.

providers will be making clinical decisions on the basis of these visualizations and the underlying data, we will need to store the relevant data and static views of the visualization (likely as a .pdf) in the EMR as the legal medical record.

The excitement around wearable sensors is understandable. The vision of real-time healthcare and wellness preservation that this easily accessible, timely data and information could enable is truly fascinating. If we can manage to survive the hype, identify valid technologies, and integrate them into meaningful workflows, healthcare will never be the same. We will have moved two big steps closer to *Star Trek*'s Dr. McCoy and his Tricorder.

Two powerful forces that will come out of this space are the "Big Data" that the sensors and devices will be generating and the analytics that the data will enable (addressed in Richard F. Gibson's Chapter 9, "Business Intelligence Reporting and Analytics: Tools, Resources, and Governance"). The large data sources will provide rich, deep data on large populations and will be an important participant in creating the new data stores that will power the Precision Medicine of the 21st century (http://www.nih.gov/precisionmedicine/, https://www.ucsf.edu/news/2015/04/125111/california-launches-initiative-advance-precision-medicine) (see Figure 16.2).

A truly intriguing by-product of these new data and analytics will be the inevitable reassessment of our clinical knowledge base in these monitored spaces. It is quite possible that our understanding of how best to treat common diseases, derived from clinical trials on selected populations

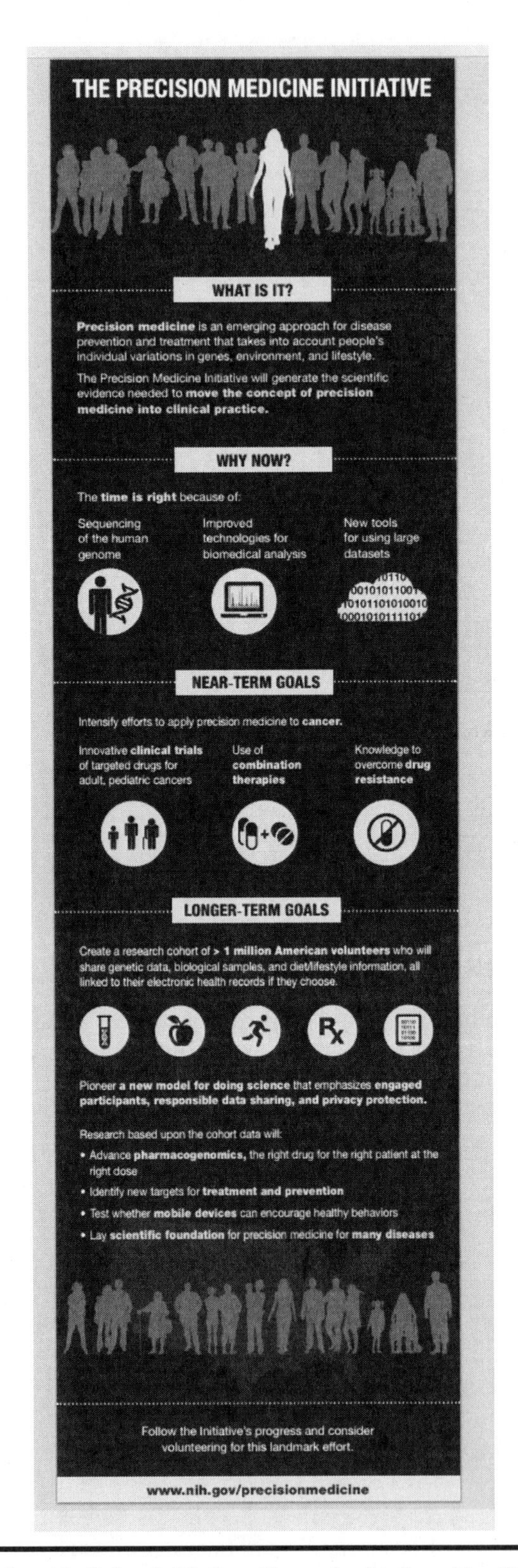

Figure 16.2 The Precision Medicine Initiative. (From the National Institutes of Health website.)

and typically adjudicated based on infrequent in-office measurements, is not entirely correct. For example, we may find that blood pressure during activity or trends throughout the day and night are important and underappreciated. Similarly, response to medications may be different than we have thought. We may find that our targets, based on healthy populations, are not correct for each individual. Essentially, the new data may allow us to rethink how we manage patients as individuals rather than an average statistic to be treated within a generic population-based guideline.

Finally, it is quite possible that these new data sets will uncover novel "vital signs" that we have not previously appreciated. For hundreds of years, we have assessed blood pressure, heart rate, respiratory rate, and temperature because they were easily accessible with the existing technology. There is no reason to limit ourselves to those descriptors of physiology. It is quite possible that advanced sensing and analytics may uncover novel, robust individual or composite values that are highly predictive and actionable, augmenting or even replacing these traditional vital measures of health and illness. Skeptics will point out that we have already tried this with measures such as heart rate variability (HRV), a dynamic assessment of heart rate rather than a static value, and that we have not been able to demonstrate improved prognosis or care delivery. While it is true that HRV assessment has yet to demonstrate convincing clinical value, the studies were mostly from the prewearable sensor era, and it is a single variable metric, albeit trended and analyzed. Additionally, it is not clear that the story for HRV is completely written yet. Regardless, I remain optimistic that access to fantastically richer, deeper data on far larger populations will add new insights and understandings of human health and fundamentally change our ability to assess and improve health and wellness.

Social Media and Mobile

So the question becomes, how do we leverage the social-mobile phenomenon in healthcare while maintaining the privacy that our patients continue to value and expect?

The advent of social media and mobile technologies has forever changed the fabric of society. Our fundamental expectations around connectedness (and not just technologically) have changed as has the way we spend our time. As reported on CNBC, "The United States spent 121 billion minutes on social media sites in July 2012 alone, according to Nielsen's annual Social Media report. That's 388 minutes—or $6\frac{1}{2}$ hours—per person (if every person in the U.S. used social media). Altogether, that's 230,060 years we spent staring into the glaring screen of so-called sharing."[1] We expect to be continuously connected to our social communities regardless of location and activity—we expect our technologies to be mobile and seamlessly support social interaction. Interestingly, while we have become accustomed to posting nearly every detail of our lives online (particularly the Millennials and younger), we seem to be resisting the urge to go public with our healthcare data. Certainly, some people have posted their healthcare data on Facebook (and sometimes providers have inappropriately done so), but in general, people seem to be maintaining a privacy barrier between their healthcare information and the rest of their online social lives. So the question becomes, how do we leverage the social-mobile phenomenon in healthcare while maintaining the privacy that our patients continue to value and expect?

While healthcare organizations continue to struggle with this issue, on the patient side, there have been several interesting advances. One of the earlier developments was for patients and caregivers with uncommon or rare diseases. Patients Like Me (https://www.patientslikeme.com) is one of the leading sites in this space and supports communities of patients and their caregivers. The site provides health tracking tools and connects users with researchers in their disease space. Smart Patients (https://www.smartpatients.com/) is another successful example that initially focused on the cancer space (has since expanded) and allows patient communities to discuss treatment options, experiences, and research that individuals might not otherwise be able to access. Interestingly, the site is relatively self-policing and rarely needs moderator intervention to remove quackery.

Likely attributed to security and privacy concerns as well as older architectures, the provider spaces have been slower to adopt mobile and social technologies. While tethered patient portals are ubiquitous and most have mobile app access, collaboration and community between providers and between providers, patients, and families are still very limited. This unfortunate state is clearly exemplified in the space of provider communications. Almost unbelievably, healthcare providers, who are generally technophilic (despite their mixed feelings about EMRs), are still relegating to use the 1970s technology of pagers to communicate. While there has been a move toward text messaging and smartphones, privacy regulations make that problematic unless a secure texting system such as Tiger Text (http://www.tigertext.com) is implemented by the organization, which can be costly. Still, simple text messaging does not harness either the power of social collaboration or the value of EMR integration. Healthcare has transitioned from a series of individual, parallel workflows of nurses, providers, care managers, discharge coordinators, patients, and families to a team-based undertaking. All members of the team (social group) need to know what the others are thinking and doing in order to optimize their interactions and deliver the best possible, most efficient, and satisfying outcome to the patient/family-customer.

In an attempt to harness the power of social, mobile, and EMR integration, at the UCSF Center for Digital Health Innovation, we have developed the CareWeb Messenger system (http://centerfordigitalhealthinnovation.org/careweb/) that integrates with the Epic EMR and supports those patient-centric communications. Initially developed for the in-patient environment, user feedback has been very positive, and we are now expanding support into the ambulatory and clinically integrated network environments. With the movement by the EMRs to develop and expose APIs that allow connectivity to third-party apps, we are anticipating rapid proliferation of collaborative social tools like CareWeb Messenger in the very near future.

Behavior

A chapter on digital technology innovation in healthcare would be incomplete without at least a brief discussion of patient behavior. It is well recognized that a tremendous amount of the burden of chronic disease is driven by patient behavior—obesity in diabetes, heart disease, hypertension, and joint disease; smoking in cancer, heart disease, and stroke; medication noncompliance; alcohol consumption and drug use; the list goes on. In fact, some public health experts have stated that if we could get people to stop smoking, moderate their alcohol consumption, exercise modestly, and improve their diets, we would eliminate so much chronic disease burden that it would resolve the issues around national healthcare costs. The point is behavior and behavior change are critical to influencing the health of our population.

The problem is that it is very hard to accomplish.

We can develop and implement all of the technology that we can imagine, but without the ability to affect behavior, we will have limited, if any, success. Early signs are concerning as the retention rate (continued use) of new digital technologies in healthcare is poor—more than half of the activity tracking devices end up in a drawer in less than 3 months. Improving the retention rate is key to ensuring the impact of these new technologies. Doing so will require more sophisticated approaches to development and better alignment with healthcare organizations and providers so that patients can perceive lasting value from the sensor, device, or app.

We see too many "solutions" developed around a technology rather than thoughtfully designed around a patient to address a clinical need as part of a healthcare ecosystem. Design Thinking (https://hbr.org/2008/06/design-thinking/)—developing a solution based on both the technical use case and the user and their specific needs must be more broadly adopted. Early involvement from experts in health, wellness, and healthcare technology (not just your father's friend who is a doctor) is critical as is technical and process validation of the technology (as discussed above). Finally, the new technology somehow needs to integrate with the individual's health experience. That means engaging the person's trusted advisors—friends, health coaches, trainers, nurses, PAs, or physicians, and that engagement has to be far more elegant, integrated, and workflow driven than "log in to my cool website."

There is promising early data in the space. Apps that can utilize social networks and behavioral health providers to help patients with depression have been created. The apps provide "gamified" therapy and notify the relevant team members when markers of worsening depression such as social isolation are detected. Even some particularly challenging populations such as schizophrenics may benefit from digital apps. An example is the PRIME app from the UCSF DRIVE lab, which was developed in conjunction with the design firm IDEO to target both of these challenging populations by investigating motivation, cognition, and reward processing (http://drive.ucsf.edu/news/drive-lab). Hopefully, the outcomes of these studies and others will provide guidance to technologists and clinicians in how to best design and deploy these innovative technologies so that they can deliver on their promise.

Reference

1. Helen A.S. Popkin, CNBC, December 4, 2012, http://www.cnbc.com/id/100275798.

Index

Page numbers with f and t refer to figures and tables, repectively.

T

U

V

W